The Paradox of Democratic Capitalism

The Paradox of Democratic Capitalism

Politics and Economics in American Thought

DAVID F. PRINDLE

The Johns Hopkins University Press
Baltimore

This book has been brought to publication with the generous
assistance of the Pribram Fund.

© 2006 The Johns Hopkins University Press
All rights reserved. Published 2006
Printed in the United States of America on acid-free paper
2 4 6 8 9 7 5 3 1

The Johns Hopkins University Press
2715 North Charles Street
Baltimore, Maryland 21218-4363
www.press.jhu.edu

Library of Congress Cataloging-in-Publication Data
Prindle, David F. (David Forrest), 1948–
The paradox of democratic capitalism : politics and economics in
American thought / David F. Prindle.
p. cm.
Includes bibliographical references and index.
ISBN 0-8018-8411-x (hardcover : alk. paper)
1. Political science—United States—History. 2. Economics—
United States—History. 3. Democracy—United States.
4. Capitalism—United States. I. Title.
JA84.U5P73 2006
320.0973—dc22   2005032617

A catalog record for this book is available from the British Library.

*To my brother and sister,
Ken Prindle and Robin Ritts,
siblings and friends*

Contents

Preface   ix
Acknowledgments   xvii

1 Origins, 1690–1776   1

2 The Founding, 1776–1819   18

3 Democracy and Capitalism, 1819–1862   54

4 Industrialism and Its Discontents I, 1862–1898   98

5 Industrialism and Its Discontents II, 1898–1932   139

6 New Paradigms, 1932–1974   178

7 Dissent, 1932–1974   211

8 Democracy and Capitalism, 1974–2001   236

9 Present and Future   268

Notes   297
Bibliography   327
Index   357

Preface

If you want to look over the collection of books on the history of political thought in the Perry-Castaneda Library on the campus of the University of Texas at Austin, you must walk to section L on the fifth floor, on the northwest side of the building. If you prefer to peruse books on the history of economic thought, you must go down to the fourth floor and move to section E on the southeast side of the building. If you decide that you want to examine books on the history of legal thought, you have to travel to a different library, a third of a mile to the northeast on the edge of the campus.

This physical separation nicely represents the intellectual separation that the development not only of intellectual history but of the disciplines of political science, economics, and jurisprudence has imposed on social thought. The divisions are not absolute. Inevitably, discussions of economics, especially in Marxist thought, but also, to a much lesser extent, in the dominant neoclassical tradition, include asides about politics. Similarly, economic issues are acknowledged by writers on politics to be part of their subject matter, and legal scholars never deny that the substance of their discipline partly consists of both politics and economics. Still, the differences of philosophical assumptions and methodologies of the three scholarly disciplines, reinforced by separation of departments, conventions, and journals, is so great that any experience of the three disciplines must compel the conclusion that their practitioners inhabit different mental worlds. In the vernacular of contemporary scholarship, we are dealing with separate discourses.

My purpose in this book is to overcome the separation of political, economic, and legal discourses and create a comprehensive history of their mutual development through American history. In order to accomplish this task, I draw upon not only the thinking in the three areas, but also historical, philosophical, and journalistic writing. I have tried to translate a variety of discourses into one that is a common denominator for all of them, and this must inevitably consist of my own mode of thought and expression.

In order for any such project to avoid degenerating into a catalog of names and quotations, I offer three major guiding themes. First, there is the unfolding of classical liberalism—capitalism and democracy—through American history. I argue that Louis Hartz's famous 1955 thesis that liberalism has dominated intellectual development in the United States is both true and false.[1] It is true because, although liberalism has never constituted the only ideological tradition in America, it has been the most important in political, economic, and legal thought. The thesis is false because Hartz characterized the liberal tradition as a consensus tradition; instead, as I demonstrate, capitalism and democracy, while they have been ideologically inseparable, have always been in tension. As a consequence, the liberal tradition in America is one of fundamental internal conflict, not consensus.

Second, there is the development of classical, then neoclassical, economic thought for two and a quarter centuries, which I see as constituting the dominant liberal form of natural law thinking in American history. The discourse of natural law is a form of argument that identifies certain facts about the nature of physical reality, relates them to human life, and explicitly or implicitly infers moral rules from them. Human beings, having free will, are at liberty to violate the laws of nature, but if they do they will pay a price in poverty and tyranny. When thinkers identify natural law, therefore, they both describe what they believe are the inner workings of reality and prescribe correct behavior to other people. For me, this is a perfect summary of neoclassical economic thought.

Neither of these two motifs is new. Even before Hartz's book in the 1950s, Robert McCloskey had argued that the two parts of the American creed of capitalism and democracy were fundamentally in tension, and in 1960 E. E. Schattschneider wrote that "the mixture of capitalism and democracy in the American regime presupposes tension."[2] I am not a disciple of McCloskey, being both more friendly to the partisans of capitalism and more skeptical of the partisans of democratic regulation of the economy. And as much as I admire Schattschneider, his analysis of the tension represents only about two pages in a short book. Nevertheless, I agree with McCloskey's and Schattschneider's basic premises and follow some of their arguments. Further, even in the nineteenth century, many opponents of neoclassical economic theory recognized its pretensions to the prestige of natural law.

Third, as a citizen as well as a scholar, I consider it to be my function to relate the history of political and economic thought from a critical point of view; to analyze and assess assumptions, premises, reasoning, and use of evidence; to draw out implications; and to judge the overall plausibility and persuasiveness of arguments.

It is not my direct purpose to summarize and take sides in scholarly controversies. Every point of interpretation of American history, every government policy, every personality, every era, every conflict, agreement, and compromise has been subjected to clashing interpretations and evaluations. To attempt to present the various arguments over methodologies and evidence over roughly three centuries of politics and economics would make for an endless, and endlessly tedious, book. While it has been necessary for me to immerse myself in these controversies in order to construct my own interpretations, I do not feel the obligation to cite every authority and list every opinion. Sometimes I recount scholarly controversies, because scholarly controversies are part of the story. By and large, however, I have tried to avoid cluttering my own narrative with the different narratives of others.

Having made clear my intention to offer a personal interpretation and evaluation of an immense amount of historical and theoretical material, I feel obligated to give my readers some clues to my own philosophical biases. It is no secret that the intellectual enterprise has fragmented in the last generation, so that there are now literally dozens of approaches to scholarship, some employing mutually incompatible assumptions and methodologies, some adhering to subtle but crucial differences. Indeed, the varieties of scholarly experience are so numerous that some scholars of scholarship have made charts categorizing all the available options of epistemology and methodology.[3] So let me locate myself within this intellectual kaleidoscope.

Philosophically, I am a realist; that is, I believe that reality is largely independent of human thought. At one time, this stance would have been completely conventional in social scholarship. Over the past generation, however, the ideas of several philosophers, of whom the best known are Michel Foucault, Jacques Derrida, and Richard Rorty, have had wide influence over thinking in the social sciences and humanities. These philosophers, and the methodologists influenced by them, reject the "foundational" assumption that there is an objective world beyond the human mind and that it is the job of the scholar to understand that world ever more accurately.[4] For example, Foucault argued that humans perceive all reality through "the dimension of discourse"; that is, that they interpret their entire experience through verbal, conceptual constructions.[5] It is therefore futile to attempt to understand the reality behind human thought; discourses constitute all that humans can know of the world. Even such an enterprise as natural science "finds its place in a discursive regularity."[6] Since the 1970s, many American scholars have elaborated the notion of discursive practices into the blanket assumption that all reality is socially or linguistically constructed; or, in other words, that there is no such thing as a universe separate from human consciousness, but only a series of discourses that have no objective referent.[7] Economist Robert Clower's declaration that his scholarly purpose is "to emphasize the essentially fictional nature of the stories that scientists tell" is a representative statement of this important theme in modern scholarship.[8]

This book is not the place for me to explore the nuances of, and problems with, the view that reality is socially constructed. Still, my own position is that reality is not all of one kind. Many abstract concepts that humans use—"virtue," "honor," and "international law" might be three—are crucially dependent upon verbal convention, and could be said to have no "reality" in an objective world. Other concepts—"spirochete," "hydrogen bomb," and "volcano," for example—are objective phenomena that only fools believe are socially constructed. A third category—"law of supply and demand," "public opinion," and "defensive war," for example—consists of concepts that are a blend of social construction and objective reality. Analyzing the extent to which these phenomena are partly objective and partly a discursive contrivance is one of the tasks of scholarship, or should be. Thus my assumption is that, with some exceptions, we humans do not create reality by interpreting it. Our knowledge is often true or false according to how well it conforms to the way the external world really is.[9]

The fact that I believe that the world exists independently of human consciousness has a decisive implication for my position on methodology. Methodologically, I am an empiricist; that is, I believe that all claims to understanding should be related to evidence. This does not mean that I abjure interpretation, for such a stance, in a chronicle of intellectual history, would make for a short book. Interpretation is always necessary. It does mean that I prefer interpretations that are anchored in something observable. As a consequence, I endorse the "principle of scientific internalization," summarized by Christopher Lloyd as "[e]very aspect of our beliefs ought, wherever possible, to be formulated, and to be brought into relation to well-founded beliefs, in such a way that it will be possible to test that aspect."[10] As a consequence of this methodological preference, I sometimes have harsh things to say about neoclassical economic theory, whose practitioners present their discipline as a scientific approach to studying social phenomena, but, as I discuss, too frequently display an at best casual attitude toward empirical evidence.

Ontologically, I endorse the point of view that Lloyd calls "structurism." I accept neither the individualist premise that only discrete human atoms are real, nor the holistic premise that individuals are derivative of social structure. Instead, I believe that we must understand human reality as consisting of the interactions of personality, intentions, and actions with culture and institutions.[11] This point of view can sometimes lead to difficult choices between conflicting approaches to explanation. On the one hand, I agree with Rogers Smith, who has urged political scientists to insist that human beings have "agency"; that is, that they are "viewed as causally potent, morally responsible actors guided by their own intentions, not external forces."[12] On the other hand, I also concur with a statement made by the young Marx before he succumbed to dogmatic holism: "Men make their own history, but they do not make it just as they please; they do not make it under circumstances chosen by themselves, but under circumstances directly encountered, given, and transmitted from the past."[13] Teasing out the extent to which Americans have had historical agency, and the extent to which they have been constrained by circumstances transmitted from the past, is part of my purpose in this book.

In terms of the political conceptualization of American society, since the end of World War II political science has generated a huge literature about "who governs"—about the extent to which a single capitalist class, or shifting groups of elites, or interest groups, or individual politicians, or the people generally, are able to make their preferences prevail in national politics. I review and analyze some of this literature in chapters 6, 7, and 8. Here, let me state that I am a pluralist; that is, I think that decisions and policies are, by and large, the result of a complex, ambiguous, and largely indeterminate struggle among individuals, groups, classes, masses, and institutions, all of it mediated by ideology, interpersonal relations, and the technologies of information, and all of it evolving over time. I do not think that a single, capitalist class always prevails in American politics, although I believe that the case can be made that it did prevail in the period from the end of the Civil War to the 1930s. I do not think that there is always a certain set of winners and losers in American society, although there are biases in the political system—toward organized as opposed to unorganized groups, for example—that tend to give some types of actors a systematic advantage over others.

As a citizen of the United States in the early years of the twenty-first century, I identify with neither the Right nor the Left in domestic politics, at least in regard to economic issues. I think that partisans on both wings of the spectrum have characteristic blindnesses that disqualify them as guardians of the public interest. What is the public interest? Very briefly, it is the organization of society that recommends that, after creating a physically secure nation, we attempt to optimize individual liberty, and national prosperity, and social justice, and democratic accountability, always recognizing that the pursuit of one—and especially that the maximization of one—may interfere with the achievement of another. Attaining such an optimum requires trade-offs, balancing, compromise, and a great deal of raucous dispute. It mandates that we generally embrace the direction of the economy by private individuals, but accept significant amounts of government regulation and redistribution. It implies that we recognize the necessity of material inequality, but attempt to keep it from becoming so extreme that it threatens social peace and political equality. Finally, the pursuit of the public interest, in my world, necessitates that we always remember that there is only one theory of governmental legitimacy that resonates in American ears, the theory of the consent of the governed, and that when people in power forget that moral principle, they create serious trouble for themselves and for the polity.

Readers who are familiar with American social thought will probably be surprised that they do not encounter the ideas of Alexis de Tocqueville in this book. The absence of his perspective does not mean, however, that I have no respect for the Frenchman. On the contrary, I concur with the general opinion that his 1835 analysis of the young North American polity, *Democracy in America*, is the best book ever written about the United States. Nevertheless, for two reasons, I have omitted discussion of that book's ideas from my own effort.

First, Tocqueville was not an American, and this is a book about American social thought. I discuss foreign theorists in this book, because American thinking cannot be understood without an understanding of its world context. The foreigners I do discuss, however, are important because their ideas influenced American thinkers. Tocqueville is significant because his ideas have influenced scholars of American thought, not theorists or politicians themselves. It is not unusual, when reading the speeches or essays of real politicians, to come upon a reference to Smith, Locke, List, John Stuart Mill, Keynes, or a variety of other foreign writers. Tocqueville does appear occasionally in the written thoughts of Americans, but not nearly as much as his ubiquity in scholarship might lead one to believe.

Second, and more important, *Democracy in America* is such a masterpiece, containing such compelling analysis of the national character, that it has thrown a dominating shadow over subsequent discussions of the American mind. It is almost impossible to pick up a scholarly book on any American topic without observing the way the author's interpretations have been influenced by Tocqueville. I have read whole books simply devoted to applying the master's ideas to modern experience. I have read others, not ostensibly about Tocqueville's ideas, in which every chapter is headed by an epigraph from his classic. So hegemonic is the legacy of *Democracy in America* that I have sometimes suspected that scholarly specialists in Americana have allowed the Frenchman to do their thinking for them. I am not the only one who has been given that impression. James Morone has complained in print about the way "the Tocquevillean views have petrified into assumptions," and James McWilliams has concurred that "there's something sadly needy about our slavish dedication to this precocious Tocqueville kid."[14]

Without necessarily concurring with McWilliams's negative attitude toward Tocqueville, I agree with him and with Morone that *Democracy in America* has exercised too great an influence over our vision of American history. When I began this project, I decided that I wanted to construct my own vision. This book is at least an attempt to create a non-Tocquevillean interpretation of American thought.

Acknowledgments

While I was mulling over the issues discussed in this book, I had many conversations with scholars and friends about its substance, organization, and style. I am particularly grateful to Bruce Buchanan, Walter Dean Burnham, James Galbraith, Paul Lyon, Alessandra Lippucci, Melvin Hinich, William Alex Rennie, Jay Wilbur, John Wilbur, and my wife, Angie Prindle, for sharing their time and wisdom with me. Portions of the manuscript were read by David Braybrooke, Robert Brigham, James Fishkin, and Benjamin Gregg. All made suggestions that saved me from factual or interpretive error, and I thank each of them.

I am particularly grateful to Thomas Schwartz and Peter Ordeshook, who permitted me to audit their graduate public choice theory classes when they were my colleagues in the Government Department at the University of Texas at Austin. In this book, I criticize public choice theory, but I have nothing but praise for Schwartz's and Ordeshook's ability to explain that theory, and for their generosity in helping me.

The Paradox of
Democratic Capitalism

CHAPTER ONE

Origins, 1690–1776

The great question of politics is the question of legitimacy: how can a moral authority be established that will oblige the citizens to obey? The great question of economics is the question of prosperity: how can a system of production and exchange be constructed that will increase the wealth of the citizens? These two questions seem distinct, but in practice their differences blur. Answers to questions about political authority inevitably encompass economic activity, and answers to questions about prosperity unavoidably involve the justifications of power. So it has always been in the United States.

Starting long before the struggle in which they founded a nation, Americans have been involved in quarrels about the proper relation of politics and economics. The arguments employed in these disputes have rested on both shared and conflicting assumptions. Looked at from one point of view, Americans have seemed to think and speak from within a consensus on fundamentals—a consensus I will term "liberal," despite some qualms about the term. Looked at from another, the contending sides have seemed to argue from incompatible premises. Americans have seemed to agree on the positive value of "equality," "individualism," "liberty," "capitalism," and "democracy" and the negative value of "tyranny," "monopoly," and "aristocracy," yet they have disagreed, sometimes violently, on the meaning of all these terms, and on their applicability to specific circumstances. Scholars reporting on the arguments have tended either to emphasize consensus, and thus portray American thought as a tradition that has closed off too many social alternatives, or to emphasize conflict, and thus agree with Richard Ellis that "cultural dissensus" is "an enduring and defining attribute of the American past."[1]

One of my theses here is that both the scholars of consensus and the scholars of dissensus are partly right. My argument is that the American tradition of discourse about political economy rests on a basic consensus, but one whose main elements are in irreconcilable tension. Briefly, that tradition embraces the themes of democracy and capitalism; yet a significant number of Americans have never been sure that democracy and capitalism are compatible. Some thinkers have endorsed one side or the other of the discourse, a few have tried to reconcile them; a very few have rejected one or the other or both. But for all the controversy, and for all the progress made in society and social theory, in the first decade of the twenty-first century the two sides are not close to reconciliation. Indeed, the Right and the Left in America may be redefining the terms of debate so as to emphasize their irreconcilability.

Despite, or perhaps because of, the continuing tension, the story of the fight within the American ideological family is worth telling. If, as David Carr advises, historical understanding arises when we tell ourselves a story about ourselves, there may be some value in telling this particular story from the beginning to the present.²

POLITICAL LIBERALISM

By the time their quarrel with George III and Parliament came to a head in 1776, the American colonists had been witnesses to, and participants in, a series of political, religious, and economic controversies that had sometimes caused the usual polemics of social conflict to rise to the level of philosophy. As intelligent and educated observers, American leaders had been much influenced by the various strands of controversy coming out of England and had themselves adopted a common set of principles of political legitimacy. Among the principles, those cohering into the system of beliefs and values that history has termed liberalism were the most important.

Liberalism's greatest spokesman had been John Locke, whose *Second Treatise of Government* in 1690 became the single most important source of American political ideas. Although it was written to justify a specific action within specific circumstances—the Glorious Revolution of 1688 in England—the *Second Treatise* summarized a more general argument about legitimacy in one articulate framework that became enormously influential on the western side of the Atlantic.

Among Locke's major points were that men were all equal children of God, that they thus possessed God-given natural rights to life, liberty, and property, but that threats to these rights were unavoidable inconveniences in any natural, pre-social setting. Governments had been instituted to preserve natural rights while suppressing the threats to their existence that lurked in the state of nature. It followed that governments could be evaluated according to their success in defending the good while eliminating the bad from nature. Because of their equality and their mutual need to evaluate government actions, men were morally required to consent to, or as a practical matter, participate in, the running of their own government. Legitimacy thus rested upon the free choice of the citizenry, making democracy the only legitimate form of government. Government had no authority over the citizens—Parliament had no power to tax the residents of the American colonies—unless those citizens were represented as voting participants in the decision-making process. Governments that violated their democratic compact with the citizens by revoking natural rights or seeking to free themselves from popular control could be justifiably overthrown by violent means.[3]

This summary and evaluation of the importance of Locke's theory to the American founding was once a commonplace of scholarly opinion. Carl Becker's characterization of the Revolutionary generation in 1922 that "most Americans had absorbed Locke's works as a kind of political gospel" was for many decades the consensus view.[4] "No taxation without representation" was assumed to be both the core slogan of the Revolution and the unassailable residue of Locke's influence. Since the mid-1960s, however, a revisionism has set in that both deprecates Locke's impact on the American revolutionaries and endorses other influences on the founding. No one denies that the Declaration of Independence was inspired, passage for passage if not word for word, by the *Second Treatise*. And indeed, it would be difficult to deny the evidence of Jefferson's early paragraphs, with their assertion of human equality, inalienable rights, government by consent, and the right of revolution.

But many recent authors have argued that Jefferson was unusual in his fidelity to Lockean thinking and that other important revolutionaries were heavily influenced by other writers, particularly the English Whigs. In the light of the contemporary effort to demote Locke's writing as an American political gospel, it will be helpful to reexamine some of the evidence.

In 1984 Donald S. Lutz published a compilation of all American political writings from 1760 to 1805, analyzing the frequency of occurrence of all named citations. In the decade of the 1760s, Locke was the most cited author, with Montesquieu a respectable second. In the 1770s Locke and Montesquieu were tied in importance. Throughout the twenty years, Lutz concluded, writers appealed to Locke when discussing the foundations of legitimacy and to Montesquieu when discussing constitutional design. Other significant citations were to

Pufendorf, who is consistent with Locke, and to the legal writings of Edward Coke, who was heavily influenced by him.[5]

The named citations, however, are only part of the story, and not necessarily the most important part. By the time of the controversy that led to the Revolution, Americans had so absorbed Locke that they referred to his ideas without bothering to name the source. Some of them may not have known the origin of their opinions. Prerevolutionary writing is saturated with Lockean assumptions, Lockean language, and Lockean claims:

> [I]t is supposed an undoubted right of Englishmen, not to be taxed but by their own consent given through their representatives. (Benjamin Franklin, 1754)[6]

> [I]n a state of nature, no man can take my property from me without my consent. If he does, he deprives me of my liberty, and makes me a slave. (James Otis, 1764)[7]

> Our liberty is being subjected to laws that we had no share in making; our property is being taxed without our own consent. (William Goddard, 1765)[8]

> Among the natural Rights of the Colonists are these: First, a right to *Life*; Secondly, to *Liberty*; thirdly, to *Property*. . . . All Men have a Right to remain in a State of Nature as long as they please; And in case of intollerable Oppression, Civil or Religious, to leave the Society they belong to, and enter into another. (Samuel Adams, 1772)[9]

> [I]n a state of nature, no man has any *moral* power to deprive another of his life, limbs, property, or liberty . . . the origin of all civil government, justly established, must be a voluntary compact, between the rulers and the ruled; and must be liable to such limitations, as are necessary for the security of the *absolute rights* of the latter; for what original title can any man or set of men have, to govern others, except their own consent? (Alexander Hamilton, 1775)[10]

> [A]ll men are by nature equally free and independent, and have certain inherent rights . . . namely, the enjoyment of life and liberty, with the means of acquiring and possessing property . . . elections of members to serve as representatives of the people, in assembly, ought to be free; and . . . all men, having sufficient evidence of permanent common interest with, and attachment to the community, have the right of suffrage, and cannot be taxed or deprived of their property for public uses, without their own consent, or that of their representatives. (Constitution of the state of Virginia, 1776)[11]

> All men are born free and independent, and have certain natural, essential, and unalienable rights, among which may be included the right of enjoying and defend-

ing their lives and liberties; that of acquiring, possessing, and protecting property . . . the people alone have an incontestable, unalienable, and indefeasible right to institute government, or totally change the same, when their protection, safety, prosperity, and happiness require it. . . . But no part of the property of any individual can, with justice, be taken from him or applied to public uses without his own consent or that of the representatives of the people. (Constitution of the state of Massachusetts; principal author John Adams, 1780)[12]

The leaders of the Revolutionary generation were generally erudite men whose reading had been wide and deep. Scholars who find other themes in the founders' thinking besides the Lockean, such as the ideas of the classical Greeks, or the Scottish Enlightenment, or the "republican" English Whigs, are quite correct. The claim here is not that the *Second Treatise of Government* was the only inspiration for the American discourse of legitimacy, only that it was the most important one. Further, it continued to be the major—though not the only—basis for American political ideas at least through the nineteenth century.

Although Locke's arguments had triumphed in America by 1783, however, they had not solved every political problem forever. The world of the *Second Treatise of Government* contains both ambiguities and implications of a political nature. These would provide fertile soil for disagreement over interpretation in the coming centuries.

Locke's writings had economic implications, also. His emphasis on property rights was not only part of his political theory but had been turned by the British legal commentators Coke and Blackstone into a foundation for the common law.[13] By the time Louis Hartz published *The Liberal Tradition in America* in 1955, it was taken for granted that Locke's legacy could be summarized in two words: democracy and capitalism. Hartz, however, amplified the prevailing wisdom to its extreme. His thesis was that the *Second Treatise of Government* offered "the master assumption of American social thought."[14]

Hartz's book had a powerful and long-lasting impact on the disciplines of history and political science. It was possibly one of the most influential pieces of scholarship of the twentieth century. A multitude of students wrote essays on *The Liberal Tradition in America* during their first semester of graduate school. Part of its influence was due to Hartz's cunning in never defining "Lockean liberalism." By clear implication, it consisted of democracy plus capitalism, but since that contention was never explicitly stated, analyzed, or defended, Hartz forestalled the attacks of pesky scholars who might want to quibble with a more conventional exegesis.

Moreover, Hartz's writing style is indirect, allusive, and witty, taking almost everything important for granted and playing with ideas rather than explaining them. Almost all 309 pages of *The Liberal Tradition in America* consist of epigrams rather than arguments, and epigrams are impossible to refute. Such assertions as "Law has flourished on the corpse of philosophy in America," and "[T]he success-failure ethos . . . was a silent quality in the national atmosphere, not so much blocking alien decisions as preventing them from ever being made," and "An irreversible ethic made all problems technical" can provoke and inspire, but they can only pretend to explain.[15] Hartz's ideas were powerful but unmeasurable. Because Hartz's concepts had never been reliably defined, they could neither be rejected nor proven on the basis of evidence.

Hartz had maintained, or been understood to maintain, that the Lockean tradition of discourse in America is so all-encompassing that it makes American arguments superficial. American conflicts are not over fundamentals. On fundamentals, consensus reigns. American disputes, however loud, are mere epiphenomena, squabbles over "who gets what" that never involve anything so dangerous as an idea. Thus America has had no true Left, no true Right, and no deep injustice. Once one has read Locke, one has absorbed all one needs to know about American history.

It may seem odd that an untestable theory should have exercised so much power over American scholarship. Perhaps the explanation lies in the fact that *The Liberal Tradition in America* seems to answer a question that has been one of the most enduring scholarly concerns of the last century and a half: why has there been no socialism in America? Looking at Europe, intellectuals saw large and powerful socialist parties; looking at the United States, they saw two liberal parties dominating all elections. Casting about for an explanation for "American exceptionalism," they found Hartz. By his account, the one-dimensional liberalism of Americans prevented them from hearing the appeals of socialist ideology. The great exception was thereby explained. Socialism was impossible in a society dominated by a liberal consensus.

I am less than satisfied with this answer. There is no doubt that the question of why the United States does not have a strong socialist tradition addresses a bona fide historical problem. Many scholars have attempted to answer it, and I attempt my own answer over the course of this book. But it seems to me that the thesis that America is the exceptional case in world history derives from the habit of looking at the problem through the wrong end of the telescope, so to speak.

Wherever the development of capitalism has taken a society into and through the Industrial Revolution, it has sparked opposition, both from the older agricultural classes and from the newly created proletariat. In Europe, when this opposition came from the proletariat, it often adopted the voice of socialism. In the United States, opposition to capitalism rarely adopted such a voice. Hartz sought to explain the lack of socialism by, in effect, denying that there had been authentic opposition. But as I demonstrate over the course of this book, such an approach is mistaken. There have been many different types of opposition to capitalist development in the United States. Much of American social commentary, for most of our history, has consisted of attacks on, and the defense of, some particular form of capitalist development. As Sean Wilentz has shown, there was even a species of class consciousness developed by New York workers as early as the first half of the nineteenth century.[16]

However, as Eric Foner has observed, the question as to why there is no socialism in the United States assumes that socialism is somehow the "default setting" of political ideology, and that the American case is thus deviant from the European model, which is "normal."[17] But a strong socialist tradition is no more a given of political history than a strong Buddhist tradition, or a strong tradition of tribal warfare. As James Kloppenberg has recently pointed out, the last twenty years have witnessed the European parties of the Left converging toward the American pattern, rather than the other way around.[18] Within a decade it may be possible to say that European politics, not American, constituted the historical aberration, and that the post-FDR American Democratic Party always was the most appropriate model for a democratic party of the Left. If that happens, we will be able to see that the question of American socialism was backward—the real question should have been "Why socialism in Europe?" More analytically, we will see that conflicts arise in a historical context and must be analyzed within that context.

Whether or not they wondered about the lack of socialism in the United States, however, many scholars in the last forty years have tried to prove Hartz wrong. The effort that recruited the largest number of scholars is the group of "republican" historians I will discuss shortly. The most influential recent effort within political science has probably been by Rogers Smith, who pointed out in his 1997 book, *Civic Ideals*, that the United States has a long history of excluding women and people from disfavored races, religions, and nationalities from full citizenship. Thus national citizenship laws "have always expressed illiberal, undemocratic ascriptive myths of U.S. civic identity."[19] Smith's point was not that the United States has no liberal tradition, but that Hartz had mistaken one thread of the national political culture for the entire garment.

Smith's "multiple American traditions thesis" was greeted with exultation by a younger generation of scholars who were tired of having to study "America's suffocating liberal consensus" and wanted instead to examine "a great dialectic between the familiar liberal tradition and its illiberal ... opposite."[20] And much of the praise is justified, for Smith is surely correct that American history has witnessed a long parade of nonliberal or antiliberal movements, philosophies, and parties. Skepticism of Rogers Smith, however, is as justified as skepticism of Louis Hartz. For one thing, the nonliberal, ascriptive rules that Smith uses as examples seem all to have eventually been overcome by American equality and inclusiveness. Slavery was abolished; then, after a long struggle, African Americans were afforded full civil rights. Women achieved the vote. Exclusionary immigration policies gave way to the nondiscriminatory laws now in effect. American Indians now fleece Anglo customers at dozens of casinos. All of Smith's examples of ascription appear to have been defeated by liberalism, albeit after decades or centuries. For another, there is an ambiguity in the idea of what exactly "liberalism" implies and what it doesn't. This is an elemental lack of clarity, and Hartz might be blamed for it. Still, it is possible to argue that some of the practices Smith identifies come from within the liberal tradition itself—especially from within capitalism. As James Morone has commented, "the real world of market liberalism has proven an eager accomplice to the ascriptive strain in American life."[21]

And so, without rejecting the insights of the research tradition inaugurated by Rogers Smith, it seems to me that there is a better way to approach the history of American arguments about politics and economics. This other approach takes off from the realization that *The Liberal Tradition in America* includes both a fundamental insight and a fundamental mistake; it is both right and wrong. Hartz is right that American society, by and large, has been politically and economically liberal. He is wrong in implying that the liberal tradition is a consensus tradition. It is, instead, profoundly and irreversibly one of dissensus, conflict, and ideological struggle. American history, therefore, is a pageant of disagreement over fundamentals embedded in agreement over fundamentals. To study American thought is to study, largely although not entirely, the tension within the liberal tradition between its political and economic halves, between democracy and capitalism.

Half of that tradition is so far undiscussed. When Hartz made Locke the paradigmatic thinker of liberalism, he emphasized that tradition's political, as opposed to its economic, half. In doing so he skewed the collective memory, for Adam Smith, the founding philosopher of economic liberalism, is as important to American opinions about the good society as John Locke.

ECONOMIC LIBERALISM

Adam Smith, the retired professor of logic at Glasgow University, had several purposes in the 1770s. He wished to kill the notion, derived from the Christian natural law tradition, that the individual interest is always opposed to the social, a belief that implied that people's behavior must be eternally watched and directed by authority. He wanted to show that mercantilist assumptions that national wealth was to be measured in bullion were fundamentally flawed and that the policies flowing from those flawed assumptions—government regulation and subsidization of the economy—were consequently counterproductive, leading to poverty rather than wealth. He planned to demonstrate that human economic activity, if directed into competition rather than subsidized and protected, yielded a harmonious and fruitful system of public-benefiting behavior that created an "opulent" society. And he planned to do all this with an analytical, scientific method, which he modeled on the approach of Isaac Newton.[22]

In political matters, Smith explicitly rejected Locke's hypothesis about agreements made within the context of an ahistorical state of nature.[23] Although he wrote no political treatise comparable in scope to his economic classic, in general Smith followed his friend David Hume in arguing that political matters were to be explained and analyzed with reference to history, custom, and institutional machinery.[24] But because Smith's fundamental purpose was to argue for greater individual liberty, his economic theory was liberal and tended to be embraced by the same people who were convinced by Locke.

Smith's book of Newtonian economics, *The Wealth of Nations*, appeared in 1776. It is an analysis of the long-term forces that lead to the development of a national economy. Like Newton, (and, ironically, Locke), Smith finds that he can best illustrate the principles at work in economic life if he abstracts away the details of reality and situates his economic actors in an ideal, imaginary economy. He creates, in other words, a state of nature, although he does not use the phrase. Smith assumes that the population of his natural economy consists of self-interested, equal individuals.

Despite their fundamental equality, the economic actors in Smith's social vacuum are diverse. They have differing tastes and talents. In the ideal economy, where there is no government to hinder human inclination, this diversity leads every producer to specialize. The economy instantly generates a division of labor, in which each producer does one thing well and exchanges goods or services for the goods and services of all the others. In order to facilitate exchange, money is introduced. With each producer spending time at what he does best, and trading for everything else, the economy as a whole is optimally efficient; that is, no other scheme of organization could bring forth more products for fewer hours worked. With the economy optimally producing, national opulence increases at the fastest possible rate.

Smith takes some pains to point out that the individuals in his natural economy are not consciously attempting to increase the common wealth. They are motivated solely by the hope of their own advancement. "It is not from the benevolence of the butcher, the brewer, or the baker that we expect our dinner, but from their regard to their own interest. We address ourselves, not to their humanity but to their self-love, and never talk to them of our own necessities but of their advantages."[25] It turns out that if correctly structured, self-love can become a mighty engine of the public interest.

Self-interest leads economic individuals to buy at the lowest price they can discover and sell at the highest that will draw customers. As a consequence, they compete with one another. When the quantity of any good falls short of demand, prices rise, because customers compete for the remaining stocks by offering ever-higher amounts of money. The rise induces people to create more of that good, and as supply increases, the reverse process occurs as competition forces producers to lower prices. There is thus a "natural" long-run price for any product that is based on the quantity of labor it contains—that is, the sum of the costs that go into it—and a market price that reflects the balance between supply and demand for that product. Over the long run, competition is always forcing the market price down to the natural price.

Consequently, if the market is allowed to operate unhindered, its inner principle of competition will compel prices to fall to a minimum and supply to rise to a maximum, resulting in the optimum situation for any economy: the most goods at the least cost. Moreover, the market mechanism has the marvelous quality of bringing about this ideal result without direction from any human authority. As the natural laws in the Newtonian universe create a system of cosmic harmony, the natural laws in the Smithian economy create a system of national prosperity. Competitive markets coordinate themselves, to the betterment of all, and without government direction. Smith summarized his insight in the most famous passage in economic literature: "As every individual . . . by directing that industry in such a manner as its produce may be of greatest value, intends only his own gain, he is in this as in many other cases led by an invisible hand to promote an end which was no part of his intention. . . . By pursuing his own interest he frequently promotes that of society more effectively than when he really intends to promote it."²⁶

This simple but revolutionary theory has a variety of implications for people thinking about the relationship of politics and economics. As Donald Winch has shown, Smith's ambiguities and ambivalence on many topics, and especially the value of self-interested economic behavior, have tended to be overlooked in favor of his apparently clear pronouncements about the value of free markets.²⁷ And as Emma Rothschild has demonstrated, the generations that followed Smith "picked and chose" among his principles so as to distort his teaching in systematic ways. Among the several tendencies of this distortion, the most important for our purposes was to overemphasize the importance of the free market and underemphasize the need to subject economic actors to competition.²⁸ Thus the lessons that most readers took away from Smith were not ambiguous.

By demonstrating that national wealth consisted of goods, not money, Smith had exposed a central assumption of mercantilism as dangerous nonsense. By invoking the image of the invisible hand that miraculously directed selfish behavior into publicly beneficial channels, he had removed the moral taint under which profit seeking had always labored. By describing economic systems as self-correcting and tending toward opulent harmony, he had dissolved the automatic tendency to suppose that human activity had to be directed by government. Henceforth, government regulation of the economy would have to be justified and defended, not assumed. Similarly, by emphasizing that the principles of free market competition applied between as well as within nations, Smith had brought into question the notion that international commerce should be regulated. Thus violations of free trade acquired an intellectual odium that increased in intensity over the generations after Smith.

The way Smith came to be understood had a paradoxical implication. In a sense, his objective had been anticapitalist. The business classes of his day sought government sponsorship and subsidy, with results that Smith believed were usually contrary to the public interest. He was greatly concerned with advancing public and private morality, as he had already shown in *The Theory of Moral Sentiments* and his university lectures on jurisprudence.²⁹ In advocating that merchants be forced to compete, he hoped to create what Rothschild has termed a "system of secular virtue."³⁰

Nevertheless, by its apparent validation of self-seeking behavior, the ultimate consequence of his economic theory was to stamp the imprimatur of morality onto private enterprise. A moral theory endorsing market outcomes and legitimating egotistical striving could not but become the philosophy of the class that invested and pursued profit. Against his own intentions, therefore, Smith became the patron saint of capitalism.

Smith's immediate influence on the thinking of Europe and America can be exaggerated. Gide and Rist's assessment that "Smith persuaded his own generation and governed the next," which once expressed the scholarly consensus, should now be considered both too strong and somewhat misleading.[31] Similarly, Robert Shalhope's more recent assertion that Smith "articulated inchoate beliefs that had permeated American society for decades" misses the opposition that *The Wealth of Nations* has provoked all through American history.[32] Smith's counsel to let the market alone was not in 1776, and has never been, endorsed by all important factions, parties, and individuals. Nevertheless, despite the fact that it did not always function as a guide, *The Wealth of Nations* immediately and permanently took its place as a touchstone of economic thinking, to be endorsed or rejected, but never ignored. In the succeeding centuries, some American thinkers agreed with Smith, and some did not. Even those who wanted to repudiate his assumptions, arguments, and conclusions, however, always felt obliged to pay them the respect of attempting to refute them. Smith joined Locke as one of the two central thinkers of liberalism. Individualism, equality, democracy, private property, competition, and the free market became, and have remained, fundamental American values. Americans, however, have not always realized that these values can sometimes contradict one another.

REPUBLICANISM

For some time, beginning in the 1960s, a group of scholars urged another interpretation of early American political thought besides the acceptance of the influence of liberalism. They accepted the Hartzian claim that liberalism was a consensus ideology, but argued that Hartz was more fundamentally mistaken, because liberalism was not the dominant discourse of American ideological disputes. Thus America did not have a "consensus tradition," and American colonial society was not so very different from European society of the same era.[33] Freed from the need to explain American exceptionalism, these scholars were so successful in discovering social conflicts in early American history that Isaac Kramnick could comment in 1988 that "contemporary scholarship seems obsessed with forever ridding the college curriculum of the baleful influence of Louis Hartz."[34]

Historians who rejected the liberal tradition as the dominant discourse in American history found a number of nonbaleful influences on the thought of the American founders. The most important of these is a group of historians, of whom the best known are Bernard Bailyn, Gordon Wood, and John Pocock, who interpreted the revolutionaries as heirs to the "republican" tradition.[35]

"Republicanism" is that thread of moral assessment of politics that arises with the ancient Greeks, was revived and elaborated by Machiavelli and Guicciardini in Italy during the sixteenth century, and came to full flower in the writings of the English Whigs during the first half of the eighteenth century. Republicans address the second great question of political philosophy: How can any polity achieve the public interest? In addressing this question, Republicans based their political evaluations on two antinomic concepts, "virtue" and "corruption."

To the republicans of the founding epoch on either side of the Atlantic, the major problem of politics lay in the difficulty of inducing both ordinary citizens and those in power to pursue the public interest. Virtue lay in a polity in which human beings would forego the temptation to view all issues through the prism of their selfish desires and instead act so as to enhance the common good. But virtue was fragile and tenuous, for all people, in office and out, were vulnerable to the temptation to put their individual welfare before the welfare of the whole. The rulers were particularly liable to yield to personal weakness, because, being closer to power, they were subjected to stronger temptations. Republicans lived by Lord Bolingbroke's dictum that "the love of power is natural; it is insatiable; it is whetted, not cloyed, by possession."[36] When either the mass of the people or most of the rulers succumbed and allowed their personal desires to govern their actions, the polity became corrupt. The result was a collective moral anarchy, a sort of nonviolent war of all against all within the confines of civil society, in which politics degenerated into a simple struggle over spoils. The task of society's moral guardians, urged republicans, was to encourage all historical forces tending to strengthen civic virtue and resist all forces tending to create civic corruption.

According to the theorists of republicanism, one of the necessary preconditions for virtue was personal independence. Men whose livelihood depended on another's pleasure were unable to exercise virtue because they must support the interests, not of the public, but of their master. Therefore, social trends that led to personal independence, such as wide dispersal of property, especially in land, were to be encouraged. Social trends that led to masses of men being subject to the authority of others, such as the growth of a rootless, impoverished mob, the members of which were liable to follow anyone who would employ them, were to be opposed.

According to the republican scholars' version of the Revolution, the American colonists interpreted Britain's attempts to impose taxes upon them without their consent as evidence of a veiled conspiracy, the purpose of which was to eliminate their autonomy and reduce them to corrupt dependency. Their assertion of independence was a defense of their political virtue. The writing of the Constitution was an attempt to structure a polity that would hinder corrupt men from gaining power and to encourage virtuous government.

There is much to be praised in the research of the historians of republicanism, not least the quantity, quality, and sensitivity of their scholarship. Their books and articles have rightfully modified the view we have of the founding generation, and forever prohibited an interpretation of that generation as influenced solely by liberalism. They explain, first, in a way that a knowledge of Locke does not, the founders' obsessive suspicion of power. Hamilton's famous assertion in the constitutional convention of 1787, "Give all power to the many, and they will oppress the few; give all power to the few, and they will oppress the many," is better interpreted with reference to republicanism than with reference to liberalism.[37]

Second, the founders' preference for a wide distribution of land is also better understood with reference to English Whig republicanism than to Locke or Smith. James Harrington's contention in *The Commonwealth of Oceana* (1656) that "equality of estates causeth equality of power, and equality of power is the liberty not only of the commonwealth, but of every man," for example, is the precursor to many statements in the writings of Jefferson and Adams.[38]

Third, a knowledge of some of the secondary concepts of the republican discourse adds insight to a discussion of American party struggles of the 1790s. In particular, Lord Bolingbroke, spokesman for the English "Country" opposition to the Walpole regime in the 1720s and 1730s, had launched a series of widely read polemics against the "stockjobbers" and speculators who were a pillar of that administration. Bolingbroke's fulminations against mobile (corrupt), as opposed to landed (virtuous), property, were taken up by the Jeffersonians in their struggle with Hamilton. The peculiar dread the Jeffersonians showed for Hamilton's class of entrepreneurs is inexplicable except when viewed against the background of Bolingbroke's writings.

The scholars of republicanism have thus added a great deal of texture and nuance to our understanding of the nation's founding. Yet as a force in the history of American thought as a whole, liberalism is still the most important interpretive key. For one thing, republicanism is not a theory of legitimacy. It does not engage people looking for the underpinnings of political authority as does liberalism.

Probably for this reason, the actual evidence from the founders' own recommendations and readings gives republicanism a secondary place to liberalism. For example, when Jefferson was asked in 1790 by Thomas Mann Randolph to recommend a list of fundamental readings to form the foundation for his legal education, the first name the secretary of state put on the list was Locke, not one of the Whigs. His third choice (after *The Federalist*) was James Burgh's *Political Disquisitions*, a mixture of Lockean and "Country" ideas.[39] When, in 1824, he drew up a list of books to form the basic curriculum in the school of law, government, and political economy in the new University of Virginia, his first choice was again Locke, followed by Algernon Sidney's 1698 *Discourses on Government*, a republican classic.[40] Similarly, in Lutz's calculation of the colonists' citations in their polemic literature, the three most cited authors are Montesquieu, Blackstone, and Locke, with Hume, an anti-Whig writer, in fourth place. Two Whig collaborators, John Trenchard and Thomas Gordon (authors of *Cato's Letters*), were in seventh place, while Bolingbroke placed sixteenth.[41] Consistently, the evidence suggests that Whig ideas were important but of secondary impact.

For another, the founders used the term "republican" in diverse and ambiguous ways. As Joyce Appleby has commented, "It would be surprising if scholars were able to agree upon the meaning of a word that contemporaries themselves used in disparate contexts."[42] This problem was compounded when the Jeffersonians adopted the label "Republican" for their party during the 1790s. Thereafter, the term rapidly became a synonym in common usage for "democracy" and lost its classical connotations.[43]

For another, the meaning of the component concepts of republicanism evolved rapidly, so that by the turn of the nineteenth century, for example, "virtue" tended to be used more as a description of private character rather than a public ideal.[44] As a consequence, once the spotlight moves away from the founding generation into the nineteenth century, the value of a republican explanation for the thought of important American actors diminishes. It has never quite faded entirely. For example, in 1997 Thomas Goebel wrote a thoughtful analysis of the beliefs of the Populists of the late nineteenth century, making a partially convincing case that much of their rhetoric could be interpreted as republican.[45] But the decay, fragmentation, and transvaluation of republican concepts during the 1790s must render such efforts somewhat quixotic. The very fact that scholars have had to write long, complicated, and subtle books retrieving republican usages from obscurity is evidence enough that the discourse is nearly extinct.

During the 1990s, several political philosophers, most notably Michael Sandel, attempted to revive republican concepts and language.[46] However successful this effort eventually proves to be, it is only further evidence of the deadness of republican discourse, for only that which is gone can experience a renaissance.

RELIGION

The study of politics and economics in American thought would be complicated enough if it only had to consider the various shadings and ambiguities of liberalism and republicanism. As a plethora of scholars have reminded us over the years, however, Americans have subscribed to a variety of religions, each contributing its set of beliefs and values, many politically and economically relevant. As James Kloppenberg summarized in 1998, "The pervasiveness of religion, whether manifested in varieties of orthodox or dissenting Protestantism or, in a few notable cases, reformulated by Deists, conditioned the reception of European ideas in America."[47]

The New England Puritans have been studied most thoroughly over the decades. The basic conclusion to be derived from the work of several generations of scholars is that Puritan theology, for all its severe aspects, evolved in a direction that by 1776 had made it a moral underpinning for democratic theory.[48] The fact that John Locke was a Puritan has made this interpretation highly plausible.

The Puritans, however, were only one segment of the population in one region of the settled area that would become the United States. Moral assumptions derived from many other Christian or Deist religious beliefs were everywhere part of public and private discussion of political issues. As the nation aged, immigration and cultural changes added many varieties of religious and secular ideologies to its foundational public opinion.

An investigation of all the ways in which religious beliefs have underlain and informed American public discourse would point this book away from its central theses. As a general strategy, therefore, I have chosen to deal with the economic and political arguments themselves, without going deeply into the religious assumptions from which they may derive. At specific points in the narrative, religious organizations and worldviews become such an overt influence on economics and politics that they must be noticed. The Populists, for example, are unexplainable without attention to their evangelical underpinning. Moreover, whenever political positions are profoundly moral, as in assertions of human equality, religious assumptions probably are playing a part. Nevertheless, as an overall design I have chosen to address myself to predominantly secular arguments.

THE LIBERAL VISION

At the beginning of their collective history as a nation, Americans were not all liberals. Various other theories and perspectives challenged those of Locke and Smith. But the story of the evolution of American public discourse is largely an account of the gradual triumph of the two great liberal theories of legitimacy and prosperity. That evolution was not the placid process it has sometimes been portrayed as being, however. Intense conflict occurred, not only between liberalism and other social theories but, more important, within liberalism itself.

American thinkers were not always consistent or clear in their use of the terms "capitalism" and "democracy." Nevertheless, if I am to discuss these concepts, I must offer my own understandings. When I use "capitalism," I mean an economic system that relies upon private investment within a relatively free market, most of the time and under most circumstances. When I use "democracy," I mean a political system that relies upon the free participation of citizens for its legitimacy and requires as corollaries freedom of expression, equality under the law, tolerance of opposition, and the assumption of majority rule with minority rights.

A variety of other scholars have identified a permanent tension in American life as the key concept in understanding the dynamics of national history. As mentioned in the preface, during the 1950s Robert McCloskey suggested that there were contradictions between capitalism and democracy.[49] In the 1980s J. David Greenstone argued that America suffers from a "fundamental bipolarity," being divided into humanist liberals, who assign a central place to people rather than a deity, and reform liberals, who focus on the development of human faculties.[50] In 1990, in *The Democratic Wish*, James Morone submitted that American history is the result of the struggle between the citizens' yearning for direct democracy and their dread of public power.[51] The same year, Eldon Eisenach detected an "antistory" tradition in the study of American political thought, one that "endlessly reproduces inherent tensions between liberty and democracy."[52] In 1995 Richard Ellis proposed that, not two, but five different value systems are perennially struggling for dominance within American culture: individualism, egalitarianism, hierarchy, fatalism, and hermitude (personal withdrawal).[53]

It would be pointless and ill-mannered for me to attempt to refute these thinkers' arguments and demonstrate that my approach to American thought is superior. A better strategy would be to simply proceed with the analysis of our intellectual history, and so I do.

CHAPTER TWO

The Founding, 1776–1819

The first census of the United States in 1790 revealed that the country had almost 3,000,000 inhabitants, of whom only about 114,000, or 2.7 percent, lived in cities. The people were temporarily concentrated along the eastern seaboard. The "frontier line," defined as those areas with between two and six persons per square mile, ran through upstate New York, central Pennsylvania, and the Appalachian crest, but was advancing westward rapidly. The business of America was agriculture. The most important crop, and therefore the most important source of wealth, was tobacco, cultivated in the Southern states, but the nation also exported rice, wheat, and corn. In the North the crops were tilled by free labor, but in the South black slaves did most of the work.[1]

Modern industrial capitalism was in its infancy. There were only three banks in the country in 1787. Americans relied on Britain for most of their manufactured products. Domestically manufactured items came almost entirely from farm families using their slack time during the winter to augment their incomes with handicrafts.[2] The first large, modern industrial firm was not founded until Francis Lowell built a textile plant at Waltham, Massachusetts, in 1814.[3] There were entrepreneurial interests in the larger cities, hungry to grow, but these were a tiny percentage of the population in 1776 and 1790.

Government and law in 1776 reflected the heritage of a rural, agricultural society that was still negotiating the transition from feudalism to capitalism and democracy. Following Locke, property was considered to be the keystone of personal and political liberty. When Arthur Lee of Virginia declared in 1775 that "the right of property is the guardian of every other right, and to deprive a people of this, is in fact to deprive them of their liberty," he spoke for virtually all Americans who mattered politically.[4] Their understanding of property, however, was premodern. In a rural society, property was held to consist of real, tangible things, mainly land. American common law, descending from the English, supposed the moral and political primacy of landowners. "Property" was assumed to be landed, and "property rights" largely referred to the power of an owner to prevent his neighbors from employing their own real estate in any manner that conflicted with his quiet enjoyment. The common law thus favored a nonindustrial conception of ownership over a conception that might encourage productive use and development.[5]

In politics, also, land ownership defined the relevant members of the community. All states in 1790 limited the right to vote, although the rules varied widely and were more or less restrictive depending on the power structure of each state and the amount of easily acquired land it offered in the West. Generally, from 50 to 75 percent of America's adult white male population was entitled to vote by 1776—a small percentage by modern standards, but far more democratic than any contemporary society, including Britain.[6]

Already by the Revolution there were arguments within the political class about whether to expand the franchise. The progressives of the era, such as Thomas Jefferson, favored including as many as possible in the voting polity, arguing to Edmund Pendleton during the summer that America declared its independence that "either the having resided a certain time, or having a family, or having property, any or all of them," should qualify a man for citizenship. Pendleton, the conservative, insisted that no, only the owning of "fixed Permanent property" should be acceptable.[7] Jefferson lost the particular argument in 1776 on the framing of the Virginia constitution, but the issue would live on.

The ideology of the thinking classes in this small, rural society was a mixture of liberalism, republicanism, mercantilism, physiocracy, and the concepts of individual theorists. The blend of ideas endorsed by any one person, of course, tended to depend on the interests he represented.

Adam Smith's great work was very influential, especially after Jean Baptiste Say added a crucial concept to his analysis in 1803. Modern scholars have sometimes doubted whether Say actually meant what other people understood him to mean.[8] Nevertheless, the world took "Say's Law" to prove that too much production of goods, and therefore general unemployment, was impossible in a society that refrained from interfering with the free market. The manufacture of anything, argued Say, requires labor. Labor must be paid. Workers receiving their wages from firm A will spend it on the goods made by firm B; workers receiving their wages from firm B will spend it on the goods made by firm A. Multiplied across a whole economy, the production of all goods creates a demand for all goods. Thus supply creates its own demand, and full production will always create full employment, in the absence of government or labor unions suppressing market forces. Disposing of what we would today call "macroeconomics" in one simple theory, Say confirmed Smith's point about the beneficence of the unmolested market and freed economic thinkers to ignore problems of society-wide unemployment until the Great Depression inspired John Maynard Keynes to rain on everyone's theoretical parade in 1936.[9]

Thinkers in the republican tradition, contemplating civic virtue and corruption, had also evolved economic views that resonated with many Americans. The one with the most lasting power was a distinction that arose about the turn of the eighteenth century in England, and that two hundred years later in America would come to be labeled the difference between making money and making goods. The distinction originated in republican contempt for "stockjobbing"—the speculative manipulation of the market values of shares in the English public debt. It seemed to republicans that speculators were pursuing their own individual good at the expense of the nation. They accused stockjobbers of constantly attempting to goad the country into war, in order to enhance the value of their securities.[10] With the single and crucial exception of Alexander Hamilton, contempt for speculators was a frequent prejudice of the founders.

In the United States, by the time of the adoption of the Constitution in 1787, the republican dislike of stockjobbing had evolved into a distaste for paper money. The paper of the time consisted partly of circulating notes issued by banks and partly of the sort of money issued by the Continental Congress during the Revolution. Either type of circulating medium tended to fluctuate widely in value and thus offer opportunities for speculators. Republicans were unable to see what now seems obvious—that speculators in currency or anything else, by their willingness to take risks, were supplying society with necessary investments that were unavailable from most of the risk-averse population. Republicans viewed speculators in public securities as corruption incarnate. Further, because banks issued private securities that both attracted speculators and could cause the value of publicly issued money to decline, the hostility to paper evolved into a suspicion of banks. To many prominent Americans of the founding generation, banks and paper money were the tools corruption used to subvert economic virtue.[11] As a result, the "property" most Americans revered did not include the more abstract and less republican forms of ownership. Although no important American ever put it quite this way, they believed that there was virtuous property and corrupt property.

From the dawn of the Republic, a set of social cleavages combined, overlay, and contradicted ideological tendencies, so that politics, as usual, was loud and confusing. Nevertheless, in the 1790s the anarchic particularity of political conflict congealed into a bipolar system of interests and ideologies. On the one hand, agrarians in the South, small business owners in the North, and recent immigrants everywhere tended to gravitate to the Democratic-Republican Party coalition, while the larger merchant and banking interests, together with the people who much later would come to be known as nativists, favored the Federalists.[12]

One issue was conspicuously absent from the political contest that lasted from Washington's first administration to 1820. The economy of the Southern states was largely based on slave labor, especially after 1793 when the introduction of the cotton gin heralded the beginning of the region's dominant industry.[13] Even before the Revolution there had been some agitation in the northern colonies to outlaw the ownership of human beings, and in the 1790s there were various antislavery societies in the North, particularly New York.[14] In 1787 Congress forbade slavery in the territories north of the Ohio River and east of the Mississippi River in the Northwest Ordinance, although this prohibition did not presume to discourage the institution where it already existed.

The reliance of their economy on the labor of slaves troubled the consciences of many prominent Southerners. Jefferson and Madison wrote of their distaste for the system on which their own livelihood depended, although they were not troubled enough to free their own slaves.[15] Given the manifest contradiction between the principles for which Americans supposedly fought the Revolution and the realities of human bondage, it might have been expected that there would have arisen a serious antislavery movement in the North.

It did not happen in the founding era. The Constitution embodied a series of compromises, not least between slave and free states, and there was very little sentiment anywhere to renege on the bargain. Northern politicians were easily convinced that an antislavery effort would destroy the new nation and were determined to placate Southern fears. A few Southerners were presciently unconvinced that Northern antislavery sentiment would always be so easy to discourage. Nevertheless, in this era the slavery issue was inconsequential.

Despite the determination of Northern and Southern elites to ignore slavery, during the period from 1776 to 1820 Americans engaged in a series of great conflicts within a basic consensus. The consensus is relatively easy to describe. With a certain number of qualifications and ambiguities, Americans believed in the legitimating power of citizen participation. Again with some quibbles of interpretation, they believed in the sacred rights of liberty and property. In general, they believed that a natural and productive economy based on agriculture would thrive if left to itself. In contrast to their agreements, however, their disagreements were complex, abstruse, and subtle. The disagreements require more analysis.

THE INVISIBLE HAND OF JAMES MADISON

Because of two essays he wrote in 1787, recommending ratification of the Constitution to the people of New York, James Madison is the most famous political philosopher that the United States has produced. Yet there is disagreement among scholars about what Madison actually advocated in *Federalist* #10 and #51. Was Madison the liberal prophet of "the method of counterpoise," in which individuals, interests, and institutions were forced to check one another so as to obstruct tyranny?[16] Or was he a republican statesman, designing a system in which "[t]he people, since *they* were virtuous, would choose wise and virtuous rulers who would exercise power benignly"?[17] Was the constitutional system designed to thwart bad people or recruit good ones? The answers to these questions lie at the heart of the national interpretation of the founding.

To one school of thought, Madison is the liberal architect of mechanistic politics, describing the Constitution as a device to pit ambitious men against one another until they exhaust themselves, and therefore have no remaining energy to oppress their fellow citizens. In Morton White's words, Madison "views the three branches of government as potential enemies who must be provided with weapons that they know how to use as well as motives that will lead them to use those weapons without impediment if and when they must be used."[18] To these scholars, the great extent of the new republic, as recommended in #10, and the opposed institutions analyzed in #51, add up to "a harmonious system of mutual frustration," in Richard Hofstadter's summary.[19]

According to the alternative interpretation, however, Madison, as an heir to the "republican" Scottish and English writers of the eighteenth century, viewed the new constitutional system as a device to ensure that the wisest, most public-spirited citizens would be chosen to govern. According to Gordon Wood, Madison "did not expect the new federal government to be neutralized into inactivity by the pressure of numerous conflicting interests." Instead, he planned that the structure of institutions that he and the other framers had constructed would bring forth representatives of enlightened views and virtuous sentiments.[20] Jack Rakove agrees that the Madisonian system is designed to "recruit a superior class of legislators qualified to act as 'proper guardians of the public weal.' "[21]

Scholarly discourse since the mid-1970s has alerted researchers to the possibility of a binary meaning in Madisonian theory, and so all writers of the past three decades or so have recognized it. Yet while acknowledging the duality in theory, in practice researchers have tended to strongly emphasize one of the facets of Madison's argument.

This dual nature of the arguments in *Federalist* #10 and #51 is significant because they are, along with the Declaration of Independence, the Gettysburg Address, and a few paragraphs and phrases from other speeches and papers, the foundation texts of Americans' self-understanding—the "ur-text of the polity" in Philip Abbott's picturesque phrase.[22] Consequently, differing interpretations of Madison are, in the muted and elevated discourse of scholarly controversy, a set of dueling myths about the formation of the Republic. And as even a cursory inspection of op-ed pages of newspapers or cable television public affairs talk shows will affirm, mythical understandings of history are frequently used as rhetorical weapons in contemporary political controversy. What Madison really meant in 1787 is of relevance today.

A contemporary scholar who attempts to evaluate previous interpretations of Madison runs into two puzzlements. The first is that there is abundant and convincing evidence, not only in the two *Federalist* essays but also in his additional writings, that Madison intended the constitutional system to be both a mechanistic frustrator of selfish interests and a generator of public-spirited officials. The best-known sentence from #51, "Ambition must be made to counteract ambition," is clearly mechanistic and is accompanied by many similar pronouncements.[23] The famous passage in #10, in which Madison argues that in a large republic, even factions whose members "will have a common motive to invade the rights of other citizens" will be stymied because "it will be more difficult for all who feel it to . . . act in unison" is similarly mechanical.[24] Yet there are other passages that unarguably refer to the production of virtuous representatives, such as the paragraph in #10 in which Madison asserts that a large national area will bring forth "a chosen body of citizens, whose wisdom may best discern the true interest of their country, and whose patriotism and love of justice will be least likely to sacrifice it to temporary or partial considerations."[25]

Moreover, Madison's emphasis on both mechanism and virtue cannot be attributed to the fact that he was hastily constructing a propaganda tract to persuade a small group of voters in one state to endorse the Constitution. The twin themes appear consistently in both his pre- and postconstitutional thinking. For example, in April 1787 he wrote a paper commonly entitled "Vices of the Political System of the United States" (that being, of course, the Articles of Confederation), in which he expressed his hopes for a new government that would encompass both principles:

> The great desideratum in Government is such a modification of the Sovereignty as will render it sufficiently neutral between the different interests and factions, to controul one part of the Society from invading the rights of another. . . . An auxiliary desideratum for the melioration of the Republican form is such a process of elections as will most certainly extract from the mass of the Society the purest and noblest characters which it contains.[26]

Thus any close study of Madison's writings must lead to the conclusion that he harbored hopes for both a mechanistic and a republican solution to the problem of good government. Evidently, the scholars who have interpreted Madison as advocating endorsement of the Constitution because of its obstructionism and those who have interpreted him as recommending it because it will produce public-spirited leaders are both right.

But this conclusion brings forth the second puzzlement. The two principles would seem to be contradictory. If one is so convinced of human depravity that one builds a system of organized obstruction in order to abort tyranny by thwarting action, why would one bother to worry about the recruitment of trustworthy citizens? Conversely, if one is designing a plan of leadership recruitment that will enlist the wisest and most public-spirited citizens to govern, why would one want to frustrate them once they achieved office? It is perhaps this apparent incompatibility of the two principles that has led scholars to emphasize one or the other. The alternative would seem to be to accept the conclusions that Madison was in fact an incoherent thinker and that the most famous pieces of political advocacy in American history are unintelligible.

Can a scheme of government designed to frustrate people in power be consistent with a plan to bring virtue to the fore? Political scholarship would tend to lead one to think not. However, there is a third way to interpret *Federalist* #10 and #51, a way that will reconcile the seemingly irreconcilable. That way involves realizing that there is an economic dimension to Madison's political theory. By thinking of *The Federalist* as the application to politics of the principles embodied in *The Wealth of Nations*, we will see that Madison, like Adam Smith, believed that the forces of competition could be structured so as to transform self-interest into public-spirited behavior.

The evidence that Madison was applying Smith to politics must be indirect. Learned men of the era had not yet adopted the modern habit of identifying many of their influences. It was considered presumptive to proclaim one's intellectual mentors.[27] There is, however, no doubt that Madison was familiar with *The Wealth of Nations*, and respected the ideas it contained. When the Confederacy Congress of the 1780s asked him to draw up a list of books to be the founding collection of the national library, *The Wealth of Nations* was among the hundred he recommended.[28] Furthermore, when commenting on specifically economic topics Madison often showed himself to be a close student of Smith. For example, writing of the best way to ensure prosperity for the arts and agriculture, city and countryside, in 1789, he opined that "all are benefitted by exchange, and the less this exchange is cramped by government, the greater are the proportions of benefit to each. The same argument holds good between nation and nation, and between parts of the same nation."[29] In 1791 he specifically cited Smith as an authority when giving a speech on banks on the floor of Congress.[30] For the rest, we must rely on what Samuel Fleischacker calls "verbal echoes."[31]

Federalist #10 contains a very loud verbal echo. In Book V of *The Wealth of Nations*, Smith discusses the application of his principles to religious factionalism. The problem for the sovereign is that "times of violent religious controversy have generally been times of equally violent political faction," and factionalism both weakens the state and saps its revenue.[32]

Governments have often attempted to head off such schisms by creating an established church. For a variety of reasons, however, Smith argues against such a solution, maintaining that while it may seem useful in the short run, it is certain to weaken the state in the long run. He counsels against the government involving itself in religion at all, but instead maintains that the sovereign should deal "equally and impartially with all the different sects," which will have the effect of encouraging them to multiply.[33] As a consequence, their competitive proselytizing will tend to force them to become tolerant and moderate:

> The interested and active zeal of religious teachers can be dangerous and troublesome only where there is, either but one sect tolerated in the society, or where the whole of a larger society is divided into two or three great sects. . . . But that zeal must be altogether innocent where the society is divided into two or three hundred, or perhaps as many as a thousand small sects, of which no one could be considerable enough to disturb the public tranquility. The teachers of each sect, seeing themselves surrounded on all sides with more adversaries than friends, would be obliged to learn . . . candour and moderation. . . . Provided those sects were sufficiently numerous . . . the excessive zeal of each for its particular tenets could not well be productive of any hurtful effects, but on the contrary, of several good ones.[34]

Although Smith does not use the word "competition" or the phrase "market forces" in this discussion, in this relatively short passage he is plainly relying upon the same principles for the social sphere that he recommends many times in the same book for the commercial sphere. Self-interested competition among religious sects, provided that they are sufficiently numerous, leads to public-spirited mutual respect. The invisible hand provides the solution to the problem of religious factionalism as it provides the solution to the problem of national prosperity.

In *Federalist* #10, Madison compared the means of handling religious and political selfishness in words that might have been lifted out of this passage in *The Wealth of Nations*. Like Smith in his discussion of the same topic, Madison did not actually use the word "competition." Viewed against the backdrop of Smith's passage on the handling of religious factionalism, however, Madison's analysis clearly refers to the political benefits of creating a mutual struggle among groups:

> Whilst all authority in it [the proposed federal republic] will be derived from and dependent upon the society, the society itself will be broken into so many parts, interests, and classes of citizens, that the rights of individuals, or of the minority, will be in little danger from interested combinations of the majority. In a free government, the security for civil rights must be the same as that for religious rights. It consists in the one case in the multiplicity of interests, and in the other the multiplicity of sects.[35]

In a similar vein, reading Madison's two essays with *The Wealth of Nations* in mind produces an interpretation of his argument that, except for the lack of the actual phrase, makes his a coherent theory of the value of market competition in politics. Human beings are not to be trusted in the great game of power. Differing economic interests will produce various political factions, defined as "a majority or minority of the whole, who are united and actuated by some common impulse of passion, or of interest adverse to the rights of other citizens, or to the permanent and aggregate interests of the community."[36] Further, once in power, ambitious individuals will attempt to use the authority of institutions to aggrandize themselves at the expense of the public good.[37] It is not possible to remove the causes of factional and individual misbehavior, for they are sewn into the nature of society and of humans. The problem, then, is to somehow control the effects of group and individual striving after power.

The solution to the problem is competition. Factions will compete for power. If a faction achieves a majority, it will use its authority to exploit the minority. The larger the republic, however, the more factions will enter the competition and the more difficult it will be for any of them to capture a majority. Further, the institutions of government under the Constitution rest upon separate power sources, yet require coordination to get anything done. This need for coordinated behavior will cause the men in charge of the various institutions to compete against one another for control over public policy. As in the Smithian market, within the constitutional structure the self-interested behavior of individuals and groups will set up a dynamic of people striving against one another.

The consequences of competition in politics, however, are different from the consequences of competition in economics. In Smithian economics, competition drives prices down and supply up. In Madisonian politics, the outcomes are more subtle. First, because the factions must compete for the people's votes in an extensive republic, they cannot make narrow campaign appeals. They must offer candidates of wide vision and noble impulse, because the large electoral arena will make it "more difficult for unworthy candidates to practice with success the vicious arts by which elections are too often carried."[38] As if directed by an invisible hand, candidates will be forced to advocate the public interest in spite of themselves. Further, one way to present one's party as the champion of the public weal will be to offer candidates of true moral worth. The competitive system will thus produce, not just more virtuous campaigns, but more virtuous candidates. The result will be wiser and more public-spirited members of the government who will be able to "refine and enlarge the public views" and "whose wisdom may best discern the true interests of their country, and whose patriotism and love of justice will be least likely to sacrifice it to temporary or partial considerations."[39] In other words, competition among many groups will improve the quality of government deliberation, which will in turn make for a more virtuous republic. Moreover, the larger the republic, the more factions will arise and be forced into the public arena, giving rise to stronger competitive forces, which will result in ever-more-virtuous deliberation.

Second, the competition for power within the government will make every public official jealously suspicious of every other, turning each into a "sentinel over the public rights." Each will be eager to advance his own career by exposing the malfeasance of other independent officials, and thus earning the approval of the electorate. Within the context of a governmental structure divided against itself, individuals with "opposite and rival interests" will constantly be monitoring one another, enlisting "personal motives" to the cause of public virtue.[40] Ambition must be made to counteract ambition because when it does, government officials must compete in a contest of virtue. The purpose of the famous mechanism of #51, then, is not to frustrate government officials but induce each to attempt to surpass every other as a faithful representative of the public interest.

When *The Federalist* is looked at this way, the apparent contradictions in Madison's thought are reconciled. Scholars who have interpreted Madison as the philosopher of the mechanism of frustration and those who have interpreted him as the philosopher of the public-spirited elite are both partially correct. As with Smith, it turns out that given the right sort of social order, the evident tendency of men and women to pursue their own interest is a boon, not a problem. Smith does not have to argue that butchers become virtuous when subjected to market forces, and Madison does not have to argue that people become angels in politics. Both theorists maintain that people are forced to act *as if they are angels* by the pressures of competition. The self-interested humans serving in the various parts of the national government respond to the pressures of institutional competition in precisely the same manner as the self-interested humans nominated to office respond to the pressures of electoral competition, and in the same manner as the self-interested humans selling their wares in the economy respond to the pressures of market competition: they attempt to advance their own causes by giving the people what they want. It turns out that Madison is both a liberal and a republican. He combines the values and styles of thinking of both traditions to design a competitive but virtuous republic.

The cases of Adam Smith and James Madison teach us that there is no necessary contradiction between a liberal and a republican social philosophy. Liberals, too, are pursuing the public interest. Whereas eighteenth-century republicans relied upon moral exhortation to persuade their fellow citizens to subordinate their self-interest to the common good, liberals fashioned institutional mechanisms to channel self-interest in a public-regarding direction.

As has been the case with *The Wealth of Nations*, there has always been a group of dissenters who refused to buy Madison's argument that the public good will arise from a governmental structure based on self-interested conflict. "If the administrators of every government are actuated by views of private interest and ambition, how is the welfare and happiness of the community to be the result of such jarring adverse interests?" asked "Centinel," a Pennsylvania anti-Federalist, arguing against ratification in 1787.[41] Centinel's plaint is echoed in more modern dissents.[42]

Despite Centinel's and many other critiques of the Constitution, however, it was ratified and formed the legal basis for the new nation. Madison became the dominant figure in the first House of Representatives that convened in 1789, and his collaborator on *The Federalist*, Alexander Hamilton, was appointed by President Washington to be secretary of the treasury. Within three years inherent social conflicts had split apart the two comrades. Madison joined with his fellow Virginian Thomas Jefferson in creating a Democratic-Republican Party that drew most of its supporters from the South, although there were important exceptions to this general rule, including Albert Gallatin, to be discussed shortly. Hamilton became the leader of the Federalist Party primarily based in the North, although with similarly important exceptions. The policies advocated by the leaders of the nation's first two parties, and the reasons they gave for them, formed traditions of argument that have retained their importance through American history.

THE HAMILTONIAN TRADITION

Hamilton was startled and offended in 1792 when Madison began to cooperate with Jefferson to try to undermine his influence, but he should not have been surprised.[43] Hamilton was the progenitor of the tradition of attempting to use governmental power to nurture commerce and industry, a direction of national policy that Madison and Jefferson, as agrarians, were certain to oppose. Moreover, while Hamilton officially endorsed the notion that the people were the fountain of legitimacy, in practice he was profoundly suspicious of the masses and unflagging in his belief that businessmen were the most useful citizens. On the one hand, democracies were always vulnerable to demagoguery, for ordinary people were "liable to be duped by flattery, & to be seduced by artful and designing men" into supporting vicious policies, such as schemes to redistribute wealth.[44] On the other hand, whereas elites were not more moral as individuals, they could be made useful to the nation. "Look through the rich and poor of the community," he had said in a speech at the New York constitutional ratifying convention. "Where does virtue predominate? The difference indeed consists, not in the quantity, but kinds of vices, which are incident to the various classes; and here the advantage of character belongs to the wealthy. Their vices are probably more favorable to the prosperity of the State than those of the indigent, and partake less of moral depravity."[45] Between the two wings of the liberal creed, Hamilton chose to emphasize capitalism rather than democracy. Madison and Jefferson, without explicitly opposing capitalism, chose to emphasize democracy.

The major reason Hamilton wanted to harness the vices of the rich to serve the new United States was that he was an intense nationalist. As one of his biographers, John C. Miller, observed, Hamilton was a hard-eyed realist when it came to human nature, but a misty-eyed romantic when it came to his country.[46] He wanted to make the United States powerful so that it could make itself prosperous, and prosperous so that it could make itself powerful. Focusing on government activity to achieve his goals, he was skeptical of Adam Smith's advice to leave the market alone, writing in 1801 that "this favorite dogma, when taken as a general rule, is true; but as an exclusive one, is false, and leads to error in the administration of public affairs . . . practical politicians know that [industry] may be beneficially stimulated by prudent aids and encouragements on the part of government."[47]

The policies that Hamilton championed before, during, and after his tenure as secretary of the treasury from 1789 to 1795 were systematically designed to harness the rich to the support of the new United States; make it a powerful trading, commercial, and industrial country; and suppress the common people's influence over their government. In the long run, which he did not live to see, he succeeded in the first two goals and failed in the third, although that failure did not occur for a century and a third after his death.

Hamilton agreed with all the measures designed to restrict suffrage to property owners.[48] Of more lasting importance to American thought, however, were his plans to simultaneously bind the power of the entrepreneurial spirit to the service of the nation, and to prevent the people from interfering with that spirit.

On January 14, 1790, Hamilton submitted the first of his famous reports to Congress. His "Report on Public Credit" was written in the context of the national discussion over what to do about the debts the Confederacy government and the states had incurred during the Revolution. In the fourteen years since the country had declared its independence, the national government and the states had dithered and stalled, so that by 1790 the new republic owed slightly over $50 million in principal and interest to its domestic and foreign creditors, while the states owed about $25 million—although these numbers were imprecise because the record-keeping had been lax to nonexistent.[49] Moreover, the seemingly interminable wait for repayment had persuaded many of the original creditors—often soldiers or farmers—to despair of ever getting their due. Many of these creditors had thereby been persuaded to sell their securities to speculators at some payment far below the original face value.

Both Hamilton's nationalism and his sense of fiscal propriety insisted that the federal government redeem its debts at full value. His model was the Bank of England, which had never defaulted on an obligation or arbitrarily reduced the rate of interest on its securities. As a result, Hamilton believed, Englishmen trusted their government as "an article of faith," and its credit everywhere was unshakeable.[50] He proposed that the federal government institute an impost or uniform tariff on imported goods, using the revenues thereby created to repay the Republic's debts at full value over a period of decades.

There was some grumbling over this part of the plan, but the serious opposition was engendered by the second part. The Constitution had authorized the federal government to redeem not only its own but also the states' debts. There was, however, warm disagreement, both over whether the national government should take on the extra $25 million debt as its own and over whether this should be done at the original value or at some lesser fraction. The situation was complicated by the fact that most of the speculative holders of state obligations resided in the North. When the national government paid them off, therefore, the many would be taxed (indirectly, through the impost) to reimburse the few, and the South would be taxed to reimburse the North. There was thus strong sentiment among the many, and in the South, to minimize the repayment. Before Hamilton's "Report," very few Americans, except those actually holding the securities, favored redemption at 100 percent of the original value.

To Hamilton, however, the "Report" offered an opportunity to implement his strategy of cementing the commercial classes to the Republic. In the first place, he argued, it would be an injustice, as well as imprudent, to penalize a speculator who had been willing to take an economic risk. Indeed, such a speculator ought to be rewarded, for "he paid what the commodity was worth in the market, and took the risks of reimbursement upon himself. He, of course, gave a fair equivalent, and ought to reap the benefit of his hazard—a hazard which was far from inconsiderable, and which, perhaps, turned on little less than a revolution in government."[51]

Hamilton was a close student of the Scottish philosopher David Hume, who had asserted that capital was only useful to a national economy if it was concentrated under the control of people who were disposed to invest it. On the other hand, it was unproductive "if it is dispersed into numberless hands, which either squander it in idle show and magnificence, or employ it in the purchase of the common necessaries of life."[52]

In the second place, Hamilton argued, assumption of the debts is a useful means of creating a class of people who defend rather than intrigue against the new government, because "[i]f all the public creditors receive their dues from one source, distributed with an equal hand, their interests will be the same. And, having the same interest, they will unite in the support of the fiscal arrangements of the Government."[53] Following Hume, Hamilton hoped to make the entrepreneurial class of society the foundation of the Republic's economy.

Despite the widespread opposition to his assumption plan, Hamilton's arguments, plus the disorganization of the dissenters, plus a deal he cut with Jefferson and Madison to site the national capital in Virginia in return for their support, enabled it to pass. Its success, of course, united present and future economic risk-takers not only behind the new government but behind the secretary of the treasury. Henceforward until he was killed by Aaron Burr in a duel in 1804, Hamilton was the undisputed leader of the commercial classes.

The assumption plan was not the only means by which Hamilton hoped to give the new United States a firm economic grounding. In December 1790 he submitted two more reports to Congress. One of these, in which he recommended an excise tax on whiskey, is of comparatively little historical importance. In the second, however, he ignited a political firestorm with the suggestion that Congress establish a national bank.

In this report Hamilton offered a variety of reasons for establishing such an institution that seem obviously persuasive and uncontroversial to a modern observer. The bank would provide a paper currency, furnish a safe place for keeping public funds, act as a fiscal agency for the government in such transactions as the sale of bonds, and so forth. But Hamilton had a private reason as well as the ones he endorsed publicly. In 1781, in a letter to Robert Morris, he had first floated the idea of a national bank. There he had been forthright about a major purpose of this institution:

> To ... give individuals ability and inclinations to lend, in any proportion to the wants of government, a plan must be devised, which by incorporating their means together and united them with those of the public, will ... erect a mass of credit that will supply the defect of monied capitals and answer all the purposes of cash, a plan which will offer adventurers immediate advantages analogous to those they receive by employing their money in trade ... and which will not only advance their own interest and secure the independence of their country, but in its progress have the most beneficial influence upon its future commerce and be a source of national strength and wealth.[54]

Thus the political—as opposed to the administrative—purpose of the bank was to be identical with the goal of the debt-assumption plan, to intertwine the future fate of the United States with the destiny of economic "adventurers." The new republic was to become the United States of entrepreneurs.

Given the passions that still surround Hamilton, at least in the scholarly community, it is important to remember that he saw entrepreneurs as means, not as ends. Lance Banning's statement that "he never meant for monied men to use the government. He intended the reverse," is accurate and fair.[55] Nevertheless, there are alternative ways for governments to stimulate economic activity. Hume's belief that capital must be concentrated is not necessarily accurate; as we shall see, there is another strategy. By placing his faith in elites, Hamilton left himself open, then and now, to the charge that he favored the few over the many.

Moreover, in his "Report on a National Bank," Hamilton made an argument that is still strongly contested when discussion turns to the Bank of the United States' historical heir, the Federal Reserve Board. Although it was to be a public institution, the Bank of the United States was to be "under a *private* not a *public* direction—under the guidance of *individual interest*, not of *public policy*."[56] The people's representatives were not to be allowed to direct the use of the people's money. Politicians could never be trusted to hew to a wise, long-run (and presumably hard-money) course. It could be anticipated that there would be an eternal clamor among the people for inflation, and "what government ever uniformly consulted its true interests in opposition to the temptations of momentary exigencies? . . . It would indeed be little less than a miracle, should the credit of the bank be at the disposal of the government, if, in a long series of time, there was not experienced a calamitous abuse of it."[57] In American history, this is probably the first assertion by an important public official that capitalism must be protected from democracy. It is worth noting, in this context, that Hamilton's ostensible model for the Bank of the United States, the Bank of England, was an entirely public institution controlled by public officials as an instrument of public finance. Hamilton's "national" bank, by contrast, was a private business run for the profit of its stockholders.[58]

Hamilton submitted his third significant report, "On Manufactures," in December 1791. Once again, the secretary of the treasury was attempting to persuade Congress to form an alliance with economic adventurers, this time with those involved in making things rather than those involved in finance and commerce. Perhaps chastened by the opposition of the agrarians to his previous efforts, Hamilton spends some time attempting to placate them. Yes, he concedes, "the cultivation of the earth" is "the primary and most certain source of national supply" and creates a situation "most favorable to the freedom and independence of the human mind."[59] But that doesn't mean that a country should be exclusively agricultural. After all (with a bow to Adam Smith), the division of labor is a good thing. To increase the number of components of this division can only spur the economy as a whole, and thus help farmers, also. There follows a variety of arguments all tending to the same conclusion: manufacturing is good for everybody.

Left to itself, the United States will become a manufacturing nation sooner or later. But normal human inertia may result in the community turning to industry more tardily than would be consistent with the interests of either individuals or society. "To produce the desirable changes as early as may be expedient may therefore require the incitement and patronage of government."[60] In order to produce an effective patronage,

> the confidence of cautious and sagacious capitalists, both citizens and foreigners, should be excited. And to inspire this description of persons with confidence, it is essential that they should be made to see in any project which is new—and for that reason alone, if for no other, precarious—the prospect of such a degree of countenance and support from governments, as may be capable of overcoming the obstacles inseparable from first experiments.[61]

At this point, the reader has been prepared for a theoretical argument in favor of a protective tariff. But Hamilton veers off, suggesting instead that a series of "bounties," what today would be called subsidies, be adopted to nurture infant industries. The recommendation is puzzling. Not only is a tariff the apparently logical outcome of Hamilton's argument, but it would have been far more politically palatable, since tariffs are indirectly paid by consumers, whereas bounties would have had to come out of government revenue. A modern scholar, John Nelson, has maintained persuasively that Hamilton was at least partly insincere in this report. Nelson suggests that it was part of an elaborate ploy on Hamilton's part to procure a government subsidy for an investment consortium of which he was a member.[62]

But no matter. The world has accepted at face value the "Report on Manufactures" as a heartfelt plea for government support of industry. Scholars have often disregarded the absence of the logical conclusion and discussed the report as though it was an explicit advocacy of protective tariffs.[63] In the event, Congress refused to endorse its recommendations. For our purposes, the important aspect of the report is that it once again displayed Hamilton's determination to tie the Republic ever closer to entrepreneurs. Granting Nelson's interpretation, then Hamilton himself was hoping to become an entrepreneur. If so, he was greatly disappointed. The consortium he may have been trying to help failed in 1796, and he died insolvent.[64]

Hamilton's intention, however, was not merely to urge the new republic to supply entrepreneurs with resources and refrain from hindering their development but also to erect constitutional buffers against popular interference with the prerogatives of property. His contributions to *The Federalist* essays, like Madison's, are full of foreboding about the potentially destructive whims of the populace and the difficulty of checking the legislative expression of those whims.

Hamilton did not disagree with Madison that the multiplicity of factions and the independence of the three branches would generate a competitive checking that would preserve the public interest. He emphasized, however, one aspect of the Madisonian structure, the judiciary.

The problem, as Hamilton stated it in *Federalist #78*, was to fashion an institution that would guard the Constitution against "the encroachments and oppressions of the representative body . . . [such as] injury of the private rights of particular classes of citizens, by unjust and partial laws."[65] The solution was twofold. First, the courts must be acknowledged to be the final arbiters of the meaning of the Constitution, because somebody must have the authority to keep the members of the legislature "within the limits assigned to their authority."[66] Second, federal judges must serve for life and be removable only with great difficulty, because "nothing can contribute so much to [the judges'] firmness and independence as permanency in office."[67] Placing *Federalist #78* within the context of Hamilton's other writings, there is no doubt that he intended the function of the judicial branch to be to shield his precious entrepreneurial class against democratic envy. When, in 1803, in the case of *Marbury v. Madison*, Hamilton's friend Chief Justice John Marshall successfully asserted the power of the Supreme Court to declare acts of Congress unconstitutional and therefore void, Marshall solidified the ability of judges to protect property from the people's representatives. Within a century this power had metastasized into perhaps the most significant aspect of the American polity.

Although only some of Hamilton's policies were enacted, although his party was cast out of national power forever in 1800, and although he died young, the political tradition he inaugurated is of robust importance in American history. While paying formal obeisance to Lockean notions of legitimacy, in practice the tradition reveres capitalism and is suspicious of democracy—it suspects that entrepreneurs are more worthy of power than the masses. Some of the Hamiltonian devices for shielding public policy from the people—a restricted franchise, for example—no longer exist. However, some—keeping the direction of fiscal policy at least a step removed from popular control and an independent judiciary—are very much with us.

When the Jeffersonians accused Hamilton of being a monarchist at heart, he reacted with offended surprise. "I give it to you with the utmost sincerity," he wrote to Edward Carrington in May 1792, "I am *affectionately* attached to the Republican theory."[68] And many scholars, over the course of the two centuries since his death, have shown a similar frustration that what they deem to be Jeffersonian slanders of Hamilton have lodged permanently in the national memory. In 2002 Stephen Knott tried again to demonstrate that Hamilton's alleged utterance, "Your people sir . . . your people is a great beast!" was simply another example of the willingness of scholars to propagate, and the people to swallow, pernicious myths about a great man.[69] "The image of Hamilton fashioned by Jefferson and his allies has endured and flourished," complained Knott. "Never has such a resilient description of a political figure, based on so little evidence, been circulated and accepted by so many."[70] Meanwhile, on another front, various historians studying American "state-building" hail Hamilton as the first American statesman to have a "comprehensive vision" of the potential greatness of the United States.[71]

But one does not have to deny Hamilton's greatness of vision and accomplishment in order to endorse the opinion that his basic attitude was antidemocratic. Yes, he was a republican and a Lockean liberal in that, at some theoretical level, he endorsed the necessity of grounding government on the people's participation. In the details of governance, however, he was the progenitor of the politician whose mind is full of schemes to separate power from the influence of the masses and place it at the disposal of elites. He authored, in his report on the bank, the classic argument in favor of insulating national monetary policy from popular influence. He authored, in *Federalist* #78, the classic argument in favor of insulating the national judiciary from popular control and, by implication, using that institution to shield property. When Jefferson was out of power, he attempted, with a public relations campaign and an organizing drive, to persuade the people to support his party. When Hamilton was out of power, in 1804, he complained to Theodore Sedgwick that "our real Disease, which is DEMOCRACY," was a "poison" in the body politic.[72] Therefore, despite the fact that Hamilton has no doubt been treated unfairly in some of the scholarly literature, and in the national imagination, the basic image of him as the paladin of those who revere capitalism and are skeptical of democracy is substantially accurate.

THE JEFFERSONIAN TRADITION

The inside walls of the Thomas Jefferson Memorial in Washington, D.C., are inscribed with quotations the designers thought the public would find edifying and inspirational. All of these inscriptions deal with the legitimacy of government or the necessity of personal liberty, especially freedom of thought. None, except possibly the one expressing Jefferson's (entirely theoretical) opposition to slavery, address economic questions. These choices are appropriate. On the subject of the politics of individual liberty, Jefferson was a remarkably modern thinker. On the subject of economic policy, his ideas were oddly retrograde. Yet the political and economic ideas were combined into a personal ideology that somehow expressed the common sense of the American people during their first four score and four years.

To Jefferson, the ideal society was one that offered its citizens Lockean individual natural rights and consent-based government combined with opportunities for republican virtue. This society would be composed mainly of small farmers, because such an arrangement would be the one most likely to support that personal economic independence that permitted true participation in the public order. Industry, and especially manufacturing, by depriving people of their self-sufficient residence on the land, concentrating them in cities, and making them dependent upon the decisions of capitalists, deprived people of the prerequisites of authentic citizenship. It vitiated democracy by foreclosing the opportunity for independent judgment. The Lockean ideal of citizens legitimating their government by choosing their representatives in free elections, therefore, could only be realized in a society dominated by yeoman farmers. The farther the nation moved away from such a model, the closer it would approach the anti-ideal of intrinsic corruption.

Fortunately, the ideal was attainable through laissez-faire public policies. In his list of recommended readings for a legal education in 1790, Jefferson wrote that "in political economy, I think Smith's *Wealth of Nations* the best book extant."[73] It may be, as Joyce Appleby has commented, that it was not so much Smith's vision of prosperity as his idea of "the economy's ordering of society with minimal compulsion that stirred the Jeffersonian imagination."[74] But whether they found its primary appeal in visions of opulence or the expectation of liberty, the Jeffersonians believed that if government would simply stop helping the sterile mercantile segments of the economy and allow agriculture to grow naturally, prosperity and justice would flourish together. Very little positive decision was necessary. The purpose of attaining power was to enable the laissez-faire forces of virtue to block the mercantilist forces of evil. Thus in Jefferson and his associates, the conviction that the party of the people should be the party of inaction took deep and profound root.

The Jeffersonian utopia would rest on four pillars: the agrarian, the democratic, the laissez-faire, and the republican. If any one of the columns of the structure faltered, the entire edifice would be threatened. Jefferson never elaborated his philosophy systematically in one place, but his most complete exposition of his idea was in a celebrated passage in a book he wrote in 1785, *Notes On Virginia*.

Those who labor in the earth are the chosen people of God, if ever He had a chosen people, whose breasts He has made His peculiar deposit for substantial and genuine virtue.... Corruption of morals in the mass of cultivators is a phenomenon of which no age nor nation has furnished an example. It is the mark set on those who, not looking up to heaven, to their own soil and industry, as does the husbandman, for their subsistence, depend for it on the casualties and caprice of customers . . . generally speaking, the proportion which the aggregate of the other classes of citizens bears in any State to that of its husbandmen, is the proportion of its unsound to its healthy parts, and is a good enough barometer whereby to measure its degree of corruption. While we have land to labor then, let us never wish to see our citizens occupied at a workbench, or twirling a distaff. . . . The mobs of great cities add just so much to the support of pure government, as sores do to the health of the human body.[75]

Not surprisingly, Jefferson and his allies greeted Hamilton's system of policy with well-articulated outrage. Here was the most important adviser to President Washington deliberately designing a scheme that would corrode all four pillars of the republican ideal: it was antiagrarian, antidemocratic, anti-laissez-faire, and antivirtue. The Constitution was still an infant, and Hamilton was trying to drown it in a sewer of corruption.

It was not necessary for the Jeffersonians to view Hamilton's financial program through the prism of English "Country" writings. There were many other possible interpretations available, including Smith's. In this area, however, they were determined to behold, not just error, but a plot to undermine the Republic. As soon as the plan to create a national bank was publicized, Senator William Maclay of Pennsylvania characterized it as "an aristocratic engine" and "a machine for the mischievous purposes of bad ministers."[76] Hamilton, wrote Jefferson after he left office and his great antagonist was long dead, was "so bewitched and perverted by the British example, as to be under thorough conviction that corruption was essential to the government of a nation."[77] Shortly after his first inauguration in 1801, he had written of Hamilton to a friend, "We can pay off his debts in 15 years, but we can never get rid of his financial system. It mortifies me to be strengthening principles which I deem radically vicious, but this vice is entailed by the first error. In other parts of our government, I hope we shall be able by degrees to introduce sound principles and make them habitual."[78]

Madison, in this as in many other instances at one with Jefferson, was equally offended at the direction taken by his one-time Federalist ally. Writing of the proposal to establish the Bank of the United States as the administrator of the national debt in 1791, he was unambiguous about who would benefit from the scheme and what that would mean to the country. He accused Hamilton of attempting to establish a government

> operating by corrupt influence ... converting its pecuniary dispensations into bounties to favorites, or bribes to opponents; accommodating its measures to the avidity of a part of the nation, instead of the benefit of the whole; in a word, enlisting an army of partizans, whose tongues, whose pens, whose intrigues, and whose active combinations, by supplying the terror of the sword, may support a real domination of the few, under an apparent liberty of the many.[79]

And so the battle was joined. It was to be agrarianism, democracy, and an inactive government versus capitalism, elitism, and an active government, at least on the battlefield of ideology. Thus in theory, if not always in practice, the Jeffersonians were antidebt, anti-Bank, and antiexcise, while remaining prodemocracy according to the rules of the era.

Jeffersonian discourse on economic topics seems stunted and myopic to a modern observer. It is easy to be misled by the Jeffersonians' constant affirmation of the sacred value of private property, for their understanding of the institution was primitive and simply lacked the conceptual categories a modern, educated person—or a Hamiltonian—would find essential in discussing economic institutions and practices. The Jeffersonian mind, refusing to go beyond the reactionary prejudices of the English "Country" party, contained no cognitive category for "entrepreneur," for example. Everyone who invested in commerce, industry, banking, or securities in the hope of reaping a future gain was a "stockjobber" or a "gambler." Despite their familiarity with the laissez-faire argument about the market marshaling self-interest on behalf of the public good, Jeffersonians seemed unable to consider the possibility that investment with the hope of profit might be an advantage to the commonweal.

Similarly, the Jeffersonians apparently lacked the ability to conceptualize a bank as anything but an organized effort by the commercial class to fleece farmers. The functions of banks as safe deposits for funds, lenders to businesspeople (including farmers) and governments, and stabilizers of currency did not enter their imaginations. When Hamilton first proposed the Bank of the United States, James Jackson, a Jeffersonian from Georgia, charged that it "was calculated to benefit a small part of the United States—the mercantile interest only; the farmers, the yeomanry of the country, will derive no advantage from it."[80] Jefferson himself wrote that "banking establishments are more dangerous than standing armies."[81] When the Bank of the United States' charter ran out in 1811, under

Madison's administration, the Jeffersonians in Congress allowed it to expire—although by that time the coalitional base of the Democratic-Republican Party had become more complicated, and the politics of the decision are not clear-cut. Be that as it may, the administration's finances fell at once into chaos, a situation that contributed to the country's largely inept performance during the war with Britain that began the next year. In 1816, chastened by their near escape from military and financial catastrophe, the Jeffersonians rather sheepishly chartered another national bank.[82]

Jefferson and his supporters were neither Luddites nor worshipers of inefficiency. By and large, they recognized the need for both commerce and manufacturing as an auxiliary to the agricultural ideal. Their view of the place of these two occupations in the Republic, however, was quite different from Hamilton's. They rejected, indeed, execrated, the notion that capital should be concentrated in the hands of a class of businesspeople in order to drive the economy. To the extent that exchange of goods was needed between decentralized individuals and states, they believed, it would arise spontaneously as a reaction to felt needs. The market would thus supply the wants of society, and Hamiltonian adventurers were not necessary. Manufacturing would not be neglected, but would be dispersed about the countryside in cottage industry. This growth and dispersal would happen authentically and beneficently if only the government would refrain from distorting the natural pattern of growth by giving privileges to one class at the expense of others. "I own myself the friend to a very free system of commerce," proclaimed Madison in a speech to the House of Representatives in 1789, "and hold it as a truth that if industry and labour are left to take their own course, they will generally be directed to those objects which are most productive, and this in a more certain and direct manner than the wisdom of the most enlightened legislature could point out."[83] Thus in the 1790s and after the Democratic-Republicans attracted the support of many Northern small businesspeople who concluded that a party dominated by laissez-faire agrarians was better than one dominated by large commercial and banking interests.

As the leader of a majority coalition spanning the thirteen states, Jefferson presided over a mosaic of individuals and interests who did not always agree with each other, or with him. Among these were a group who, in their devotion to the agricultural ideal, out-Jeffersoned their president.

Two of the most articulate and outspoken of the hyperagrarians were John Taylor and John Randolph, both Virginians. They believed that Jefferson, Madison, and the others who had sometimes been willing to compromise with commerce, banking, and manufacturing, and active government, were weak-minded dupes who did not see the essentially satanic nature of the adversary. Indeed, both Taylor and Randolph were always suspicious of Madison for having been willing to collaborate with Hamilton in writing *The Federalist*, which they saw as a reprehensible brief for despotic government. They viewed Madison as a closet Federalist and blamed him for misleading Jefferson into moderation.[84]

All commerce, argued Taylor, is "political," that is, it is based upon the creation of fictional value by government. On the other hand, property in land is real because it is created by nature. Political property, he argued in 1794, "is distinguishable from natural property. Land cannot be increased by law—paper money may. Land, being incapable of artificial multiplication, cannot by increasing its quantity, strengthen its influence—with paper the case is different. Land cannot in interest be at enmity with the public good—paper money is often so."[85]

Because the agrarians had initially not understood this difference between the two kinds of property, Taylor wrote in later publications, they had allowed Hamilton to install "a power for creating pecuniary inequalities." The Federalists had given to bankers "an irresponsible, uncontrolled, unpunishable, unelected power over the national purse" and had fashioned, in the tariff, a scheme for enriching manufacturers at the expense of everyone else. Unless the agricultural and mechanical classes could abolish these "property-transferring" laws, the country would eventually fall under the domination of a "vast pecuniary aristocracy."[86]

Randolph agreed, but was pessimistic that the virtuous landed interests could prevail against the wicked manufacturers. Anticipating arguments that would be made a century and a half later by economists who noticed that concentrated industries, already organized, had advantages of political influence over dispersed industries such as agriculture, Randolph warned his fellow agrarians in 1819 that they were up against an antagonist occupying a superior strategic position:

> The agriculturist has his property, his lands, his household goods to defend; and like that meek drudge, the ox, who does the labor and plows the ground, and then, for his reward, takes the refuse of the farmyard . . . while the commercial speculators live in opulence . . . the agriculturists are no match for them. Alert, vigilant, the manufacturing interest are collected in masses and ready to associate at a moment's warning for any purpose of general interest to their body.[87]

Whereas most of the Jeffersonians eventually became reconciled, in practice if not in theory, to the basics of the Hamiltonian system, the true agrarians never gave an inch.

Taylor, who served in the Virginia state legislature and the U.S. Senate off and on from 1779 to 1824, and Randolph, who served in Congress from 1800 to 1832, spent part of their time excoriating the hated Federalists and their descendants and part of their time chiding their putative party for its moderation and weak-mindedness. Their rhetoric was florid, satirical, and perceptive. They were for weak interpretation of the Constitution and for states' rights, and opposed to debts, banks, tariffs, foreign entanglements, and internal improvements. They castigated any Democratic-Republican who dared to compromise with the commercial interests. Inevitably, therefore, Randolph broke publicly with President Jefferson in 1806, and Taylor broke publicly with President Madison in 1812.

Although their devotion to agrarianism was sincere, underneath the rhetoric of Taylor, Randolph, and their followers one suspects another, equally basic value. This suspicion partly rests on the realization that, while backing the party of the people most of the time, they were no democrats. Explicitly rejecting Lockean notions of equality and consent, they endorsed a more hierarchical and traditional conception of rule by the propertied.[88] More fundamentally, however, at the base of their ranking of values, inextricably intertwined with agriculture, one finds slavery. At the bottom of their fear of a powerful national government is the suspicion that it might one day be used to destroy the peculiar institution. Taylor and Randolph began the Southern tradition of opposition to federal power rhetorically looping through a series of prevarications and euphemisms, all designed to deflect attention from the fact that what is actually being discussed is slavery.

Like Jefferson, each was troubled, in theory, by the reality that they and their state held humans in bondage, and like Jefferson, each began by being barely reconciled with the institution, then advanced to the position of defending it. Unlike Jefferson, each eventually evolved into a forceful and articulate public champion of the institution. Taylor's statement in 1818 that "Negro slavery is an evil which the United States must look in the face. To whine over it, is cowardly," is typical of their personal style, one in which professed ambivalence always seemed to end in an unambivalent defense of the institution.[89] Equally typical is Randolph's assertion in 1816 that "we must concern ourselves with what is, and slavery exists . . . it . . . is to us a question of life and death . . . a necessity imposed on the South, not a Utopia of our seeking."[90]

Their advocacy of principles that incidentally protected slavery and attack on policies that incidentally undermined it, however, were never ambivalent. Thus, in discussing a bill providing federal support to build roads and canals, Randolph prophesied that "if Congress possesses the power to do what is proposed by this bill, they may . . . emancipate every slave in the United States. . . . And where will they find the power? They may . . . hook the power upon the first loop they find in the Constitution."[91] And Taylor, speaking against the proposed Missouri Compromise of 1820, one of whose provisions would outlaw human bondage in the Northern territories, was quite explicit in linking the effort to limit slavery to the ongoing capitalist conspiracy: "The great pecuniary favor granted by congress to certificate holders, begat banking; banking begat bounties to manufacturing capitalists; bounties to manufacturing capitalists begat an oppressive pension list; these partialities united to beget the Missouri project."[92]

Later, when the slavery controversy came to a head, Southerners would look to Taylor and Randolph as prophets. Both had foreseen the dissolution of the Union if the federal government failed to reverse course and become a champion of agrarian rights.[93]

The hypocrisy of Jeffersonian slaveholders styling themselves the guardians of liberty did not pass unnoticed by the Federalists. "Men who can count in their train a hundred slaves, whose large domains, like feudal barons are peopled with the humblest vassals," crowed James Bayard, Federalist member of the House from Delaware, "are styled democrats. . . . These high priests of liberty are zealously proclaiming freedom on one hand while on the other they are riveting the chains of slavery."[94] It was a good point, and it applied to Jefferson and Madison as much as to Taylor and Randolph.

Nevertheless, the best of the Jeffersonians were honest hypocrites. They believed ardently in the principles of the Declaration of Independence while violating them in practice. They endorsed the agrarian republican ideal whether or not they carried out policies consistent with its demands. Without self-doubt, they confirmed that their favored policies represented the good of the whole, while Hamilton's represented the good of a narrow, unrepresentative class. If this self-image was an illusion, it was an illusion shared by the people. As Joanne Freeman has summarized, "by 1830, the idea that democracy had triumphed with Jefferson's victory was central to America's self perception as a New World haven for equality, justice, and the rights of the common man."[95] Jefferson is thus remembered, accurately, as the progenitor of the tradition in American thought that proclaims democracy while being suspicious of capitalism and that recommends an inactive government as the best guardian of democratic liberty. Because the democratic tradition has triumphed, Americans put Jefferson's face on mountain sculptures and read his words in marble monuments. They don't bother much about his economic views.

There was a time when historians tended to tell the national story as essentially a struggle between Hamiltonians, defined as the party of the elites, and Jeffersonians, defined as the party of the people. Decades ago this narrative tradition was discarded as immature and inaccurate. Nevertheless, in a more complicated intellectual world, the struggle between Jefferson and Hamilton is still instructive, although incomplete and potentially misleading if wrongly interpreted. The perspective that frets about the threats to private property and the economy from democratic meddling, which derives from Hamilton, is very much alive today. Similarly, the perspective that fears that capitalist organization and resources are threatening the sovereignty of the people, which derives from Jefferson, is commonly evident in modern public discourse. My identification of two "traditions" in American argument is not an attempt to force current disagreements into archaic molds, but to rest some helpful assumptions on the foundation of enduring values and outlooks in American thought.

Nevertheless, despite the permanent value of an approach that focuses on the struggle between capitalism and democracy, no discussion about American history can proceed without identifying alternative visions. Logically, it is possible to reject both capitalism and democracy. It is not only logical but, to my thinking, preferable to embrace both capitalism and democracy. And if we are looking for important early thinkers who exemplify the two logical alternatives, they are available.

WHY IS THERE NO ADAMS TRADITION?

John Adams was acknowledged by all, Federalists and Democratic-Republicans alike, to be one of the premier intellects of the Republic, and an honest man to boot. His *Dissertation on the Canon and Feudal Law* in 1765 had paved the way for the colonies' ideological rejection of the authority of feudalism. He had been an important propagandist on behalf of the patriot cause in 1774–1775 and had served in the Continental Congress that had declared independence in 1776. He was the principal author of the constitution adopted by Massachusetts in 1780. His *A Defense of the Constitutions of Government of the United States*, written while he was minister to Great Britain in 1786 and 1787, provided a general justification for the structural innovations of the federal Constitution during the latter year. He was president from 1797 to 1801, the second and final Federalist to hold the office. Like those of Madison and Jefferson, his career was an impressive combination of articulate thought and effective action.

And yet Adams has left barely a trace behind. If he sticks in the national memory at all, it is as a grumpy man who was defeated for reelection in 1800. None of his works is ever included, as are some of the *Federalist* essays or the Declaration, in the appendixes of introductory American politics textbooks. His face is not on Mount Rushmore, and Washington, D.C., contains no monument to his memory.

In 2001 David McCullough's biography—which emphasized Adams's character and de-emphasized his intellectual contributions—won the Pulitzer Prize, became a national bestseller, and for a few months provoked a flurry of interest on book-review pages and television talk shows.[96] But the enthusiasm proved short-lived. There is still no monument to Adams in Washington. American politics textbooks still reprint *Federalist* #10 and 51, and sometimes #78, but none of Adams's writings. There is no Adams tradition.

Part of this neglect may be a consequence of the general opinion that he was a failure as president. Yet Madison, who is also evaluated by historians as an unsuccessful chief executive, is revered. In courses on American political thought, undergraduates are assigned Madison's writings without much discussion of his shortcomings in office. Adams is generally ignored.

Adams's lack of resonance in the national consciousness can be attributed to his poor judgment in choosing the losing historical alternative in both of the great values of the liberal tradition. Hamilton is praised for being the champion of capitalism and forgiven for being skeptical of democracy. Jefferson is praised for being the champion of democracy and forgiven for being skeptical of capitalism. Adams, skeptical of both democracy and capitalism, consigns himself to ideological irrelevance.

It was not that Adams was firmly opposed to either. Politically, at the level of abstraction, he endorsed the conclusion that the people are the "fountain of legitimacy."[97] But Adams never abandoned the tradition of deducing social conclusions from the precepts of natural law. Opening a page at random in any of his works, one is likely to encounter a reference to the phrase itself or to "human nature." And the conclusion that Adams drew from his examination of the nature of man was that human beings were not to be trusted with power. Neither the few nor the many are evil. Rather, it is "weakness, rather than wickedness, which renders men unfit to be trusted with unlimited power." Therefore, the poor and unschooled, like the rich and educated, must be hemmed about with restraints in order to "check force with force. Arm a power above it and another below it; or, if you will, one on the right hand, the other on the left; both able to say to it, when it grows mad, 'Maniac! keep within your limits.' "[98] In politics, Adams believed that thought had advanced beyond the knowledge that no country could put its confidence in unrestrained power to the realization that restrained power might be induced to behave itself. He therefore strongly endorsed constitutional checks and balances to prevent abuse of power by any individual or institution.

This position may sound a great deal like that of the Jeffersonians, but it was unleavened by their rhetorical endorsement of the idea of equality. Whereas they took care to proclaim their belief that all men were created equal, Adams took equal care to distance himself from "the leveling spirit" he sensed around him,[99] and to make sure everyone understood his position that while men might be morally equal, they were certainly not equal "in natural and acquired qualities, in virtues, talents, and riches."[100] The false impression he thus created of secretly harboring a sympathy for monarchy was reinforced by his letters to friends in 1789 suggesting that the president should be addressed as "His Most Benign Highness" and predicting that the United States would one day become a hereditary aristocracy "as an asylum against discord, seditions, and civil war."[101] The suspicion that Adams was an antidemocrat was further strengthened by the fact that in 1820, at the age of eighty-five, he overcame sundry health problems in order to make a speech at the Massachusetts constitutional convention endorsing property qualifications for the suffrage.[102] The popular image of Adams as a Federalist, highly suspicious of government by the people, is thus largely accurate.

Being a Federalist by political temperament, however, did not make Adams a partisan of Hamiltonian economics. In a general sort of way, he endorsed the common reverence for the free use of private property. But his standards of economic evaluation were utterly unlike Hamilton's. Far from admiring entrepreneurs as the backbone of society, he despaired that there was "such a rage for Profit and Commerce among all Ranks and Degree of Men even in America, that I sometimes doubt whether there is public Virtue enough to support a Republic."[103] He agreed with the Jeffersonians that the debt assumption plan "was contrived to enrich particular individuals at the public expense."[104] He endorsed a national "bank of deposit"—that is, an institution in which individuals and the government could safely keep their money, "[b]ut every bank of discount, every bank by which interest is to be paid or profit of any kind made by the deponent, is downright corruption. It is taxing the public for the benefit and profit of individuals."[105]

If this statement of principle seems to be nonsense, it is because Adams's understanding of finance was no more perspicuous than that of the Jeffersonians. In economics, he seems never to have advanced beyond the English "Country" party, or perhaps even the natural law tradition. He believed that commerce, like politics, should be ruled by the principles of public-spirited justice and that individual profit seeking was opposed to the common good. Thus Adams is known to have agreed with a 1793 pamphlet by John Taylor attacking banks as the instrument of the devil, and he wrote to a friend in 1809 that "the Funding system and Banking systems, which are the work of the Federalists, have introduced more corruption and injustice, for what I know, than any other cause."[106] He never understood or endorsed capitalism. Indeed, in his personal life he candidly admitted his ignorance of "coin and commerce," and his wife, Abigail, upon failing to convince him to invest in government securities, told a friend that he "held to his faith in land as true wealth."[107] Given his ignorance of and hostility to their own values, by the end of his presidency most of his fellow Federalists despised him. It was fitting that in 1811, after both their administrations had ended, he rekindled a warm friendship with Jefferson.

But if Jefferson and Hamilton each endorsed half of the winning side of American history, and Adams chose both losing sides, there would seem to be a logical opportunity for a fourth ideologue. Someone who championed both capitalism and democracy would surely be a great American hero. Has anyone left a legacy of correctly identifying the direction of history?

THE FORGOTTEN STATESMAN

When Meriwether Lewis and William Clark paused in their epic journey of exploration to the Pacific Coast in 1805 to name the three streams that joined to form the Missouri River in what is now Montana, they chose as inspiration the leaders of their political party. Thus the three watercourses, good-sized rivers in their own right, were named the Jefferson, after the president, the Madison, after the secretary of state, and the Gallatin, after the secretary of the treasury. The names of Jefferson and Madison will cause no surprise. But Albert Gallatin's name in the midst of such company may not be expected, for he has slipped even farther from the national consciousness than John Adams. In truth, he was one of the illustrious men of the day.

In the governing coalition of which Jefferson held the center, Gallatin represented the wing opposite John Taylor and John Randolph. The only actual businessman in Jefferson's intimate circle—he was a partner in a glass factory and a firearms manufacturing firm in western Pennsylvania—he shared only a few of the agrarians' economic assumptions and none of their moral pretensions. He extolled capitalism, believed the government should build roads and canals, and never missed an opportunity to praise the Bank of the United States. Yet he managed to remain respected and esteemed not only by people in the center of the coalition but also by the hyperagrarians. Even after Randolph's rupture with Jefferson in 1806, for example, he remained friends with Gallatin, praising the secretary on the floor of the Senate as a "commanding statesman . . . second to none for vigorous understanding, and practical good sense."[108] What magic did Gallatin possess to survive as the only important procapitalist leader in a party of militant agrarians?

Gallatin's eminence among the Democratic-Republicans demonstrates the complications and subtleties within the politics of the founders, for despite his fondness for industry, Gallatin did share important beliefs and values with the Jeffersonians, and these, combined with high intelligence, unquestioned integrity, and an affable personality, enabled him to establish an influence out of proportion to the number of votes he commanded or the clout of the interests he advanced.

In 1796 Gallatin forever endeared himself to the Jeffersonians when, as a member of the House of Representatives, he published *A Sketch of the Finances of the United States*, a root-and-branch attack on the Hamiltonian debt assumption scheme. With detailed calculations, he argued that assumption of the state debts had been mishandled, so that the nation was carrying a burden of $11 million more than it would have had to meet if Hamilton had not bungled the job. More important, he attacked the conceptual basis for assumption, asserting that "every nation is enfeebled by a public debt" and that the present system of obligations represented the triumph of a faction—Hamilton's adventurers—rather than a benefit to the nation.[109]

When Jefferson appointed him secretary of the treasury in 1801, Gallatin devised a plan for accelerating payment of the debt by reducing expenditures on the military. As a result of the adoption of this plan, Congress cut defense spending from $6 million to $1.6 million a year. Although, as a result of the Louisiana Purchase and the war against the Barbary Pirates, national expenditures were back to Federalist levels by 1805, Gallatin had proven himself a champion of frugality and an enemy of Hamiltonian policy.[110]

His position on the debts is indicative of Gallatin's general economic ideas and permits an explanation of his Republican, as opposed to Federalist, membership. The first ideologue of democratic capitalism, he envisioned an economy in which agriculture, commerce, and manufacturing were all valued, and all assisted, when necessary, by government. Unlike the Jeffersonians, who tolerated trade as a necessary evil, Gallatin respected commerce as the cornerstone of the economy. Crucially, however, in contrast to Hamilton's view that capital must be concentrated in order to be effective, Gallatin believed in offering economic opportunity to as many people as possible. His democratic ideal was thus commercial, rather than strictly political. He rarely bothered to think about the suffrage, worrying instead about ways to expand property ownership.

In regard to the disposition of the public lands, for example, in the 1790s there were a variety of opinions in Congress. Easterners in general and Federalists in particular opposed a sale, arguing that it would dilute the population, leaving settlements open to American Indian attacks, as well as depressing property values and tightening the labor market. Developers wanted to turn the land over to companies and the wealthy, who would be able to guarantee full payment and "orderly" development by selling large parcels. Gallatin opposed both these positions, contending that westward expansion would diminish the Indian menace and insisting that the lands be sold in small tracts. "The happiness of a country," he maintained, "depends more ... on the poorer class of people having it within their power to become freeholders at a small expence, and being able to live comfortably, and dependent only on their industry and exertions."[111] As secretary of the treasury, he devoted much of his energy to devising means to make the public lands as widely available as was feasible.[112]

Because the Jeffersonians trusted in his fundamentally democratic economic views, they not only tolerated Gallatin's advocacy of policy positions they would have condemned if uttered by a Federalist but allowed him to influence their own thinking. Thus Gallatin was able to function as the protector of that hated symbol of Hamiltonianism, the Bank of the United States, without losing his credentials as a good Democratic-Republican. Jefferson periodically resolved to abolish the "monopoly" by transferring government funds to state banks, in order to "make all banks Republican by sharing deposits among them in proportion to the dispositions they show."[113] Gallatin successfully resisted these intentions, although he wrote ruefully, years later, that his boss had "lived and died a decided enemy of the banking system generally, and specially to the bank of the United States."[114] Once, Gallatin ignored Jefferson's request that he devise an independent treasury system.[115] In 1809, with Madison newly inaugurated, Gallatin wrote "Report on the Bank of the United States," in which he attempted to refute every criticism of the institution and demonstrate that it was a useful helpmate to the country's economy.[116] Two years later he exerted himself mightily in a losing effort to have the bank rechartered.[117]

Gallatin lost other important battles, also. In 1808 he authored a report urging the federal government to build an intricate system of roads and canals tying all parts of the nation together.[118] In 1810 he offered his "Report On Manufactures," in which he recommended that the government lend capital to business firms at a low rate of interest.[119] Neither of these schemes came to anything.

A government activist in economic thinking but a democrat by sentiment and conviction, Gallatin was an anomaly, a man ahead of his time. Although he was respected and admired within his party, and held the top economic post in two administrations, his main achievement was to blunt and modify the more pixilated intentions of the Jeffersonians. Because of Gallatin, the nation never discovered what life would be like under pure agrarian republican government. Instead, he taught the governing party that democratic capitalism could complement agrarian republicanism.

THE GREAT ISSUE

Besides the controversies over the debt, the excise, public lands, and the Bank, the years immediately following the founding witnessed the arrival of an economic issue that would never go away. It is interesting not only because of its continuing importance in American politics but because of the light it sheds on the beliefs and practices of the founders.

By taxing imports, tariffs add to their transportation costs, raising their price to consumers. When imports are thus rendered more expensive, domestic suppliers are enabled to pad their own prices. The general price level rises, and high-cost domestic manufacturers that would otherwise be forced out of business are able to prosper. Consumers are made to indirectly subsidize domestic industry. The ideology that holds that tariffs are good for a country because they create jobs and prosperity is called the philosophy of "protection." The counterideology, called "free trade," maintains that tariffs are almost always bad for the overall national economy, however helpful they may be to specific industries.

In theory, most of the founders were free-traders, even before Adam Smith made a systematic case against the mercantilist rationale for protection in 1776. Two years earlier, Benjamin Franklin had argued that commerce should be "as free between all the nations of the world as it is between the several counties of England. . . . No nation was ever ruined by trade, even, seemingly the most disadvantageous."[120] His position was broadly typical of the founders, with the proviso that many of them, especially Madison, reserved the right to discipline nations that discriminated against American goods by imposing retaliatory tariffs.[121]

In order to pay for his assumption plan, in 1789 Hamilton recommended a uniform impost on imported goods of 5 percent. Instantly, the general consensus on overall freedom of trade disintegrated as representatives of various interests flung aside their notions of the public good in an effort to gain advantages for their own constituents. Representatives argued that imports of products that were either luxuries or that smacked of moral turpitude (never the goods coming out of their own districts) should be subject to higher duties. Southerners, for example, generally favored a uniformly low tariff, but asked for an extra percent on molasses. As this product was used almost entirely to manufacture rum, they argued that it was a morally dubious luxury. Because it was New England's principal import, however, representatives from that section recognized the threat and responded imaginatively. They invented a legislative maneuver that political scientists have termed "logrolling," a species of vote trading in which representatives barter individual advantage at the expense of the whole. New Englanders announced that they would join with any other members who objected to any duty on anything, swapping support for a reduction on the molasses duty for support for a reduction on the other items. Eventually, the duty on molasses was reduced to 4 percent. Meanwhile, Pennsylvanians wanted to eliminate the tax on loaf sugar, Southerners advocated an increase in the duty on salt, New York City and Philadelphia demanded higher rates for imported beer, Maryland requested protection from imported glass, and so on. In the end, although the Federalist leadership managed to hold the line on most items and establish a generally uniform impost, the law as passed named eighty-one articles for special protection.[122]

The country's first tariff was thus not a persuasive indicator that the ideology of the public interest would be heard more loudly in Congress than the cry of individual economic interests. However much the eighteenth-century discourse of republican virtue had resounded in public discussion, in practice, when Congress made a law, it turned governing into a series of maneuvers for individual advantage. During the next two centuries, legal theorists wrestled with means by which to base law on defensible principles. All of the literature of jurisprudence, however, would be fashioned within the context of the knowledge that very frequently, lawmaking was guided by self-interest rather than principle.

Madison and Jefferson had been troubled by the idea of an impost from its inception, because they wanted the federal government to be able to use tariffs as a weapon to pry equal trade treatment from other governments. Although they understood and endorsed the Smithian rationale for free trade, as political animals they were sensitive to the logic of international power. They did not believe that other nations could be brought to treat American exports fairly unless the United States stood ready to pass reprisals, tariff for tariff. As a consequence, their trade policy always emphasized reciprocity rather than simply low duties. In 1796 Madison had unsuccessfully attempted to persuade the Washington administration to support the idea of passing retaliatory tariffs to coerce Great Britain into ending its policy of seizing American ships that were trading with France.[123] In 1807 President Jefferson imposed a complete embargo on all incoming and outgoing commerce to try to force Britain and France to stop their unofficial war against American commercial shipping. The embargo did not accomplish its intended purpose, and Jefferson abandoned it just before leaving office in early 1809.[124] The Jeffersonians retained their trade philosophy, however, blaming the failure of the embargo on America's lack of political leverage rather than rejecting the concept of reciprocity.

The issue came to a head again in 1816. The two-year War of 1812 between the United States and Britain had, by disrupting commerce, stimulated the growth of sundry manufacturing enterprises in the United States, especially textiles. Britain determined to throttle these infant industries, using a strategy that in the twentieth century came to be known as "dumping." The country deliberately offered textile imports to the U.S. market at prices below cost, thereby endeavoring to drive the new American manufacturing firms out of business, after which assassination the prices would be raised back to profitable levels. The British government did not even have the guile to attempt to conceal this assault from its intended target. As the chancellor of the exchequer declared publicly, the purpose of British trade policy was "to incur a loss upon the first exportation [after the war] in order, by the glut, to stifle in the cradle these risky manufactures in the United States, which the war had forced into existence contrary to the natural cause of things."[125]

Responding to this peaceful warfare that had succeeded the violent kind, President Madison endorsed a protective tariff. Explaining himself to a friend in 1819, he wrote, "There are practical exceptions to the Theory [of free trade] which sufficiently speak for themselves. The Theory itself requires a similarity of circumstances, and an equal freedom of interchange among commercial nations, which have never existed."[126] With infant industries undoubtedly in peril, the country in an economic downturn caused by a postwar deflation, and the population still experiencing a wave of nationalism, all sections united to support a protective tariff. In Congress, William Lowndes and John C. Calhoun of South Carolina, later the uncompromising opponents of protection, led the campaign for its enactment. The tariff as passed imposed duties ranging from 7.5 to 30 percent on various items, giving special protection to textiles, iron, and other manufacturing products stimulated by the recent war.[127] Making trade policy would never again be so easy.

By the end of 1816 Jefferson's party had taken over most of Hamilton's program: encouragement of manufactures, the Bank of the United States, a large military, and a national debt. A leader of the vanishing opposition party, Josiah Quincy, accused the Democratic-Republicans of having "out-Federalized Federalism."[128] Jefferson had seen it coming, and knew himself singed by the ironies of history. In 1814 he had complained in a letter to William Short that "our enemy [the dead Hamilton] has indeed the consolation of Satan on removing our first parents from Paradise: from a peaceable and agricultural nation he makes us a military and manufacturing one."[129] Indeed, Hamilton had sown the seeds, Gallatin had watered many of them, the British had provided plenty of manure, and industrialism was beginning to sprout.

THE LEGACY OF THE FOUNDERS' POLITICS

By the end of the founding period, the major patterns and themes of American political controversy were largely set. Even in the preindustrial period, public discourse encompassed the values of capitalism and democracy, intertwined yet in tension. On the one hand, the Jeffersonian tradition, still embracing the ideal of an agricultural economy, rhetorically endorsed democracy while hedging about its approval of capitalism with many qualifications. On the other hand, the Hamiltonian tradition, very much alive in society although defeated as a party, endorsed capitalism and officially accepted democracy while remaining deeply skeptical in practice. Thus the liberal tradition dominated American political thought, but the two halves of that tradition coexisted in uneasy alliance.

This contradiction at the heart of the American public ideology was joined by other, somewhat less central but nevertheless politically significant confusions. By 1820 a variety of economic and political notions without any necessary connection to one another had nevertheless coalesced with the two dominant political ideologies. Democracy had joined in the American political mind with the doctrines of agrarianism, slavery, and an inactive federal government. Suspicion of democracy, dominant in the commercial classes, had become allied with faith in an active government. In Europe, the nineteenth century saw the partisans of democracy join with the advocates of strong central government to form a socialist coalition that eventually, in the twentieth century, exercised a dominant influence over much of the western countries on the continent. In the United States, however, democracy was stuck to the twin tar babies of laissez-faire ideology and social reaction. It would take decades of political controversy, a civil war, and the industrial transformation of society before Americans realized that the various elements in the two ideological coalitions were not logically associated, and began to separate and recombine them. It would take another century before they began to suspect that the deeper fusion between capitalism and democracy was also adventitious.

CHAPTER THREE

Democracy and Capitalism, 1819–1862

The United States seemed to be a success. In 1820 its population was officially counted as 9,636,453, almost twice what it had been in 1800. There would be over 31,000,000 Americans by 1860. The latter figure would include about 13 percent immigrants and 14 percent slaves. The rapid growth of population from both births and immigration was an indicator of the present and future riches of the country. Real income was growing at a rate of 1.3 percent a year, so that by 1860 the United States was among the wealthiest nations on Earth. If the two sections with their differing economic systems had been separate countries, then in that year the North would have had the second highest per capita income in the world, after Australia, and the South would have ranked fourth, after Great Britain. Despite the general prosperity and progress, however, riches were not equally distributed, and economic progress not steady. Throughout the first half of the nineteenth century, wealth became more concentrated—that is, although almost everyone was getting richer, those at the top were getting richer faster, leading to ever-greater economic inequality. Moreover, there were economic panics in 1819, 1837, 1839, and 1857, all of which ruined thousands of people and raised the general anxiety level.[1]

The ongoing accumulation and concentration of wealth were not unrelated to the fact that while America was still predominantly agricultural, the economic base was changing. In the Middle Atlantic and New England states, trade and banking had been established for some time; now lumbering, flour milling, textiles, and iron manufacturing were evolving from family-based artisan shops into large manufacturing enterprises.[2] Various inventions and creative applications of previous inventions were increasing industrial efficiency and expanding the market—the reaper, telegraph, railroad, steamboat, sewing machine, and cotton gin, among others. As factories sprouted in the Northeast, so did cities, and the nature of the landscape changed. In 1820 less than 5 percent of the population lived in cities, and only two cities had a population over 75,000. By 1860, the urban percentage had more than tripled; there were seven cities with populations over 75,000 and three with more than 250,000.[3]

Meanwhile, however, the South remained proudly rural and agricultural, its economy tied ever-more tightly to the farming of cotton. The soft white fibers comprised the country's largest single crop, made up about 20 percent of the value of all crops, and accounted for roughly half the value of all its exports by the 1830s. As a result, the South sowed ever more fields with cottonseed. In 1820 the region produced slightly over 300,000 bales (each five hundred pounds) of cotton; but by 1860 production had jumped to 3.8 million bales. The number of slaves grew as the size of the crop expanded. There had been about seven hundred thousand slaves in 1790, but there were almost four million in 1860. In the 1790s prominent Southerners had often expressed the hope that the peculiar institution could one day be abolished. Such Southern antislavery sentiment had disappeared by the end of the 1830s. Thus Northern and Southern societies, while sharing one overall political system, were evolving in directions that promised increasing economic dissimilarity.[4]

The differing industrial development in the two regions of the country was partly the cause, and partly the result, of divergent cultural values. The North was unabashedly a business civilization. Foreign travelers, immigrants, and temporary residents who wrote of their observations in the Northern states almost invariably described a people obsessed with the pursuit of material gain. Already in this era of the bare beginnings of an industrial society, Americans were so eager to get whatever there was to get while the getting was good that they were perpetually in a hurry. Foreign travelers remarked upon the national propensity to grab a "quick lunch" and then get back to work.[5] Immigrant Francis J. Grund noticed in 1836 that in the North, "[b]usiness is the very soul of an American; he pursues it, not as a means of procuring for himself and his family the necessary comforts of life, but as the fountain of all human felicity."[6]

The uninhibited industrialization of the North not only offended some foreign visitors but began to create class antagonisms. The first attempt to form a labor union, by the Philadelphia cordwainers (leather shoemakers) in 1806, had been legally suppressed, but workers kept trying. Mechanics in the City of Brotherly Love founded the first federation of labor in 1827 and the first workers' political party the next year. From 1833 to 1837 a wave of strikes swept through the cities of the eastern seaboard. The hard times that followed the panic of 1837 destroyed virtually all labor organizations, but with the return of prosperity in 1842, the workers' movement revived. Printers formed the first national union in 1850, an organization that is still functioning. Although a general labor shortage often made management amenable to demands for shorter hours and higher wages, whenever and wherever they could, employers used laws, police, and public opinion to squash unions. Throughout the decades prior to the Civil War, American labor in the North—there was no labor movement in the South—faced the paradoxical situation of generally rising wages and improving working conditions coupled with ruthless determination among business leaders and their allies in the political structure to throttle the labor movement before it could achieve actual power.[7]

The West, an arena of geography and myth that was constantly moving away from the Atlantic seaboard, was culturally a segment of the North, although frontier areas in the South were often temporarily western in outlook. Westerners displayed their own variant of Northerners' obsession with business. While westerners could be serious farmers, or occasionally serious merchants, they were more noteworthy for their preoccupation with land speculation. In the popular mind, the West was a classless region—for white males, of course—where anyone could strike it rich, and the way to realize that particular American dream was to move beyond the Alleghenies, buy land, sell it to the next wave of settlers, then move farther west and repeat the process.[8]

Southerners, however, tended to enshrine different ideals. Although they were by no means antimoney, and although such scholars as Robert Fogel, Stanley Engerman, and Gavin Wright have demonstrated that much of the behavior of Southern planters can be understood using hypotheses derived from economic theory,[9] the Southern cultural pattern was somewhat different from that of the North. As a culture, Southern whites prided themselves in pursuing less material ends. The rich, poor, and middling often adopted an aristocratic contempt for the meanness of trade and subscribed to the Jeffersonian model of landed gentry and yeoman farmers living in an agricultural utopia. Moreover, the defense of their slave society, which increasingly preoccupied Southerners after 1820, acted to suppress innovation in all areas of life. As a consequence, young white Southern males aspired not to become businessmen, but country squires who would live by preindustrial notions of honor. Southerners boasted that their quiet region lacked the bustle of the North. They were proud of the fact that the South contained few establishments catering to travelers, for example, for travelers meant business activity, and business activity meant social change. They proclaimed their immunity "from the bane of hotel life and the curse of boarding-houses." An absence of such places showed that Southerners stayed put, and every citizen was a landholder with strong "home feeling."[10]

Thus the North became dominated, in imagination and in fact, by commerce and industry, while the South remained agricultural in both. By 1860 the South contained fewer than a fifth of the number of manufacturing establishments in the North and created an annual value of manufacturing products that was less than 10 percent of the $1.6 billion generated in the New England, Middle Atlantic, and western states. The region contained only 29 percent of the country's population, and, since 30 percent of Southern residents were slaves, the white population was seriously outnumbered by its counterparts in the North.[11]

This rapidly growing country, already encompassing a great geographic extent; featuring general prosperity but increasing inequality and periodic economic downturns; containing two different societies with incompatible social structures and clashing values; needing, like all developing countries, capital and infrastructure; and generating class resentments with its industrial progress and ethnic and religious hostilities with its stream of immigration, naturally developed a profuse variety of political conflicts. There were controversies about "hard" (metallic) currency versus paper, laws permitting banking and incorporation by individuals versus general laws, slavery versus abolitionism, slavery in the territories versus territories that forbade slavery, banks versus no banks, state banks versus a national bank, protectionism versus free trade, distribution of tariff revenues to the states versus use of that income for internal improvements, restriction of the franchise to property owners versus universal adult white male suffrage, cheap public lands in small parcels versus expensive lands in large parcels, nativism versus immigrants, Protestants versus Catholics, internal improvements versus no improvements, internal improvements by the federal government versus improvements by the states, a national bankruptcy law versus no such law, and prolabor versus antilabor, to list only the socioeconomic, and not the constitutional, quarrels.

Moreover, until the election of 1860 polarized the country along geographic lines, there was no natural, stable coalition sustainable between partisans on various sides of the myriad issues. As historical progress, individual ambition and imagination, ideological reasoning, economic vicissitude, and party maneuvering advanced, societal and, therefore, congressional groupings in particular combined, dissolved, and recombined in kaleidoscopic patterns. There is thus no important political figure in this era who does not reverse his position on a major issue, or contradict his stated principles by his actions in office. Daniel Webster began his career as an eloquent free trader, but soon turned into an equally eloquent protectionist. John C. Calhoun navigated the same reversal over the same time period, but in the opposite direction. Henry Clay made a fiery speech against the Bank of the United States in 1811, a position that caused him acute embarrassment when he became one of the Bank's chief defenders in the 1830s. Andrew Jackson generally presented himself as an advocate of free trade, yet he allowed his supporters to fashion the Tariff of Abominations in 1828, which imposed the highest duties in American history, then presided over another tariff in 1832 that, despite promises to the contrary, reduced rates so slightly that it almost caused South Carolina to secede. Martin Van Buren virtually created the Democratic Party in 1827—the first mass party in the world—on the basis of an alliance between Northerners and Southerners, the main purpose of which was to suppress discussion of the slavery issue, yet he ran for president in 1848 as the candidate of an antislavery third party. Stephen Douglas almost single-handedly destroyed the Union by persuading Congress to repeal the Missouri Compromise with his Kansas-Nebraska Act in 1854, yet became an outspoken unionist upon the South's secession in 1861. It was an era of social turmoil, ideological contradiction, and personal incongruity.

This is not to say that there were no consistent economic ideas, only that politicians never adhered to them consistently. The era was in fact awash in theory, so much so that there was a saying that economics was the favorite science of the day. Practically every college included a course.[12]

The starting point for most efforts at serious economic discussion was *The Wealth of Nations*. In 1821 Clement Biddle of Philadelphia published Jean Baptiste Say's textbook on political economy, which Biddle edited for American readers. Say's book contained a shorter and punchier version of Adam Smith's doctrine of laissez-faire, along with a few improvements, such as Say's own theory that in a well-ordered economy, a general glut of production, and therefore widespread unemployment, was impossible. This book went through several editions and was probably the most widely read exposition until 1837.[13]

Also during the same period, the writings of British classical economist David Ricardo were becoming familiar to educated American readers. Unlike Smith, who had written his book to attack mercantilist and natural law theories of the seventeenth and eighteenth centuries, Ricardo was addressing social conflicts in nineteenth-century Britain. He was the partisan of the rising industrial classes. His celebrated major work, *The Principles of Political Economy and Taxation*, appeared in 1817 and took its place among the rhetorical weapons of British capitalist spokespersons in their struggle with the landed aristocracy. On the western side of the Atlantic, those who preferred not to engage Ricardo's turgid and obscure prose turned to John McCulloch, a doctrinaire disciple with a more accessible writing style. According to Paul Conkin, McCulloch joined Adam Smith as the economist whom representatives quoted most often on the floors of the houses of Congress between 1820 and 1850.[14]

Ricardo emphasized deductive reasoning from a small number of abstract principles. His assumptions and logic, and the ways in which his methodology derived from or contradicted Adam Smith, need not concern us, but some of his conclusions had considerable impact in America. His argument in favor of free trade was more compact than Smith's and emphasized the point that countries should eschew tariffs even if their own products were the target of protection by other countries. He was opposed to labor unions, viewing them as a pernicious interference with efficient economic functioning, insisting that "like all other contracts, wages should be left to the fair and free competition of the market," which would tend to put them at a level at which laborers could survive and reproduce, but no more. Similarly, he opposed all welfare (the British "Poor Laws") as meddlesome economic inefficiencies.[15] Ricardo also came to various pessimistic conclusions about the inevitable tendency of profits to fall, and the baneful effects of hereditary landowning on national prosperity, but these were at first much less influential in the United States.

In 1848 appeared the last of the great treatises in British classical economics, John Stuart Mill's *Principles of Political Economy*. Despite displaying the customary lack of imagination in his title, Mill was a somewhat more entertaining writer than Ricardo, and probably for this reason his book was enormously successful and influential on both sides of the Atlantic for several decades.[16] Like Smith, Ricardo, and Say, Mill excoriated protectionism, labeling it a "false theory" that attempts to evade the "laws and principles of the production of wealth."[17] Unlike his predecessors, however, he made an analytical distinction between production and distribution. The principles of *production*, he declared, "partake of the character of physical truths" and are consequently as much beyond human intervention as Newton's laws. But the rules of *distribution* are (in the language of a much later era) socially constructed. Being the product of "human institution," they are subject to human intervention. In brief, redistribution of wealth by government would not violate natural law.[18]

While Mill's first conclusion about free trade was completely conventional liberalism, his second argument marked a considerable step toward reorienting the liberal creed. For if redistribution was not a guarantee of moral and economic poverty, then government activism on behalf of society's lower orders might have a legitimate defense. The minimalist state of Smith, Say, and Ricardo, while still necessary to generate wealth, could be replaced by an activist state in the distribution of wealth. Here was the most influential economic thinker of the second half of the nineteenth century demolishing a good part of the intellectual foundations of the doctrine of laissez-faire. Economic theory had turned a corner.

But Americans were not careful readers. During the era I am discussing, and afterward, it was Mill's conventional defense of free trade that received the attention. The implications of his argument about distribution were mostly ignored. The natural laws of the market were believed to be antigovernment on both the production and distribution sides. It would be decades before respectable, educated Americans realized that government activism could be compatible with the tenets of orthodox economic theory.

Americans did not rely only on Europeans for their systematic accounts of economic theory. There were many obvious and important differences between British and American social conditions. In Britain, land was scarce, whereas in America (if one disregarded the American Indians, which most Americans did when thinking about economics), the amount of available arable land seemed limitless. In Britain, land ownership was extremely concentrated, whereas in the United States it was highly decentralized. In Britain, laws of primogeniture, entail, and various other feudal remnants made the subdivision and sale of most land difficult, whereas New World laws encouraged land sales. In Britain, the people who owned land were almost completely separate from the merchant and industrial classes, whereas the opposite was the case in the United States, at least in the northern and western states. In Britain, there was a superabundance of labor in relation to the available employment, leading to a national pattern of subsistence wages, whereas in America there was a chronic labor shortage, leading to a national pattern of high wages. In Britain, depressed wages led to relatively high profits in industrial concerns, which in turn led to a relative indifference to technological innovation, whereas in the United States high labor costs led to an intense emphasis on the search for technological replacements for labor.[19]

All of these differences made it necessary for American theorists to adapt European arguments to American conditions. Americans tended to ignore or downplay a great many of the subjects that occupied the British, such as the conflict between the rising industrial classes and the traditional landed gentry, concentrating instead on producing popularized writings on the subjects that were relevant to the Unites States, preeminently the tariff.

The first systematic economic treatise produced by an American was Daniel Raymond's *Thoughts on Political Economy*, which appeared in 1820. Raymond explicitly rejected Adam Smith's enshrinement of the market mechanism, arguing that to withdraw government sponsorship and protection from an economy was to establish a system that forced a war of all against all. What was needed instead was a regulated economy in which everyone—traders, industrialists, farmers, and workers—would be given a fair allotment of the national product. As inspiration, Raymond looked to Alexander Hamilton, although he did not adopt Hamilton's concentration on the entrepreneurial class as the linchpin of the economy. Instead, it was the secretary of the treasury's vision of what would today be called national industrial policy that appealed to Raymond. As the centerpiece of his own version of such a policy, he recommended a high protective tariff, one that would virtually guarantee a self-sufficient economy that could be democratically regulated for the benefit of all.[20]

Over the course of the next four decades, a variety of other writers, whom historians have labeled "the nationalist school," picked up on Raymond's themes, especially his endorsement of protectionism. Some of these followed Raymond in emphasizing the internal economic justice of a closed and regulated system. The most influential writers in this genre were Matthew Carey and his son Henry, whose main argument was that there was a "harmony of interests," not a conflict, in regard to tariff protection.[21] Others, such as German immigrant professor Friedrich List, resembled classic mercantilists in their insistence that national power and foreign trade must be conceptualized as one entity.[22] Their efforts were often subsidized by pro-protectionist organizations and read carefully by Whig and then Republican politicians.

Free trade could boast a stable of serious spokespersons, also. The most popular American-authored textbook in the first half of the century was John McVickar's *Outline of Political Economy*, first published in 1825. McVickar followed Smith and Ricardo in recommending laissez-faire and opposing tariffs, bounties, and monopolies, and he emphasized that "the national interest is best consulted by letting individuals be unrestrained in the pursuit of profit, since the national wealth is only the sum of individual wealth."[23] McVickar was also forthright in his endorsement of the principle that political economy functioned not merely as a science but also as a device for the "moral instruction of nations."[24] A legion of authors—Samuel Newman, Francis Wayland, Henry Vehake, Jacob Cardozo, Thomas Cooper—followed McVickar in translating classical economics into popular laissez-faire, free trade doctrine for Americans.

Two other themes, of secondary importance to the argument over the tariff but arising from deep roots in American history, wind through the arguments of the antebellum political economists. James Harrington's assertion from *Oceana* that social liberty depended upon a wide dispersion of property, so influential on the founders, was not forgotten. Raymond, Theodore Sedgwick, and Thomas Skidmore all incorporated some version of it into their analyses. Skidmore, the most radical, argued in 1829 for the equal division of land among men and a ban on inheritance of property.[25]

The second theme, one that had also resonated with the founders, was the suspicion of banks, especially their issuance of paper money. William Gouge's *A Short History of Paper Money and Banking in the United States*, a best seller in 1833, spoke to the old republican suspicion of anything but hard money, blaming paper currency for inflation and speculative booms.[26] To the extent that Andrew Jackson cared about scholarly endorsement of his economic prejudices, Gouge gave it to him.

For the many interests and individuals who began to blend into two unstable, internally quarreling, but nevertheless recognizable party coalitions in the late 1820s, therefore, there was available a menu of concepts, arguments, and whole ideologies from which to choose. On the one side were the Democrats, who won the presidency under the leadership of Andrew Jackson in 1828 and 1832 and who were the "normal" majority party thereafter until 1860. In general, and making allowances for local variations, partisan hypocrisy, and individual eccentricity, Democrats in the North were the party of the "out groups," those who thought either that government policy up to that time had enriched others more than themselves or who felt threatened by some potential sociopolitical hostility. They were businessmen who felt shut out of the opportunity to found corporations and banks, immigrants who felt threatened by nativist antagonism, Catholics who felt besieged by Protestant hostility, and farmers and workers who saw themselves as victims of capitalist power. In the South, however, the Democrats tended to be the in-groups—the slaveholding planters.

This coalition of strange bedfellows was held together by a mutual devotion to laissez-faire ideology, at least when applied to the federal government, and, in the North, by the rhetoric of democracy. Democrats styled themselves defenders of the ordinary "honest and industrious" folk against the depredations of "aristocrats" representing "wealth and privilege." Democratic thought on political economy was thus a blend of Adam Smith, John Locke, and John Taylor—general faith in the free market allied to confidence in the legitimating power of mass participation, augmented by a general suspicion, at least at the rhetorical level, of the commercial classes. Because they conceived the elites as having gotten into a position of undeserved prominence through manipulation of government authority, the Democrats offered a twin solution: expand the franchise so that the common man could combat the power of elites, and drain national government of authority so that it could no longer be used to enrich the few at the expense of the many. In regard to the latter point, Democrats always seemed to be arguing that the way to combat any social ill was for government to do less:

> As a general rule, the prosperity of rational men depends on themselves. Their talents and their virtues shape their fortunes. They are therefore the best judges of their own affairs, and should be permitted to seek their own happiness in their own way, untrammelled by the capricious interference of legislative bungling. (William Leggett, 1834)[27]

> what shall government do? Its first doing must be an undoing. There has been thus far quite too much government, as well as government of the wrong kind. The first act of government we want is a still further limitation of itself. (Orestes Brownson, 1840)[28]

> Under a proper organization (and even to a great extent as things are) the wealth and happiness of the citizens could hardly be touched by the government—could neither be retarded nor advanced. Men must be "masters unto themselves," and not look to Presidents and legislative bodies for aid. In this wide and naturally rich country, the best government indeed is "that which governs least." (Walt Whitman, 1847)[29]

Democrats opposed property qualifications for voting, because such restrictions interfered with democratic legitimacy. They were suspicious of laws of incorporation, because these seemed to provide economic privileges to a favored few. They opposed tariffs, because these taxed the many consumers for the benefit of a small number of producers. They criticized plans by the federal government to build roads and canals, because such things offered development to some areas at the expense of others. And, of course, Southern Democrats reacted strongly against the mere whisper of an idea that anything should be done about slavery.

It is easy to become carried away with the terms in which Democrats expressed their ideology, and thus interpret the entire antebellum period as one in which governments at all levels did almost nothing. However, historical research has demonstrated that, whatever the Jacksonian rhetoric about governmental activity, the actual relationship of politics and economics during the period was both more ambiguous and more contradictory than mere intellectual history would lead us to believe.

First, there was a disconnect between frequently antigovernment beliefs pitched at the level of national economic policy and progovernment assumptions in regard to health, safety, and morals at the local and state levels. These governments habitually used the "police" power to enforce regulations governing fire codes, gunpowder, prostitution, liquor, and public health.[30]

Second, there was at the subnational levels a much greater willingness to foster economic development by government activity. From the mid-1820s to the early 1840s, many states, inspired by New York's success with the Erie Canal, sponsored similar projects.[31]

Third, historical and technological evolution interacted with one another to effect changes in public attitudes. Citizens who had been eager to underwrite canal building through the 1830s had often become chastened by the spectacle of failure and bankruptcy by the 1840s. The advance of the railroad as a more hopeful engine of progress, combined with public disillusion with direct governmental funding, led state legislatures to devise schemes to encourage the laying of tracks by private corporations. And as a general pattern, the 1840s witnessed a retreat from interventionist economic policies by state governments.[32]

Fourth, these factors affected each other in different mixes within each state, so that while one state or group of states was retrenching in regard to public activity, others might be expanding. While the Middle Atlantic and midwestern states were rejecting governmental activism in the 1840s, for example, Virginia and North Carolina were launching public works projects.[33]

Nevertheless, the theoretical arguments that concern us were directed at the level of the nation. Political economists did not bother themselves with theorizing about state-level economies. Scholars and polemicists were able to carry on warm controversies about what the national government should be doing, regardless of what was going on at lower rungs of the federal ladder.

Furthermore, it is not a historical myth that the national government during this era was small and inactive by today's standards. Except for short periods during the wars of 1812–1814 and 1846–1848, federal spending as a proportion of gross national product during the entire era never broke 5 percent.[34] In contrast, for the last half of the twentieth century and first few years of the twenty-first, it has been standard operating procedure for the federal government to spend more than 20 percent of gross national product each year.[35] Thus, when Democrats and Whigs argued over the scope and direction of federal activity, it was not a sham battle.

Because they were the usual majority, Jacksonians were able to ratchet national government down to a minimum, at least in most domestic policy areas. They retained the Post Office, a bureaucracy that was large even by European standards, because that institution was supremely useful as a source of party patronage.[36] But in many other ways they trimmed government activity to what they considered to be virtuous levels. By 1838, New York Democrat Theodore Sedgwick could proclaim, with only a smidgen of exaggeration, that Adam Smith's "voice has been ringing in the world's ears for sixty years, but it is only now in the United States that he is listened to, reverenced, and followed."[37] The Democrats were so much opposed to activity by the national government that when the English chemist James Smithson died in 1835 and left the United States half a million dollars to enhance knowledge among its citizens, they defeated Whig efforts to create a scientific and literary institution in Washington. It took a concentrated, implacable campaign by Whig John Quincy Adams to save the money from being frittered away on ordinary government expenditures and finally used to found the Smithsonian Institution in 1846.[38]

For their part, in the North the Whigs tended to be an alliance of the propertied classes—both business and landed—with evangelical Protestant nativists. Both sides of this coalition had reasons to desire activist government at the federal and state levels, and both had reasons to prefer to keep the franchise restricted. Businesspeople needed a legal system and infrastructure spending that supported capitalist development, while evangelicals wanted laws that would allow them to reform drinkers, immigrants, Masons, slaveholders, and Catholics. At the economic level, Northern Whigs demanded tariffs and internal improvements, and at the social level, they generally supported the hot reform movement of the moment, although they tended to waffle on the issue of slavery in deference to their Southern wing. In the South, Whigs tended to represent the commercial classes, and therefore endorsed the economic programs of their Northern brethren. However, Southern Whigs tried to steer clear of anything smacking of reform, for that would inevitably bring them into collision with slavery. In fact, when the nation polarized over the issue of extension of slavery into the territories in 1854, the Northern Whig faction threw in its lot with free soil, and the Southern Whig faction promptly disintegrated. The Northern Whigs were then absorbed, along with the antislavery Free Soil Party, and the anti-immigrant American ("Know Nothing") Party, into the new Republican Party.

Even such a brief sketch of ideological tendencies during the era of 1819 to 1860 supplies us with hints as to why the United States did not develop a strong socialist presence during the first half of the nineteenth century. The party of the Left, the Jacksonians, continued the tradition inaugurated by the Jeffersonians of believing that the solution to elite domination was less federal activity. The more radical the Jacksonian, the more he urged the national state to limit itself. Socialist ideology could find no sustenance in such a climate of opinion.

DEMOCRACY

Despite the complete absence of a socialist menace, a specter was haunting the American ruling classes—the specter of the Declaration of Independence. Since the Revolution, Americans had proclaimed as an ideal that all men were created equal, yet they denied all men the right to vote. Ideals are pesky things. Comfortably situated citizens are normally not overly sensitive to the gap between ideal and reality, but those on the outside of the elite circle are apt to use the hypocrisy of ruling groups as a weapon to try to force their way in. In the 1820s men who were kept from voting by laws requiring property ownership for the suffrage began to demand that the ideals of the Declaration be honored. The result was a series of intelligent debates in which the forces of reaction were compelled to attempt to justify their departure from the aspirations of the Declaration, and the forces of democracy were able to maneuver the country one step closer to the ideal.

The arenas for the debates on the suffrage and the property qualification were efforts by three big states to write new constitutions. In Massachusetts in 1820 and 1821, New York in 1821, and Virginia in 1829 and 1830, one of the major topics at issue was whether each state should retain the requirement that a citizen must own some specified amount of landed property in order to be able to vote, or whether the new constitution should enshrine the principle of universal adult white male suffrage.

The conservative argument was noteworthy for its clarity and frankness. Conservatives held that Jefferson had been a prophet, in *Notes on Virginia* in 1785, when he had warned that industrialism would create cities, and cities would create mobs of unrooted men who would become the tools of demagogues. It had come to pass. Industrialism was only in its infancy, yet "[e]verything indicates," in the words of Josiah Quincy of Massachusetts, "that the destinies of the country will eventuate in the establishment of a great manufacturing interest.... There is nothing in the condition of our country, to prevent manufacturers [that is, industrial workers] from being absolutely dependent upon their employers, here as they are everywhere else. The whole body of every manufacturing establishment, therefore, are dead votes, counted by the head of their employer."[39] James Kent of New York agreed as to the fecklessness of urban workers, but he doubted the problem would be one of industrialists directing the vote of their employees. The probabilities were far more frightening:

The tendency of universal suffrage is to jeopardize the rights of property, and the principles of liberty. There is a constant tendency in human society, and the history of every age proves it; there is a tendency in the poor to covet and to share the plunder of the rich; in the debtor to relax or avoid the obligation of contracts; in the majority to tyrannize over the minority, and trample down their rights; in the indolent and the profligate, to cast the whole burthens of society upon the industrious and the virtuous; and *there is a tendency in ambitious and wicked men, to inflame these combustible materials* . . . universal suffrage never can be recalled or checked, but by the strength of the bayonet. We stand, therefore, this moment, on the very edge of the precipice.[40]

In Jefferson's home state of Virginia, although there were no predictions of industrial expansion, the conservative message was very similar. Demagoguery, asserted the antidemocratic faction, was an ever-present possibility, kept in check only by the monopoly of power by the freeholders—the landowners. The great advantage of the landed property qualification for suffrage, asserted Philip Nicholas, is that

> it keeps the Government in the hand of the middling classes. . . . But place power in the hands of those who have none, or a very trivial stake in the community, and you expose the poor and dependent to the influence and seductions of wealth. . . . You [now] hear nothing of the bribery and corruption of freeholders. . . . But extend the Right of Suffrage to every man dependent as well as independent, and you immediately open the flood-gates of corruption.[41]

The conservative argument was powerful. It flattered the self-image of landowners as the pillars and ballast of society, while it also alluded to actual historical experience in the United States and elsewhere, not only of mob attacks on property but of the efforts of debtors to seize political power and legislate away their obligations. The most impressive example of the latter occurrence had been Shays's Rebellion in Massachusetts in the 1780s. Daniel Shays had become the bogeyman who stalked American property owners in their nightmares, the personification and proof of the latent tyranny of the impoverished majority in every republic.

The advocates of universal white male suffrage, however, had two answers to the conservative attack, one that looked to American ideals, the other that reasoned from human nature. The first was simply to demand that the nation live up to its professed commitments. The most coherent example of this argument was "The Memorial of the Non-Freeholders of the City of Richmond," a petition present to the Virginia convention.

If we are sincerely republican, we must give our confidence to the prin[c]iples we profess. We have been taught by our fathers, that all power is vested in, and derived from, the people, not the freeholders; that the majority of the community, in whom the abides the physical force, have also the political right of creating and remoulding at will, their civil institutions . . . to deny to the great body of the people all share in the Government; on suspicion that they may deprive others of their property; to rob them, in advance of their rights; to look to a privileged order as the fountain and depository of all power, is to depart from the fundamental maxims, to destroy the chief beauty, the characteristic feature, indeed, of Republican Government.[42]

It was a difficult argument to meet, for to deny its validity required a rejection of most Americans' descriptions of themselves throughout their history. And the profranchise forces had another important answer to the fears of the property owners, one that soothed their apprehensions rather than challenged their intellectual integrity. Repeatedly and vehemently, prosuffrage speakers in all three states denied that an enlarged electorate would threaten property—quite the contrary. In fact, they insisted, universal suffrage was the best guarantor of property. John Cooke of Virginia offered the most vivid summary of this position:

[W]e are asked to believe that . . . the love of property is the great engrossing passion which swallows up all other passions, and feelings, and principles; and thus not in particular cases only, but in all men. The poor man is fatally and inevitably the enemy of the rich, and will wage a war of rapine against him, if once let loose from the restraints of the fundamental law. A doctrine monstrous, hateful, and incredible! If it be contended that man is greedy and avaricious, it will, still, not be denied, that he is a reasoning and calculating animal. When he desires to *attain* property, it is in order that he may *possess* and *enjoy* it. But if he join in establishing the rule that the right of the strongest is the best right, what security has he that he, in his turn, will not soon be deprived of his property by some one stronger than himself? Sir, the *very* desire for property implies the desire to possess it *securely*. And he who has a strong desire to possess it . . . will be a firm supporter of the laws which secure that possession, and a decided enemy of every systematic invasion of the rule of *meum* and *tuum* [mine and yours].[43]

This was more than an appeal to reason. It was a wider vision of what America could be than the conservatives had permitted themselves to entertain—a formula for reconciling the defense of property with the sovereignty of the people. The secret to making property secure was to democratize it. If everyone has a chance of becoming a property owner, then everyone will become a conservative. The movement to extend the franchise, then, was part of a vision of American society that looked to far more than political rights. It is no accident that many of the people who spoke in favor of universal suffrage at the conventions soon became Democrats, or that many of the antisuffrage speakers were former Federalists and future Whigs. The Democrats had many flaws in their economic thinking, but they were irresistible because they were the party of the political future.

The movement to make the suffrage an aspect of citizenship, rather than property, gradually triumphed. In New York, the new constitution retained a taxpaying qualification for voting, but that was erased by an amendment in 1826. Massachusetts eliminated the landholding qualification, but kept a poll tax. Virginia discarded the freehold qualification in 1830 and dropped its taxpaying requirement in 1851. Other states followed suit: Pennsylvania abandoned property qualifications in 1838, New Jersey in 1844, Ohio in 1851, and so on. Manhood suffrage was not universal, as there were still various kinds of ballot discriminations against free Northern blacks and immigrants, and a variety of registration schemes were adopted (mainly by Whig legislatures) to discourage voting by the working class. Nevertheless, by 1860 property had been eliminated as a qualification for voting in almost every state.[44]

The widening of the franchise, combined with the ongoing organizing efforts of the political parties, prompted voter turnout to rise. In the bewildering four-way presidential contest of 1824, only 26.5 percent of the country's electorate managed to register their preference at the polls. In 1828, 56.3 percent cast ballots, and that percentage held fairly steady for the next two elections. Then in 1840, amid intense party organizing efforts and great public interest, turnout jumped to 78 percent, and it remained at comparable levels to the end of the century.[45]

Rising participation rates, in turn, compelled the democratization of issues. Whigs found themselves competing with Democrats to endorse policies that pleased the people. Suddenly, for example, it no longer seemed politic to imprison people for debt. New York repealed its imprisonment law in 1831; Vermont, Ohio, and Michigan in 1838; Alabama in 1839; New Hampshire and Tennessee in 1840; Pennsylvania and Connecticut in 1842; and even stodgy old Massachusetts in 1857. Elites, traditional and newly arrived, cautious and reckless, ignorant and learned, conservative and progressive, North and South, were having to learn a new democratic vocabulary.[46] The change in discourse begun under the Jeffersonians during the 1790s was completed during the Age of Jackson.

One writer who well illustrates this transmutation of discourse is the Massachusetts philosopher Ralph Waldo Emerson. Among the many entries in his journal that capture his enunciation of the democratic ideal as they also portray his ambivalence about its current implementation by the Democrats are these two, the first from 1834, the second from 1836:

> Democracy. Freedom, has its root in the sacred truth that every man hath in him the divine Reason, or that, though few men since the creation of the world live according to the dictates of Reason, yet all men are created capable of doing so.
>
> When I ... speak of the democratic element, I do not mean that ill thing, vain and loud, which writes lying newspapers, spouts at caucuses, and sells its lies for gold; but that spirit of love for the general good whose name this assumes.[47]

Democracy, to many of the founders a dangerous beast that must be tamed with clever government mechanisms in order to be safely paddocked with the public interest, was now synonymous with the public interest. Participation by ordinary people, which had always been the only legitimate means to the end of good government, had now become the end itself.

Similarly, the definition of one of democracy's essential components evolved in both its political and economic meanings. "All men are created equal" had been a statement of faith about moral equivalence; now it became a demand for political equivalence, specifically on election day. Economic equality, which had always been interpreted as leveling, and always execrated, was converted into a common permission to acquire property. Whigs tended to state this last belief as "equality of rights," while Democrats tended to state it as "equality of opportunity," but the differences of phrasing were not significant. Both parties agreed on the principle that all white men might assert the privilege to enter an equality of striving, but did not possess a claim to equality of results.

Although the ideology and the reality of democracy expanded during this period, they both halted short of their logical conclusion. In 1848 some two hundred women and about forty men met at the first women's rights convention in Seneca Falls, New York. The Declaration of Sentiments they produced was a perfect parody of the Declaration of Independence, beginning its argument with the words, "We hold these truths to be self-evident: that all men and women are created equal," and progressing to chastise half the population for not applying its avowed principles to the other half. The ideological force of the parody was little appreciated, however. Most of the male democrats of the day met the Seneca Falls demands with patronizing rejection. Female suffrage would not be realized until the next century.[48]

CAPITALISM

Within the context of the general national argument over politics and economics that took place in the years 1819 to 1861, there were a series of specific conflicts that both modified the ideological discussion and were modified by it. Chief among these were disagreements over the tariff and the Bank of the United States.

Everyone accepted the fact that the country needed at least a minimal tariff to raise revenue for the federal government. The disagreement was over whether some level above this base to protect domestic producers from foreign competition was justified. This quarrel spawned volumes of writing, decades of angry rhetoric, feverish organization, frenzied lobbying of Congress, and, in 1832, threatened secession.

To Democrats in general and Southerners in particular, a protective tariff was simply a scheme to squeeze the great majority of the population for the benefit of the manufacturing elite. Antitariff agitators marshaled all the reasoning of Smith, Ricardo, Say, and Mill, as well as their American epigones, to prove that protectionism served to transfer wealth within the country from the many to the few, while retarding overall economic advance. As Senator John Rowan of Kentucky stated during the debate over the 1828 tariff, as reported in the *Register of Debates* (there was as yet no *Congressional Record*), "he was opposed to the tariff, as a system of bounties, for the encouragement of certain classes of industry. He considered the protection, which it extended to one class of industry, as a correspondent depression upon other classes. Its professed object was to tax one part of the community for the benefit of another."[49]

The free traders' analysis of the politics of the tariff, however, was anything but simple, for there was a logical problem with the assertion that tariffs were a scheme by the minority to misappropriate economic benefits for themselves while transferring costs to the majority: why would not the majority vote down the plan in Congress? The tariffs of 1828 and 1832, which drove Southerners to despair, were passed by majority votes in both houses. How could they be tools of the minority? Free traders answered this question with a modern analytic eye. The protectionists, complained the Southerners, had acquired a political power out of proportion to their economic or population percentage through the use of organization. By pooling their resources, hiring lobbyists, and perhaps bribing legislators, industries wanting protection had been able to artificially manufacture majority votes in Congress. Thus in 1828 the Alabama state legislature sent a "Remonstrance" to the U.S. House of Representatives containing the observation that

> already has the manufacturing interests assumed an organized form, and exhibited a concert and systematic combination against all the other great interests of the nation. Unions of councils and immense wealth enable the manufacturing corps to sustain a set of agents to attend the sessions of Congress to importune and press their claims upon the attention of the National Legislature. . . . The inevitable tendency of such a system is to accumulate the wealth of the country into a few hands.[50]

The Southern charge that the tariff was the result of a minority-in-majority's clothing had an additional, and ominous, political implication. Educated by the writings and speeches of John Randolph and John Taylor, the majority agrarians were quick to see that, once reduced by political legerdemain to a policy-making minority, they could then be expropriated of every right and possession by the false majority in Congress. This belief allowed Southerners to suggest implicitly that they were the victims of the tyranny of the minority while they were asserting explicitly that they were the victims of the tyranny of the majority. "We are the serfs of the system," proclaimed John C. Calhoun in 1828, and he set about attempting to devise an alternative mode of government that would protect the South from Northern domination.[51]

Arguments in favor of the tariff followed two major strategies. The first was to deny that protection was the policy of any one class, industry, or region. Protection was good for everybody. One of the leading protariff writers, Henry Carey, asserted that the "harmony of interests" of all classes in a society formed a self-contained, steadily expanding economy. Carey seems to anticipate John Maynard Keynes in his emphasis on effective demand as the mainspring of the economy, but unlike Keynes, who rejected Say's Law, Carey embraces it. It is "the power of production" that creates demand, and therefore, "[t]he more is produced, the more must be consumed."[52] Carey surveys the available statistics over the previous several decades and concludes that times with high tariffs were good for all industries, including agriculture, and all regions, including the South. In contrast, as he reads the evidence, times of low tariffs were bad for all industries and all regions.[53] This historical experience merely illustrates a general law, that when nations "sell their own products, their power to purchase from others is equal to the whole amount sold. When they sell the products of others . . . their power of purchase is only to the extent of the difference between the price paid and the price received."[54] In sum, a thoroughly protected economy with constantly increasing industrial production would create an expansion that fed on itself. Moreover, its always-growing wealth would be ever-more-equally distributed, because Carey had a theory that as industry expanded, labor constantly became more valuable. Therefore, as the tariff-protected economy grew, wages would rise in relation to capital, which would equalize wealth. The constantly growing standard of living among industrial workers would increase demand for agricultural products (including cotton), which would spread the prosperity to the nonindustrialized areas of the country, even as the growing power of all laborers would gradually lead to the emancipation of the slaves. Rising prosperity would lead to greater equality for women. Without foreign markets to worry about, the nation would never have a reason to fight a war. Thus utopia could be achieved if only the country would put up a high enough tariff wall.[55] Finally, the business cycle is caused by the instabilities of foreign trade; if the nation would rely upon its own protected resources, financial crises and depressions would disappear.[56]

Since Keynes in the 1930s, economists consider any analysis that relies on Say's Law to be fundamental nonsense. As a consequence, Henry Carey is apt to be treated roughly by modern economic historians, if he is noticed at all. In his own day, however, he was a celebrity. He was called "The Master" by a group of disciples, and business interests subsidized the reprinting and distribution of his writings. Horace Greeley, publisher of the influential Whig *New York Tribune*, popularized Carey's views through the columns of the newspaper. New York University gave him an honorary degree, while Harvard's president, Thomas Hill, called him one of the greatest philosophers of the time.[57] Carey illustrates the temporary glory that can come to scholars whose ideas seem to legitimize the interests of powerful groups. If tariffs were good for everybody, then their partisans were not, as the agrarians charged, flacks for narrow special interests, but misunderstood prophets of the public weal.

Protectionists were particularly intent upon proving to industrial labor that high tariffs did not exploit its members as consumers, but benefited them as employees. Daniel Webster made many speeches in the Senate about trade policy, and he never failed to draw the connection between tariffs and jobs, as in the following excerpt from the debates of 1846:

> I am looking, not for a law such as will benefit capitalists—they can take care of themselves—but for a law that shall induce capitalists to invest their capital in such a manner as to occupy and employ American labor. I am for such laws as shall induce capitalists not to withhold their capital from actual operations, which give employment to thousands of hands. I look to capital, therefore, in no other

view than as I wish it drawn out and used for the public good, and the employment of the labor of the country.[58]

It was a persuasive argument. Although workers in the northeastern cities voted Democratic as a general rule, on the specific issue of tariffs they were more likely to support Whig positions. As a result, congressional representatives of both parties from the industrialized sections of the country tended to support protectionist trade policy.[59]

The protectionists' second general rhetorical strategy was to maintain that classical economic doctrines about the benefits of free trade might be true in some wholly abstract theoretical world, but not in the real world of ruthless, self-interested nations. Like Jefferson and Madison before them, they argued that in the actual world, nations had to be ready to fight trade discrimination with discrimination, and to trade a relaxation of duties for reciprocal relaxation.

One of the gurus of nationalist trade policy turned out to be a visiting professor from the University of Tübingen in Germany, Friedrich List. After having offended the rulers of Tübingen, he found it expedient to leave the country, and he arrived in the United States in 1825. Here he allowed himself to be subsidized by protariff interests while he wrote voluminously on economic matters.

List takes as his rhetorical antagonist not the writers of his own day, but Adam Smith himself. He gives Smith credit for having invented "the analytical method" of economic discussion, thereby enabling political economy to become a science.[60] But Smith's methodological individualism blinded him to a crucial aspect of economy. He was "unable to combine individual interests in one harmonious whole," and in particular, he "ignores the very nature of nationalities, [and] seeks almost entirely to exclude politics and the power of the State."[61]

This is a fatal error, for "power is more important than wealth" because it creates the rules within which wealth is accumulated. Individual self-interested striving, as such, is not useful to the commonwealth unless it is disciplined for public purposes. Under conditions of the free market, it is just as likely to direct itself into crime as into wholesome commerce. Therefore, "[i]n a thousand cases the power of the State is compelled to impose restrictions on private industry."[62] Rather than attempting to deny this truth, countries should frankly pursue national economic policy.

Nevertheless, List argues that Smith is correct about the power of an unfettered market to bring forth the most efficient distribution of goods, and therefore create wealth rapidly. But Smith's discussion is excessively abstract. Free trade works only under the conditions of "a universal confederation and a perpetual peace."[63] But in the real world, with uncooperative nations that are willing to exploit each other's naive conformity to theory, unqualified free trade is a self-destructive policy.[64] Furthermore, the balance of industry and agriculture in any society should not be left to chance. Government must determine whether infant industries should be founded and nurtured, and by what levels of support. Just as not enough protection will stifle economic growth, too much will waste resources. Therefore, intelligent policy is needed to judge how much protection is needed for which sectors at any one time. In general, a country will achieve optimum power and wealth by striving to import raw materials and export finished products, but this rule is subject to specific application under specific circumstances.[65] In other words, nations should adopt a national industrial policy.

In regard to the United States, List proposes that the economy, in the 1820s and 1830s, should be viewed as having achieved a rapid level of manufacturing development behind tariff barriers. Like Carey, he interprets the economic crises of the previous decades as having been the result of free trade, and the surges in prosperity as having been caused by protection. He is certain that if the country will hew to the protectionist policy, it will soon become a major manufacturing power. On the contrary, if it persists in pursuing free trade, it will forever remain an economic colony of Great Britain. Therefore, the country should pursue a system in which the purpose is to create "not only wealth as in individual and cosmopolitan economy, but power and wealth, because national wealth is increased and secured by national power, as national power is increased and secured by national wealth."[66] The crucial principle underlying this national economic strategy is protectionism.

The irony of a foreigner giving Americans advice on nationalism did not escape the free traders. "We appear to have imported a professor from Germany," jeered James Hamilton of South Carolina, "in absolute violation of the American system."[67]

Irony aside, industrialism blossomed behind the tariff walls. Modern economic historians are not in agreement as to whether, on balance, the nation gained or lost more wealth in the aggregate from trade policy during those forty years. There is no quarrel, however, about the distributional consequences of the tariff policy of the era. Southerners were perfectly correct in charging that the effect of high duties was to redistribute national wealth from the agricultural to the industrial regions of the country. The agricultural South was forced to subsidize the industrialization of the Northeast.[68]

The second great economic controversy of the era concerned banks, and, in particular, the Second Bank of the United States. Then as now, banks served essential functions. They were intermediaries between savers, who desired to set aside part of their income, earning interest, in a safe place for later use, and borrowers, who wanted to invest that surplus income. Banks were thus crucial in providing capital for economic growth, especially of an industrial nature. As part of this process of financial mediation, banks also created money. When a bank gives a loan to a business, it does not normally hand over a box of cash. It establishes a line of credit. With an accounting fiction, it increases the amount of money in circulation by the size of the loan. This increase in the supply of money can be a good thing for the economy if there is not enough circulating medium to lubricate commerce, but it can be a bad thing if the increase in bank credits outpaces the supply of goods, resulting in a general inflation. In the United States of this era, there were constant arguments about whether banks were increasing the national money supply by too much or not enough.

The Second Bank of the United States, headquartered in Philadelphia, performed other vital functions for the economy as a whole. As the official fiscal agent for the United States, it held tax receipts, paid bills, and loaned money to the government. In addition, its federal charter permitted it to operate branches in every state, whereas all other banks were restricted to conducting business within one state. The fact that it possessed a large sum of deposits, plus the fact that it was the only bank with a national reach, made the Bank of the United States incomparably more important than the state banks, to which it often lent money. Because of its power to lend or not to lend at an institutional level, it evolved into a quasi-central bank, policing the activities of the smaller state banks and attempting to stabilize the national currency by regulating their lending practices. It performed these functions of public economic stabilization despite the fact that it was a private organization intent upon the pursuit of profit. Although government representatives sat on its board, their suggestions and questions were mostly ignored by the bank's president, Nicholas Biddle.[69]

As the federal loan policeman, the Bank of the United States naturally engendered resentment among the state bankers, who tended to believe that it was too conservative in its fiscal policies—that is, that it did not put enough money into circulation because it did not lend them enough. Discontent was especially prevalent in the western states, where investment capital was in short supply and the speculative spirit was unconstrained.

Greatly enhancing and complicating the conflict between the rest of the country and the giant Philadelphia institution was the anticorporation ideology of the times. In 1819 there were no general incorporation laws as we understand them. To receive a charter, an entrepreneur had to apply individually to a state legislature for a specific grant. The very act of incorporation, therefore, was a special grant of economic privilege. As such, it seemed to a great many Americans to be unjust at its core. Moreover, because banks had a particularly concentrated kind of economic power—the power to create money—they were especially noxious to democratic ideologues. "What is this but the monarchical principle in government?" asked Benjamin Hallett in 1841. "For whatever form or administration of government establishes in the state, directly or indirectly, a sovereignty independent of the people, is essentially monarchical. It is immaterial whether this sovereignty, this exclusive and irrepealable power, is held by a single man or by a privileged few-by a king or an aristocracy—by nobles or by corporations—by a divan or a bank."[70]

The Bank, therefore, for all its undoubted usefulness to the country, had a serious legitimacy problem. It exercised crucial public functions without being responsible to the public. The problem was made worse by the fact that Biddle, while he was acknowledged by everyone to be honest and competent, could never understand the nature of the resentment against the institution he managed.

In 1829 Andrew Jackson became president. Jackson was himself as suspicious as Thomas Jefferson or John Taylor of the irresponsible power of the Bank of the United States. Once, in personal conversation, Jackson informed Biddle that "I do not dislike your Bank any more than all banks."[71] Moreover, many of Jackson's political allies had financial ties to state banks, and thus were constantly intriguing against the Bank of the United States. Given this sort of political situation, it would have been wise for Biddle to have professed his democratic principles, followed all suggestions from the White House, and done his best to present himself as a humble public servant. Because he did not understand the Bank's legitimacy problem, however, his words and deeds helped Jackson turn his institution into a symbol of elitist economic oppression.

In 1832, at the urging of Senators Henry Clay of Kentucky and Daniel Webster of Massachusetts, the Bank of the United States petitioned to have its charter renewed four years ahead of schedule. Congress passed the recharter bill, and President Jackson vetoed it. His veto message to Congress read in part:

> Distinctions in society will always exist under every just government . . . but when the laws undertake to add to these natural and just advantages artificial distinctions . . . to make the rich richer and the potent more powerful, the humble members of society—the farmers, mechanics, and laborers—who have neither the time nor the means of securing like favors to themselves, have a right to complain of the injustice of their Government. . . . If we can not at once, in justice to interests

vested under improvident legislation, make our Government what it ought to be, we can at least take a stand against all new grants of monopolies and exclusive privileges.[72]

Jackson thus addressed his rhetoric, not so much to the outright functions of the Bank, but to its legitimacy. In so doing, he turned it into a national villain, a symbol of everything the average American resented about rich insiders making deals for the benefit of each other. The Bank's partisans detected the strategy, but grossly underestimated its appeal. Daniel Webster, the first to make a speech in the Senate after the veto, precisely identified the purpose of Jackson's rhetoric:

> Congress passed the bill, not as bounty or a favor to the present stockholders ... but to promote great public interests.... If a bank charter is not to be granted, because it may be profitable, either in a small or great degree, to the stockholders, no charter can be granted.... [The veto message] sows, in an unsparing manner, the seeds of jealousy and ill-will against the Government of which its author is the official head.... It manifestly seeks to influence the poor against the rich. It wantonly attacks whole classes of people, for the purpose of turning against them the prejudices and resentments of other classes.[73]

He was exactly right, but it did not matter. Ever since Alexander Hamilton, businesspeople had been arguing that fiscal decisions of large public import, employing public funds, had to be made by private individuals. Such a stance was no longer tenable. Jackson destroyed the legitimacy of the Hamiltonian solution to the problem of national finance. His veto message, and his subsequent actions, however, did not solve the problem of how to manage national fiscal policy in a manner responsible to the public. His presidency was more noteworthy as a destructive than as a constructive force. Jackson did what had to be done, but he left two problems behind.

The first problem involved how to allow banks to carry out their useful private lending functions without inciting public suspicion of their elitist character. The solution proved to be easy and obvious, once the question was clearly posed. In 1837 Michigan passed the first "free banking" law, which allowed anyone to set up a financial institution, provided that they backed the issue of notes with securities kept on deposit with the state banking authority. By 1860 a majority of states had passed similar statutes. These were all in the North and West, for Southerners retained their antibank prejudices even with the new rules—in 1845 Texas even entered the Union with a constitution that forbade banking absolutely. As a result of the statutory evolution in the Northern states, whereas there had been 307 state-chartered banks in 1820, there were 1,601 in 1860, the great majority in the North.[74]

During the same period, most of the Northern states also passed general incorporation laws, making this tool of business at least theoretically obtainable by all white men. The response to the controversy over banks and corporations as creatures of special privilege, therefore, was to democratize access to them, at least in the North. Southerners, still deeply suspicious of commerce and industry no matter how widely accessible, held their agrarian ground.[75]

The second problem was the puzzle of how to create an institution that could set national fiscal policy while satisfying the requirements of democratic legitimacy. This one was more difficult, entangled as it was in national party passions. In 1836 Jackson's vice president, Martin Van Buren, was elected president in his own right. Less than a year later the Panic of 1837, the United States' first full-fledged depression, descended on the country. There was a recovery in 1838, then another crisis in 1839, from which recovery was slow. Economic historians can engage in lively debate about whether Jackson's destruction of the Bank caused the economic troubles, or whether they were caused by forces external to the country and outside of any president's control.[76] Whatever the truth, the Whigs, who loathed Van Buren almost as much as they hated Jackson, never doubted that the Democrats had crippled the country's economy by extinguishing the Bank. Whigs were unrestrained in informing the people of their opinion.

Jackson's practice of depositing federal money in selected state banks (termed "pet banks" by the Whigs) was generally viewed as unsatisfactory because it made the government vulnerable to the charge of corrupt favoritism—and not without reason, because some of the president's advisers had financial ties to the chosen institutions. Van Buren proposed another system. In 1837 he endorsed an idea sponsored by the "Loco-Foco" or left wing, of the Democratic Party, by calling for the establishment of an "independent treasury" system. This plan involved having the government keep its money in its own treasury vaults rather than those of private banks, insist on collecting all its revenue in specie (gold and silver), and pay all its debts in specie, using its own officials. There would be no regulation of banks by the federal government, that is, no effort to place limits on their ability to create money by making loans and issuing notes. Their only constraints would be applied, potentially, by the states. Thus, said Van Buren in his message to Congress, there would be no "blending [of] private interests with the operations of government" and no provisions for "relieving mercantile embarrassments," for such measures would not only be unconstitutional but "would not promote the real and permanent welfare of those they might be designed to aid." The plan was, in other words, the logical culmination of the Democrats' antigovernment ideology. The federal government would abjure all responsibility for regulating the nation's money supply—it would not have a fiscal policy. This would be laissez-faire on steroids.[77]

Loco-Foco Democrats were ecstatic. William Leggett editorialized in the *New York Evening Post* that the plan would finally "separate the government from all the injustice, favouritism, casualties and fluctuations of the banking system." Frank Blair of Missouri hailed the president's message as "the boldest and highest stand ever taken by a Chief Magistrate in defense of the rights of the people . . . a second declaration of independence." A. H. Wood of Boston said of Van Buren that "like his predecessor he now stands at the head of radical democracy."[78]

Not surprisingly, most Whigs were rendered apoplectic by the plan to abandon national fiscal policy. It seemed to them that Van Buren had decided to declare war on government itself, which was not far from the truth. "He has identified himself wholly with the loco-focos—come forth as a champion of the most destructive species of ultraism—and aimed at the vital interests of the country a blow," editorialized the *Boston Atlas*, "which if it do not recoil upon the aggressor, must be productive to the country of lasting mischief, perhaps of irretrievably anarchy." "I feel as if I were on some other sphere, as if I were not at home," lamented Webster, "as if this could not be America when I see a scheme of public policy proposed, having for their object the convenience of Government only, and leaving the people to shift for themselves." Clay compared Jackson and Van Buren to the British kings whose insatiable grasping for power had precipitated two revolutions during the seventeenth century. Looking forward to the American version of revolution, the next general election scheduled for 1840, Clay prophesied that "our deliverance is not distant, and . . . on the 4th of march, 1841 [inauguration day], a great and glorious revolution, without blood and without convulsion, will be achieved."[79]

The independent treasury bill passed Congress in 1840. As Clay had predicted, however, the Whigs won a great victory in the election that year, placing William Henry Harrison in the White House and garnering majorities in both houses of Congress. In 1841 they repealed the treasury plan and passed a bill establishing a new national bank. Here, however, one of the random accidents of history interacted with one of the eccentricities of the American constitutional system to overthrow all reason and sanity in national self-government. Striving for a maximum popular vote, the Whigs had created a "balanced ticket" in 1840 by nominating former Virginia senator John Tyler as Harrison's vice-presidential running mate. Very much like Calhoun, by ideology Tyler was a states' rights agrarian, and a Whig only by virtue of his opposition to Jackson's use of presidential power. In the vice presidency, this divergence between Tyler's values and the purposes of his party would not have mattered. When Harrison died after only a month in office, however, Tyler, who opposed virtually all the congressional Whigs' policies, became president. He vetoed the bank bill. For four years the Whigs were stymied by their own president. When the Democrats regained the White House in 1844, the chance of resurrecting a national bank was gone forever.

In 1846 the Democrats reestablished the independent treasury. As a result, the country went into the Civil War years with no national currency, no organization of nationally regulated paper money, and no central influence over inflation and deflation or effective restraint on risky or fraudulent banking practices. By 1860 there were an estimated nine thousand different kinds of bank notes circulating in the United States.[80] On the one hand, this system of purposeful anarchy led to dangerously boisterous economic times, with speculation running wild and periodic panics in which many banks failed, causing substantial losses to note holders and depositors. On the other hand, the unrestrained business energies of the country created a generally prosperous and rapidly growing economy.[81]

In short, the cumulative effect of the political choices of this era was to allow the economy to develop with a minimum of government interference, albeit within tariff walls, and the result was a quarter century of explosive industrial growth punctuated by periods of acute and unevenly distributed retrenchment and pain. As the economy progressed, the competing ideologies of the time tended to converge. At the level of politics (although not, as we shall see, at the level of law), democracy, laissez-faire, and capitalist economic advance all became dissolved in a rhetorical stew. By the 1850s both major parties generally endorsed mass participation for white males in both the ballot box and the economy. Furthermore, the traditional agrarian opposition to commercial and industrial capitalism was becoming less important with each passing decade. Whether political developments would have resulted in the peaceful spread of democratic capitalism to the entire country is impossible to say. Before such an evolution could be fairly under way, another issue obliterated the American consensus and changed the terms of the debate.

SLAVERY

Slavery was an economic imperative confronted by a moral mandate. Although only about a quarter of the 1.6 million white families in eleven Southern states in 1860 owned slaves, the institution was in fact far more important to the region than this percentage might suggest. The South's economy was absolutely dependent upon agriculture, and agriculture was absolutely dependent upon slave labor. Not only King Cotton but the South's other staple crops, tobacco and rice, would have been impossible to cultivate without gangs of field hands disciplined by the lash—or so white Southerners believed. Moreover, not only Southern interests rested upon the institution. Northern textile and shipping companies were part of the Southern economic orbit. To contemplate an end to slavery was to envision an economic disruption that would not be exclusively sectional.[82]

In a speech on the floor of the House of Representatives in 1836, Congressman James Hammond of South Carolina sought to remind his Northern colleagues of these economic facts of life. "It could scarcely be expected that this Government would undertake to free our slaves without paying for them," he assumed, plausibly. Since there were that year about 2.3 million slaves, their annual increase was about sixty thousand, and they were worth about $400 each, their monetary value "would amount to upwards of nine hundred million. The value of their annual increase, alone, is twenty-four millions of dollars; so that to free them in one hundred years, without the expense of taking them from the country, would require an annual appropriation of between thirty-three and thirty-four millions of dollars." Given the fact that the total annual receipts of the federal government were only about $25 million, "The thing is physically impossible."[83]

Neither Hammond nor any of his listeners had the ability to foresee that when the time came for the federal government to forcibly free the slaves, the act would cost $6.6 billion, plus the lives of six hundred thousand young men. The monetary price of the Civil War would have been enough to purchase the freedom of all the slaves at 1860 market value, buy each one a forty-acre farm and a mule, and still have $3.5 billion left over.[84] If Americans had been able to foretell the future in 1836, they might have considered the emancipation price of $900 million a bargain. Because no one could imagine the coming catastrophe, however, the economic imperative of the slave system dictated the politics of the South and both major parties until 1854.

To the abolitionists, of course, cost-benefit analysis was irrelevant. Their opposition to slavery was moral. The institution was an intolerable evil and must be extinguished. Their opposition rested on two foundations, Christianity and the ideals of the Declaration of Independence.

As Southerners frequently pointed out, slavery was a practice endorsed by implication in the Bible, and Jesus, who condemns many other institutions and habits, never criticizes it.[85] But Christianity also emphasizes the equality of all souls, and antislavery Northerners took this part of the creed and used it to condemn slavery as a moral abomination. When William Wirt, attorney general under John Quincy Adams, argued before the Supreme Court in the 1825 case of the South Carolina Negro Seaman's Act that slavery was "inconsistent with the laws of God and nature," his statement expressed one of the most powerful strains in abolitionist thinking.[86]

By far the most effective contribution of Christian polemics to the antislavery cause was a novel, *Uncle Tom's Cabin or Life Among the Lowly*, published by Harriett Beecher Stowe in 1852. It appeared in an era before mass marketing, electronic communications, or chain bookstores, yet it sold four hundred thousand copies its first year in print and two hundred thousand more by the end of the decade. It became required reading among the educated classes in Europe and is given partial credit for preventing Britain from entering the Civil War on the side of the South. Harriet Beecher Stowe became an international celebrity.[87]

Uncle Tom's Cabin is the story of a group of slaves who engage in two divergent journeys over the course of the novel. In the first movement, some individuals escape their servitude, first to the North, then to Europe or Africa. Although these escapes lend hope to the story, and have provided the best-remembered images from the book, they do not give the novel its moral punch. That is supplied by the second movement, consisting of the more unfortunate of the group, especially Tom, the title character. Tom and the others gradually descend from their relatively benign (and relatively Northerly) condition at the beginning of the novel through successively more infernal (and more Southerly) conditions until, near the end, Tom arrives at the innermost circle of hell, Simon Legree's plantation in Louisiana. The central horror of the novel, as expressed in the plight of this second group of slaves, is not bondage, terror, whipping, starvation, or rape, although the book has all of those, but the sundering of families. Stowe makes it clear that the forced separation of spouses from each other and children from their parents should be at the heart of the Christian's condemnation of slavery. In her moral universe, the destruction of families for economic reasons is the ultimate, unforgivable social sin. The reception given her book outside the South suggests that it spoke to a crucial concern in the culture of Western civilization. By thus weakening any hope of justifying slavery on religious grounds, she made Southerners turn to other rhetorical strategies.

Over time, the pious fervor of the antislavery cause blended with what was becoming the American civil religion to produce a righteous and wrathful application of the Declaration of Independence to the practice of human chatteldom. It is not surprising that Frederick Douglass, an escaped slave, should excoriate white Americans for their hypocrisy in proclaiming democratic ideals while permitting slavery:

> Would you have me argue that man is entitled to liberty? That he is the rightful owner of his own body? You have already declared it.... How should I look to-day, in the presence of Americans, dividing, and subdividing a discourse, to show that men have a natural right to freedom?... What, to the American slave, is your 4th of July? I answer: a day that reveals to him more than all other days in the year, the gross injustice and cruelty to which he is the constant victim. To him, your celebration is a sham.[88]

But to increasing numbers of Northern whites, also, the Declaration decreed a goal that was no longer to be deferred. In 1839 "sundry inhabitants of Boston" sent a petition to the House of Representatives asking Congress to remove the seat of government from the District of Columbia to some point farther north, where the ideals of the Declaration were "not treated as a mere rhetorical flourish."[89] Southerners did not appreciate the sarcasm. They had no way to stop the transformation of culture that was taking place in the North, however. By 1860 the antislavery cause combined Christianity and the Declaration into a civil faith that vibrated with the intensity of a jihad. De Witt Leach, Republican from Michigan, perfectly expressed the combination of ideas, values, and fervor that defined his party in a speech to the House of Representatives in 1860. The Republican Party, he announced,

> holds the political faith of the fathers of the Republic. We believe that all men have an inalienable right to "life, liberty, and the pursuit of happiness." We believe—nay, we *know*, that slavery, socially, morally, politically, is a blighting and a withering curse.... We know it impedes the progress, as it corrupts the morals and perverts the doctrines, of the Christian religion. We know it is surely, and with fearful rapidity, undermining the very foundations of our Government.[90]

When, in February 1861, President-elect Abraham Lincoln stated that "I have never had a feeling politically that did not spring from the sentiments embodied in the Declaration of Independence," he was affirming a personal creed that, if it was not exactly dominant in the North, had at least come to play a crucial role in all public discourse. He had already been elected running on a platform that affirmed the self-evident truths of the Declaration as the foundation of the nation and the party.[91]

None of this meant that Northerners were ready to embrace the ex-slaves as social or economic equals. Racial hostility was common in the North, and Republicans, including Lincoln, always had to stress publicly that they did not support the extension of civic equality to African Americans. Given the racial attitudes of the day, an endorsement of full equality would have prevented any candidate from being elected, especially at the presidential level. Republicans assembled a majority coalition by emphasizing their opposition to the spread of slavery into the western territories.

It was an article of faith in the North that the systems of slave labor and free labor—industrial or agricultural—were incompatible.[92] If slavery were allowed to spread to the territories, it would snuff out the possibilities of free agriculture and industry. The Missouri Compromise of 1820, by forbidding slavery in the unsettled (except by American Indians) land in the Northwest, permitted white Northerners to dream of moving there and growing rich with the country. As long as the compromise held, abolitionists would never be able to persuade the bulk of the Northern citizenry to destroy the Union by striking at slavery where it already existed.

Meanwhile, through the decades of mounting attack, Southerners elaborated a defense of their institution. At the level of polemic, at the level of analysis, at the level of law, at the level of congressional disputation, and, after 1852, when there was a felt need for a rejoinder to *Uncle Tom's Cabin*, at the level of fiction, the South produced a massive quantity of proslavery literature. At first, until Stowe dug the moral ground out from under them, Southerners disputed the abolitionists' contention that slavery was un-Christian. They rejected the ideals of the Declaration of Independence—by 1830 only Virginia among the Southern states retained in its bill of rights a phrase affirming all men's inalienable rights to life, liberty, and property.[93] They proclaimed that slavery was an unalloyed and positive good—good for blacks, good for whites, good for the economy, good for labor, good for agriculture, good for the family, good for the legal system, good for morals, good for character, good for the country. Furthermore, argued Thomas Roderick Dew in 1833, slaves know that slavery is good. Far from being resentful of their condition, they actually admire and even love their masters. In fact, in Dew's home state of Virginia, "they form the happiest portion of society."[94]

In the North, the reception afforded such arguments ranged from the skeptical to the derisory. Lincoln's comment in 1854 that "although volume upon volume is written to prove slavery a very good thing, we never hear of the man who wishes to take the good of it, *by being a slave himself*," summarizes the general Northern attitude to most Southern apologetics.[95]

There was one Southern argument defending the slave system, however, that was so powerful and credible that it not only caught the respectful attention of many Northerners but convinced some of them. This was the contention that slavery, even with all its flaws, was yet a more just and humane economic system than Northern free labor. Although slaves might lack personal liberty, they were well cared for. Using the liberal assumption of the rational pursuit of profit, Southerners compared slaves to valuable farm animals: while such creatures might be worked hard, it was in the self-interest of their owners to see that they were well fed, well housed, cared for when sick, and otherwise tended as the important investments they were. Just so, because slaves were a valuable investment, slave owners were driven by an invisible hand to treat them as well as they possibly could. There were, of course, occasional sadists who mistreated their slaves, just as there were a few pathological eccentrics who beat their farm animals. But such behavior was rare, and in no sense representative of the system. In the North, by contrast, employers were obliged only to pay wages as high as the market would bear and could ignore the workers' health, safety, and general well-being. In fact, systematic abuse was essential, because kind employers would have higher costs, and therefore be at a competitive disadvantage. Mistreatment of workers was thus an essential component of the capitalist labor market.

John Taylor, with his usual prescience, was the first to make this argument, in 1821. As industrialism advanced in the North, and created an urban working class with visible poverty and labor strife, other Southern writers picked up on the theme. In 1834 John C. Calhoun made a speech in which he drew an invidious distinction between the Northern and Southern labor systems. In 1837 Francis Pickens, also of South Carolina, threatened to circulate among Northern workers, abolitionist-style, with incendiary pamphlets urging social revolution. "When gentlemen preach insurrection to the slaves, I warn them ... that I will preach ... insurrection to the laborers of the North!"[96] After *Uncle Tom's Cabin* diminished the credibility of other Southern arguments in 1852, the allegedly greater humanity of the slave system became the dominant theme in Southern speeches and publications.

If slavery was a superior system of labor, then why not introduce it into the North? Southern writers constantly led their readers right up to this conclusion, then neglected to actually pronounce the recommendation. Probably the advocate who came the closest to outright endorsement of Northern industrial slavery was Edmund Ruffin, in his book *The Political Economy of Slavery*, in 1853. Discussing the analyses and demands of Northern and European socialists, Ruffin insisted that every measure of welfare and justice that those reformers commended to industrial societies was already available to Southern slaves. He therefore advised socialists that if they truly believed their own propaganda, they must begin to support slavery for workers. A modern reader might be tempted to suppose that Ruffin's tongue was in his cheek were not a great many other Southern writers making almost the same suggestion.[97]

The most forceful and sustained exploration of this theme of the inferiority of free labor to slave labor from the standpoint of the worker came from George Fitzhugh of Virginia. Fitzhugh is a favorite of modern scholars because he gives the impression of having a sufficiently powerful intellect that, if his subject had not been so constrained and his cause so unsympathetic, he could have been an important philosopher. In his fearless clarity, he is sometimes reminiscent of Hobbes; in his attachment to order and his suspicion of unfettered human desire, he is often similar to Burke; in his celebration of the strong and insistence that the weak should be governed by the strong, he anticipates Nietzsche. His master assumption is that always and everywhere, exploitation of labor is the basis of economy. Liberty for the masses is a myth; in every social system the majority of the working population is under the domination of elites. An honest evaluation of political economy, then, will not perpetuate the illusion that there is a "free labor" system in the North and a "slave labor" system in the South. It will frankly admit at the beginning that white wage slavery prevails in the North and black legal slavery in the South, and attempt to discover which system of exploitation is better for the mass of the citizens who must live under it.

When the problem is posed this way, says Fitzhugh, the choice is clear. Northern capitalists "are masters without the obligations of masters, and the poor are slaves without the rights of slaves." But "Negroes are immensely valuable, and increase rapidly in value and numbers when well treated. The law of self-interest secures kind and humane treatment to Southern slaves. All the legislative ingenuity in the world will never enact so efficient a law on behalf of free laborers."[98]

Southerners thus tried, and with considerable success, to use the economic half of liberalism—its assumption of individual pursuit of self-interest—to combat the political half—the Lockean assumptions of equality and liberty as embodied in the Declaration. In this one area of the proslavery intellectual campaign, they were often joined by Northern writers. Looking around them at the beginnings of industrial misery and discord, Northerners frequently agreed that free workers seemed to be worse off than slaves. It was often difficult to discern, in some of these publications, if the writer was penning a Swiftian satire of the free labor system, comparing it unfavorably to slavery in the hope of stimulating reform, or actually agreeing with Southerners that slavery, as the more humane system, should be let alone. Thus, during the 1840 presidential campaign, Orestes Brownson wrote a much-noticed essay, "The Laboring Classes," for the *Boston Quarterly Review*, in which he opined,

> In regard to labor, two systems obtain: one that of slave labor, the other of free labor. Of the two, the first is, in our judgment, except so far as the feelings are concerned, decidedly the least oppressive. . . . The laborer at wages has all the disadvantages of freedom, and none of its blessings, while the slave, if denied the blessings, is freed from the disadvantages. . . . One thing is certain: that, of the amount actually produced by the operative, he retains a less proportion than it costs the master to feed, clothe, and lodge his slave. Wages is a cunning device of the devil for the benefit of tender consciences who would retain all the advantages of the slave system without the expense, trouble, and odium of being slaveholders.[99]

Despite the power and plausibility of this argument, however, it contained a fatal flaw. As was frequently the case with proslavery talking points, the crucial weakness in this one was detected and articulated by Abraham Lincoln. Southerners "insist that their slaves are far better off than Northern freemen," he declared in a speech in 1856. "What a mistaken view do these men have of Northern laborers! They think that men are always to remain laborers here—but there is no such class. The man who labors for another last year, this year labors for himself, and next year he will hire others to labor for him."[100] It was thus the social mobility promised by the capitalist labor system that refuted the Southerners' comparison, for no one disputed that slaves would always be slaves, and so would their descendants. According to Eric Foner, Republicans as a group "viewed social mobility as the glory of northern society."[101] In the future, the possibility that workers, or their children, could rise out of the proletariat would remain a central defense of the capitalist system, albeit in the face of other antagonists.

That the party also expressed the attitude of Northern workers is well illustrated by their political behavior. They were willing to endorse the invidious distinction between Northern and Southern labor, but unwilling to accept the logical conclusion of the argument. When Southerners such as Calhoun, Pickens, and Hammond made speeches in Congress comparing the two labor systems to the disadvantage of the North, they received many letters from Northern workers thanking them for exposing the injustice under which "free" workers labored. But no Northern worker ever publicly expressed the desire to be a slave. Labor's purpose in congratulating Southern reactionaries was to spur Northern reforms, not spread Southern institutions.[102]

Nevertheless, Southerners convinced themselves that the expansion of slavery would be a good thing. In 1854 they collaborated with Senator Stephen Douglas of Illinois, a "northern man with southern principles," to pass the Kansas-Nebraska Act, which repealed the Missouri Compromise and opened up the western territories to the spread of slavery by popular vote. Instantly the North exploded in outrage, the Whig Party disintegrated, and legions of ordinary people of no particular ideology joined with committed abolitionists to form the Republican Party. The Republicans did not elect a president in 1856 because the Know Nothing Party—an anti-Catholic, anti-immigrant party—drained enough of their support that James Buchanan, the Democratic candidate, managed to win five states in the North as well as all of those in the South.[103]

In 1857, however, the Supreme Court handed down its *Dred Scott* decision, in which it declared, in essence, that the Missouri Compromise had been unconstitutional because Congress had no power to prevent people from taking their property anywhere, including the territories. Because slaves were property, they could not be kept out of the territories, the free states, or anywhere else. The Court was confronting a bona fide constitutional problem, for Article IV, section 1, declares that "Full Faith and Credit shall be given in each state to the public Acts, Records, and judicial Proceedings of every other State." Today, the clause presents a problem in regard to marriage of gays and lesbians—if the citizens of one state choose to legalize such unions, how can that preference not also be imposed on the other forty-nine? In 1857, Chief Justice Roger Taney believed he saw an analogous problem in regard to slavery. As Robert Meister has reconstructed Taney's thinking, the chief justice "found that as long as slavery is permitted in any state, no state could subsequently confer citizenship on former slaves in a way that would be legally recognizable in other states . . . given the facts of American history, the Constitution is not, and cannot be, neutral regarding the continuing existence of slavery."[104] Therefore, Taney wrote in *Dred Scott*, African Americans "are not included, and were not intended to be included, under the word 'citizen' in the Constitution, and can therefore claim none of the rights and privileges which that instrument provides" and that neither a state nor the federal government can interfere with an owner's property rights in his chattel.[105]

In a sense, the Court under Taney did to the free states what Southern propagandists had been accusing Northerners of attempting to do for seventy years—impose a national rule about rights on a nation that was intended to be an amalgam of local rules and rights. Taney therefore betrayed the deepest principles of the region he was ostensibly defending. In a cockeyed way, abolitionists should have welcomed the decision, for it cleared away the middle ground of possible compromise and traditional muddling through and mandated a showdown. After

Dred Scott, it was actually true, as Lincoln perceived, that the United States could not continue to exist half slave and half free.

Lincoln's perception was widely shared in the North. *Dred Scott* became the evidence that convinced a majority of the Northern public that there was a conspiracy to subjugate all Northern society under slavery. The Know Nothing Party dissolved into the Republicans, Lincoln was elected president, eleven Southern states seceded, and, during four years of civil war, Southern society was smashed and its peculiar institution ended.

The national debate over slavery exposed for the first time a major tension within the liberal creed. An ideology based upon both individual freedom and equality would have trouble addressing the realities of inequality. The Republicans offered social mobility as the ultimate refutation of Southern claims that slavery was the more humane system. But industrialism and its attendant social effects cast doubt on that assumption. The poor lived and sought employment under a set of constraints that were, to an increasing number of observers on the left, demonstrably coercive. In their mutual recognition of this potential contradiction within the premises of liberalism, the preindustrial Southern Right and the industrial Northern Left shared a historical moment of ideological concurrence. When the South was removed from the national political debate, the Left discovered itself weaker and more vulnerable.

LAW

While citizens voted; while parties formed, died, and reformed; while scholars theorized; and while the state and national legislatures afforded arenas for the struggles of great interests, another development was unfolding concerning the relationship of politics and economics. The legal system was the forum for a community of discourse that was connected to, yet separate from, the wider political arena. Unlike the battlefield of electoral politics, on which masses of ordinary citizens were key combatants, in courtrooms battles were fought out between highly paid counsel almost exclusively representing powerful economic and governmental institutions. Under any of three conditions, these clashes of elites could substitute for the ostensible policy-making bodies and replace democratic with legal decision making.

The first condition that could lead to government by judges and lawyers occurred when legislatures, and especially Congress, were paralyzed by an inability to form a governing majority on an important policy issue. Bankruptcy legislation is the best example. The commercial classes had been trying and failing to pass permanent national laws regulating insolvency since the 1790s. The contest had begun as a classic struggle between the commercial and industrial versus the agricultural states. As the economy developed, the differing interests and opinions mutated from two to many, and instead of a bipolar struggle to exhaustion, almost every year Congress witnessed a confused melee of shifting positions, coalitions, and arguments. Some representatives hewed to the traditional belief that bankruptcy should permit only individuals to wipe their financial slate clean and start anew, while others decided that the law should contain provisions for corporations, also. Some argued for a law that applied to everyone, others for protection restricted to those who contracted debts after the passage of the statute. Some insisted that bankruptcy should be a measure that creditors could force on debtors, others that it should permit voluntary action by debtors only. In one masterful episode of logrolling, coalition building, and manipulation of congressional rules in 1841, Henry Clay managed to maneuver a bill through to passage, but it was repealed the next year. From 1842 to the outbreak of the war, the issue was again mired in futility.[106]

But while Congress deadlocked, judges acted. In 1819, in *Sturges v. Crowninshield*, the U.S. Supreme Court decided that the passage in Article I, section 8, of the Constitution granting Congress the authority to pass uniform national bankruptcy laws was not exclusive, and that therefore the states could proceed to address the problem. Chief Justice John Marshall also concluded, however, that because New York's 1811 statute relieved bankrupts of the obligation to pay debts contracted before the measure was passed, it violated the passage in Article I, section 10, that forbade the states to impair the obligation of contracts, and was therefore void. New York then passed a law that covered only debts incurred after the date of enactment. When, in 1827, in *Ogden v. Saunders*, the Court sustained this law, the states were free to move.[107] This piecemeal and inconsistent approach to the problem was inferior to a single, uniform strategy, but it was better than the nothing offered by Congress.

The second circumstance that could lead to courts substituting for legislatures in policy making concerned the development of the common law. This judge-made law was an intricate summary of a tradition of judicial rule making that stretched back many centuries into English history. It dealt with the gaps and ambiguities of statutory law, supplying interpretation where legislative command was absent or problematical. In the case of economic development, American judges played a crucial role in deciding among contending interests in this realm that was removed from the pronouncements of legislatures.

The development of American common law was greatly influenced by the growing, if tacit, alliance between the legal profession and the commercial classes. Over decades after 1790, merchants and industrialists came to see that their enterprises could be rationalized if they consented to submit disputes to the arbitration of judges. For their part, lawyers and judges were delighted to act as the guardians of property against potential regulatory or confiscatory movements in return for augmentation of their own wealth and power.[108] Federalists, Whigs, and Republicans all saw this alliance as the best means of protecting wealth from democratic excesses—which is why they consistently supported the independence of the judiciary. Democrats tended to be more conflicted, supporting property rights but endorsing more control over judges by legislatures. The differences were more of emphasis than of kind, but over time the differences of emphasis had some important consequences.

One indicator of the manner in which judges positioned themselves to shield property from potential democratic disruption is the decline of the jury in the early nineteenth century. The eighteenth-century view, in the words of a treatise written in 1795, was that "the jury [are] the proper judges not only of the fact but of the law that [is] necessarily involved." But juries, being composed of the people, were potentially dangerous to property. Eighteenth-century juries had the power, for example, to overturn contracts on the basis of their evaluation of the equity of the exchange. Juries could and did decide that a contract was void if the parties to the agreement were of such unequal power, wealth, and position that their relationship was essentially coercive. By 1810, however, many Northern states had mandated a distinction between the facts of the case and the law pertaining to it. The law had become the exclusive domain of the judge. By the 1840s the question at issue in contract cases was whether an agreement had been reached voluntarily. Juries were not allowed to form an opinion as to its equity.[109]

As the nineteenth century advanced, judges marked out more areas of law from which juries could be excluded. In 1852, for example, Daniel Webster (still practicing law despite the fact that he was secretary of state) convinced the members of the Supreme Court, in the case of *Goodyear v. Day*, that judges should not submit questions of fact in patent cases to juries, but should decide the cases themselves. Webster's argument, endorsed by the Court, was that inventors' rights would be safer in the hands of judges than in those of juries whose members might be swayed by popular prejudices against patent holders as monopolists.[110]

Having assumed the role of the friendly arbiter of business by about 1815, state and federal judges proceeded to modify a variety of common law doctrines, inherited from the English and all tending to protect agricultural landed property rights, so that they could be used to sponsor and defend capitalist development. American water law, for example, reflecting its English origins, had been based on the doctrine of prior appropriation—whoever first owned the land around the river determined its use along its entire length. In the context of a feudal society in which the first use of water was certain to be nonindustrial, this rule could easily operate to suppress development. The first landowner could forbid a later owner upstream to build a mill on the stream, for instance. In 1805, however, a New York court held for the first time, in *Palmer v. Mulligan*, that an upper riparian landowner could build a mill and obstruct flow, despite the objections of downstream landowners. In 1827, in *Tyler v. Wilkinson*, the Supreme Court decided that the "reasonable use" of water by a developer might, under some, not clearly stated, circumstances, override an original owner's right to the resource. By 1856 and the Vermont case of *Snow v. Parsons*, most courts had decided that competing needs for water should be subject to a balancing test, making "reasonable use" of a stream "depend on the extent of detriment to the riparian proprietors below." As it happened, American judges generally decided that any planned industrial development was a reasonable use and trumped the downstream owner's previous right to all the undeveloped water he or she wanted. In an age when most industrial power was supplied by rivers, the common law of water thus became an engine of capitalism's progress.[111]

State court judges also attempted, at first with success, to use the common law to help business by suppressing labor unions. From the first New York case in 1806 to the early 1840s, judges simply brought all unions under the common law doctrine of conspiracy and declared them outlaws. Sometimes the courts held that a combination of workers was illegal per se, and sometimes they contented themselves with ruling that, although the organization itself was permissible, every possible deed it performed to raise wages or constrict the number of people applying for work was a criminal act. Labor gained a somewhat ambiguous first victory in 1842 when, in *Commonwealth v. Hunt*, the Massachusetts Supreme Court ruled both that, under the common law, a labor union was a lawful organization and that the means it used could also be permissible. Because Chief Justice Lemuel Shaw also upheld the general doctrine of conspiracy, however, the ruling still allowed unions to be subjected to a great deal of harassment and suppression.[112]

The third manner in which judges could block governmental action inconvenient to business was to declare it a violation of the Constitution. With the single exception of *Dred Scott*, all the Supreme Court decisions striking down government decisions on constitutional grounds in this era targeted state legislation.

One landmark was *Dartmouth College v. Woodward*, decided in 1819. The college had received a charter from King George III in 1769, but this original document had been amended by the New Hampshire legislature in 1816, which increased the number of trustees and vested the future power of appointing trustees in the governor and his council. The original trustees sued but lost in the state courts. The U.S. Supreme Court, however, decided that the legislature's actions had violated the contract clause of the Constitution. Writing the majority opinion, Chief Justice Marshall asserted that a state charter is a contract. Although a corporation is undoubtedly "an artificial being . . . the mere creature of law" brought into existence by public authorities for "benefits to the public," still, "it is no more a state instrument than a natural person exercising the same powers would be." It is a private entity and thus possesses the natural right to be let alone. Under the Constitution, a state has no more authority to interfere in the contract that created this public, fictional person than it would have to interfere in the contracts of a private, biological one. Therefore the original trustees must get their college back.[113]

The *Dartmouth College* decision established an important principle in the judicial protection of business from democratic interference. After 1819, not only educational but all types of corporations could claim the protection of the contract clause against regulation by state governments. The Democratic suspicion of corporations as elitist monopolies, expressed in both the legislative and executive spheres of government, thus ran up against Federalist protection of corporations in the judicial sphere. A concurring opinion by Justice Joseph Story in the *Dartmouth* case, however, provided a framework for softening the absolutism of Marshall's opinion. Story pointed out that legislatures, in granting corporate charters, could insert clauses retaining the right to modify them. Soon all the states included such clauses in their chartering statutes. As a result, the potential sweep of the *Dartmouth* case was diminished, and the authority of the states to regulate the institutions they created remained a battleground.[114]

Another crucial Supreme Court ruling in the contentious judicial discussion of the authority of state legislatures to regulate business was *Charles River Bridge v. Warren Bridge*, decided in 1837. By that date, John Marshall had died, and had been succeeded as chief justice by Roger Taney. Taney and the Democrats were no less concerned about the protection of property than the Federalists (or, by 1837, the Whigs), but their interest was more subtle and complicated. As the representatives of rising economic classes, they did not want previous economic privileges to be able to stifle new business—that purpose had been part of their motivation for their recent war against the Bank of the United States. Furthermore, they were ideologically committed to allowing public authorities to have control over the public institutions of economic development. The Bank of the United States' stubborn resistance to public direction had been another reason for their hostility to its existence. Whereas the Marshall Court had been liable to give lip service to public responsibilities while affirming private rights, in this particular instance the Taney Court rhetorically endorsed private rights while upholding a public authority's power to infringe an implied contract.

The case involved the Charles River Bridge Company, which in 1785 had been granted the right, by the Massachusetts legislature, to construct a bridge over the river between Boston and Cambridge and collect tolls for forty years (later extended to seventy). In 1828 the legislature chartered another toll bridge over the Charles, situated sufficiently close to the first bridge to deprive it of its revenue. The owners of the first bridge sued, claiming that the original charter had been an implied contract guaranteeing them a monopoly. The original owners lost in state court and appealed to the federal courts.

The U.S. Supreme Court upheld the Massachusetts court, rejecting the claim of an implied contract in the original grant. "While the rights of private property are sacredly guarded, we must not forget that the community also have rights," wrote Taney, thus reversing the Federalist judges' emphasis. The argument of the plaintiffs, he continued, would, if endorsed, result in bringing economic progress to a halt. Any business, anywhere, could assert that its profits were being harmed by some new state road, land grant, canal, harbor, or other enterprise.

> [W]hat would be the fruits of this doctrine of implied contracts, on the part of the states? ... If this court should establish the principles now contended for, what is to become of the numerous railroads established on the same line of travel with turnpike companies, and which have rendered the franchises of the turnpike corporations of no value? Let it once be understood, that such charters carry with them these implied contracts ... and you will soon find the old turnpike corporations awakened from their sleep and calling upon this court to put down the improvements which have taken their place. ... We shall be thrown back to the improvements of the last century, and obliged to stand still, until the claims of the old turnpike corporations shall be satisfied, and they shall permit these states ... to partake of the benefit of those improvements which are now adding to the wealth and prosperity, and the convenience and comfort, of every other part of the civilized world.[115]

And so, in order for the economy to advance, judges must permit governments the latitude to abridge the absolute rights of past economic privileges. It was a pro-property decision, but it looked to the future rather than the past.

Apparently, however, Taney did not understand all the potential implications of such a doctrine. Some of his opponents did understand. Justice Story dissented, but the most penetrating critique of the implications of Taney's argument came from another old Federalist, James Kent of New York. He remarked that upon reading the opinion he "dropped the pamphlet in disgust and read no more." Kent saw, more clearly than Taney, that "if the Legislature can quibble away, or whittle away its contracts with impunity, the people will be sure to follow."[116] While Taney was thinking of legislatures sponsoring projects to encourage development, Kent understood that such a path could lead in more than one direction. If legislatures could modify charters at the behest of new companies, they could certainly modify them at the behest of democratic majorities envious of economic success. Taney's decision could sow the seeds for what would certainly please most business interests in the short run, but might very much displease them in the long run.

By 1862 the general American, and two specialized public discourses, the legal and the economic, were traveling in opposite directions. Making allowances for inconsistencies, hypocrisies, and unrealized implications, the overall rhetoric, and also the practice, of Americanism was toward an ever-greater realization of democratic participation in both government and the economy. The economic barriers to full participation in the vote had fallen, and sundry citizens were realizing that the ideals they had used to expand the franchise now mandated yet further expansion. The opportunity to create business corporations had been extended to all white males. Slavery was on the road to extinction. In the White House was a politician who understood that the war then in its early months was a struggle "to clear the paths of laudable pursuit for all—to afford all, an unfettered start, and a fair chance, in the race of life."[117]

Like Albert Gallatin before him, Lincoln believed that democracy and capitalism were marvelous things, avenues to a society both wealthy and just. In the two generations before he spoke, Americans had been creating a society in which the impediments to both democracy and capitalism were being removed. Lincoln believed that the way to improve American society was to clear away still more hindrances to equal participation in politics and economics. Not everyone, however, not at the time he spoke, or later, was so confident that democracy and capitalism was a marriage made in heaven.

In the discourse of the legal profession, now allied with industrial capitalism, the suspicion of democratic majorities was intense, erudite, and resourceful. There was not yet an overall philosophy of legitimacy, or a juridical doctrine, to justify suppressing the ability of majorities to interfere in the decisions of capitalists. But the democratic victories of the previous decades had alarmed legal thinkers, and they would soon make themselves busy finding rationales for the restraint of democracy.

Meanwhile, the evolution of the sibling professions of philosophy and economics was about to bring them into a position where they would become useful to judges in their campaign to undermine democracy. Adam Smith, so long the nemesis of industrial capitalism, was about to become its best friend.

CHAPTER FOUR

Industrialism and Its Discontents I, 1862–1898

After the end of the Civil War in 1865, industrialism exploded across the northern and eastern states. Machinery, textiles, iron and steel, food processing, alcoholic beverages, chemicals, leather, paper and printing, and, preeminently, the railroads pushed the United States into the "takeoff phase" of industrial development that had already been experienced by Britain two generations earlier. As transportation, communication, and financial webs spread across the continent, business became nationalized and sometimes internationalized, and the United States burgeoned into an economic behemoth. By 1870 it had the largest economy in the world, and its per capita real income was expanding at a rate of 1.6 percent a year.[1] New machinery and new processes grew exponentially; the federal government issued 25,200 patents in the decade prior to the war, then 85,910 from 1860 to 1870, and 234,956 from 1890 to 1900.[2] By 1894 the United States produced more manufactures than any other country.[3] The expansion was accompanied by a general shift in production locations from small workshops, often with family members as workers, to large factories.

Technically, agriculture was still the dominant sector through the 1880s, but the 1890 census revealed that, for the first time, the value of manufactured goods surpassed that of agricultural commodities. Not surprisingly, the percentage of the population employed in agriculture declined from 53 percent of all working Americans in 1870 to 42 percent in 1890, and continued to go down thereafter.[4]

The takeoff phase of industrial capitalism was accompanied by, and certainly facilitated by, a national culture that seemed to many observers to be obsessed with the accumulation of wealth. A scramble for riches appeared to be the American's vocation and avocation, at least among males. Many observers concurred that in the United States, the moral worth of all men was conflated with their personal economic success, and "work, whiskey, and cards," in Henry Adams's words, consumed their lives.[5] The emphasis upon material success seemed also, to many critics, to be accompanied by a collapse of moral rules, as individuals and their governments discarded all ethical standards except economic advance.[6]

The mushrooming national wealth created by kinetic industrial capitalism showed three patterns of development. The first was increasing inequality of distribution, as the entrepreneurs who created the new industrial enterprises captured an ever-larger share of the burgeoning national product. There are no systematic, reliable statistics, but as a liberal estimate, the United States may have had 400 millionaires at the end of the Civil War, and many of those were slaveholders who were soon ruined. By 1892 the *New York Tribune Monthly* could name 4,047 alleged members of the magic circle. Chicago alone boasted 280. One writer estimated in 1889 that two hundred thousand people controlled 70 percent of the nation's wealth.[7] Certain neighborhoods in large cities became entirely filled with mansions, and whole resort cities, the most famous being Newport, Rhode Island, were transformed into concentrations of palatial estates where the rich congregated.

The second pattern was the undeniable increasing prosperity of many members of the industrial working class and some farmers. From 1865 to 1890, there was both a general price decline and a general increase in wages. Real wages over that period rose more than 100 percent in industry and 70 percent in agriculture.[8] While the rich were becoming fabulously wealthy, most people, over most of this era, were becoming, if not rich, then more prosperous than they had been.

The third, however, was a pattern of geographic skew to the trend of economic progress for farmers, with those in the South and the plains states not sharing in the prosperity enjoyed by their fellow husbandmen in the Northeast and Midwest. The South, in particular, went into a long economic decline after the war, and fell into a pattern of sharecropping and "debt peonage" for both black and white farmers that resulted in an average personal income in the region that by 1890 was only half of what it was in the Midwest.[9] The South's misery was worsened by discriminatory policies pursued by both the federal government and great industrial combinations. Northerners seemed to decide to punish Southerners for their recent rebellion by reducing them to "colonial" status and exploiting them ruthlessly. The protective tariff in effect taxed Southern farmers for the benefit of Northern industrialists. Railroad rates on raw materials from the South and West to the Northeast were lower than in the reverse direction, thereby helping to keep these regions in vassalage to the Northeast. Rail lines, in league with Pennsylvania interests, established rates that encouraged the development of the steel industry in Pittsburgh and suppressed its development in Birmingham, Alabama.[10] The behavior of post-Civil War white Southerners in attempting to abuse and oppress black Southerners in every way possible should not be allowed to eclipse the exploitation of Southerners of both races by Northerners over the same period. Throughout the latter years of the century, the South was impoverished, subjugated, and resentful.

Although growing prosperity, outside the South, was a dominant economic fact of American life during this era, the good times were not unbroken. There was a period of economic contraction that lasted from 1873 to 1878, another leveling off of business activity from 1883 to 1886, and a severe depression from 1893 to 1897. During these downturns, the lack of government help for destitute individuals created a reservoir of the downtrodden who could not be reassured that their own misfortune was all for the best. Further, the visible contrast of the few conspicuously opulent with the struggling masses, inoffensive during the prosperous years, seemed intolerable during hard times, and gave rise to rhetoric about "tramps and millionaires." The country thus harbored more resentment about economic inequalities than might have been expected from knowledge of its overall prosperity.

Along with industrialism in the North and East came urbanization. The country's population more than doubled from 1860 to 1900, going from 31.4 million to 76.9 million, and the proportion of Americans living in incorporated municipalities during that period doubled, from 20 to 40 percent of the total.[11] The most startling urban growth was in Chicago, which exploded from a population of thirty thousand residents in 1850 to over a million in 1890, by which time it was the sixth-largest city in the world.[12] But Chicago was only the most spectacular representative of a general phenomenon. During the decade of the 1880s alone, 101 American cities at least doubled their size.[13]

The growth of cities outpaced all efforts to make them livable. Communication, transportation, sanitation, and habitation lagged far behind the influx of bodies. Cities stank from primitive sewage disposal systems. Government reports of the era record many examples of overcrowding, unhealthy conditions, and desperate poverty.[14] The words "tenement" and "slum" entered the American vocabulary.

The problem of crowded poverty in the cities seemed to be made worse by the tide of immigration. More than twenty-eight million people moved from Europe to the United States between 1860 and 1920, most of them settling in the urban areas. By 1900 foreign-born residents constituted about 40 percent of the population of the twelve largest cities in the country, while another 20 percent were second generation.[15] Progressives of the period worried about the squalid, exploited lives of immigrants. In contrast, conservatives, such as the *New York Herald*'s editorial writer in 1877, tended to worry that the immigrants were "men incapable of understanding our ideas and principles," that is, American reverence for property.[16]

The battle for the adult white male suffrage had been won the previous generation, but conservatives were still echoing Chancellor Kent's warnings about the certainty of the have-nots using their votes to rob the haves. In the 1870s the defenders of property began to fill the intellectual air with the cry that Kent had been right, and something had to be done to tame the foreign, urban beast that was slouching toward socialism. Among these alarums, historian Francis Parkman sounded the clarion call about the menace to property inherent in the new urban democracy in an article in the *North American Review*: "Here the dangerous classes are most numerous and strong, and the effects of flinging the suffrage to the mob are most disastrous.... [In cities, democracy] hands over great municipal corporations, the property of those who hold stock in them, to the keeping of greedy and irresponsible crowds, controlled by adventurers as reckless as themselves, whose object is nothing but plunder."[17]

It was not just the intellectual classes in the 1870s who were dismayed by the potential of democracy to render property insecure. Politicians, too, examined foreigners and urban machines and found them a threat. Thus future president James Garfield, in a letter to a friend in 1875, confided, "It has long been my opinion that universal suffrage is a failure as applied to municipal corporations.... The root of the difficulty is this: one naturalized foreigner can by his vote neutralize the vote of A. T. Steward [millionaire New York merchant]. Thus two men without a dollar can dispose of the pecuniary interests of a man worth many millions."[18]

Immigrants and machines were not the only threat perceived by the propertied. Organized labor was equally frightening. To a historian looking back through more than a century of industrial relations, it is obvious that the employers were much more of a threat to the employees than vice versa. The generally rising prosperity of the era still left many workers at the mercy of bosses who ignored their health and safety, worked them killing hours, and inflicted all manner of private despotisms upon them. As a consequence, the industrial takeoff of capitalism after the Civil War spawned a parallel effort by workers to organize so as to protect themselves from such private power.

The first conflict to startle propertied opinion was the Railway Strike of 1877, during which workers battled Pennsylvania militia and federal troops and set fire to numerous buildings and railroad installations. By the time order was restored, property damage was upward of $10 million, and hundreds of people had died.[19] An even more unsettling event occurred in 1886, when in the midst of a strike against the McCormick Harvester Works in Chicago, someone detonated a bomb on the outskirts of a mass meeting in Haymarket Square, killing one policeman and injuring perhaps sixty other people. The remaining police opened fire on the strikers, killing ten and injuring fifty. Respectable opinion in the United States became anxious at the alleged criminal intent of labor unions.[20] The anxiety was only heightened by a cresting of labor strife in the 1890s. In 1892 alone, there were four violent strikes, in Pittsburgh; Coeur d'Alene, Idaho; Buffalo, New York; and Tracey City, Tennessee, in all of which the strikers were suppressed by either state militia or federal troops.[21] Between 1893 and 1898 there were 7,029 strikes, or about 1,171 per year. The average number of employees refusing to work in each of these years was 280,708.[22] Regardless of the realistic balance of power between labor and capital, to many respectable citizens it seemed, in the final third of the nineteenth century, that free enterprise itself was under siege by a powerful enemy.

In the years immediately following the war, party politics emphasized the sectional cleavage that had caused the conflict in the first place, now centered around the issue of the tariff, with northeastern interests, as represented by Republicans, usually supporting protection and Southern interests, as represented by Democrats, generally opposing it, and with both sides bidding for the support of the Midwest and West. This cleavage line, however, was sometimes overlain and sometimes crosscut, both by a variety of social issues—including sectional antagonisms based on memories of the war, prohibitionism, religious conflicts, and ethnic hostility—and by specifically economic issues, especially the currency question. If there was one area of common ground on which the two major parties stood in this era, it was their shared enmity toward organized labor. In general, major party leaders attempted to suppress, evade, and diffuse the discontents created by industrialization, and largely succeeded until the 1890s. Questions of the value of unrestrained capitalist expansion did not become part of the major party battle until the 1896 presidential election.[23] This is not to say that the state and federal governments never addressed the issues of industrialism. When they did so, however, it was on an ad hoc basis, not part of an overall party strategy, a stable set of interests, or a counterideology.

The dominant social theory of the age thus permeated the ideas and values of the leaders of both major parties, and was endorsed by executives, legislators, and, inevitably, judges. This ideology combined satisfaction at the undoubtedly impressive achievements of American capitalism with genuine fear at what appeared to be a serious challenge to the system that had created those achievements, all conditioned by the accepted thinking of previous generations. It was not an era of intellectual distinction, but it was an era of ideological coherence.

NATURAL LAW REDUX

During the last four decades of the nineteenth century, most educated Americans believed that the human intellect had solved the major problems of economics and politics. Informed people could learn the right way to structure society; that is, the way that would produce legitimacy, prosperity, and justice. Because they took for granted that legitimacy, prosperity, and justice were good things, they concluded that the right way was the moral way and that people who opposed the right way were immoral. Science, in the form of liberal social theory, could instruct humankind on the way to become both rich and good. Respectable Americans believed, then, in natural law, and their wrath at those who would deliberately violate that law could be righteous and terrible.

The dominant textbook of economics during this entire period, in both Britain and the United States, was John Stuart Mill's *Principles of Political Economy*.[24] Mill both summarized the thinking of previous classical economists and made many theoretical innovations that expanded on or corrected their principles in such areas as the concept of noncompeting groups in labor markets, the treatment of economies of scale, and the idea of opportunity costs. Despite Mill's intellectual eminence, however, he was internally conflicted; his head was at war with his heart. While endorsing and elaborating many of the tenets of the theory deriving from Adam Smith, his compassionate conscience was greatly troubled by the real-world excesses of the actual economic system that owed much of its vitality to Smith's theory. Yet he was not a great enough thinker to be able to break out of the classical mold and fashion a new theory based on new premises.

Mill's strategy for dealing with his personal muddle was more stylistic than substantive. He would typically begin a discussion of a given question with a clear endorsement of some classical postulate, and then qualify it at great length until very little was left of it. Thus he usually began with a short, unambiguous statement advocating the classical position—"laissez-faire, in short, should be the general practice; every departure from it, unless required by some greater good, is a certain evil" is an excellent example.[25] Then he would expand on the qualification—"unless required by some greater good"—making concessions and restatements over many pages until his position seemed to become, although obscurely and ambiguously, that the world was full of greater goods justifying interference with the market.[26]

To understand Mill in his entirety, however, required both the patience to wade through hundreds of pages of increasing ambiguity and the subtlety to follow his reasoning. Most readers, on both sides of the Atlantic, didn't bother. They absorbed the easy, intelligible paragraphs and avoided or daydreamed through the rest. Thus Mill, who is now seen as a transition figure between classical economics and socialism, was understood throughout the period as the man who had improved on, while confirming, the theories of Smith, Ricardo, and Say.

During the last three decades of the century, however, academic thinkers were making theoretical advances that would eventually supersede classical economics altogether. W. Stanley Jevons in England, Carl Mengers in Austria, and Leon Walras in Switzerland began to create the theory of marginal utility during the 1870s, and Alfred Marshall in England and John Bates Clark in the United States expanded and refined it during the 1890s. Their "neoclassical economics," as it is now termed, assumed that humans attempt to maximize their subjective "utility," or welfare, at the margins of choice. This new basic assumption allowed economists to model many market problems that the classicists had been unable to handle. Just as important, if utility was the standard of judgment in economics, then it was possible to evaluate whether a wholly free market, or some more controlled economy, might result in more total social utility. Neoclassical economics thereby opened the intellect to imagine how state regulation might produce a more "opulent" society than Smith's free market.[27]

This aspect of neoclassical economic theory, however, had very little effect on American thinking until the twentieth century. Even Clark, America's only prominent nineteenth-century neoclassical economist, managed to recast marginalist theory so that it became entirely hostile to government regulation.[28] The respectable view—the opinion of academics, elite journalists, and scholars generally—was thus that natural law, as discovered by Smith and refined by Mill, constituted a system that combined scientific and moral truth. In 1889, for example, Francis Amasa Walker, president of the Massachusetts Institute of Technology (MIT), attested that a belief in laissez-faire "was not made the test of economic orthodoxy, merely. It was used to decide whether a man were an economist at all."[29]

Popularizers found this an easy test to pass. Arthur Latham Perry's book, *Elements of Political Economy*, which first appeared in 1873, was the most widely used American-authored text of the last quarter of the century.[30] Perry has none of Mill's qualms. He announces that "the laws of exchange are based on nothing less solid than the will of God . . . it is a high-handed infringement of natural rights, a blow aimed at the life and source of property, when any authority whatever interferes to restrict or prohibit the freedom of exchange."[31] The giant intellect who had been able to intuit God's laws was Adam Smith, who "contributed more, by the publication of this single work [*The Wealth of Nations*], toward the happiness of man, than has been effected by the united abilities of all the statesmen and legislators of whom history has preserved an authentic account."[32] Then why not simply read Smith, rather than Perry? For two reasons. First, Smith committed one confusion in arguing that there were two types of value, natural and exchange. A little more thought, says Perry, would have convinced Smith that there is only one type of value, created by exchange.[33] Second, Smith's theory was usefully augmented by J. B. Say, who provided "the important demonstration that there cannot be a general glut of production—a general over-production," unless, of course, some sinister force intervenes to obstruct the workings of free exchange.[34]

But sinister forces are abroad, and they must be denounced. Labor unions, for one, are organizations created with the specific intention of interfering with the free exchange of employers and employees. Their very purpose is "to destroy the freedom of personal action" that underlies God's economy, and therefore "[t]he spirit of Political Economy, which is the spirit of freedom, is against such associations."[35] In particular, the chief weapon of a union is contrary to natural law, for "strikes are false in theory and pernicious in practice."[36]

In addition, however, government obstructs the free market with tariffs. These are abominations, for "foreign trade is just as legitimate as domestic trade; it rests on the same ultimate principles in the constitution of man and the providential arrangements of Nature."[37]

So, repeal all tariffs and outlaw labor unions, and the naturally beneficent market will reign supreme.

As the century aged and various elements of the population expressed their disgruntlement with laissez-faire policies, other authors felt it necessary to freshen Perry's thesis. Thus Henry Wood, in *The Political Economy of Natural Law*, which appeared in 1894, in the second year of a serious depression, addressed the criticisms of classical economics that had begun to be heard more persistently and more loudly: "Economic evils, now so prominent and universal, are not the outcome of the present 'social system,' but of the abuses which fasten themselves to it, consequent upon general moral delinquency. They are not a real part of it, but are like barnacles on the bottom of a ship."[38]

What are these barnacles on the ship of opulence? First, of course, are labor unions, which seem to be eternally multiplying despite the fact that they are contrary to natural law. Second is charity, which also violates natural law, and is "worse than useless" because it "breeds dependence" rather than forcing people to get up and go exchange things.[39]

Wood is particularly concerned to counter one canard made by socialists against the capitalist system. The "great and mischievous fallacy" the enemies of this system keep repeating is that "wealth is created by labor, and therefore, belongs to the laborers who produced it." In a technical sense, he says, the assertion is true. Wealth is created by labor. But it is not the sort of labor the socialists think. It is *mental* labor, the entrepreneurial element, that organizes chaotic energy and creates economic activity. The regular laborers, the employees, are merely drones who have no creative power. It is a great effrontery to think that they are in some sense responsible for a business concern. They deserve nothing but their wages.[40]

Finally, Wood addresses the cry against bigness that was a prominent part of the political rhetoric of the 1890s. The trend of large factories replacing small workshops, of mergers making ever-larger firms, of holding companies and trusts, he says, seems to be scaring many people out of their wits. But "the menace to government and to citizens by great business combinations is much overrated" because such combinations are disciplined by market forces. It doesn't matter how big a firm is, as long it is subject to the laws of exchange. And since all firms of whatever size are so subject, there is nothing to worry about.[41]

The orthodox American economic theory of the age was accordingly an endorsement of Smith's original principles, with their ruthless implications emphasized and their moral force explicitly enhanced by conflation with "natural" morality. There was nothing surreptitious about this political and economic conservatism. Leading American economists frankly proclaimed themselves to be apologists for industrial capitalism. Thus Walker, in his presidential address to the American Economic Association in 1890, was disturbed by the fact that "our economists, as a body, should be able to do little in stemming the tide of socialism which has set in so strongly of late." His advice to his fellow scholars was that "our first duty is to see to it that this political and industrial experiment [the competitive order] does not fail."[42]

But "political economy" was not the only important social theory of this era. Natural law also made another entry, out of biology by way of philosophy. In social

Darwinism, the propertied classes found a justification for some industrial trends that were not covered by classical economics.

Charles Darwin was neither a political nor an economic philosopher, and all his life remained cautious about drawing social implications from his theory of natural selection as the mainspring of biological evolution.[43] And indeed, a direct application of Darwinian theory to economic development would not be comforting to defenders of the industrial order. Superficially, the doctrines of Smith and Darwin are not only compatible but complementary, for both posit competition as the activity that winnows less competent individuals, thereby causing the whole to progress. But there is a crucial difference between the two theories that makes them incompatible at a more profound level. According to Smith, competition increases the opulence of living humans. He emphasizes quantity of production as a means to the end of quality of life, and the production he discusses is nonbiological. In contrast, Darwin emphasizes that life has no end but biological quantity. Both species and individuals of a species prevail in the struggle for existence by reproducing; the more offspring, the more successful the individual or the species. Biological evolution is unconcerned with the happiness, power, wealth, beauty, or any other quality of individuals' lives. All that matters is the number of their surviving children.[44] In industrial or any other kind of society, however, the poor are notoriously more fecund than the wealthy. Therefore, by a strict application of Darwinism to industrial society, the poor, not the rich, are history's winners.

This problem was solved by Herbert Spencer, an English philosopher who began creating a politically conservative theory of social evolution even before Darwin published *The Origin of Species* in 1859. As soon as Darwin's book came out, however, Spencer seized upon its central idea and began adding or subtracting concepts according to their usefulness to a defense of laissez-faire. It was Spencer who coined the phrase "survival of the fittest" (although Darwin endorsed the idea, beginning in his fifth edition), in order to introduce an element of moral approval into the notion of evolution. By the later decades of the century he had fashioned an elaborate theory of the progress of inanimate matter, biological organisms, and human social systems.

Spencer argues that the principle of conservation of energy, which he terms "persistence of force," is at work everywhere to produce a uniform direction of development in all matter, living and nonliving. This "law of evolution" consists in a tendency to advance from the small and simple to the large and complex. Moreover, the principle of persistence of force results in a pattern in which nature progresses from energy to life, from life to mind, from mind to society, from society to civilization, and thence to more highly differentiated and integrated civilization.[45] This natural progression is both inevitable and tending toward the improvement of humanity. To oppose it is both ignorant and wicked.

Despite the thousands of pages of exposition he published over the decades, Spencer never coherently explained the way that his conclusions necessarily followed from his premises. Exactly how the conservation of energy led to "multiplicity and heterogeneity," or how biological adaptation led to moral progress, or how all this related, at least in the early stages, to competition, was never clear even to his disciples. His large body of stilted and incomprehensible exegesis inspired the English mathematician Thomas Kirkman to offer a parody summary of Spencer's theory in 1876. Evolution, proposed Kirkman, is "a change from a nohowish untalkaboutable all-alikeness to a somehowish and in general talkaboutable not-all-alikeness by continuous stick-togetherness and somethingelseifications."[46]

Nevertheless, despite the logical obscurity at its core, Spencer's theory had, and has, a surface plausibility. Anyone looking about themselves in late-nineteenth-century America could see that in economy, in politics, and in society in general, the country was evolving from the small and simple to the large and complex, and that the shape of things had something to do with competition. A philosopher who had predicted it all beginning in the 1850s had to be on to something.

Furthermore, the details of Spencer's theory of the natural law of social evolution were intensely agreeable to the new captains of industry and their academic apologists. It was gratifying to think that science had proven that they were the fittest who had survived, and that their dominance was good for everybody. As Andrew Carnegie wrote in 1889:

> The price which society pays for the law of competition, like the price it pays for cheap comforts and luxuries, is . . . great, but the advantages of the law are also greater still . . . while the law may be sometimes hard for the individual, it is best for the race, because it insures the survival of the fittest in every department. We accept and welcome, therefore, as conditions to which we must accommodate ourselves, great inequality of environment, the concentration of business, industrial and commercial, in the hands of a few, and the law of competition between these, as being not only beneficial, but essential for the future progress of the race.[47]

There was, of course, the problem of the unfit. Here Spencer was far more useful to the propertied classes than Darwin had been. Unflinchingly, he explained that the poor had lost the evolutionary race. The worst thing to do would be to provide them with some sort of relief. That would be anti-Darwinian; it would ensure the survival of the incompetent. Spencer attacked the weak-minded sentimentalists who advocated such measures as the English poor laws: "Blind to the fact that under the natural order of things society is constantly excreting its unhealthy, imbecile, slow, vacillating, faithless members, these unthinking, though well-meaning, men advocate an interference which not only stops the purifying process, but even increases the vitiation—absolutely encouraging the multiplication of the reckless and incompetent by offering them an unfailing provision."[48]

So the rich were good and should be applauded, and the poor were bad and ought to be excreted. In specific regard to the treatment of industrial workers, Spencer, unlike many of his followers, was quite frank in acknowledging their exploitation. Liberty of contract "amounts in practice to little more than the ability to exchange one slavery for another.... The coercion of circumstances often bears more hardly on him than the coercion of a master does on one in bondage." Since this point was exactly the criticism made by progressives of the labor relations of the time, it might be supposed that Spencer's own logic would lead him to advocate some sort of state protection for workers. But no. "It seems that in the course of social progress, parts, more or less large, of each society, are sacrificed for the benefit of the society as a whole." In earlier human history, that immolation consisted of warfare, but in the present state of civilized development, "the sacrifice takes the form of mortality entailed by the commercial struggle.... In either case, men are used up for the benefit of posterity."[49] Both government intervention on behalf of workers and labor unions interfere with the natural process of using up men and women for the benefit of posterity, and so, while they both may appeal to short-run sentimentality, they are damaging to society in the long run. Spencer turned Smith's moral uneasiness about the fate of workers in a free market into a positive conviction that the exploitation of labor today was the road to widespread prosperity tomorrow.

The grand conclusion of all this detailed examination of the benefits of social evolution was that undiluted laissez-faire, resting on absolute and unhindered freedom of contract, was an economic and political imperative. In addition to his opposition to public and private welfare projects and any efforts to ameliorate the conditions of industrial workers, Spencer criticized state-supported education, regulation of housing conditions, government licensing of doctors, tariffs, state banking, and government postal systems. Anything that interfered with "nature," or that stopped human beings from agreeing among themselves under any circumstances, was an impediment to human progress.[50]

Today, the fallacies of this line of reasoning are obvious. Accepting Spencer's own premises, to take a simple example, if the poor unite, kill the rich, and take over the means of production, then *they* are the fittest, and by that fact, justified. Might makes right, by the "law of competition."

With a few significant exceptions, most American intellectuals and journalists of the era failed to detect the obvious problems with social Darwinism, or, more correctly, Spencerism, as a world-encompassing philosophy. Probably, they read Spencer's political essays, were impressed by them, and assumed that their philosophical underpinning was sound. At any rate, he became the philosopher of the age. The sales of his books from their first publication in the 1860s to 1903 totaled 368,755, far ahead of anything else by a professional philosopher or sociologist.[51] He was lauded as the man with the most capacious intellect of all time, whose genius surpassed that of Aristotle and Newton as the telegraph surpassed the carrier pigeon, whose revelations were more effective than those from Sinai.[52] Politicians, scholars, and judges regularly appealed to him as the authority on political and economic policy.

The most influential American social Darwinist was Yale sociologist William Graham Sumner. Sumner not only shared crucial premises and conclusions with Spencer, admired him personally, and borrowed some of his terminology, but his writing style is remarkably akin to Spencer's polemical mode. Although his ideas are derivative, his clarity and force of expression make Sumner a figure still worth reading.

Like Spencer, Sumner frequently tossed around the phrase "survival of the fittest," and always identified the fittest with the wealthy. Like the English philosopher, he believed that the industrial configuration of the late-nineteenth-century economy was based upon unfettered competition among freely contracting individuals, whose choices had necessarily—although inadvertently—produced the outcome that was the best for that society in that stage of its development. Like Spencer, he opposed all plans for ameliorating the condition of the unfit, or for interfering with the rights of contract, believing that such schemes retarded social progress. And like the Englishman, he insisted that these ideas were but a statement of natural law, partaking of both scientific truth and moral righteousness.

Further, Sumner, like Spencer, produced critiques of the progressive arguments of the day, and his polemics were, if anything, an improvement upon his master's—intellectually identical but expressed in a more concise and pithy style. Sumner was perhaps the first American conservative who paid the critics of capitalism the compliment of reading them closely, analyzing their arguments, exposing their assumptions, and drawing out their implications. His criticisms of progressivism are, in fact, more convincing than his own, or Spencer's, celebration of laissez-faire.

For example, progressives criticized social Darwinists for their assumption that human beings are responsible for their own fate. In the new industrial reality, progressives argued, people are at the mercy of economic developments beyond their control and cannot be blamed for the conditions into which they fall. Although the phrase "blaming the victim" did not come into common usage until the 1960s, postwar progressives accused Spencerians of unfairly placing the blame for recessions, depressions, and panics on the little people who were ruined by them, and of insisting that the poor, whether industrial or agricultural, had brought their poverty on themselves. On the contrary, insisted progressive critics, farmers crushed by the crop-lien system and workers exploited by industrial tyranny were the small victims of large social forces.

Sumner elaborated on Spencer's point that this progressive critique drained men of responsibility for their own behavior, thus depriving them of a reason to behave in a socially useful manner. When the progressives are in power, he implied, people will no longer be punished for bad behavior or rewarded for good behavior, so why should we expect them to behave well?

> We cannot get a revision of the laws of human life.... These are very wearisome and commonplace tasks. They consist in labor and self-denial repeated over and over again in learning and doing.... For the mass of mankind... the price of better things is too severe, for that price can be summed up in one word: self control.... Almost all legislative effort to prevent vice is really protective of vice, because all such legislation saves the vicious man from the penalty of his vice. Nature's remedies against vice are terrible. She removes the victim without pity. A drunkard in the gutter is just where he ought to be, according to the fitness and tendency of things. Nature has set up on him the process of decline and dissolution by which she removes things which have survived their usefulness.[53]

While twentieth- and twenty-first-century scholars have often pointed out that there is much truth in the progressives' critique of social Darwinism, they have just as often forgotten to remind their readers that Sumner's critique of progressivism is equally potent. People must be held accountable for their behavior. If they are not, they will often behave irresponsibly. How can a society be based on the principle that people may behave irresponsibly without penalty? Progressives have not done a good job answering this question, and Sumner deserves more credit for asking it in such a trenchant manner.

But Sumner was not only astute in his discussion of the effects on behavior of removing its consequences. Like Spencer, he also perceived the problems with state action on behalf of individuals many decades before such problems were generally acknowledged by progressives. "As an abstraction, the State to me is only All-of-us. In practice—that is, when it exercises will or adopts a line of action—it is only a little group of men chosen in a very haphazard way by the majority of us to perform certain services for all of us. The majority do not go about their selection very rationally, and they are almost always disappointed by the results of their own operation."[54] This insight anticipates an important thread in late-twentieth-century scholarly thinking about government action. In fact, it turns out that majorities, for a variety of reasons, often do not go about the task of picking democratic authorities in a very rational manner. Governmental action launched into with the best of intentions many times goes awry. Often it would have been better to subject a social problem to benign neglect.

Moreover, experience has demonstrated that once progressives achieve power, the administrative machinery they create can then be turned to goals its creators did not intend. Sumner saw this potential clearly:

> Let the reader note for himself with what naivete the advocate of interference takes it for granted that he and his associates will have the administration of their legislative device in their own hands and will be sure of guiding it for their purposes only. They never appear to remember that the device, when once set up, will itself become the prize of a struggle; that it will serve one set of purposes as well as another, so that after all the only serious question is: who will get it?[55]

Finally, Sumner saw clearly that the essence of the state was coercion, and that a democratic state no less than other forms threatened liberty. Progressives, he pointed out, talk endlessly about inequality, but the only way to achieve equality is by having government force people to do things they don't want to do, especially give up income they have earned. Therefore, "we shall find that every effort to realize equality necessitates a sacrifice of liberty,"[56] and "if the principle of equality is what we aim at we can probably get it—we can all be equally slaves together."[57]

Sumner was esteemed by the capitalist classes both for his defense of their ascendancy and for his critique of their critics. Their support was not unalloyed, however, for his intellectual integrity and consistency led him to become a vocal critic of protectionism, which he classed with socialism as schemes to employ state power to shelter favored individuals from the beneficent law of competition.[58] As it turned out, most businesspeople were only social Darwinists, in favor of nature red in tooth and claw, when it benefited their bank accounts; they were all for state interference in the market when that promised to be profitable to themselves. They swore fealty to Sumner's ideas in general, while ensuring that they would not be implemented on trade policy.

Sumner's problems with the tariff were indicative of the whole era. The combination of classical economics and social Darwinism became a quasi-official antigovernment ideology, with most of the respectable people pledging allegiance in public. There was no coherent, acceptable alternative system of ideas and values. But this does not mean that there was no criticism of the dominant ideology, or that public policy was always consistent with it. Both state and federal governments during this era passed many measures that contradicted the professed beliefs of the politicians who voted for them. Protectionism is unusual in that people who proclaimed their loyalty to the ideal of the unfettered market actually elaborated a set of justifications that allowed them to explain their votes as being due to the exceptional nature of international trade. More often, politicians who allegedly endorsed the free market and abhorred mercantilist interference supported policies that violated these principles on an ad hoc basis, because of momentary political expediency reinforced by intellectual sloth. Two good examples are the establishment of Yellowstone National Park and the institutionalization of pensions for Union Civil War veterans.

A park is a socialist establishment, so a national park would seem to violate the public ideology of the late nineteenth century in an egregious manner. There was no such thing as a national park in any other country. The United States invented the institution when it established Yellowstone in 1872. The politicians of the day, however, did not think of themselves as practicing innovative socialism; quite the contrary.

Various government explorations and reports in the late 1860s and early 1870s had created public interest, wonder, and enthusiasm for the region in northwest Wyoming territory that contained the world's largest concentration of geysers, a spectacular waterfall and canyon on the Yellowstone River, and abundant wildlife. Jay Cooke, owner of the Northern Pacific Railway, whose route passed just north of this natural marvel, saw the potential tourist market for a sort of official recreation spot that would have to be reached on his line. Cooke hired public relations specialists to give lectures and write articles touting the value of a park, thereby encouraging public support, and employed his lobbyists to persuade Congress of the virtues of such a policy. During the debate on the bill establishing a park, its advocates argued that there was no disadvantage to rendering two and a half million acres of land undevelopable, because it was useless for any purpose but recreation: it was too high, cold, and rocky to be of value for agriculture, and it probably contained no minerals worth mining. When congressional representatives passed the law authorizing the park and President Grant signed it, they thus thought of themselves as furthering, not interfering with, capitalist commerce.[59]

Pensions for Civil War veterans would seem to be an even more flagrant violation of classical economics/social Darwinist public ideology, for they consisted of direct governmental payments to individuals. Again, however, the politicians discussing them did not conceptualize them in those terms. The pensions were instituted in 1862 for Union soldiers who had incurred disabilities as a direct consequence of military duty. The program was gradually expanded, until by the turn of the century it had become a general system of disability, old-age, and survivors' benefits for anyone who had served the North during the war. As such, it was exactly the sort of support for society's weak that Spencerians execrated.

Politicians, however, did not see it that way, or at least they claimed not to see it that way. The Republican Party, the party of industrial capitalism and the law of competition, was particularly enthusiastic about expanding the pensions. This attitude was politically expedient in the extreme, for almost all of the program's possible beneficiaries were resident in the northern states, and thus potential GOP voters. Moreover, high tariff schedules, supported by the party, had provided the federal government with an embarrassingly large budget surplus, and it helped the protectionist cause to find something to do with the money. Republican candidates explicitly linked protariff and liberalized pension appeals during their election campaigns. They thus pursued a political strategy of economic "cross-subsidization," in Richard Bensel's apt phrase.[60]

Regardless of the unabashed political tradeoff the party was advocating, however, it never tried to sell the pensions as a welfare program. They were justified as compensation to men who had risked their lives to save their country. The pensioners, in other words, were not recipients of welfare; they had earned their rewards through meritorious service, and the country was merely fulfilling its obligations under a social contract.[61]

In like manner, both the federal and state legislatures passed many measures during these years that technically violated the ideology of most of the people doing the legislating. In addition to establishing Yellowstone and passing veterans' pensions, Congress created the Interstate Commerce Commission in 1887, with power to investigate railroad rate complaints and forbid discrimination among customers; passed the Sherman Antitrust Act in 1890, which outlawed economic combinations "in restraint of trade"; encouraged railroad expansion with land grants and the steamship industry with postal subsidies; maintained the tariff; and, in 1894, passed a national graduated income tax law. State governments established workmen's compensation programs, instituted industrial safety inspections, created minimum-wage and maximum-hour legislation for women and children, established their own commissions to regulate railroads, undertook to police various occupations through licensing laws, and passed pro-union legislation, such as forbidding the practice of making a worker pledge not to join a union as a condition of employment, among other measures. Industrialists, traders, and bankers of the era endorsed a policy violation of the respectable ideology when it helped them, as with the tariff and railroad grants, and denounced it as a wicked violation of natural law when it helped others, such as workers and farmers.

The relationship of public ideology and public policy during this era was thus shot through with hypocrisy, contradiction, and sometimes simple stupidity. There was no counterideology to the amalgamation of Smith and Spencer; the number of outright socialists in the country was infinitesimal, and the ideas of progressivism were in their infancy. Bits and pieces of Christian notions of concern for the downtrodden, remnants of the old republican emphasis upon the public weal, persistent attacks by dissenters, simple humanitarian impulses, and competition for votes caused the dominant ideology to be insecure in legislatures. Especially, politicians who represented the less favored classes, such as farmers and workers, or the less favored geographical areas, such as the South, responded to the outcries of their constituents with legislative initiatives that threatened the hegemony of the reigning ideology with death from a thousand exceptions.

The capitalist industrialist class therefore needed an institution that would courageously implement the Smith/Spencer ideology when it served their interests, and ignore it or permit exceptions when that course of action would be useful to them. Legislatures, however, although often subject to influence by lobbying and bribery, were treacherously democratic. As Hamilton had warned a century earlier, the people's representatives were often more sensitive to the people's whims than to the needs of business. And as Hamilton had foreseen, judges wielding the power of judicial review were the best means of protecting capitalism from democracy.

UN-NATURAL LAW

After the close of the Civil War, the judiciary continued and intensified its practice of fashioning the American version of the common law to favor property in industrial development over property in pastoral enjoyment. As Charles Doe, chief justice of the New Hampshire Supreme Court, put it in a ruling in 1889, the function of the courts was to protect the rights of people "in a society dedicated to progress through free enterprise."[62] Scholars have traced the growing power of the right to engage in free enterprise, for example, through the evolution of the law of eminent domain—the authority to confiscate private property for publicly approved uses. Early in the nineteenth century, the judicial doctrine of the power of eminent domain held that only public authorities could legitimately seize private land, and only for a bona fide public use. Before the Civil War, some state legislatures had empowered private corporations to take private land for public purposes. In the 1860s and 1870s, however, judges and legislatures modified both state constitutions and the common law so as to allow the taking of private property for private purposes. They accomplished this feat by defining almost any business activity as a beneficial public use. The U.S. Supreme Court largely upheld this evolution, although it did apply the Fifth Amendment's "just compensation" clause to the states.[63] In this and many other ways, judges sought to provide a legal environment that was encouraging to industrial capitalism.

The development of eminent domain law was merely a tiny part of the general movement of American legal thinking during the era. As representatives of the intellectual classes, lawyers and judges were well aware of the ideological trends of the day, and, in fact, participated in forming them. During this period, various publications, including the *North American Review*, the *Yale Review*, and the *Princeton Review*, acted as intellectual forums for the exchange of ideas by the intellectual, legal, and business elite. Political economists, lawyers, judges, journalists, historians, philosophers, and, in general, other scholars contributed to and read these reviews, so that the dominant ideology influenced thinking on the law, and vice versa. Moreover, the founding of state bar associations (New York being first in 1870) and the American Bar Association in 1878 enabled the formation of communications networks that allowed members of the legal profession to exchange information, debate issues, and create, if not a consensus, at least a dominant view on most topics.[64] So it was that legal scholars, in their treatises and articles; attorneys, in their briefs; and judges, in their opinions, occasionally cited Smith, Mill, Spencer, and Sumner by name, and, more frequently, used such phrases as "survival of the fittest" and "the right to contract" without attribution.[65]

In the late 1880s and early 1890s, in addition to their alarm at such threats to authority and property as the Haymarket Riot, members of the legal profession became increasingly dismayed at the challenges to ideological orthodoxy posed by state and national legislation regulating business, offering relief to the losers of industrial society, and, in particular, favoring labor. To the grumblings about the excesses of universal suffrage among the propertied classes generally, legal thinkers added particularly intense and programmatic criticisms. Christopher Tiedeman, in his greatly influential 1886 treatise *Limitations of Police Power*, stated the case plainly:

> [T]he doctrine of governmental inactivity in economical matters is attacked daily with increasing vehemence. Governmental interference is proclaimed and demanded everywhere as a sufficient panacea for every social evil which threatens the prosperity of society. Socialism, Communism, and Anarchism are rampant throughout the civilized world. The State is called upon to protect the weak against the shrewdness of the stronger, to determine what wages a workman shall receive for his labor, and how many hours he shall labor. . . . Contemplating these extraordinary demands of the great army of discontents, and their apparent power, with the growth and development of universal suffrage . . . the conservative classes stand in constant fear of the advent of an absolutism more tyrannical and more unreasoning than any before experienced by man, the absolutism of a democratic majority.[66]

Tiedeman was not alone; in fact, he was typical. As early as 1872, John Appleton, chief justice of the Maine Supreme Court, had authored a decision in which he proclaimed that the law should not "submit [property rights] to the will of an irresponsible majority," because to do so would mean "the robbery and spoliation of those whose estates, in whole or in part are thus confiscated."[67] By the early 1890s legal journals and conventions were full of antidemocratic rhetoric. In an 1890 article in the *American Law Review*, New York attorney Charles Marshall asserted that "it is apparent that against the whim of a temporary majority inflamed with class-prejudice, envy, or revenge, the property of no man is safe."[68] Frederick Judson, a St. Louis corporation lawyer, read a paper to the 1891 meeting of the American Bar Association in which he warned against "the competition of reckless politicians for the unthinking vote."[69] In his 1892 presidential address to the American Bar Association, John Dillon prophesied that "the era of the despotism of the monarch, or of an oligarchy, has passed away. If we are not struck with judicial blindness, we cannot fail to see that what is now to be feared and guarded against is the despotism of the many—of the majority."[70]

But majority despotism could not simply be swatted down according to the prejudices of individuals. Legal decision-making requires a set of broad, defensible principles that can be explained to the specialized community of lawyers and judges, consistently applied across jurisdictions, and plausibly derived from precedent. At the close of the Civil War, the American judiciary did not have such a set of principles that would allow them to deal with industrialism and its discontents. Over the next three decades, however, they constructed a set of doctrines that allowed them to accede to the government activity they thought proper, suppress the government activity they thought improper, and, in addition, make war against such nongovernment organizations as labor unions that they believed to be subversive of a just society.

The difficulty of the intellectual task adopted by the judiciary is illustrated by the tortured nature of the key doctrine they adopted, the concept of "substantive due process." The very phrase is an oxymoron, for "substantive" refers to goals, and "due process" to means. Nevertheless, judges were searching for some phrase in the Constitution that would enable them to invalidate government action that seemed morally wrong, and, when the Fourteenth Amendment was ratified in 1868, began to focus on its admonition that "No State shall . . . deprive any person of life, liberty, or property, without due process of law," which applied to the states the identical interdiction applied to the federal government by the Fifth Amendment. Jurists gradually translated this guarantee of fair procedures into a prohibition of interference with property rights, while expanding the notion of such rights to cover almost anything a business might do in the present or want to do in the future.

Their project began the same year as the amendment was ratified, with Thomas Cooley's *A Treatise on the Constitutional Limitations Which Rest upon the Legislative Power of the States of the American Union*, which was, along with Tiedeman's book, one of the two most influential American legal treatises in the latter part of the century. Cooley cites Chancellor Kent, the 1803 *Marbury v. Madison* decision, Daniel Webster (who himself was repeating Hamilton's argument in *Federalist* #78), and Alexis de Tocqueville on the dangers from an unrestrained legislature and the right of the judiciary to check its excesses.[71] After a long and detailed discussion of state laws, constitutions, and misbehaviors, he begins the process of alchemy by which procedure was to be transformed into substance:

> When the government, through its established agencies, interferes with the title to one's property, or with his independent enjoyment of it, and its act is called in question as not in accordance with the law of the land, we are able to test its validity by those principles of civil liberty and constitutional defense which have become established in our system of law, and not by any rules that pertain to forms of procedure merely. . . . Due process of law in each particular case means, such an exertion of the powers of government as the settled maxims of law sanction.[72]

Some of the "maxims of law" that Cooley elaborated, in his famous treatise, his other publications, and in his court decisions as justice on the Michigan Supreme

Court, were, first, the fundamental principle of individual liberty, generally defined in terms of property rights.[73] Second, "it is not the business of the state to make discriminations in favor of one class against another," or, in other words, redistribution is unconstitutional.[74] And third, the state must attempt to treat all individuals with perfect equality, which means that a graduated income tax, for example, is not taxation but "confiscation," and therefore void.[75] In general, the impact of Cooley's thinking was to propose that laissez-faire be institutionalized as a fundamental constitutional principle.

Taking off from Cooley's suggestions, lawyers and judges developed a set of doctrines that had fused classical economics and social Darwinism into an elaborate and coherent judicial ideology by the mid-1890s. It is clear that jurists did not think of themselves as taking the side of one class against another when propounding this creed. They thought of themselves as protecting natural rights and human liberty against the tyranny of the majority. And indeed, when legislation designed to help business interests ran afoul of the principle of substantive due process, judges did not hesitate to extinguish it. Federal and state courts frequently invalidated state professional licensing statutes, business subsidies, and laws to shield in-state business from out-of-state competition, on the basis of substantive due process. None of these decisions can be interpreted as being intended to protect established economic interests; quite the contrary. When capitalists attempted to use the legislature to protect themselves from the free market, with the one outstanding exception of the tariff, the courts did not hesitate to intervene.[76] Furthermore, they upheld far more national and state statutes than they voided during this era.[77]

Nevertheless, the predominant result of the development of the dogma of substantive due process was to suffocate democratic regulation of business activity. The leading jurist in providing a detailed rationale for such oversight was Stephen Field, who served on the U.S. Supreme Court from 1863 to 1897, during which time he wrote 620 opinions, then a record for any justice, and several famous and influential dissents.[78]

Field began to Cooley-ize American constitutional law in 1873 with his dissent in the *Slaughter-House Cases*. In 1869 the Louisiana legislature had granted a monopoly to a slaughterhouse company within the city limits of New Orleans. Various butchers sought an injunction against the act, and, after losing in state and federal lower courts, their attorney argued to the Supreme Court that the monopoly violated the Fourteenth Amendment. The five-member majority of the Court disagreed, holding that Congress had not intended the amendment to apply to this type of legislation. Field, writing for three other justices, objected:

"the amendment refers to the natural and inalienable rights which belong to all citizens. . . . What, then, are the privileges and immunities which are secured against abridgement by state legislation? . . . Clearly, among those must be placed the right to pursue a lawful employment in a lawful manner, without other restraint than such as equally affects all persons."[79]

So people had an inalienable right to not be bothered by the state in their economic activities. In 1877, in *Munn v. Illinois*, the Supreme Court again upheld the authority of states to regulate industry, this time in regard to the regulation of grain elevators. Field again dissented, asserting that "the principle upon which the opinion of the majority proceeds is, in my judgment, subversive of the rights of private property, heretofore believed to be protected by constitutional guarantees against legislative interference."[80] But over the following decades, Field and his views gradually prevailed. In 1886 the Supreme Court held that a corporation was a person and therefore entitled to substantive due process protection under the Fourteenth Amendment. Therefore, corporate property rights could be protected from state interference.[81] In 1890 it forbade Minnesota to establish a commission regulating railroads and warehouses, because, in the words of Justice Samuel Blatchford, writing for the majority, "If the company is deprived of the power of charging reasonable rates for the use of its property, and such deprivation takes place in the absence of an investigation by judicial authority, it is deprived of the lawful use of its property . . . without due process of law."[82] In 1897, in *Allgeyer v. Louisiana*, the Court fully adopted Field's notion that substantive due process included a "freedom of contract" protecting individuals from state economic regulation. The decision was written by Justice Rufus Peckham. Voiding a law prohibiting a person from contracting with an out-of-state marine insurance company for the insurance of property within the state, Peckham wrote that the statute "deprives the defendants of their liberty without due process of law."[83]

While they were developing the doctrine of substantive due process, the courts were elaborating parallel notions into a general support of whatever business wanted to do, and a general suspicion of all government attempts to control it. For example, the concept of "freedom of contract" was closely allied to substantive due process. Workers, reasoned judges, had an inalienable right to accept whatever employment terms were offered to them. It was therefore a violation of substantive due process for the state or federal government to attempt to regulate their job conditions in order to protect their health or safety or limit the hours they might be worked. In 1885, for instance, the New York Court of Appeals explained in *In Re Jacobs* that the state legislature could not interfere with "the application of [the worker's] industry and the disposition of his labor, and thus ... depriv[e] him of his property and some portion of his personal liberty."[84] The most famous case developing the freedom of contract concept during this era was *Ritchie v. People*, in which the Illinois Supreme Court held that an 1893 statute limiting women's hours in workshops or factories to eight in a day or forty-eight in a week violated women's liberty to contract for the best possible job arrangements.[85] The climactic development of this line of reasoning came in the next decade, at the national level, and will be discussed in chapter 5.

To take another example, during this era property came to be conceptualized in an increasingly abstract manner and began to include the possibility of future profits as well as present control. Once defined as tangible things, by the 1890s property had become a set of "probable expectancies." In other words, the courts began to hold that businesses had the right to expect a profit, and anything that violated that expectation, therefore, violated their right to property. Because both government regulation and labor union activity might affect a business's future revenues, both could be, and were, defined as constitutionally impermissible.[86]

Beginning in the late 1880s and thence into the 1890s, state courts applied the doctrines of substantive due process and liberty of contract to nullify quantities of economic regulatory statutes. They voided acts in West Virginia, Illinois, and Missouri prohibiting payment of wages in company scrip, overturned a Los Angeles ordinance prescribing the eight-hour day for employees of municipal contractors, tossed out an Illinois law regulating the computation of wages to miners, killed a Texas statute requiring railroads to pay all back wages within eight days after termination of employment, negated a Massachusetts law forbidding employers to fine or reduce the wages of weavers because of allegedly inferior work, and much more. The decisions explaining these acts of abrogation were frequently composed of appeals to laissez-faire ideology, as when the West Virginia Court of Appeals denied the right of the state to regulate labor contracts because the legislature did not have the authority "to do for its people what they can do for themselves. The natural law of supply and demand is the best law of trade."[87]

The courts' deductions of antigovernment and anti-union conclusions from substantive due process, freedom of contract, and laissez-faire premises grew so rigid by the last decade of the nineteenth century that modern scholars have come to speak of an era of "legal formalism,"[88] one of a number of "constitutional doctrines" that have structured legal thinking in American history.[89] Law students were trained to think of their vocation as a science based on logic, whose purpose was to determine the relations between immutable principles.[90] By 1911 Joseph Choate, who during his career had been president of the Bar of the City of New

York, the New York State Bar Association, the American Bar Association, and the Harvard Law School Association, could assert that "among all the learned professions," the bar "is the one that involves the study and pursuit of a stable and exact science," without much fear of contradiction from within the community of jurists.[91]

The apogee of federal imposition of laissez-faire according to formalistic principles during this era came in 1895. In that year the U.S. Supreme Court struck down the congressional law passed the previous year establishing a graduated income tax on the grounds that it violated the provision of Article I, section 8, requiring that all taxes be uniformly imposed. Even more impressively, it eviscerated the Sherman Antitrust Act when it invalidated the application of the law to a trust that controlled over 90 percent of the sugar refining in the country on the grounds that the act applied only to commerce, not manufacturing, and manufacturing was an activity that affected commerce "only incidentally and indirectly." Justice John Harlan, in dissent, accused his colleagues of reducing the Constitution to "a condition of helplessness . . . while capital combines . . . to destroy competition," which is exactly what they had done.[92]

The 1895 Court also upheld the use of the injunction to suppress strikes. This ruling was typical; in fact, the area in which the courts were the most active was not in invalidating government regulation, but in repressing labor unions. This is understandable, given the belief of both classical economists and social Darwinists that unions were a perversely intentional violation of natural law. The decision by federal judge William Howard Taft during a strike by the Brotherhood of Locomotive Engineers in 1893 well indicates the dominant attitude of the judiciary by that decade. "A man has the inalienable right to bestow his labor where he will," intoned the judge, sounding very progressive. However, if any man uses his own labor "for the purpose of inducing, procuring, or compelling" another man to strike, then "the withholding or bestowing of his labor for such a purpose is itself an unlawful and criminal act," and therefore the whole union is "a criminal conspiracy against the laws of their country."[93] Men might quit, and they might even quit in a mass, but if they attempted to persuade their brethren to quit, by that act they became criminals. There was a right to strike, but only if the strikers did not plan it or exhort others to join it. Since the essence of a labor union is its potential for organized work stoppage to bring pressure on management, Taft's ruling outlawed the very activity that made unions useful to workers. Moreover, the judge did this all by himself, without pretending that he was interpreting a statute. He was applying the common law—judge-made law—to criminalize activity the legislature had not criminalized.

Judges soon systematized the Taft rationale and used it to justify their application of the labor injunction to stop strikes. When a strike began, the company would apply to a federal court to enjoin the union leadership to cease their attempts to persuade their members to stop working, the judge would comply, and the union leaders, upon their refusal to tell their men to go back to work, would be imprisoned. It was a strategy practically guaranteed to turn moderate labor leaders into radicals.

A case in point is Eugene V. Debs. A leader of the American Railway Union that struck on May 10, 1894, to protest the treatment of workers at Pullman, Debs was served with a federal injunction on July 4. He refused to obey its order to stop "compelling or inducing by threats, intimidation, persuasion, force, or violence, railway employees to refuse or fail to perform their duties," and was arrested and indicted three days later.[94] Other unions chose not to support the strike, and it was suppressed by federal troops sent by President Cleveland.

Debs's trial on criminal conspiracy charges came to nothing, but he was sent to jail for six months for contempt of court for ignoring the injunction. The U.S. Supreme Court upheld this conviction, stating that "a combination and conspiracy exists to subject the control" of American "transportation to the will of the conspirators," of whom Debs was one, and the federal government, by virtue of its constitutional control over interstate commerce, has the authority to prevent the conspiracy.[95] The Court glided over the point that Congress, not the judiciary, had the constitutional power to regulate commerce, and that institution had done nothing about the strike. More impressively, coming the same year as the Court's holding in the *E. C. Knight* case that the government could not touch a firm that had created an explicitly illegal national monopoly over sugar processing because manufacturing was only indirectly related to commerce, the argument of *In Re Debs* that a strike was so directly related to commerce that a court could intervene in the absence of statutory authority creates the impression of either serious hypocrisy or ideological blindness. Additionally, Debs was jailed without a jury trial; the judge who issued the injunction decided that the union leader had violated it, and decided what punishment to impose. He had, in effect, acted as prosecutor, judge, and jury. And it was all in the name of constitutional rights.

None of this was lost on Debs. Upon his release from a Chicago jail on November 22, 1895, he gave a much-remembered speech to a crowd of over one hundred thousand listeners: "I stand in your presence stripped of my constitutional rights as a freeman and shorn of the most sacred prerogatives of American citizenship, and what is true of myself is true of every other citizen who has the temerity to protest against corporation rule or question the absolute sway of the money power."[96]

He had a right to be anguished, for there was much truth in his rhetoric. After brooding over the situation for a little over a year, Debs decided that the alliance between industrial capitalism and an unelected judiciary was too corrupt to redeem, and too strong for democracy, as it then existed, to overcome. Prior to the struggle at Pullman, he wrote years later, "I had heard but little of Socialism." But during the strike, "in the gleam of every bayonet and the flash of every rifle *the class struggle was revealed.*"[97] He publicly announced that he had become a socialist.

That the alliance between industrial capitalism, elected representatives of the Republican Party, and the American judiciary was not accidental was illustrated by the actions of the representatives. In 1875 a Republican-dominated Congress passed the Judiciary and Removal Act, which redirected civil litigation involving national business interests from the state to the federal courts. In 1891 another Republican Congress passed the Evarts Act, which restructured the federal court system so as to reduce local pressures on Supreme Court justices. Meanwhile, during this era Republican presidents were appointing judges and justices who were certain to endorse the Cooley/Field jurisprudential regime. After his review of the fifteen justices appointed between 1870 and 1893. Richard Bensel concluded that they "were selected by presidents and confirmed by senators who carefully noted both their devotion to party principles and 'soundness' on the major economic questions of the day."[98]

Within the legal profession as a whole, allegiance to the Smith/Spencer/Cooley/Field theory of economic jurisprudence, and to the legal formalism that was its stylistic expression, was not unanimous. A minority of attorneys, using the *American Law Review* to express their views, reviled and rejected laissez-faire, substantive due process, and liberty of contract. "What mockery to talk about freedom of contract!" exploded Seymour Thompson, St. Louis judge and editor of the *American Law Review* from 1890 to 1894, in a talk to the Kansas Bar Association in 1892, "where only one of the contracting parties is free! What mockery to talk about the freedom of contract as between the corporation which has everything and a day laborer who has nothing!"[99] C. B. Labatt, a San Francisco attorney, explained the origins of the contemporary direction of judicial thinking quite clearly in another article. Recent court decisions, he wrote, are "breathing the very spirit of Mr. Herbert Spencer," are "distorted by class prejudices," and could "scarcely fail to strengthen the impression which is already widely prevalent among workingmen, that the courts are a mere stronghold of capital."[100]

There were also more consequential criticisms. Most important, future Supreme Court justice Oliver Wendell Holmes began a series of attacks that lasted for decades against the jurisprudential regime of his era. In a celebrated introductory passage in *The Common Law*, published in 1881, he wrote "The life of the law has not been logic; it has been experience. . . . The law embodies the story of a nation's development through many centuries, and it cannot be dealt with as if it contained only the axioms and corollaries of a book of mathematics."[101] In a sense, Holmes's attack was misdirected, for the problem with American law of the 1880s and 1890s, and later, was not so much its logical approach as its premises. To develop any body of law, judges need to reason, and logic is indispensable to reasoning. The problem with the American judiciary was that its members insisted on reasoning from a theoretically specious and empirically flawed set of natural law axioms, not that they did so with rational consistency. Nevertheless, Holmes's rebuke, unsatisfactory as it was, became the pioneer attack in a rebellion that, almost half a century later, finally overthrew the dominant approach to American jurisprudence.

Nevertheless, Holmes's voice during 1880s and 1890s was a relatively mild and unimportant one. The truly significant political and economic discontent in the latter decades of the century was not being expressed in the law journals or courtrooms of the cities, but in the churches and meeting halls of the prairies.

DISSENTERS

The most intense, persistent, and noisy critics of the reigning ideology of triumphal industrialism were the farmers of the South and the plains states. Scholars have disagreed on the nature of the agrarian discontent, and whether it can be justified, as much as they have differed on the interpretation of any subject in American history. According to several prominent researchers, the farmers' revolt, sometimes called "the antimonopoly tradition," but more often Populism after the nickname of the Peoples Party of the 1890s, was the voice of genuine victims of economic policies imposed upon them by a political elite, and represented a grassroots attempt to control capitalism with democracy.[102] According to others, however, Populism was essentially an irrational response by agriculturalists to the imposition of industrialism and the mass market on the Jeffersonian image of the self-sufficient yeoman. The rebelling farmers were no more victimized by the free market than any other sector of American society, but they were offended that they were not accorded immunity, and chose to attribute their troubles to a conspiracy.[103] I am inclined to agree with pro-Populist scholars, but the issue is complicated, and the contrary view has some theoretical and empirical force.

The essence of the farmers' problem was the government's currency policy. In

1863, seeking to bring order to the country's finances to enable the government to prosecute the Civil War, and also to nationalize the economy for the betterment of capitalism, the Republican Congress ended the Jacksonian "wildcat" banking era by beginning to charter national banks, and by issuing a uniform paper currency. At first, the treasury caused the number of these "greenbacks" to grow faster than the advance of the national economy, which created inflation. Shortly after the end of the war, however, the treasury made the rate of expansion of the currency begin to lag behind the rate of expansion of the economy. This trend was reinforced in 1879 when Congress put the country on a de facto gold standard. Then and for another two decades, there was a worldwide gold shortage. Unable to acquire more gold, the federal government could not issue more dollars, which, in the context of an expanding economy, inevitably led to deflation. From the end of the Civil War to the middle of the 1890s, the purchasing power of the dollar tripled.[104]

In general, inflations favor debtors; deflations favor creditors. Specifically in the post–Civil War period, the larger banks and industrial capitalists in particular valued the gold standard because it stabilized the value of the dollar in international trade and thus guaranteed the flow of European investment.[105] Meanwhile, however, every farmer supported a mortgage, and had to pay it off in ever-more-valuable dollars. A person who borrowed in order to begin farming in 1868 would have had to grow twice as much wheat to earn the same mortgage payment twenty years later, and still more every year the deflation continued.[106] Farmers understood clearly that federal policies were sacrificing their interests to those of eastern banks; furthermore, they could see that the class discrimination was also a sectional discrimination. As Populist Party senator William Allen of Nebraska put it in 1896, speaking for the West, "We feel that, through the operation of a shrinking volume of money, which has been caused by Eastern votes and influences for purely selfish purposes, the East has placed its hands on the throat of the West and refused to afford us that measure of justice which we, as citizens of a common country, are entitled to receive."[107]

To this giant, overriding grievance were attached various subsidiary but nevertheless important complaints. Railroads, Populists believed, discriminated against small shippers, and against products from the South and West. In a like manner, operators of grain elevators used their monopoly power to pay farmers less than they would have received in a truly free market. Similarly, under the crop-lien system, those merchants who generally held a monopoly position in an area of the South used their position to extort outrageous mortgage rates and to forbid those in their power to raise anything but cotton, thus undermining farmers' capacity to feed their families. Northeastern industrial interests obtained tariffs allowing them to raise their prices, but no public policy supported farm prices; when farmers complained about low commodity prices, they were informed that they were the victims of nothing but their own overproduction. Finally, all these favored business entities used the wealth they had partially expropriated from farmers to bribe legislators and obtain even more favorable government policies.

To the southern and western farmers, Populism was far more than an economic revolt; it was a moral crusade. They were the people, and their wealth as well as their democratic voice was being brazenly looted. It was no accident that rural Protestant churches were frequently the focus of organization for Populism, for the farmers' indignation was theological in its fury. Kansas Populist congressman John Davis summarized the whole movement when he reported on the floor of Congress that "the battle is between God's people and worshipers of the golden calf."[108] Even when Populist rhetoric was not specifically religious, its moral fervor easily matched that of the social Darwinists. Ignatius Donnelly of Minnesota, writing the preamble to the Peoples Party platform in 1892, combined several types of righteous indignation:

> We meet in the midst of a nation brought to the verge of moral, political, and material ruin. Corruption dominates the ballot box, the legislatures, the Congress, and touches even the ermine of the bench. The people are demoralized. . . . The newspapers are subsidized or muzzled; public opinion silenced; business prostrate; our homes covered with mortgages, labor impoverished, and the land concentrating in hands of capitalists. The urban workingmen are denied the right of organization for self-protection. . . . The fruits of the toil of millions are boldly stolen to build up colossal fortunes for a few, unprecedented in the history of the world, and the possessors of those, in turn, despise the republic and endanger liberty. From the same prolific womb of governmental injustice we breed the two great classes—tramps and millionaires.[109]

In their quest to find arguments to persuade the rest of the country to adopt new public policies based on new moral values, Populists began to reject many of the economic assumptions of American liberalism. Thomas Goebel has argued that in their quest for an alternative to the reigning public ideology, they reached back to the principles and rhetoric of classical republicanism. Their "language of protest," he says, "was republican in its understanding of the relations between politics and the economy, in its model of political economy," and in "its trust in the mass of the people to correct the faults in the American polity."[110]

I find this position unconvincing, because by the era of the Populists, "republican" ideas had come to mean many different things. As Joyce Appleby has demonstrated, by the turn of the nineteenth century republican ideas had evolved, degenerated, and combined with other traditions and rhetorics. Even in the 1780s, American politicians themselves infused the word with disparate meanings. During the 1790s the Jeffersonians had caused the general populace to identify republicanism with democracy, rather than with the older British Whig discourse from which the concept had originally made its way into American thought.[111] While Goebel is therefore not exactly mistaken in tracing Populist rhetoric back to the protest tradition of a previous century, I find it more illuminating to consider the ways the Populists looked forward rather than backward.

Advocating democracy, Populists found themselves abandoning laissez-faire capitalism. "The trouble has been, we have so much regard for the rights of property that we have forgotten the liberties of the individual," proclaimed Lorenzo Lewelling, Populist governor of Kansas, in 1894, in the process severing two concepts that liberal opinion had heretofore considered an identity.[112] "The tendency of the competitive system is to antagonize and disassociate men," asserted an 1894 editorial in the *Farmer's Almanac*, thereby committing heresy against another sacred American concept. "The actual state of society today is a state of war, active irreconcilable war on every side, and in all things. Deny it if you can. Competition is only another name for war."[113] Thus Populists rejected competition—one side of the liberal mantra—in the name of the other side—government of, by, and for the people. As an editorial in the *Farmer's Alliance* had put it in 1891, the Populists "shall make of this nation an industrial democracy in which each citizen shall have an equal interest."[114]

The policies Populists recommended were consistent with the intellectual emancipation they had achieved. Their 1892 platform contained the expected demand for an increase in the money supply, to be brought about by a return to a bimetallic standard; an endorsement of several goals sought by organized labor, including an eight-hour-day law for government workers; an advocacy of some institutional reforms, such as a limitation of the president to one term, direct election of senators, and adoption of the Australian ballot; and other fairly tame promises. But it also launched into waters that were, for Americans, definitely radical. "We believe that the power of government—in other words, of the people—should be expanded . . . as rapidly and as far as the good sense of an intelligent people and the teachings of experience will justify, to the end that oppression, injustice, and poverty shall eventually cease in the land," and "We believe that the time has come when the railroad corporations will either own the people or the people must own the railroads," and the reference to corporate strikebreakers as "hired assassins of plutocracy" were statements guaranteed to freeze the blood of any good social Darwinist.[115] With Populism, the conflict between capitalism and democracy, long papered over in America, stepped onto the forefront of the national political consciousness, at least temporarily. When the party committed suicide by endorsing William Jennings Bryan, the Democratic candidate for president, in 1896, some of its leaders, aghast at this concession to American orthodoxy, gravitated to the Socialist Labor Party. It was only a short journey.

Given the number of potential voters in a coalition of farmers and industrial workers in the 1890s, it might seem surprising that the Populists did not blossom into a major party. They were up against insurmountable external and internal difficulties, however. Externally, the Populists' attempts to unite black and white farmers in the South in a class-based, color-blind party was met with skepticism from both races and fraud and violence from the reigning Democrats.[116] Additionally, when Populists did manage to get elected to state offices, as they did in some plains states, the two major parties cooperated in obstructing their ability to govern.[117]

Equally important was a primal conflict within the coalition the Populists hoped to construct. Northeastern union leaders were not convinced that the party's rhetorical endorsement of labor's goals was a true representation of the farmers' views. Although the Knights of Labor, already in decline, attempted to work with the Populists, the rising American Federation of Labor (AFL) was wary. Declaring an alliance between industrial workers and farmers "unnatural," the AFL's president, Samuel Gompers, wrote in 1892,

> Composed, as the People's Party is, mainly of the *employing* farmers without any regard to the interests of the *employed* farmers of the country districts or the mechanics and laborers of the industrial centers, there must of necessity be a divergence of purposes, methods, and interests . . . before there can be any hope of the unification of labor's forces of the field, farm, factory, and workshop, the people who work on and in them for wages must be organized to protect *their* interests against those who pay them wages for that work.[118]

Gompers was right; it was an unnatural alliance. It did not hold. When both farmer and labor forces won representation in state legislatures, they experienced great difficulty in concerting their efforts.[119]

The Populists, however, were not the only dissenters during this era. There were also urban journalists, scholars, and clergymen who refused to endorse the dominant ideology. With a few significant exceptions, their critiques did not approach the Populist level of a counterideology to liberal economics. They tended to attack the excesses, injustices, and absurdities of the dominant ideology, without offering a systematic alternative. Nevertheless, three types of dissenters did offer a systematic alternative. There were, of course, the socialists, whose utter moral rejection of capitalism was buttressed by an elaborated ideology largely imported from Europe. Socialists were scarce in the northern states and virtually absent in the South and West, so they were largely irrelevant. Two other, more homegrown ideologues, however, attracted large and vocal followings.

In 1879, just after at the end of the depression of that decade, journalist Henry George published *Progress and Poverty*. To say that the book was a smash would be an understatement. It sold in the millions; it inspired a network of clubs designed to spread George's influence; its ideas were praised by many famous and influential people, including Theodore Roosevelt, Leo Tolstoy, Woodrow Wilson, and George Bernard Shaw; it turned its author into a personal political force, who ran for mayor of New York City.[120] It was the first radical American treatise on political economy that was written so as to be accessible to the ordinary reader, and its huge success demonstrated that the dominant national ideology was largely an elite phenomenon.

As a thinking response to industrialism, however, *Progress and Poverty* is entirely unpersuasive. Its thesis is that all the problems of society are caused by the fact that increasing population causes land prices to rise, and that therefore, landowners siphon off all the wealth produced by the other classes. Thus "[i]t is not in the relations of capital and labour, it is not in the pressure of population against subsistence, that an explanation of the unequal development of our civilization is to be found. The great cause of inequality in the distribution of wealth is inequality in the ownership of land."[121]

That being the problem, the solution is to confiscate monopoly rents. George advocates abolishing all taxation except the taxation of rent at 100 percent of its value, a panacea he called the "Single Tax." After this reform, there will be no incentive for speculation in land, which will be owned only by people who can put it to productive purposes. Both industry and labor will be freed from their slavery to rent, and everything will be copacetic.[122]

Professional economists from George's day to the present have branded this theory a mess of contradiction, ambiguity, ignorance, and error. Their critiques are persuasive. No doubt some people who own strategically located land exploit those around them, no doubt real-estate speculation sometimes causes booms and busts, and no doubt workers in large cities have to pay high rents. But to say that unequal land ownership causes all the irrationalities and miseries of industrial society, and that socialization of land will solve all its problems, is preposterous. If a corporation builds a factory on its own land, how does its nonpayment of rent prevent it from offering its workers the lowest wages the market will bear? If all rent is to be confiscated, why would anyone ever go to the administrative trouble of collecting it; if it would never be collected, how would the government get any revenue? And so on. Possibly William Graham Sumner was thinking of George when he boasted that he had rescued several generations of Yale undergraduates from "the domination of cranks."[123]

The Single Tax, however, was not the only eccentric, native radicalism to attract a following during this era. In 1888 another journalist, Edward Bellamy, published *Looking Backward*, a utopian tract in the form of a fantasy novel. Bellamy's hero falls asleep under somewhat magical conditions in the year of the book's publication and is revived in the year 2000 to discover that the United States has been transformed into a socialist paradise. His hosts explain to him how and why the change came about, and how the new society functions.

Like George's book, Bellamy's was a publishing and political phenomenon. It influenced such disparate thinkers as John Dewey, Charles Beard, Eugene V. Debs, Norman Thomas, and Thorstein Veblen. Between 1890 and 1891 at least a 165 "Bellamy Clubs" sprang up around the country to work for the day when the author's utopia could be realized. A group of prominent intellectuals, making a list of the most influential books of the late nineteenth century, ranked *Looking Backward* second, after *Das Kapital*. In contrast with George's work, Bellamy's found favor among many other strands of American dissent. Populist newspapers, for example, gave away copies as subscription prizes.[124]

The assumptions embedded in Bellamy's vision of the future were, and are, among the most important premises shared by the political Left. Captains of industry have done nothing to deserve their wealth; entrepreneurship is not an activity worthy of reward. Neither is the business of designing and building an economy a creative task—it requires no more imagination than pulling a cart along a road. Anybody could do it, so there is no rational basis to differential income. The matter of who is rich and who is poor is a product of chance, and consequently, merit is unconnected to remuneration. The Right typically agrees with Sumner that the drunk in the gutter is where he ought to be, and that the tycoon in his mansion is where he belongs, also, while the Left typically believes that the wealth and power people possess are due to accident, especially the accident of birth, and that therefore the good things of life ought to be redistributed regularly.

Complementing this moral point, in *Looking Backward*, is the analytic point that the free market system does not, as the classical economists maintained, result in the public good. Markets do not coordinate efficiently; they lead only to irrationality and waste. "It was the sincere belief of even the best of men of that epoch," lectures the hero's informant, speaking of the nineteenth century,

> that the only stable elements in human nature on which a social system could be safely founded were its worst propensities. They had been taught and believed that greed and self-seeking were all that held mankind together.... In a word, they believed... the exact reverse of what seems to us self-evident; they believed, that is, that the antisocial qualities of men, and not their social qualities, were what furnished the cohesive force of society.[125]

The ideal society of 2000 embodies these notions and their implications: the economy is controlled and directed from a central authority, and each person receives the same pay every month. There is a species of industrial democracy. All members of society work until they are forty-five years old (with a nod to Plato), then retire and devote themselves to serving the collective. The retirees elect the administrators in the industry in which they spent their work lives. Because everyone receives the same pay, people are attracted into trades on the basis of adjustment of hours of employment (with a nod to Fourier). If more workers are needed to make shoes, the employment hours of each shoemaker are reduced. There is no advertising to stimulate false needs. Items are priced according to the number of hours of labor needed to produce them (with a nod to Ricardo). There is no envy, corruption, or dissatisfaction; everyone joyously serves the whole: "With us, diligence in the national service is the sole and certain way to public repute, social distinction, and official power."[126]

Bellamy's utopia rests on the assumption that the disadvantageous attributes of human nature—greed, selfishness, and perhaps violence—are created by society. With a different sort of social arrangements, people will behave differently than they have behaved in every known large society up to now. They will put others before themselves, and the good of the whole before their own advancement. Especially, the administrators will not develop an interest separate from the rest of society. They will not seek to aggrandize their own power or channel an exceptionally large portion of the national wealth to themselves. History in general, and the record of socialist countries in particular, suggests that this assumption is mistaken to the point of delusion. The historical record suggests that the nation's founders, with their intense suspicion of human motives, were far wiser than socialists such as Bellamy who optimistically expected to be able to turn men and women into angels with a little institutional tweaking. Because he assumed that his new social organization would create a new type of good citizen, Bellamy did not have to address the problem of those people who refused to be reformed, and kept behaving the old-fashioned selfish way. He thus did not have to discuss prisons, reeducation camps, and gulags, although history suggests they would be part of his utopia, also.

Additionally, it is difficult to see how Bellamy's society could produce change and creativity. He wants to take an industrial structure manufactured by swashbuckling adventurers, often fashioned from nothing by audacity, leaps of imagination, stupendous exertions, anxiety, bribery, corner-cutting, and violence, and turn it over to an army of bureaucrats. These will simply administer the wealth-producing machine. Apparently, they will not have to adapt to change, except perhaps to squirt a drop of oil into the mechanism now and then. They will certainly not have to respond to price signals, or make risky investments, or adjust to variations in the supply of raw materials, or adapt to changing consumer tastes. No entrepreneurs will test the market for new products, because all "authentic" needs will already be satisfied. It is a static vision, and in economics, stasis means death. Merely to ask how Bellamy's bureaucratically rigid economy would respond to the international market is to perceive that it would die of paralysis.

Taken together, the Populists, Henry George, and Edward Bellamy illustrate a crucial point about critics of the dominant liberal paradigm in the United States. It is one thing to make a trenchant critique of imperfect reality, and another thing altogether to design a plausibly superior alternative. When measured against its own ideals, actual liberalism looks pretty disappointing. When measured against the available alternatives, its virtues suddenly appear much brighter, and its vices more tolerable.

AGAIN THE TARIFF

Representatives from the industrial Northeast and the still-agricultural South continued to quarrel about protectionism throughout this era. Most of their arguments were simply restatements of positions the two antagonists had been repeating for close to a century. Republicans, who revered classical economists when they served useful purposes, expressed contempt for their theories about the value of free trade. "While our wiseacres are reading British books of forty years ago with the emotions of great discoverers," observed Thomas Reed of Maine, Speaker of the House of Representatives in 1896, "what do the English themselves say about the actual facts? They come here in shoals."[127] Meanwhile, southerners reiterated positions that could have been written by Jefferson or Calhoun. "No amount of juggling, no amount of sophistry, no amount of theory," proclaimed Charles Crisp of Georgia, future Speaker, in 1890, "will prevent them [the people] from understanding really what this protective system is; that its effect is to take from one class to give to another, to take from the masses to give to a class."[128]

Despite its basic unoriginality, however, new notes entered the debate over protectionism in the 1890s. Tariffs had always, by definition, been part of foreign policy, and most American statesman had been quite aware of their coercive potential. Now, however, partly to pursue nationalist dreams of glory and partly to find expanding markets for expanding industry, northern Republicans began to think in expansive terms. As part of a general movement toward imperialism, they decided that Americans needed access to consumers in other countries, especially those in South America and the Caribbean. "Reciprocity," or offering to trade tariff reductions, seemed to be a good lever to pry open potential markets. Meanwhile, southern Democrats, who depended upon European markets for their agricultural products, were made nervous by talk of naval buildups, territorial acquisitions, and efforts to displace British influence in Latin America. The fight over the tariff therefore was joined to a larger fight over America's strategy for creating a place for itself in the world.[129]

Moreover, both parties were attempting at the same time to fashion arguments and policies that would defuse the farmers' revolt. Republican secretary of state James Blaine appealed to wheat and corn growers in the early 1890s with a promise to expand their markets south of the border by offering to trade a lowering of American tariffs on sugar and coffee for a lowering of Central and South American sugar and coffee tariffs. Meanwhile, Southern politicians were attempting to frighten potential Populist voters with the bogeyman of a widening racial menace. Not only would a Populist vote threaten white supremacy in the South, they warned, but it would inevitably strengthen Republican imperialist plans for, say, annexing the Hawaiian Islands, which would in turn subject the United States to immigration from "inferior races."[130]

In the end, western representatives allied with northeasterners to turn the country Republican, industrial, proreciprocity but high tariff, and imperialist. The South had lost another civil war.[131]

THE ELECTION OF 1896

In the midst of the second worst depression in the nation's history, the Democratic Party was partially captured by the spirit of Populism in 1896. Repudiating the policies of its own incumbent president, the conservative, hard-money New

Yorker Grover Cleveland, the party gave its nomination to a thirty-six-year-old Nebraskan, former Democratic congressional representative William Jennings Bryan. Because the Republicans could count on campaign contributions from most of industry, the Democrats were forced to emphasize an issue that could unite the concerns of many potential voters with the concerns of a reliable source of financing. That issue was a demand to resume a bimetallic standard, coining silver and gold coins at the ratio of sixteen to one. By promising inflation, this stand appealed to the farmers, and by promising massive government purchases of silver, it appealed to both entrepreneurs and miners in the Rocky Mountain states. "Free silver" was therefore the central issue of the campaign. At the convention, Bryan explained it to the nation in a speech that beautifully preserved the Populist combination of economic democracy and Protestant moralistic fervor:

> There are two ideas of government. There are those who believe that if you just legislate to make the well-to-do prosperous that their prosperity will leak through to those below. The democratic idea has been that if you legislate to make the masses prosperous, their prosperity will find its way up and through every class and rest upon it. . . . Having behind us the commercial interests and the laboring interests and all the toiling masses, we shall answer their demands for a gold standard by saying to them, You shall not press down upon the brow of labor this crown of thorns. You shall not crucify mankind upon a cross of gold![132]

Although free silver was the dominant plank in the Democrats' platform, they did not neglect various other causes. They denounced "government by injunction" as a weapon against labor, endorsed the resurrection of the income tax recently interred by the Supreme Court, recommended a tariff only high enough to fill the government's revenue needs, and proclaimed that "the absorption of wealth by the few, the consolidation of our leading railroad systems, and the formation of trusts and pools require a stricter control by the Federal Government of those arteries of communication."[133] It wasn't exactly Populism, but it was definitely left wing. It was, in fact, so frightening to the propertied classes that Bryan felt obliged, when visiting New York, to emphasize that he was not a socialist and had no intention of repealing American individualism: "Our campaign has not for its object the reconstruction of society. . . . Property is and will remain the stimulus to endeavor and the compensation for toil. We, believe, as asserted in the Declaration of Independence, that all men are created equal, but that does not mean that all men are or can be equal in possessions, in ability, or in merit; it simply means that all shall stand equal before the law."[134]

Bryan did not endorse all possible reforms. As a Democrat who counted on the solid support of the white South, he never mentioned the most glaring injustice in American society, the systematic oppression of African Americans in that region—unlike the Republicans, who denounced southern racial lynching. Moreover, his potential coalition of the victims of industrial capitalism failed to attract one of its wings. If he had been able to add northern industrial working-class votes to his farmers' and miners', Bryan might very well have been able to win crucial battleground states in the Midwest, and thus the presidency. But labor, like its leader Samuel Gompers, was as skeptical of these new Democrats as it was of Populists. In the first place, many industrial workers were of foreign stock, and a generous percentage were adherents of such liturgical religious groups as Catholicism and Lutheranism. Bryan's perfervidly pietistic Protestant style caused a massive revulsion within these groups, many of whom had been traditionally Democratic.[135] In the second place, despite the rhetorical endorsement of labor's aims in the Democratic platform, the candidate never displayed much understanding of the situation of industrial workers, or much sympathy for their causes. During a speech about free silver at Lynn, Massachusetts, for example, a worker in the audience asked Bryan to discuss the anti-injunction plank in the Democratic platform. The candidate replied lamely that he hoped that in time arbitration would replace the injunction as a means of settling such disputes.[136] He was, in other words, unable to apply his talent for eloquent moral rhetoric to the plight of industrial workers, because he could not relate to that plight. Bryan was the voice of one of the two groups of dissenters to industrial capitalism. Dissent would not advance until a candidate would arise who could appeal to both sides.

Meanwhile, Republicans were just as capable as any Populist of portraying an economic controversy as a battle between evil and righteousness. In 1893 Massachusetts senator George Hoar had written that "a sound currency is to the affairs of this life what a pure religion and a sound system of morals are to the affairs of the spiritual life."[137] Now some Republicans ramped up their moralistic rhetoric to match Bryan's. "Free silver alone does not, of course, mean anarchy," wrote Curtis Guild for the Republican Club of Massachusetts, invoking the specter of the Paris Commune,

> but a government without an army or navy, or supreme court, or fixed tenure of public service, or national banks, or power to borrow money or suppress riots is no government at all. . . . It was no mere coincidence that his [Bryan's] chief supporter in Massachusetts offered to vote down the Christian religion, if need be. . . . Though we fight not with bullets, but with ballots, we nevertheless face to-day the issue that

the young republic of France faced in '71.... They have hoisted the red rag of the Commune. We fight for the Stars and Stripes.¹³⁸

The Republican candidate himself, however, was considerably more cautious in his campaigning than some of his advocates. Not only was William McKinley, governor of Ohio and former member of the House, more temperamentally moderate than Bryan, but he had no wish to frighten workers by appearing to be the creature of capitalist interests. He consistently maintained that he represented a party and set of issues that were good for labor. Democratic low tariffs had caused the depression, he argued, while Republican high tariffs would restore prosperity. Democratic free silver would destroy business confidence and create unemployment, while the Republican gold standard would ensure well-paying jobs for everyone. He summarized his party's appeal in a single sentence which, if it did not have Bryan's flash, still made the point eloquently: "Not open mints for the unlimited coinage of the silver of the world, but open mills for the full and unrestricted labor of American workingmen."¹³⁹ Besides declaring the party unreservedly for protectionism and "sound money," the Republicans promised to control the Hawaiian Islands, build a canal across Nicaragua, buy some Danish islands in order to establish a naval base on them, aid the people of Cuba in their fight for independence from Spain, enlarge the navy, and, in general, make the United States into an imperial power.¹⁴⁰

Election day saw the highest voter turnout in American history-almost 90 percent of adult males outside the South, and close to 60 percent in the South, where suppression of the African American franchise lowered the overall totals.¹⁴¹ As expected, Bryan won the South and the plains and the Rocky Mountain states; McKinley won the Pacific Coast, the New England and Middle Atlantic states, and, crucially, most of the Midwest. It was a victory of the industrial future over the agricultural past. In general, business went for McKinley and farmers for Bryan, although, of course, there were local variations. Industrial workers, partly because they felt repelled by Bryan's cultural appeal, partly because they were never convinced that the Democrats were a viable alternative to the capitalist-dominated Republicans, partly because they were persuaded that free silver would be bad for them and high tariffs would be good for them, and partly because they blamed the Democrats for the depression, voted for the party of industrialism. They decided the election.¹⁴² McKinley entered the White House, and the Republicans controlled both houses of Congress.

The upheaval of 1896 was a "critical election" in that it set a new pattern for American politics. This relative durability was undoubtedly partly based on a returning prosperity in 1897 as the business cycle ran its course and newly discovered supplies of gold flooded into the country, easing the currency crunch. It may also have been partly caused by the Democrats' failure to learn from their mistakes, remaining under the domination of southern agriculturalists, and even nominating Bryan for the presidency in two more losing campaigns. After 1896 until at least 1912, the Republicans were the "normal" majority party in Congress, the White House, and all the federal courts, and procapitalist policies prevailed everywhere.[143] The agriculturalists and the urban working class were relegated to minority representation.

The policy consequences of the defeat of farmers and irrelevance of labor were evident quickly. McKinley had been in the White House only a few weeks when he called a special session of Congress, which passed the Dingley tariff, jacking up rates across the board.[144] In 1898 Congress finally passed a lasting national bankruptcy act, which permitted the involuntary seizure of property, including agricultural land.[145] In 1900 it passed the Gold Standard Act, formally establishing that metal as the sole backing for the dollar.[146] The United States embarked upon a career as an imperial power. The judiciary entered an era during which it seemed to be convinced that Herbert Spencer had authored the U.S. Constitution. After 1896, Americans saw what democracy dominated by capitalism looked like.

CHAPTER FIVE

Industrialism and Its Discontents II, 1898–1932

As the nineteenth century merged into the twentieth, the United States was rich and getting richer. The depression that began in 1893 ended in 1897, and national wealth continued its temporarily interrupted climb. New sources of gold from strikes in the Yukon and South Africa enabled the federal government to increase its supply of dollars, which lubricated business expansion. Although the country experienced a brief financial panic in 1907 and recessions in 1913–1914, 1920–1921, and 1927, until the Great Crash of 1929 the trajectory of the American economy was spectacularly upward. The increasing wealth provided a strong underpinning for increasing population as the country's 76 million inhabitants in 1900 increased 62 percent to 123 million by 1930, by which date almost exactly half lived in urban areas.[1]

The technological transformation experienced by a now unabashedly industrial and urban America caused a more-or-less continuous rise in the productivity of labor. In general terms, people living in 1929 produced about four times as much as their grandparents living in 1865. In other words, the amount of goods and services available to each person was steadily growing, or, in still other words, the standard of living was rising. The growing wealth, as always, however, was not equally distributed. From 1897 to 1920 real wages only held their own, although they then rose noticeably during the 1920s. Still, even with rising general prosperity, a large percentage of the population remained in poverty. According to a study by the Brookings Institution, almost 60 percent of American families earned less than the "poverty level" income of $2,000 in 1929. Meanwhile, 5 percent of the families controlled more than a third of all the country's wealth.[2]

While the United States was growing richer and more populous, the structure of its economy was evolving. A great wave of mergers from 1898 to 1904 created monopolies or oligopolies in key sectors, so that by the latter year one or two giant firms controlled at least half the output of seventy-eight different industries.[3] At the same time, the growing institution of "interlocking directorates"—businesspeople and especially bankers, sitting on more than one corporate board—tied formally separate firms into cooperating parts of functional wholes. As Louis Brandeis wrote to a friend in 1915 about the great banker J. P. Morgan,

> J. P. Morgan (or a partner), a director of the New York, New Haven & Hartford Railroad, causes that company to sell to J. P. Morgan & Co. an issue of bonds; J. P. Morgan & Co. borrow the money with which to pay for the bonds from the Guaranty Trust Company, of which Mr. Morgan (or a partner) is a director; J. P. Morgan & Co. sell the bonds to the Penn Mutual Life Insurance Company, of which Mr. Morgan (or a partner) is a director. The New Haven spends the proceeds of the bonds in purchasing steel rails from the United States Steel Corporation, of which Mr. Morgan (or a partner) is a director. The United States Steel corporation spends the proceeds of the rails in purchasing electrical supplies from the General Electric Company, of which Mr. Morgan (or a partner) is a director.[4]

A provision of the Clayton Act, passed the previous year, had prohibited interlocking directorates, but its enforcement proved inadequate. By the early 1930s Samuel Insull sat on more than eighty corporate boards, Percy Rockefeller on sixty-eight, Richard Mellon on nearly fifty, Albert Wiggin on about fifty, Charles Mitchell on thirty-two, and so on. The concentration of the economy was thus far greater than it appeared to an onlooker observing the small number of huge firms that dominated many important industries. In terms of economic power, it was not too much of an exaggeration to say that the United States was run by a few dozen men, all unelected by, and unaccountable to, the larger public, except indirectly through market forces, such as they were.[5]

Many of the chief questions of public discussion in this era were therefore directed at the fact of an economy that had become dominated by a small number of firms and a smaller number of people: Was bigness bad in itself? Why or why not? If not always, then under what conditions was big bad? If big was bad under any conditions, should the government do anything about it? A generation earlier, these sorts of questions had been almost the exclusive province of Populist provincials. Now, such questions, and the differing answers offered from the various points on the ideological spectrum, were frequently at the center of American political argument.

The economy was changing not only in structure but in scope as well. Some foreign trade had always been important to some industries in some regions, but as the new century aged a greater and greater percentage of the giant corporations that had come to dominate the economy found ever more of their markets overseas, and greater numbers of products to import. Armour, Coca-Cola, Du Pont, Ford, General Electric, Swift, Heinz, Kodak, Singer, Standard Oil, Westinghouse, and many of the big banks expanded overseas. This expansion had two great consequences. First, it encouraged American imperialist ventures, the maneuvers and shenanigans surrounding the acquisition of the Panama Canal Zone in 1903 being the best example. Second, it began to dissolve the coalition of industrialists that had made the Republican Party a bastion of protectionist sentiment.

The problem faced by the protectionists was made worse by World War I from 1914 to 1918, which turned the United States from a net debtor to a net creditor nation. The United States had lent millions of dollars to the warring European powers. Since international debts are paid with money that is earned by selling goods, America had to encourage its foreign debtors to export products to its home market. But the efforts of successive Democratic and Republican administrations to encourage American citizens to buy more foreign goods collided with American tariffs, traditionally championed by the Republican Party, and still fervently supported by many noninternationalized industries. Thus astride an untenable political coalition, through the 1920s the party struggled to hold together its high-tariff consensus, but by 1932 important segments of its base were ready to bolt.[6]

As the economy evolved, so did the labor force. Until the 1880s, the United States was an agricultural country. From the 1890s to the 1950s, it was a manufacturing country. Along with the growth in manufacturing, however, came the enlargement of the service sector of the economy. By 1919 there were fourteen million service workers, still not as many as the twenty-six million employed in mining, manufacturing, and construction, but a large enough chunk of the population to determine the outcome of almost any election. Just as important, service workers were the fastest-growing segment of the work force. As a group, these "white-collar" workers were better educated than their blue-collar counterparts, and better treated by management. Still, they were almost as much at the mercy of managerial whim as were the newly arrived immigrants in the coal mines. They formed an attentive audience for the national debates over the future of capitalism.[7]

Although most Americans were employees, however, the national aspiration continued to be one of achieving entrepreneurial independence. As a culture,

Americans were intensely materialistic, confident in the productive capacity of their economic system, and satisfied with their political system. In a society so oriented, it was only natural that the businessman should become a cultural icon. No longer was the yeoman farmer the repository of virtue in the American mythos. By the 1920s the businessman was in charge of the national imagination as well as the economy and the government. In 1925 *Nation's Business*, the organ of the U.S. Chamber of Commerce, proclaimed the American businessman "the most influential person in the nation," now occupying "a position of leadership which the businessman has never held before." "Never before, here or anywhere else," observed the *Wall Street Journal*, "has a government been so completely fused with business." There was no dissent from President Calvin Coolidge (1923–1929). "This is a business country," he had told the *New York Times* in 1924, "and it wants a business government."[8]

Writers of fiction had less faith that the problems with American society were epiphenominal. Beginning in the first decade of the century, and continuing strongly to its end, novelists portrayed a materialist culture that was corrupt at its core. The problem, according to these writers, was that American civilization rested on a collection of false values. A culture dominated by business was not an American aberration; it was a natural outgrowth of democratic aspirations.

The most successful of the early fiction-writing critics of Coolidge culture, the first American to be awarded the Nobel Prize for literature (in 1930), was Sinclair Lewis. He spent his career satirizing the boosterism, banality, spiritual emptiness, and hidden viciousness of a society that seemed to have forgotten everything except how to make a buck. His description of typical small town Americans in 1920s *Main Street* is a good example of his and many other writers' horror at the single-minded materialist outlook of their countrymen and women: "A savorless people, gulping tasteless food, and sitting afterward, coatless and thoughtless, in rocking chairs prickly with inane decorations, listening to mechanical music, saying mechanical things about the excellence of Ford automobiles, and viewing themselves as the greatest race in the world."[9]

The middle-class, white, business-oriented people lampooned in *Main Street* were not, of course, the whole story. In particular, African Americans, in the United States in general but in the former Confederate states in particular, were brutally excluded from the main street economy. With some individual exceptions, particularly in the North, they were deprived of the franchise that had theoretically been guaranteed them by the Fifteenth Amendment to the Constitution, largely relegated to menial jobs, forced into segregated housing and schools, and abused and exploited in countless ways. Even the labor unions, except those few dominated by socialist ideology, tended, as this era advanced, to exclude them from membership and, therefore, protection against management.[10]

Inclusions in the unions would have been a great advantage, for those organizations considerably expanded through the first part of this era. America's chronic labor shortage continued through the end of the 1920s, giving all workers, but especially those in skilled occupations, a bargaining power that tended to render management relatively vulnerable to demands for decent wages and working conditions, and recognition for workers' organizations. Between 1890 and 1926, aggregate wages approximately tripled. Labor unions and their umbrella organizations, of which the most important was the American Federation of Labor, expanded in membership from less than half a million in 1896 to more than five million in 1920.[11]

Employers and their partisans did not sit idly by while unions expanded. They created various organizations, most importantly the National Association of Manufacturers (NAM; founded 1895) and the National Civic Federation (NCF; founded 1900), to deal with many of their members' economic problems, including labor. The NCF, composed mainly of large businesses, was generally hostile to the labor movement, but its members would accommodate themselves to conservative unions that demonstrated discipline and resolve. The NAM, whose membership was mostly small and middle-range manufacturers, however, beginning in 1903 launched a "crusade against unionism" and remained creatively hostile throughout the period. These organizations subsidized academics and politicians who would speak and work against the labor foe, founded law firms devoted to antilabor litigation, and urged the appointment of judges who subscribed to the dominant common law doctrines that unions were conspiracies devoted to violating the natural laws of supply and demand and that picketing during a strike was an inherently coercive interference with property rights.[12]

Scholars have made much of this era as a period of "state building." According to Stephen Skowronek's influential survey, the United States was transformed from a "state of courts and parties" prior to 1877 to an administrative apparatus by 1920 in which "nationalism superseded localism; system superseded fragmentation; administrative flexibility superseded legal formalism; expert managers superseded political agitators; supervision superseded surveillance"; and "public financiers superseded private profiteers"—that is, nationally oriented administration rather than locally oriented patronage.[13] Skowronek makes much of this new state as being only weakly rational because its bureaucratic independence was continuously undermined by struggles for authority between the president and Congress, but he nevertheless emphasizes its paradigmatically different nature from the pre-1877 federal state.¹⁴ In Skowronek's wake, many scholars have investigated the nature of the bureaucratic transformation of those decades and engaged in various debates about how they should be conceived.¹⁵

No doubt, in the Weberian perspective adopted by "state" scholars, which emphasizes bureaucratic organization and authority, the federal government did change in a substantial manner from 1877 to 1920. While we are acknowledging this fact, however, we should also notice that even on the eve of World War I, the American state was very small by contemporary standards. In 1917 the federal government's share of gross national product was only about 7 percent, not much larger than it had been during most of the nineteenth century.¹⁶ Moreover, a significant number of the activities of that small state consisted of nonprogressive activities—repressing labor unions with judicial authority, for instance. The government, like the culture, was still dominated by liberal hostility to government regulation of the economy and government programs to ameliorate the condition of the economically disadvantaged. With a larger, more Weberian state or not, the U.S. government was still conservative and business dominated for much of the era.

It was, however, an era that produced both political and ideological challenges to the reigning interests. The challenges were only partially and temporarily successful, but they prepared the polity for what was to come.

THE TRANSFORMATION OF NATURAL LAW

In the 1870s the scholarly discipline of political economy had faced a crisis. On the one hand, the difficulties of the classical theory of value were becoming impossible to ignore. The classical theorists—Smith, Ricardo, and Mill, in particular—had argued that the long-run value of anything, and hence its price, was determined by the costs that went into it, especially labor costs. But the inadequacies of this explanation were becoming apparent less than a century after Smith wrote. Land, for example, became more valuable as population grew, without any labor being expended on it. Further, the theory had no way of explaining why a given consumer might buy three widgets and then go on to shop for something else; if each widget had the same value, why did she not go on buying until she was out of money?

On the other hand, the main philosophical rival to classical economics, utilitarianism, also had its problems. The utilitarians, led by Jeremy Bentham, had argued that human behavior should be both explained and justified by assuming that human beings attempted to pursue their subjective utility, or pleasure. As an ethical theory, utilitarianism argued that society should pursue the greatest aggregate utility, that is, the greatest good for the greatest number. As an economic theory, it held that value should be defined as the subjective utility of each individual. The classical economists, however, had rejected this approach because it seemed to require a method of measuring intensity of preference within each individual, and then of comparing those intensities interpersonally—how can we ever discover if Justin would value that Rembrandt more than Muffy would, or if my pain at losing a job is greater than your pleasure in gaining it? Moreover, they observed that some commodities with great use value—water, for example, in moist England—had a very low price, whereas some commodities with very little use value—diamonds, for example—sold at a high price. They did not see how a utilitarian calculus could thus account for the observed prices.

The theory of marginal utility as created by several different scholars in the 1870s had rescued the two theories by absorbing and transforming both. The marginalist theory of value posited that goods command prices equal to their value *at the margin* of subjective utility—that satisfaction declines with each purchase of a given product. That is, as people buy more of anything, each unit possesses less subjective value. The final unit purchased will be the one at which price equals marginal utility, for the next unit would have a utility below the price of the commodity. The consumer could be persuaded to buy more only by a reduction in price of the commodity. Similarly, a firm will stop producing goods when its marginal benefit (the revenue from selling one more widget) equals its marginal cost (the cost of producing one more widget), and an employee will stop working when her personal marginal cost of one more hour of labor equals the value, to her, of one more unit of pay. A consumer has achieved an optimum state when the last penny spent on any given good will add an identical amount of satisfaction, a firm has achieved an optimum state when no possible further production could increase its marginal revenue, and a worker has achieved an optimum state when no more labor could be adequately compensated. The problem of value has disappeared; things are exchanged on the basis of their marginal utilities.[17]

Having thus transformed the theoretical basis of their subject, scholars became "neoclassical" economists and proceeded to erect a massive and intricate edifice of theory. The theory by itself, however, was not enough. The early neoclassicals wanted to be able to elaborate and formalize their arguments with either mathematics or graphics. They also wanted to be able to avoid the problem of measuring and comparing subjective intensity of preference. They solved both problems by adopting as an axiom—an unproven assumption—that human beings and firms always attempt to rationally maximize their utility. The maximization assumption solves the problem of mathematics because it lends itself to both calculus and graphical presentation. It solves the problems of measuring and comparing intensity of preference by assuming it away. The fact that the vast majority of people do not, even in their economic capacities, attempt to maximize one objective was thrust aside. The maximization assumption became a "behavioural postulate" underlying the thousands of books, hundreds of thousands of articles, and countless confident pronouncements on public policy produced by the practitioners of what is now called microeconomics, straight into the twenty-first century.[18]

The adoption of neoclassical economics as the basis of much Euro-American social thought had another important consequence for the discussion of public policy. The assumption of rational maximization almost instantly became transformed from a neutral postulate into a normative standard. If a person, a group, or a firm behaved in the way the assumption demanded, that behavior was deemed rational. Rational behavior was good because it led to efficiency in exchange. Efficiency was good because it resulted in the optimum quantity of utility for everyone—or, in practical terms, the greatest wealth. Thus people who refused to behave in the efficient manner predicted by the theory stood convicted of damaging the public interest. Since the era when neoclassical economics became the standard for scholarly discussion, this normative presupposition has sometimes been stated explicitly, as in this sentence from a modern textbook: "To say that a competitive market is efficient is to say that it maximizes the net benefits to the participants."[19] More often, it is left implicit and used as a standard by which to recommend some policies and excoriate others.

The fact that the concept of "efficiency" was derived from an unprovable and empirically dubious axiom was quickly either forgotten or suppressed by the new economists. By the time the neoclassical paradigm had been codified and elaborated in Alfred Marshall's *Principles of Economics* in 1890, it had become an elegant and incisive tool with which to evaluate public policy. In the guise of science, economists were able to prescribe the right sorts of behavior for firms, workers, and governments—the efficient kind—and rhetorically condemn the wrong—inefficient—kind.

Economics had become, in other words, an updated form of natural law theory. Like the old, it purported to be derived from the rational nature of the universe. Like the old, it provided a basis by which a priesthood could judge human behavior as being either in conformity with or in violation of a standard of righteousness. Like the old, it could prophesy damnation for those who sinned against its one commandment: thou shalt be efficient! Unlike the old, however, it seemed to be secular and, more important, neutrally scientific.

Thus armed and robed, economists went forth and thought. The volume of their publications during the period from 1898 to 1932 was huge, and not always tending in one political direction. In general, and leaving out some important exceptions, the major overall purpose of the profession during these years was to demonstrate the way prices, if uninhibited, would cause society to reach an efficient equilibrium. Economists derived formal models of the way any system of human interaction—demand and supply for goods, the labor market, a firm's investment decisions, and so on—should function if the competitive price system was allowed to work without obstruction. They then demonstrated that such a result was optimal, that is, that no other system could distribute wealth more efficiently. To supplement Smith's metaphor of the invisible hand, Marshall offered his own hydraulic image of the way a market system uses wages (which are only the term used to denote the price of work) to achieve equilibrium in the labor market:

> When two tanks containing fluid are joined by a pipe, the fluid, which is near the pipe in the tank with the higher level, will flow into the other. . . . And thus the general levels of the tanks will tend to be brought together . . . and if several tanks are connected by pipes, the fluid in all will tend to the same level, though some tanks will have no direct connection with others. And similarly, the principle of substitution [adjustment by the pricing mechanism] is constantly tending by indirect routes to apportion earnings to efficiency between trades . . . which appear at first sight to have no way of competing with one another.[20]

As a group, neoclassical economists endorsed Say's Law, the idea that, because supply creates its own demand, in the absence of artificial constraints an oversupply of goods is impossible, although they advanced and expanded Say's primitive notion by grounding it in the competitive pricing mechanism. They accepted the quantity theory of money as an explanation for inflation or deflation. Valuing price stability, they approved of the gold standard because it prevented governments from cheapening the currency. As Edwin Cannan asserted to the annual meeting of the Royal Economic Society in 1924, "We do have a barbarous system of government, and the gold standard is . . . a most effective safeguard against inflation."[21] They opposed all impediments to the free interplay of prices, from government subsidies to labor unions. Because collective ownership of the means of production would, in Marshall's words, "deaden the energies of mankind and arrest economic progress," they vocally disapproved of socialism.[22]

By far the most influential American neoclassical economist, and a marginal utility thinker of international stature, was John Bates Clark, professor of economics at Columbia University from 1895 to 1923. He did not attempt to hide the normative implications of his theoretical presuppositions, instead using his free market analyses to justify decades of public advice as to how the nation and its citizens should conduct themselves. Businesspersons should, he argued, attempt to maximize their profits, because in a competitive market such behavior would maximize social as well as private wealth. This was because he had proven, to his and many others' satisfaction, that in a free market each person received in compensation an amount equal to his marginal value to someone else. Any interference with this equilibrium would only make the country poorer.[23]

This stance put Clark on the left of the political spectrum when it came to the trusts. "The regime of monopoly," he argued in 1902, is worse for the country than "a feudal tyranny," because it "checks progress in production and infuses into distribution an element of robbery.... Monopoly is not a mere bit of friction which interferes with the perfect working of economic laws. It is a definite perversion of the laws themselves." Therefore he asked that "the righteous of his generation to go forth to war" against it. The state must be enlisted "to discipline wrong-doers [and to] define and forbid the evil practices which [make] monopoly possible."[24] Clark's authoritative voice thus joined a chorus of prominent people, during the waning decades of the nineteenth century and the first decades of the twentieth, that decried the increasing concentration of private economic power and urged government to do something about it.

On the issue of labor unions, however, the same theoretical framework put Clark on the right. "With an ideally complete and free competitive system, each unit of labor can get exactly what a final [marginal] unit produces," he wrote in 1899, meaning that each worker is paid what she deserves, in terms of her marginal contribution to the national product.[25] Under such a system, wages are by definition not only "efficient" but also "fair."[26] It follows that when unions attempt to coerce employers to raise wages, they are trying to force inefficiency and unfairness, not only on the individual firm but on society as a whole. Government should no more stand for this sort of market interference than it should stand for private monopoly among capitalists.

Given his theoretical commitments, Clark was not willing to entertain the possibility that inequalities in power between employers and employees might make a worker's decision to take a given job at a given wage a matter of necessity rather than free choice—and freedom of choice, of course, is essential to a market mechanism. "In making his bargain" with the employer, Clark wrote in a footnote, "the worker has the benefit of free competition. He is virtually selling his forthcoming product, and can resort to another employer, if the present one refuses to give him the full value of it."[27] The worker has freedom of contract, so the market functions to his and everyone else's benefit.

Clark's version of marginal utility theory is thus an updating and formalization of the philosophical theory of Herbert Spencer, minus the evolutionary trappings. Freedom of individual contract, in the good society, assures the maximization of the public welfare. If government can but eliminate artificial inefficiencies, such as trusts and unions, then everyone will meet in the marketplace in a condition of perfect equality, striking bargains for goods and employment at the point at which marginal benefits meet marginal costs. The result will be an efficient societal equilibrium. If workers are not equal in power to employers, however, they do not possess the necessary freedom, and the theory, normative and analytical implications alike, falls apart. But Clark ensured that this problem would not arise by assuming it away.

From Clark's era to modern times there has been a steady criticism of his marginal theory of wages because of its assumption that the productivity of labor is fixed. If unionization raises the productivity of workers, however, then their higher compensation is thereby justified, and Clark's theory is refuted. And the question of whether unionized workers are more productive than non-unionized is an empirical, not a theoretical, question. Modern economists can get into prolix arguments about the empirical validity of the claim that unions raise productivity. In other words, the question is an open one.[28] The important point for this era, however, is that Clark functioned in American public discourse as an apparently scientific authority who had proven that labor unions are bad for the public welfare.

Neoclassical economists were not all free market purists. In fact, the substitution of marginal utility analysis for the traditional methods and concepts of the classical economists turned out to be a double-edged sword that could cut both against government activism and in favor of it. Most prominently, Arthur Pigou, who succeeded to Marshall's chair in political economy at Cambridge University in 1908, opened up several lines of inquiry in progressive directions. In one direction, marginal utility analysis convinced him that government redistribution of wealth would be a good thing. "It is evident that any transference of income from a relatively rich man to a relatively poor man of similar temperament," he wrote in 1920, "since it enables more intense wants to be satisfied at the expense of less intense wants, must increase the aggregate sum of satisfaction." Because a "transference of income" was unlikely to be accomplished by any means other than government taxes and subsidies, Pigou became an advocate of the welfare state.[29]

In another direction, Pigou pioneered the analysis of "market failure," the situations under which the pursuit of self-interest certainly and unambiguously contradict the public interest. The most conceptually clear form of market failure is an "externality," a condition under which an individual or firm is able to reap economic rewards by wholly or partially shunting the costs of production onto someone else. When a factory, for example, dumps its untreated toxic wastes into a river, it is imposing costs on the people who live downstream, which allows the firm to price its product at below true social cost. Such a situation, argued Pigou, justifies government regulation to make sure that individuals are made to pay the true costs—that is, make the marginal social costs equal the marginal private costs—of their activities.[30] The method of neoclassical economics, therefore, although based on a debatable empirical assumption, was able to inspire new and useful insights into both politics and economics.

Although Pigou and others who leaned left were major figures in the academic discipline of their day, still, neoclassical economics as expounded by Marshall and Clark unquestionably dominated the American intellectual scene. The unfettered operation of the price system, under most conditions, was good. Government activity, with a few well-defined exceptions, was bad, as were private monopolistic firms and labor unions. Because a free economy always offered everyone a job if they were willing to work for the market wage, all unemployment was essentially voluntary, and therefore not a social problem. The main legitimate purpose of government, besides defending the country, was to maintain price stability by pledging allegiance to the gold standard.[31] Thus although neoclassical economics was in language and technique considerably different from classical political economy, its differences were more superficial than profound. Its conclusions, at least in the United States, were nearly identical: with certain significant but not dominant exceptions, government meddling with free enterprise was analytically counterproductive and morally depraved. Further, focusing on a presumed system of many small independent units that were all subject to market forces, it ignored the presence of business practices, such as interlocking directorates, that created giant structures able to evade or control the market. Neoclassical theorists were therefore irrelevant to many of the questions that occupied public debate about the nature of economic power, except to function in a general way as advocates of the existing system. If the dominant public philosophy of the United States was to evolve, the impetus for the change would not come from economists.

THE GHOST OF ALEXANDER HAMILTON

Nor from judges; or at least it seemed so at the time. By 1898 the justices of the Supreme Court were openly embracing Hamilton's explicit charge that they see their duty as protecting the true spirit of the Constitution from "the encroachments and oppressions of the representative body." As the Court proclaimed in *Smyth v. Ames* that year,

> The idea that any legislature, state or federal, can conclusively determine for the people and for the courts that what it enacts in the form of laws, or what it authorizes its agents to do, is consistent with the fundamental law, is in opposition to the theory of our institutions. The duty rests upon all courts, federal and state, when their jurisdiction is properly invoked, to see to it that no right secured by the supreme law of the land is impaired or destroyed by legislation.[32]

Implicitly, it was the right to property that was to be defended. The Court's success in that department was so great that conservatives began to articulate a theory of democracy that emphasized the judiciary's imperative to check the people's representatives whenever they began to menace that most important right. In 1908 Arthur Twining Hadley, professor of political economy and the first lay president of Yale, published a much-noticed article in which he congratulated the courts for having preserved the good society by shielding capitalism from democracy. "The fundamental division of powers in the Constitution of the United States is between voters on the one hand and property owners on the other," he asserted.

> The forces of democracy on one side, divided between the executive and legislature, are set over against the forces of property on the other side, with the judiciary as arbiter between them; the Constitution itself not only forbidding the legislature and executive to trench upon the rights of property, but compelling the judiciary to define and uphold those rights in a manner provided by the Constitution itself. This theory of American politics ... has allowed the experiment of universal suffrage to be tried under conditions essentially different from those which led to its ruin in Athens or Rome. The voter was omnipotent—within a limited area. He could make what laws he pleased, as long as those laws did not trench upon property rights.... I will not go so far as to say that this set of limitations on the political power of the majority in favor of the political power of the property owner has been a necessary element in the success of universal suffrage in the United States, but I will say

unhesitatingly that it has been a decisive factor in determining the political character of the nation and the actual development of its industries and institutions.[33]

Hadley voiced the spirit of the age. The theories, not only of Hamilton, but of Spencer, Cooley, and Field, triumphed in the years after 1898. The Supreme Court did not overturn every act of Congress that attempted to regulate the economy or help organized labor, and, given the vagaries of the human mind and the different teams of justices that sat during this era, Court majorities were not always entirely consistent in the principles they applied from case to case. But they were consistent enough.

Several cases from this era stand out for their illumination of the Court's general application of antidemocratic and pro-laissez-faire principles. One of the most remarkable, and the archetype of villainy in progressive jurisprudence, is *Lochner v. New York*, decided in 1905. Lochner, a bakery owner, was convicted of violating an 1895 state law that limited the hours of employment in such establishments to ten hours a day. The conviction was upheld in the state courts, and the U.S. Supreme Court agreed to hear Lochner's appeal. Writing the decision overturning the conviction and quashing the New York law, Justice Rufus Peckham left no doubt that the Field approach to folding Spencer's notion of freedom of contract into the Constitution via the doctrine of substantive due process had been fully embraced by the Court: "The statute necessarily interferes with the right of contract between the employer and employes, concerning the number of hours in which the latter may labor. . . . The general right to make a contract in relation to his business is part of the liberty of the individual protected by the Fourteenth Amendment of the federal Constitution."[34]

As the realization that the Court had removed a large chunk of potential action dealing with the problems of industrialization from the authority of the people's representatives sank in, this decision raised a fury in the country, both among working-class spokespeople and more generally. As an editorial in the *Baker's Journal* fumed, the Court had informed the country that "everything that furthers the interests of employers is constitutional," while everything "which may be undertaken for the welfare of the working people and aims for the emancipation of the proletariat" is unconstitutional.[35]

The journal was only slightly exaggerating, but not much could be done about the situation as long as judges were appointed under the political structure of the "system of '96." Despite the outcry over *Lochner*, the Court continued to apply its Spencerian doctrines in a manner that surely pleased the Arthur Hadleys of the country. In 1908, in *Adair v. U.S.*, and in 1915, in *Coppage v. Kansas*, it forbade the federal and state legislatures to outlaw yellow dog contracts, with which firms required workers to swear not to join a union as a condition of their employment.[36] In 1918, in *Hammer v. Dagenhart*, it denied Congress the authority to prevent the interstate shipment of goods manufactured by child labor. The excuse for this decision was the alleged abuse by the national legislature of its constitutional power to regulate interstate commerce by its employment of that power to prevent local practices, but the underlying impulse was clearly Spencerian.[37] In 1923, in *Adkins v. Children's Hospital*, it overturned a federal law setting up a board to determine minimum wages for women in the District of Columbia. Affirming the Court's devotion to the equality of women, Justice George Sutherland wrote that "we cannot accept the doctrine that women of mature age ... require or may be subjected to restrictions upon their liberty of contract which could not lawfully be imposed in the case of men under similar circumstances."[38]

The Court during this era was not averse to government meddling in the lives of its citizens. It upheld national prohibition on alcoholic beverages, allowed Congress to prohibit the interstate shipment of lottery tickets, permitted the states to regulate pool halls, upheld the local censorship of motion pictures, and endorsed various other measures by which authorities regulated business in order to enforce contemporary standards of conventional morality.[39] It was only when democratic majorities threatened to interfere with such a Spencerian principle as freedom of contract that the justices applied the doctrine of substantive due process to stifle legal measures.

The Court was beset by persistent criticism during the years after *Lochner*. Various Progressive politicians, most notably Wisconsin senator Robert La Follette, proposed legislation to bring the institution under the authority of elected representatives.[40] These initiatives went nowhere. Sundry journalists and scholars kept up a drumbeat of opposition to judicial power throughout the era, all of it ineffective. By far the most incisive, and ultimately the most influential, opposition to Spencerian jurisprudence came from within the Court itself.

The first of the great dissenters within the Court was Oliver Wendell Holmes, who was appointed by President Theodore Roosevelt in 1902 and served for thirty years. In legal philosophy he was in direct opposition to the dominant strain of thinking of most of his colleagues.

There had long been, and there continues in the twenty-first century, a fundamental dichotomy in the theory of the relationship of the judge to the law. The paramount theory of American jurisprudence had always been the application of natural law, an ideal that there were timeless principles of justice by which any statute or social action should be tested. The power of judicial review is grounded in this assumption of a standard of judgment that transcends the scribbling of the moment. In American jurisprudence, natural law principles were sometimes based on interpretation of the Constitution, and sometimes derived from the heritage of common law, but in either case they allowed judges to impose their own opinions about appropriate public policy on everyone else.

Holmes, however, was strongly influenced by another tradition. Jurists who give their allegiance to the theory of legal "positivism" argue that the job of judges is to apply the statute as written by the legislature as faithfully as they can, without comparing it to some hypothetical abstraction. Positivists strongly discourage judges from substituting their own notions of appropriate policy for those of legislators. Even in constitutional jurisprudence, they counsel restraint.[41]

Although Holmes was not a thoroughgoing, always-and-everywhere positivist, he was deeply suspicious of judges who grafted philosophical theories onto the Constitution and then used the hybrid to overturn legislative enactments. Over his three decades on the Court, he wrote a series of dissents chiding his colleagues for using Field's notions to obstruct the efforts of the people's representatives to deal with the fallout from industrialism. Just as important, because he was the most lucid and powerful prose stylist in the history of the Court, Holmes's statements of American legal positivism not only rallied progressives at the time but became a sort of textbook advocacy of judicial restraint that influenced generations of law students.

"The fourteenth amendment does not enact Mr. Herbert Spencer's *Social Statics*," he dissented in the *Lochner* case. A Constitution

> is not intended to embody a particular economic theory, whether of paternalism and the organic relation of the citizen to the state or of *laissez faire*. It is made for people of fundamentally differing views, and the accident of our finding certain opinions natural and familiar, or novel, and even shocking, ought not to conclude our judgment upon the question whether statutes embodying them conflict with the Constitution of the United States. . . . I think that the word "liberty," in the Fourteenth Amendment, is perverted when it is held to prevent the natural outcome of a dominant opinion, unless it can be said that a rational and fair man necessarily would admit that the statute proposed would infringe fundamental principles as they have been understood by the traditions of our people and our law.[42]

In the succeeding years, in a host of celebrated dissents, Holmes restated and refined his argument that the Court should, unless spurred by some egregious violation of fair play, keep its hands off the regulations authorized by legislatures.

In *Coppage*, he scolded his colleagues for not realizing that relations between management and labor do not feature "the equality of position between the parties in which liberty of contract begins."[43] In *Dagenhart*, he reminded the Court of the many times it had upheld laws regulating morality, and asserted that "I should have thought that if we were to introduce our own moral conceptions where, in my opinion, they do not belong, this [child labor] was preeminently a case for upholding the exercise of all its powers by the United States."[44] In *Adkins*, he expressed his view that the words of the Fourteenth Amendment, originally merely an "innocuous generality," had been distorted by the Court into "the dogma, Liberty of Contract," and, in case his readers had missed the point, he repeated his preferred general principle that "the criterion of constitutionality is not whether we believe the law to be for the public good."[45]

It was not only his counsel of judicial restraint, however, that turned Holmes into the hero of later progressivism. His thought was inconsistent and even self-contradictory in a manner that made him more, not less, popular with the post-1930s generations. On issues dealing with the provision of goods and services, Holmes resisted the idea that the Constitution commanded adherence to an unregulated market. On issues dealing with freedom of speech, however, he eloquently argued for the opposite interpretation. The most prominent illustration of this promarket tendency was his dissent in the *Abrams* case of 1919.

In 1918 Abrams and four other Russian immigrants had thrown leaflets from the roof of a building, protesting President Wilson's decision to send American troops to eastern Russia. Exactly as the immigrants charged, the purpose of the military expedition had been to help the White Russian forces then fighting to roll back the Bolshevik revolution. Although the five criticized only the Russian campaign, they had been arrested, tried, and convicted under the Espionage Act of 1917, which made it a crime to attempt to obstruct the war effort against *Germany* with words or deeds. Holmes had already voted with the Court majority to uphold several previous convictions under the act, but balked at this one. In what was to become perhaps his most famous dissent, he employed a metaphor which, given his views on other cases, might be startling:

> [W]hen men have realized that time has upset many fighting faiths, they may come to believe even more than they believe the very foundations of their own conduct that the ultimate good desired is better reached by free trade in ideas—that the best test of truth is the power of the thought to get itself accepted in the competition of the market, and that truth is the only ground upon which their wishes safely can be carried out. That, at any rate, is the theory of our Constitution.[46]

Thus Holmes, the most effective critic of the doctrine that laissez faire is part of the substrate of the Constitution in regard to economic activity, became the most effective advocate of the doctrine that laissez faire is the bedrock principle underlying the Constitution in regard to personal expression. Sharply skeptical toward natural law in the realm of freedom of business, he embraced it in the realm of freedom of speech. In thus combining these two incompatible attitudes toward the free market into one ideology, he virtually founded modern liberalism. Modern liberals combine an intense suspicion of the unfettered market and a naive faith in government regulation, when it comes to business, with an intense suspicion of government regulation and a naive faith in the unfettered market, when it comes to speech. Holmes became an icon to later generations because he inscribed this self-contradiction into beautiful prose, thus lending philosophical dignity to incoherence.

The second great dissenter on the Court was Louis Brandeis, appointed by President Wilson in 1916 and serving until 1939. Graduating from Harvard Law School in 1878, he had become, by 1890, a wealthy and respected corporate attorney. Dissatisfied, however, with the narrow and selfish focus of the typical members of his profession, he evolved a personal philosophy that a lawyer should spend less time serving the powers that be and more time pursuing justice. By 1897 he had become, with Clarence Darrow, one of the two great "people's lawyers"—attorneys who volunteered to become advocates for individuals and causes who could not pay, but whose situations embodied larger questions of the public interest.[47]

Brandeis was no socialist, and no radical. His own well-articulated view was that the only way to avoid class warfare in the United States was for the forces of capital to compromise with and accommodate the demands of the unowning classes for at least some democratic control of business. Since power in the United States was largely a function of who had control of the law, it followed that the unpowerful must be brought into the governing process by being given access to adequate legal representation. On many occasions he repeated the message in a speech he gave to the Harvard Ethical Society in 1905:

> The next generation must witness a continuing and ever-increasing contest between those who have and those who have not. The industrial world is in a state of ferment. The ferment is in the main peaceful, and, to a considerable extent, silent; but there is felt today very widely the inconsistency in this condition of political democracy and industrial absolutism. The people are beginning to doubt whether in the long run democracy and absolutism can co-exist in the same community; beginning to

doubt whether there is justification for the great inequalities in the distribution of wealth. . . . There will come a revolt of the people against the capitalists, unless the aspirations of the people are given some adequate legal expression.⁴⁸

Brandeis spent most of his remarkably active and effective life attempting to provide that adequate legal expression to the aspirations of the people.

In his view, one of the main problems of the American political economy was that business had grown so huge it was able to suppress or evade the competition that was supposed to keep it serving the public good. It was not that Adam Smith had been wrong; it was that he had not foreseen the growth of capital into aggregations big enough to escape the control of market forces. The goal of government, then, must be not to socialize industry, but to break it up into units so small they would once again be subject to the discipline of the market, or better still, to prevent business from concentrating in the first place. This activity would not constitute government interference with competitive market forces, because "not a single industrial monopoly exists today which is the result of natural growth. Competition has been suppressed either by ruthless practices or an improper use of inordinate wealth and power. . . . Is it not irony to speak of equality of opportunity, in a country cursed with their [the trusts] bigness?"⁴⁹

Brandeis became an adviser to Woodrow Wilson during the summer of 1912, and strongly influenced his thinking. After Wilson appointed him to the Court in 1916, Brandeis joined Holmes in an intellectual partnership that, forged in persistent but not futile minority, marked out a different path for future American jurisprudence.

Although the phrase "Holmes and Brandeis dissenting" became a mantra in the history of American law, in fact the two jurists were almost as philosophically divergent from each other as they were alienated from the Court majority. Personally, Holmes was neither a champion of the underdog nor a fan of government regulation of business. He believed that democratic majorities should be allowed to experiment with social legislation, even though he frequently thought that legislation to be foolish or pernicious. His was more a philosophy of judicial restraint than of political progressivism. In contrast, Brandeis supported the social experiments of democratic legislatures because he endorsed the policies they created. His was a philosophy of judicial activism in tandem with a progressive social philosophy. It is noteworthy, also, that Brandeis joined Holmes in the *Abrams* and other dissents opposing government regulation of expression. In one of those odd convergences of ideas that makes the study of intellectual history so much fun, Brandeis's positive faith in democracy led him for sixteen years to walk in the same direction that Holmes's negative skepticism about all fighting faiths led him.[50]

THE CONSERVATIVE NEXUS

In the era from 1898 to 1932, the abstract and detailed theories of economics and law underlay, buttressed, and legitimated the simpler and more general ideology of conservatism that dominated American public discourse. All or part of the elements of this ideology could be put in a crude form, as when George Baer, president of the Philadelphia and Reading Railroad, in 1903 responded to a letter protesting the way his company was treating striking workers with the information that "the rights and interests of the laboring man will be protected and cared for, not by the labor agitators, but by the Christian men to whom God in His infinite wisdom has given control of the property interests of this country."[51] It was axiomatic that if God was procapitalism, he must be, if not exactly antidemocracy, then the next best thing: antigovernment. Although no one ever accused him of being an intellectual, President Calvin Coolidge could distill both sides of this conservative catechism into phrases that were eloquently puerile. "The chief business of the American people," he said, "is business." The corollary must be that "if the Federal Government should go out of existence, the common run of people would not detect the difference in the affairs of their daily life for a considerable length of time . . . the Government can do more to remedy the economic ills of the people by a system of rigid economy in public expenditure than can be accomplished through any other action."[52]

Although many of the proclamations of the public philosophy during the era were either, like Baer's, transparent rationalizations of class power or, like Coolidge's, the epigrams of a simpleton who knew on which side his bread was buttered, other prominent conservatives were more sensitive in their awareness of problems in the system, more troubled by its unsavory aspects, and more willing to think hard about both its justifications and its possibilities for improvement. Such a person was Herbert Hoover, secretary of commerce from 1921 to 1929 and president from 1929 to 1933.

Hoover's thought was an attempt to reconcile traditional faith in individualism and antistatist assumptions with his recognition that a complex industrial society requires an active government, both to coordinate business activities and to provide the skills the common people need to participate in the national enterprise. The primal assumption of the American philosophy, he wrote, holds that moral and spiritual advancement among men can come only through the freedom of individual conscience and opinion, and the responsibilities which of themselves come only in freedom . . . the other freedoms cannot be maintained if economic freedom is impaired—not alone because the most insidious mastery of men's minds and lives is through economic domination, but because the maximum possible economic freedom is the most nearly universal field for release of the creative spirit.[53]

Individual freedom, of course, exists only within natural laws, particularly of the economic kind. Government must respect and work within these laws, or tyranny and poverty will result. In case his readers were confused about what those laws were, Hoover offered a summary:

Economic laws may be said to be the deductions from human experience of the average response of these varied selfish or altruistic raw materials of the human animal when applied to the mass. These cannot be repealed by official fiat. . . . Those amateur sociologists who are misleading this nation by ignoring the biological foundations of human action are as far from common sense as an engineer who ignores physics in bridge building. . . . Out of . . . complex and powerful instincts and impulses human experience over generations has developed an economic system which we may define as one of private property, competitive production and distribution of goods and services in hope of profit, the payment of differential wages and salaries based upon abilities and services.[54]

This sounds very much as if Hoover was simply a popularizer of Spencer. But although he insisted that all individuals must be tested by "the emery wheel of competition," Hoover did not want to see governments content themselves with merely looking on while universal strife winnowed the unfit.[55] Instead, a new ideal must replace Spencer's, an ideal that was both more sophisticated and humane:

In our individualism we have long since abandoned the *laissez faire* of the eighteenth century—the notion that it is "every man for himself, and the devil take the hindmost." We abandoned that when we adopted the ideal of equality of opportunity—the fair chance of Abraham Lincoln. . . . we shall safeguard to every individual an equality of opportunity to take that position in the community to which his intelligence, character, ability, and ambition entitle him. . . . It is as if we set a race. We, through free and universal education provide the training of the runners; we give to them an equal start, we provide in the government the umpire of fairness in the race.[56]

Government, then, through the provision of education, was responsible, not for ending the competition that was the engine of progress, but for providing the means with which people could equip themselves for the contest. Once the life training was completed, however, government was not to extend any more help to individuals who had run poorly in the race. To do so would be to sap their self-reliance and start them on the road to dependency. In 1931 President Hoover addressed the many proposals being made to deal with the mass unemployment of the Depression by offering people government support—what was then called "the dole." In the very suggestion, Hoover detected the symptom of national decay. Once citizens begin to think that the state can be relied upon to solve their personal difficulties, he stated to the press, "we have not only impaired something infinitely valuable in the life of the American people but have struck at the roots of self-government. Once this has happened it is not the cost of a few score millions, but we are faced with the abyss of reliance in the future upon Government charity in some form or other."[57] He was right, but in the context of the immediate suffering of Americans, his cautions about the long-run consequences of government assistance to individuals seemed callous rather than prophetic.

Despite his objections to government aid to individuals, however, Hoover was an advocate of government coordination of and aid to business activity. Beginning in 1921, as secretary of commerce, he attempted to help industries rationalize their activities in order to eliminated the gyrations of the business cycle, which he considered wasteful. His Department of Commerce assisted industries by collecting and distributing statistics on production, sales, and supplies; offered specialized information to trade associations; and helped to organize associations in industries where there were none.[58] In 1931 he persuaded Congress to create the Reconstruction Finance Corporation, which would lend to banks that were in financial straits, hopefully allowing them to ride out short-run liquidity crises and thereby survive in the long run.[59]

Even with his emphasis on personal liberty and his congenital suspicion of government, therefore, Hoover was willing to sponsor state actions that helped capitalism without regulating it. Combined with his emphasis on education of the masses to prepare them for the race of life, this willingness demonstrates the nature of humane, intelligent conservatism in the pre-Depression era. While retaining a belief in the natural laws of the market, and a moral faith in the value of nurturing independent individualism, conservatives like Hoover had discarded the knee-jerk opposition to government activity espoused by neanderthals such as Coolidge, and were willing to consider the possibility that intelligent state action might be wholesomely useful.

Two other beliefs, however, crippled Hoover's response to the Depression and ensured that he would not be the standard-bearer for a modern conservatism. As a disciple of the orthodox macroeconomic thinking of the time, he made a fetish of price stability. Consequently, he was dedicated to both balanced federal budgets and the gold standard. To the neoclassical economists who dominated public discourse in America and Britain, this dedication made him prudent, well informed, and moral. Unfortunately for Hoover and orthodox economics, however, the twin idols of the balanced budget and the gold standard were about to wreck his administration. Before getting to that, however, we must examine the most sustained and coherent critique of the dominant conservative ideology during the period from 1898 to 1932.

PROGRESSIVISM

As with most other social movements, the people we now call Progressives were neither all alike in social background nor unanimous in their diagnosis as to what was wrong with the American political economy, nor united in their recommendations for its improvement. In general, however, they were urban, college educated, prosperous to rich, of old-line British stock, and mainly white-collar professionals mixed with people with backgrounds in small and large businesses. As a group they believed that both the economy and the polity were being undermined by concentrated power, and that the possibilities of economic and social advance for ordinary people were vanishing. To repel the predations of the powerful few and restore possibility to the many, they rejected the dominant antigovernment ideology and endorsed regulation, although in most instances not public ownership or management, of large businesses.[60]

Like nearly every disgruntled political observer since Thomas Jefferson, the Progressives decried the tendencies they opposed as constituting a conspiracy of the few against the many, but they modified the traditional nature of this discourse. Previously, discontented theorists had argued that they themselves represented the people, who were being denied their rightful patrimony by an unscrupulous minority. The Progressives made this charge more diffuse and abstract, disassociating themselves from any defined group of victims and associating themselves with the nation at large. To the Progressives, "special interests" in general were undermining economic justice, not necessarily some particular misbehaving interest. When Woodrow Wilson charged that "the government of the United States at present is a foster child of special interests," or Theodore Roosevelt insisted that "our government, national and state, must be freed from the sinister influence or control of special interests," or Robert La Follette opined that "the forces of special privilege are deeply entrenched. Their resources are inexhaustible. Their efforts never relax," they were speaking of an indefinite menace to individual advancement, not of a definite enemy. In any given speech, they were quite ready to cast certain individuals or institutions in the role of villain—bankers, trusts, railroads, interlocking directorates, corporations, monopolies, rich people who had inherited rather than earned their wealth, and so on. But the overall argument was one of generality, not specificity; the power of special interests as such, not the dominance of one, was the problem to be corrected. Progressives might be interpreted as having resurrected the eighteenth-century moral stance of classical republicanism, except that in the place of "virtue" and "corruption" they used more modern terms, and except that they did not fear every concentration of power. On the contrary, they believed that to overthrow concentrations of private power, a concentration of public power had become essential.[61]

When Progressives discussed the solution to the problem of special interests, they revealed a fundamental schism in their thinking, a dichotomy that continues in the mind of the Left to the present day. On the one hand, many of them, much of the time, believed that the basis of the problem in American life was not enough participation by the people, or, in other words, not enough democracy. The economy had slipped under the control of elites because elites dominated American politics and were thereby able to rig the game. If the political system could be made receptive to the authentic voice of the people, however, public policy would reflect mass rather than elite yearnings, and the economic problem could be solved. As Al Smith, governor of New York from 1919 to 1920 and 1923 to 1928, sloganized this point of view, "All the ills of democracy can be cured by more democracy."[62] Progressives thus sponsored a collection of reforms intended to shift control of the political process from professional politicians to the people at large: voter-registration laws, which, by making fraudulent voting more difficult, struck at the power of the urban machines; the secret ballot, which liberated voters from intimidation by party poll watchers; the direct primary, which wrested party nominations from the hands of professionals; the initiative and referendum, which allowed citizens to legislate directly; and so on.

On the other hand, many Progressives, much of the time, embraced principles that they never quite realized would steer them in the opposite direction. Good government, they believed, must rest upon decision making by a group of people who had no special interests to defend, and were thus free to make neutrally benevolent choices. It thus demanded administration, not politics; experts, not party hacks; scientific certainty, not human whim. Progressives therefore spent much time musing about what group might become the Platonic guardians of the public weal. Some of them followed Edward Bellamy in *Looking Backward* and endorsed a class of well-trained bureaucrats to preside over society's important decisions. Some settled on a private group of technocrats in some presumably impartial profession such as engineering.

Conservatives had been arguing for a century that such a fair-minded, neutral role could and should be played by judges, but by this era no one on the left concurred with that opinion. Yet Progressives as a group were curiously trusting that some group somewhere could be discovered whose members would make decisions in a wholly disinterested and public-spirited manner. Few of them seemed to realize that even if such a group were to be located, it could be installed in power only at the expense of the democratic principles the Progressives claimed to hold dear. Because they never faced this problem squarely, much Progressive thinking has an earnest but befuddled quality, as if the writer was sincerely concerned about the concentration of power in American society, and honestly searching for a solution, but could recommend nothing better, after long thought, than that he and his friends be given the reins of power. Thus James Morone's identification of "the Progressive oxymoron" is a faultless characterization.[63]

The most interesting and enduring Progressive theorist was Thorstein Veblen (1857–1929), an economist employed at various universities during this period. Veblen became famous with the publication of *The Theory of the Leisure Class* in 1899, a book that not only added the phrase "conspicuous consumption" to the language but inaugurated a new genre of American literature, one that might be termed scholarly satire. Prior to Veblen, there were three types of writing critical of the American political economy. There was sober analysis mixed with outrage, such as George's *Wealth and Poverty* or Lloyd's *Wealth against Commonwealth*. There were appeals to the nation's conscience, such as Riis's *How the Other Half Lives* or Steffen's *The Shame of the Cities*. And there were fictions sketching possible futures, such as Bellamy's *Looking Backward* and Donnelly's *Caesar's Column*. Veblen's books, however, were a discussion of the American economy by a man thoroughly familiar with, yet hostile to, neoclassical theory, described and analyzed with anthropological detachment, and written in a style that featured a somewhat elliptical yet ferociously deadpan humor. His work was so piercing and so sardonic that many of his readers, then and now, could be amused by his work without understanding it. An entirely serious scholar, Veblen was dogged for most of his career by the public perception that he was primarily a satirist. Yet modern economists view him with respect, he inadvertently founded a school of counterneoclassical scholars who are called the "institutional economists," and his style of exposition has been enormously influential on subsequent social critics.[64]

Although Veblen, by the end of his life, had elaborated a complex but consistent theory of political economy, he himself caused much of the misunderstanding that plagued his work by publishing it in a nonlinear manner. Like his prose style, which often neglected to develop an argument in a logical sequence, settling for ironic bite rather than clarity, his publication strategy (at least with his books) began his interpretation of American society in the middle, with *The Theory of the Leisure Class*. Yet viewed in their entirety, his ideas formed an epic whole.

Veblen entirely rejects neoclassical economics, its assumptions, its methodology, its conclusions, its affection for modern capitalism. A true science of economic behavior would be evolutionary; it would start with the assumption that humans instinctively engage in activity directed toward some end, but it would then investigate the ideological and technological development of any society to discover the boundaries within which that instinctual activity was being directed. Its main questions would be, first, how a given society in a given era had come to exhibit its particular kind of economic structures, and second, what forces—especially, what ideas—within that society were impelling it to change, and in what direction. Instead of approaching its subject matter this way, however, neoclassical economics has appropriated the beliefs and values of modern American capitalist society as givens and constructed abstract, timeless models of exchange, using the rules as they existed at the moment as though they were immutable laws. Having a static rather than dynamic concept of economic reality, it could neither explain the present system nor identify possible avenues of change.[65]

In his own discussion of American political economy, Veblen adopts a standard of judgment that is both analytic and evaluative. It is, oddly enough, one that he shares with the neoclassicals: efficiency. Whereas they assume that the capitalist system is the most efficient known or imagined, however, Veblen's whole theory is directed toward demonstrating the opposite. Left to itself, the natural human urge to create would result in the efficient provision of goods and services, for the "instinct of workmanship"—otherwise known as pride of craftsmanship—would lead people to avoid waste. Thus they would of their own accord provide their fellows with the most products at the fairest prices. But in American society, this natural tendency toward efficiency is overridden by the capitalists' ethos, which values making money above making goods. Modern capitalism has foisted the standards of value of the stockjobber upon the entire society, and thereby condemned it to chronic inefficiency.

Thus the United States has a "pecuniary culture" in which people are taught to engage in the pursuit of profit, not useful toil. Adam Smith was mistaken: the public interest is not the consequence of a gaggle of individuals all looking out for their own interests. Instead, the consequence is waste. Businessmen are schooled, not to organize industry so that it will make products, but so that it will produce the maximum pecuniary gain. "The gainful manipulation of property" becomes the end of work, with "grave and lasting consequences for the welfare of society."[66]

Because the interests of a stockjobber conflict with the interests of society, and because modern technology would, if left to itself, lead to persistent overproduction (Say's Law also being mistaken), businesspersons are led to sabotage production in order to pump up their own profits. Smith's observation that "people of the same trade seldom meet together, even for merriment and diversion, but the conversation ends in a conspiracy against the public, or in some contrivance to raise prices," becomes, for Veblen, the central principle of the culture.[67] Ironically, in contemporary America the conspirators are celebrated, and techniques of conspiracy become folk wisdom. Among the means by which entrepreneurs contrive to restrict production are the tariff, collusion on output and prices, and, among the "ordinary lines of waste and obstruction,"

(a) Unemployment of material resources, equipment and manpower . . .
(b) Salesmanship (includes, e.g., needless multiplication of merchants and shops, wholesale and retail, newspaper advertising and billboards, sales exhibits, sales agents, fancy packaging and labels, adulteration, multiplication of brands and proprietary articles);
(c) Production (and sales-cost) of superfluities and spurious goods;
(d) Systematic dislocation, sabotage and duplication.[68]

Any reader is liable to object at this point: if capitalist business is such a wasteful and antiproductive system, how has Western civilization grown so rich? Veblen's reply is that, although the pecuniary culture is censurable in many ways, it nevertheless has one redeeming facet—it values peace. War—in fact, disruption of any kind—is bad for business. Business culture, in its long and successful (this passage was written in 1914) historical mission to overcome the old aristocratic compulsion to make war on neighbors, has fostered an era in which people could pursue their interests unmolested by brigands with titles. In the pacific environment fostered by business culture, the instinct of workmanship is sometimes able to evade suppression by pecuniary forces and make an advance. The advances accumulate, so society grows richer partially because of, and partially in spite of, capitalist values.[69]

The evolution of pecuniary culture naturally creates a class of winners, rich industrialists who bask in the rewards of having successfully manipulated the system to their own advantage. At this point, Veblen introduces two more human instincts: to create invidious distinctions, and to emulate those above one on the social scale. The ultimate goal of pecuniary gain is to allow successful people to benefit from the fact that they know they are successful, and that others envy them. Any society is a great game of one-upmanship, with the markers that signify success varying from society to society.

In American society the marker is money. But merely having money is not enough; those who have it must flaunt it, or those below will not be able to measure the extent of their own inferiority. Therefore, the rich consume their wealth in the manner calculated to be the most visually impressive. Conspicuous consumption becomes the means by which the rich fix their position in the social hierarchy, and one of the best ways to emphasize the point is to be extravagantly wasteful. Social life becomes a game in which the purpose is to squander ever-larger amounts of resources in more uselessly spectacular ways. Grand balls, huge yachts, palatial mansions, expensive clothing, European vacations, and much more, are all part of the never-ending need to spend money with theatrical prodigality.[70]

Given the human need to emulate the higher classes, however, the compulsion to consume conspicuously extends down the social hierarchy, with the members of each stratum competing in waste contests within their own category. Each class comes to adopt "pecuniary canons of taste"; that is, comes to ascribe beauty and value to objects and behaviors that help to advertise the wastefulness of the individuals in the class.[71] Driven by the imperative to maintain their social status by holding their own in the consumption contest, American citizens are driven to adopt pecuniary values. The need to make money replaces the need to take pride in one's work, or to be useful to one's fellows. An ethic of universal social competition, causing anxiety, maliciousness, and greed, contaminates every human relationship.

Despite the vulgarity and insecurity that are sewn into the nature of the pecuniary culture, it would be supportable, except for a serious flaw. It is unstable and subject to business cycles. All entrepreneurs borrow in order to invest, but Americans, being essentially speculators and con artists rather than genuine investors, borrow, in effect, to begin some scheme of pecuniary manipulation. All is well for them as long as some of the speculators succeed in striking it rich, and the banks are willing to bet on the future success of the rest. As long as businesspeople can succeed in colluding to restrict production in order to prop up profits, the system is likely to hum along. But if some historical event—a surge of imports, say, or a new federal law—threatens to wreck the collusion and return the system to competition, its chronic overproduction will then cause prices, and thus profits, to fall. Falling profits threaten the ability of the speculators to repay their debts. If banks begin to suspect that their investments are insecure for any reason (and this always happens eventually), they begin to call in their loans. The speculative house of cards then collapses, knocking the whole economy into a depression. This interlude causes the familiar mass misery that always accompanies unemployment. At some point business revives, only to begin the cycle anew.[72]

Because Veblen locates the basic nature of this irrational and unstable system in the distinction between making money and making things, he relies upon the act of overcoming that distinction to rescue it. The solution to the American dilemma is to turn the national productive apparatus over to the engineers, who by temperament and training want only to make things, not money. This is Veblen's class of Platonic guardians, the group of impartial saviors on whom the country must rely, as he urged in 1919:

> [T]he progressive advance of this industrial system towards an all-inclusive mechanical balance of interlocking processes appears to be approaching a critical pass, beyond which it will no longer be practical to leave its control in the hands of business men working at cross purposes for private gain, or to entrust its continued administration to others than suitably trained technological experts, production engineers without a commercial interest.[73]

Although much of Veblen's analysis is plausible, especially his account of the way people achieve social status through their consumption habits, at its core his account of American capitalism is absurd. It is not credible that the vast productive capacity of United States society was, at the turn of the twentieth century or any other time, an achievement that had occurred in spite of rather than because of business entrepreneurs. Granted the numbers of people whose lives were given over to "pecuniary management" rather than making useful objects, granted the duplication and waste that accompany business culture, and granted the tendency of the system to generate periodic crises, still Veblen's account does not begin to give credit to the creativity and sincere effort that went into making the richest society in the world. Veblen's critique is really the jeremiad of a very smart Puritan wrenched out of his place and time, the dismayed sermon of a moralist who believes that frivolities are sinful, that everyone should act simply and virtuously, and that a system that derives prosperity from the individual pursuit of self-interest must have a wicked soul. Veblen's originality, humor, and writing skill succeeded in concealing the fact that at bottom he was merely a scold.

Moreover, his recommendation of a class of "experts" to take over the economy contains a raft of implications, all of them sinister. Like Bellamy and others, Veblen does not see that the entrepreneur is not only the spark of creativity in the system but the person who takes the risks. Entrepreneurs thrive in a milieu of uncertainty and personal daring; engineers lives are spent attempting to reduce chaos to order. A society run by engineers would be as risk averse, and therefore stagnant, as a society run by bureaucrats. Further, the endorsement of any governing class presumably answering to technical imperative rather than public demand is, by definition, antidemocratic. The experts know what is best for the people, and the people better not complain. Veblen's assertion that the engineers have no interest of their own but are only pursuing the public interest is as silly and naive as Bellamy's trust in selfless administrators. It would be one of the most common and dangerous beliefs among leftists in the future, sometimes shaken but never discredited, that some class could be found, the members of which could, unlike the capitalists, be relied upon never to consult their personal interests. Veblen's frequent evocation of "the common good," "the welfare of society," "the free movement of the human spirit," and "the community's industrial welfare" hides the fact that he is advocating rule by an elite.[74]

Veblen's analysis of the American political economy, funny, perceptive, and in many ways accurate as it is, is thus entirely unsatisfactory as either an explanation or a prescription for action. He was not, however, the only Progressive thinker, and his contemporaries managed to come up with plenty of their own ideas.

The Progressive high point as a political movement, as a diagnosis of the ills of American society, and as a prescription for reform was the presidential campaign of 1912. In that year there were four major candidates, each representing a different ideological approach to industrialism and its discontents. Being professional politicians, three of the four engaged in a certain amount of obfuscation and self-contradiction, and practiced the art of saying different things to different audiences. The exception was Eugene Debs, the Socialist candidate, who was blunt and lucid. Despite the lack of complete clarity in the speeches of the others, however, their central messages were sufficiently unambiguous that they well illustrate the contentiousness of the American mind of the era.

On the right was the incumbent president, William Howard Taft (1909–1913). The essence of the conservative position was that capitalism had to be protected from democracy rather than the other way around. Although Taft had some mild

Progressive credentials on the tariff, conservation, and trust busting, he was a conservative on anything having to do with labor, and he was backed by all the most probusiness "standpatter" elements of the Republican Party. In his four years in office he had the good luck to appoint six justices to the Supreme Court, all of whom, with the partial exception of Charles Evans Hughes, had been witless partisans of the Spencer/Field doctrines of jurisprudence. He had filled his cabinet with corporation lawyers because he felt that they were best fitted to administer government policies "without injury to the business interests of the country." He received the votes of everyone who endorsed the developmental growth of the American political economy and opposed government attempts to interfere with it, except, of course, for the tariff.[75]

In the center of the spectrum of 1912, and providing all the ideological interest, were former president Theodore Roosevelt (1901–1909), running as the Bull Moose Progressive Party candidate, and Woodrow Wilson, nominee of the Democrats. Both accepted without question that the United States was and would remain a capitalist country, but both thought that the time had come for the people's government to begin to regulate business. The subtle differences in their positions, however, reveal a good deal about the multiple ideals at the core of the Progressive approach to public policy.

To Roosevelt, it was futile to decry the concentration of industry and mourn for the lost society of yeoman farmers. Huge business concerns were an inevitable outcome of social evolution. Granted, they often engaged in behavior that ran counter to the public interest. The solution to this undoubted problem, however, was not to search for a way to break up the mammoth concerns and return the economy to a vanished state of agricultural utopia. "This is an age of combination," he had told Congress in his annual message of 1905, "and any effort to prevent combination will not only be useless, but in the end vicious, because of the contempt for law which the failure to enforce law inevitably produces."[76]

The way to defend the public interest in a realistic manner was to counter big business with big government. A powerful, neutral state, standing above but dedicated both to the nurturance and disciplining of industry, commerce, labor, and the citizens in general, could tame the antisocial tendencies of industrial capitalism and harness its energies for the benefit of all. "Industry," he proclaimed to the Bull Moose nominating convention,

> must submit to such public regulation as will make it a means of life and health, not of death and inefficiency. We must protect the crushable elements at the base of our present industrial structure. . . . What is needed is the application to all industrial

concerns and all co-operating interests engaged in interstate commerce, in which there is either monopoly or control of the market, of the principles on which we have gone on regulating transportation concerns engaged in such commerce . . . a national industrial commission should be created which should have complete power to regulate and control all the great industrial concerns engaged in interstate business.[77]

Roosevelt's vision was comprehensively nationalistic. Because he wanted the federal government to be a steward of all the people's natural resources, he had, while president, launched the first serious (and quite popular) national conservation policy. Because he wanted the entire economy to be under the watchful eye of the federal government, he supported a high tariff. Because he both endorsed the right of workers to be represented in the national dialogue and recognized the potential for unions, like business, to act selfishly and contrary to the public good, he advocated that labor organizations, also, should come under the authority of a benevolent government. As he wrote in an article in 1911, "I wish to see labor organizations powerful, and the minute that any organization becomes powerful it becomes powerful for evil as well as for good; and when organized labor becomes sufficiently powerful the State will have to regulate the collective use of labor just as it must regulate the collective use of capital."[78]

Roosevelt's ideal was thus one of a democratic leviathan with extensive powers to regulate, sponsor, and police all the parts for the benefit of the whole. As a prophecy, it was a remarkably accurate anticipation of the regime we have today, with the important exception that it lacked the suspicion of big government we have acquired through hard experience. Like many of the other Progressives, Roosevelt did not imagine that the benevolent democratic despot could itself turn into an enemy of the public interest.

The same could not be said of the Democratic candidate, Woodrow Wilson, whose early career as a political scientist studying American government had left him less confident than Roosevelt that it could be trusted. Like all previous Democratic presidential candidates, Wilson made opposition to the tariff a central part of his platform and his rhetoric. Unlike his predecessors, however, he accepted the urban, industrial world; his speeches and writings betray no nostalgia for Jeffersonian society. While acknowledging the new America, he was just as critical of its excesses and injustices as Roosevelt, and just as determined to eradicate the scourge of "special interests" from the body politic. But he was far more skeptical of the idea that huge industrial firms could be disciplined by an even larger national state.

The problem, in Wilson's view, was not that the federal government in isolation was dangerous. The problem was that gigantic industrial combinations, if permitted to continue, would have the means and motive to capture governmental power and turn it to their own advantage. Roosevelt's program seemed to him to be a recipe for augmenting the national reach of the trusts, not reducing it. As he said of the Bull Moose platform in September 1912, "what does this platform propose to do? Break up the monopolies [trusts]? Not at all. It proposes to legalize them. . . . And that looks to me like a consummation of the partnership between monopoly and government. Because, when once the government regulates monopoly, then monopoly will have to see to it that it regulates the government."[79]

Moreover, Wilson (in this belief he was heavily influenced by Brandeis) rejected the claim that concentration was the inevitable result of market forces. On the contrary, the trusts had become large and powerful by evading and obstructing, not bowing to, the market. The trusts were therefore not the end point of nature's evolution; they were the consequence of human conspiracy. Because the government had looked the other way while capitalists colluded, its own inaction, not natural law, was the cause of their ascendancy. Roosevelt was therefore merely playing into the hands of the trusts when he proposed to accept their existence but subject them to regulation. In Wilson's view, because government inattention had allowed the trusts to thrive, government attention could both destroy them in the present and prevent them in the future. "What has created these monopolies?" he asked. His answer was "[u]nregulated competition. It has permitted these men to do anything that they chose to do to squeeze their rivals out and crush their rivals to the earth. We know the processes by which they have done these things. We can prevent these processes by remedial legislation, and that remedial legislation will so restrict the wrong use of competition that the right use of competition will destroy monopoly."[80]

Wilson was therefore just as much in favor of the leviathan state as Roosevelt, but wished it to be oriented toward slightly different ends. It was to be as active in attempting to prevent concentrations of wealth and power as it was in regulating them if they nevertheless succeeded in establishing themselves. Furthermore, Wilson had a different idea about the ultimate ends for which the national government was to acquire its extra authority. "The purpose of government," Wilson had written in 1885, "is to create restraints that secure the continuation and vitality of individual interests."[81] In all of his later speeches he continued to reason from the same premises: economic or political action that stifles individual opportunity is bad, action that enhances individual opportunity is good. Like Jefferson, his basic constituent, at least rhetorically, was the ordinary person struggling virtuously in a harsh world. In Wilson, however, that ordinary person had been transformed from a farmer into a small entrepreneur or industrial worker.

Wilson's rhetoric therefore creates a far more humane atmosphere than that of the Bull Moose candidate. Roosevelt's vision was essentially of the big picture, seeing the broad contours of the nation and giving little attention to the traditional American hero, the individual. Wilson was far more attuned to those small people living fearfully on the edges of industrialism. When discussing the ways government should respond to the new economy, he was always completely clear that the point was to make sure that the little guy had the opportunity to get ahead. In this sense, Wilson leaves a more benevolent impression than Roosevelt, who sometimes seems so preoccupied with large social forces that he forgets that the purpose of an economy is to allow people to make a living.

It would be a mistake to exaggerate Wilson's humane feelings. A southerner by birth, and the nominee of a southern-based party, he ignored the injustices being perpetrated all across that region against African Americans. After his election, he imposed racial segregation on federal workers in offices, shops, restrooms, and restaurants, and gave free rein to southern postmasters to discharge or downgrade black employees. He openly endorsed the popular 1915 motion picture *The Birth of a Nation*, a racist melodrama that later came to be used as a sort of living recruiting poster by the Ku Klux Klan. Nevertheless, even taking this ugly blemish on his record into account, Wilson still represents the side of Progressivism that values individual humanity and worries about the opportunities available to the little guy. In contrast, Roosevelt often seems to value bigness, power, and prosperity while forgetting people.[82]

On the left of the spectrum in the campaign of 1912 was Eugene Debs. As a Socialist, he viewed Progressive efforts to subject capitalism to democratic regulation as fantasy. The cause of injustice and irrationality "does not lie in a maladministration of present government, but in the very nature of Society as at present constituted," he told a western audience on the campaign trail, "[a]nd the remedy must be found in a reconstruction of all existing systems."[83] The only way to cure the ills caused by the present system, he said in his acceptance speech at the party convention, was to begin from the principle that "the tools of labor belong to labor and that the wealth produced by the working class belongs to the working class." It is futile to pretend that the present political economy can be remedied; we must wake up and recognize that "capitalism is rushing blindly to its impending doom. All the signs portend the inevitable breakdown of the existing order." Once private control of the economy is ended by government takeover, the consequence will not only be "industrial and social democracy."[84] Earlier in his career, he had contended that after the Socialist utopia had been established, racism would disappear, as would sexism. The liberation from capitalist oppression would create a situation in which "all men and women and children the world around are rendered secure from dread of war and fear of want, [and] then the mind and soul will be free to develop as they never were before. We shall have a literature and an art such as the troubled heart and brain of man never before conceived."[85]

Later, Debs explicitly defended the principle of freedom of speech, and declared that "I have never advocated violence in any form. I have always believed in education . . . and I have always made my appeal to the reason and to conscience of the people."[86] During the 1912 campaign, however, his intentions were less clearly peaceful: "Deep-seated discontent has seized upon the masses. They must indeed be deaf who do not hear the mutterings of the approaching storm. . . . Social reorganization is the imperative demand of this world-wide revolutionary movement."[87]

This ambiguity aside, however, Debs's differences with the Progressives are not as great as they might at first appear. During this era, the Left, as an ideological tendency and temperament, was insensitive to the creative and risk-taking functions of business entrepreneurs. As a group, leftists give the impression that they believed that the immense wealth-producing machine in front of them somehow arose of its own accord out of the primeval swamp. That their rich and expanding society was the product of generations of people willing to hazard their capital on a dream is a truth they could not grasp. Veblen's notion that the "instinct of workmanship" among the common people had created modern society against the resistance of capitalists, which was the Progressive's only attempt to face the issue squarely, is absurd.

Similarly, Socialists and Progressives were united in their faith that government administrators would be a superior substitute, in public-regarding intelligence, for professional captains of industry. To the Progressives, their intention to have government regulate business was light-years away from the Socialist plan for government to take possession of and manage the means of production. From the perspective of eight decades later, however, the space between these two positions seems rather narrow. And the wisdom of experience must leave us less tolerant of an ideological movement that blithely assumed that its alternate organization of society would solve the problems of the present one without causing new troubles.

Be that as it may, Woodrow Wilson won the presidency in 1912 with 42.5 percent of the 14.7 million popular votes and 82 percent of electoral college votes.

Roosevelt came in second with 28 percent of the popular vote, Taft was next with 23.5 percent, and Debs, in the strongest historical showing for a Socialist candidate, received 6 percent.[88] Eight years later, for reasons having more to do with foreign than economic policy, the Republicans recaptured the presidency and Congress, and held them throughout the 1920s. When the crisis came, therefore, it was on the conservatives' watch.

THE GREAT COLLAPSE

Throughout this era, the United States was part of an international system of finance based both upon theories of neoclassical economics and historical arrangements worked out over centuries among governments and bankers. Each country fixed the value of its currency by pegging it to a given quantity of gold. The yellow metal functioned as an international as well as national standard by determining the value of each country's currency in relation to every other nation's currency. As countries traded goods among themselves, imbalances were bound to occur in the system of currency values as some countries sold more and some countries bought more. The forces of supply and demand pushed down the international value of a currency issued by a country that was buying more goods than it sold abroad and buoyed up the currency of a country that was selling more than it bought. Such imbalances were rectified by transfers of the standard metal between countries: each central bank was committed to buy gold when its country's imbalance of imports over exports was putting downward pressure on the value of its currency and to sell gold when its imbalance of exports over imports was exerting pressure to raise that value. Until 1914 the private House of Morgan attempted with partial success to perform the central banking function for the United States. After that date the partly public and partly private Federal Reserve System assumed the responsibility of a central bank.[89]

This system worked well and prosperously for a long time. It depended, however, on certain conditions: that each country had a robust capitalist economy, that each both exported and imported in an unfettered manner, and that each was committed to maintaining the value of its currency through the gold standard. After World War I, however, the conditions underlying the system began to erode, and the system began to break down. It did not collapse until 1931, but when it did the result was catastrophe.

The United States had loaned hundreds of millions of dollars to the Allied nations during World War I and naturally wished to be reimbursed. But those countries could only earn the money to service the loans by selling goods abroad.

The tariffs so beloved by the ruling Republican Party interfered with their ability to repay. Moreover, France counted on the reparations imposed on Germany at the end of World War I in 1918 to allow it to discharge its own obligations to the United States, and when Germany had difficulty paying off, France experienced even worse troubles. Lastly, Great Britain had nearly impoverished itself financing its share of the war, and its industrial production was being hampered by labor troubles. The prosperity experienced by the United States during the "Roaring Twenties" was thus not generally shared.[90]

Even within the United States, the economy was not as solid as it seemed. Agriculture was in a depression for virtually the entire postwar period. During the war years, when marching armies needed food, farmers had greatly expanded their acreage. With the war over and Europe's economy's staggering, the market for American agricultural exports contracted just as production reached a peak. As a result, prices collapsed and remained low through the 1920s.[91]

Furthermore, the fabled stock market boom of the late 1920s, which at first had some sensible foundations, became a speculative bubble that, like all such exercises in mass psychosis, was bound to burst sometime. Many people who should have known better, however, were convinced otherwise. Not only did top federal politicians make public statements urging Americans to buy stock, but even eminent economists opined that the U.S. economy had entered a "new era" in which it had achieved a "higher plateau" of securities prices—or, in other words, that it was no longer necessary for stocks to represent anything in terms of productive value.[92]

When the bubble burst in October 1929 it caused unavoidable, and severe, economic difficulties. National income, which was $321.6 billion in the third quarter of 1929, stood at $280.9 billion a year later, $266.2 billion by the same period in 1931, and $217.1 billion in 1932. During the same three years, investment fell from about 15 percent of the gross national product to less than 1 percent. The value of the dollar rose (deflated) by more than 20 percent. Unemployment went from about 3 percent to almost 25 percent of the workforce, at which point well over ten million Americans were out of a job.[93]

If such a contraction happened today (in fact, it is happening as I write this), the response of the federal government would be to attempt to expand both elite investment and mass spending power. The Federal Reserve Board would lower interest rates (as it has been doing), and Congress would both cut taxes and increase spending (ditto). In the 1920s and 1930s, however, the reigning economic theory, both in its academic form and in the cruder form understood by politicians, counseled an opposite response. The economy must take its medicine. Prices and wages must be allowed to fall until they reached a new equilibrium. The federal government must balance its budget and refrain from doing anything, such as helping labor unions, that would prevent prices from falling to their natural level. In addition, no matter what the situation overseas, it must defend the gold standard. Businesses would fail and people would be put out of work, but as soon as the economy had wrung out its inefficiencies it would right itself.

By 1932, however, with the American and European economies spiraling ever downward, there grew a consensus even among orthodox economists that governments should spend, even running a deficit, in order to stimulate the public's buying power. But as these scholars, coming from different theoretical tribes within the basic orthodoxy, could not give a coherent rationale for their recommendation, and were in fact contradicting their own former teachings, their advice lacked persuasiveness.[94] Moreover, Treasury Secretary Andrew Mellon, his education completed in orthodoxy long before, stuck with practiced stubbornness to the traditional, and mistaken, ideology. President Hoover later complained that when he had asked Mellon for suggestions as to how the government might intervene, the secretary's only advice had been to "liquidate labor, liquidate stocks, liquidate the farmers, liquidate real estate, liquidate banks, liquidate businesses."[95]

Meanwhile, however, everyone in authority, including Hoover, was doing everything wrong. On September 20, 1931, unable to stand the monetary strain of an overvalued pound, Britain went off the gold standard—that is, it declined to redeem its currency in metal. This announcement caused a run on gold in the America, and the United States lost (redeemed) about $750 million of it over the next two weeks. On the one hand, from the standpoint of stimulating prosperity, the proper thing for the Fed to be doing was to lower its discount rate (the rate it charged to the large banks). Such a cut would ripple through the economy, with the banks then lending more to entrepreneurs, who would invest more, and so on. On the other hand, in order to save the gold standard, the proper thing to do was raise rates, thus persuading speculators to hold paper rather than metal. Faced with these options, the Fed decided in early October to crucify the economy on a cross of gold. It raised the discount rate by two percentage points, the steepest rise in such a brief period in that institution's history.[96]

Meanwhile, Congress and the president were also busy making bad public policy. The Hawley-Smoot Tariff Act of June 1930 raised average rates on imported goods from 26 percent of value to 50 percent. This action contradicted, of course, the theory that the politicians supposedly supported. If they had really been believers in neoclassical economics, they would have cut, not raised, tariffs. But American politicians had been living with this hypocrisy for so long that it no doubt came naturally, and they cast their votes without thought. Other countries immediately retaliated by increasing their own rates, and world trade collapsed.[97]

In 1932 Congress passed the Glass-Steagall Act, which confirmed the national support for the gold standard. Someone might have pointed out that if representatives were willing to reject economic orthodoxy on the tariff, they might do so on gold, also. But no one did. The president concurred in the folly.[98]

Finally, despite Hoover's belief that government spending might help alleviate the Depression, he had an enduring and unbreakable faith that governments must always have a balanced budget. The fact that the argument against government deficits was that they might cause inflation, whereas the problem facing the country was a massive deflation, did not shake his belief. Late in his term he wrote that "it would steady the country greatly if there could be prompt assurance that there will be no tampering or inflation of the currency; that the budget will be unquestionably balanced even if further taxation is necessary."[99] And so when the federal government experienced a billion-dollar deficit at the end of the 1931 fiscal year, there was only one path for the legislative and executive branches to take. In June 1932 they passed a massive tax increase.[100]

It is sometimes recalled that centuries ago, medical science attempted to cure various illnesses by bleeding the victims—applying the worst possible remedy. The doctors who thus killed their patients were not evil; they simply believed in a fatally mistaken theory. After 1929, when American and other economies were ill, the "doctors" did not merely bleed it. They bled it, strangled it, and poisoned it. The patient survived, but barely. If it had succumbed, however, the result would not have been a murder. It would have been inadvertent homicide by ideology.

CHAPTER SIX

New Paradigms, 1932–1974

During the more than four decades from the election of Franklin Roosevelt to the resignation of Richard Nixon, the United States traveled from bust to boom to the edge of stagflation. The economy staggered through the 1930s, improving slightly after 1933 but failing to achieve prosperity during the decade. Real gross national product in 1939 was $100 billion, only about what it had been in 1929, and unemployment still hovered above 9 percent.[1] With the stimulus of war spending that began in the early 1940s, however, the economy took off. It continued its boom after the end of World War II in 1945, expanding to record levels until the temporary pause of the recession of 1958, then exploding to fantastic levels during the 1960s. The gross national product hit $286 billion in 1950, $506 billion in 1960, and $982 billion in 1970.[2] Although the United States grew from 151 million people in 1950 to 203 million in 1970, the economy's expansion far outpaced the population's. As a consequence, annual per capita disposable income in current dollars, $1,074 in 1945, had almost tripled by 1970.[3] In 1973, however, the hike in oil prices that accompanied the Arab-Israeli war set off a decade of economic troubles.

For all the riches it created, this fabulous expansion did not manage to eliminate poverty. Although wealth was becoming more equally distributed, it still eluded a minority of the population. Depending on the assumptions of the researchers and the definition of "poverty," between 19 and 25 percent of American citizens were poor in the early 1960s.[4] African American poverty was twice that of whites.[5] The presence of relative hardship within American affluence presented a significant social problem for intellectuals and politicians to consider, especially after President Lyndon Johnson launched his "war on poverty" in 1965.

Nor did its expanding postwar wealth guarantee that the United States was immune to other economic troubles. Except for the recession of 1958, when it reached 6.8 percent, unemployment remained at relatively low levels throughout the period, averaging below 4.5 percent during the Eisenhower years and sinking even farther during the 1960s. The high levels of employment, however, were accompanied by a chronic "creeping" inflation during the entire era. The price index had dropped by about 25 percent from 1865 to 1929—that is, a dollar bought about 25 percent more goods and services in 1929 than it had at the end of the Civil War. After the deflation of the 1930s, however, prices roughly tripled to 1971. Even more bothersome, the pace of inflation began to accelerate during the latter years of the era. In 1960 the Consumer Price Index rose 1.4 percent. By 1969 the increase was 6.2 percent, and by 1974, 12.3 percent.[6] Arguments over the causes and possible cures for inflation, and about whether inflation could be combated without bringing back unemployment, became among the most persistent and intense political controversies of the postwar period.

Among the aspects of the American economy that had political relevance during this period were its participation in the international economy and the development of the labor movement. After the massive destruction of infrastructure in Europe and Asia during the Second World War, the United States was left with the only intact industrial economy. The federal government responded with various programs—most notably the Marshall Plan—to try to help repair the shattered European economies so that they could become trading partners. American firms responded with large amounts of investment in foreign countries. The Marshall Plan was a success; Western Europe revived quickly. Partly as a consequence, the private investment was also a success. During the 1960s scholars spoke of American "multinational" firms as the backbone of the non-Communist world's economy. By 1970 American companies manufactured three times as much abroad as they exported from the United States and controlled $78 billion of the $120 billion of foreign direct investment in non-Communist economies.[7]

The postwar United States was so dominant economically that it used its own currency to lubricate and coordinate not only American investments and trade but the economies of the other non-Communist countries as well. Although the United States officially went off the gold standard in 1933, even before the war's end it had assumed the role of financial balance wheel for the free world. Under the 1944 Bretton Woods agreement, the values of foreign currencies were fixed in terms of the dollar, the value of which was pegged at $35 per ounce of gold. If another country ran a trade surplus with the United States, it could exchange its accumulated dollars for gold. In effect, the size and strength of its economy permitted the United States to offer the dollar as the reserve currency for the capitalist world.

Such was the predominance of the postwar U.S. economy that this system worked well for a quarter of a century. As other countries revived and prospered, however, and as the United States pursued its own national policies, sometimes to the detriment of Europe, the arrangement broke down. During the 1960s the Federal Reserve Board adopted low interest rates to stimulate the economy, which, combined with the budget deficits necessary to finance both President Johnson's Great Society program and the Vietnam War, threatened serious inflation. Further, the United States was running an international balance-of-payments deficit— because of military expenditures, tourism, and American investment. By the early 1970s it no longer had the metal reserves to cover its commitment to permit the unrestricted redemption of dollars for gold. The American government asked foreign governments to simply sit on their dollars and not try to redeem them. But Germany, by now an economic heavyweight in its own right, was concerned about the inflationary consequences of such a policy and refused to comply. Unable to sustain the dollar's role as the world's reserve currency, in August 1971 the Nixon administration suspended the Bretton Woods system. Henceforth, there would be no single world currency; all currencies would float against one another.[8]

The other factor of political relevance during this period was the rise and decline of labor unions. Until the 1930s unions had occupied a semioutlaw status within American society. They were not in themselves illegal, but governments did nothing to aid organizing efforts, and the courts had held a great many of their activities, and especially those associated with strikes, as a violation of common law. In 1932, however, Congress passed the Norris-LaGuardia Act, which forbade courts to issue antistrike injunctions or enforce yellow dog contracts that required workers to sign a promise not to join a union as a condition of employment. Even more helpfully, in 1935 Franklin Roosevelt's administration endorsed, and the Democratic Congress passed, the National Labor Relations Act (Wagner Act). This legislation threw the weight of the federal government behind labor's organizing activities. It established the National Labor Relations Board as an agency empowered to oversee elections among employees to determine if they wanted to be unionized; forbade employers to interfere with organizing activities; required management to negotiate in good faith with unions once established; prohibited the use of labor spies, anti-union propaganda, and blacklisting; and recognized the legitimacy of peaceful picketing, the preferential union shop, and the closed shop.[9]

With the government working with them instead of against them, unions became a significant part of the economy and polity. From a low of 2.5 million members in 1933, organized labor's membership surged to 14 million by the end of the World War II, at which time it enrolled more than 35 percent of the nation's nonagricultural workers, a percentage that held steady for a decade.[10] Unions were now an important component in the Democratic Party coalition. Their volunteer workers and campaign contributions were crucial resources for Democratic candidates. As a consequence, their leaders were consulted on policy and personnel decisions, and flattered with rhetoric. Labor had become an important player in the game.[11]

The postwar decade, however, represented a temporary high tide of union influence. The movement's difficulties were several, and some of its wounds were self-inflicted. A significant percentage of union leaders turned out to be corrupt, tyrannical, in league with organized crime, or all three, and the image of a dishonest, dangerous labor boss soon entered the popular consciousness. It did not help the image that after the war some union locals (especially in the industry-wide Congress of Industrial Organizations [CIO], as opposed to the craft-specific American Federation of Labor [AFL]) were taken over by Communists and turned into outposts of Soviet foreign policy. The CIO eventually expelled these locals, but the public relations damage was done. Moreover, the Republican Party in general and southerners in general were intensely anti-union and took whatever steps they could to cripple the movement. In 1947 the first Republican Congress in fourteen years passed the Taft-Hartley Act over Democrat Harry Truman's veto. Without actually repealing the Wagner Act, this law significantly weakened it. It banned closed shops (requiring workers to be members of a union in order to apply for work), prohibited secondary boycotts (which enabled unions to boycott the goods of antilabor companies), authorized states to pass "right to work" laws prohibiting union shops (which required workers to join a union after being hired), and enacted several other provisions that made it difficult for unions to organize and exert pressure on management if they survived. Finally, the evolution of the economy from blue-collar to white-collar employment drained unions of potential recruits, for the new middle-class workers were more individualistic and resistant to organization than the old manual classes.[12]

As a result of these trends and events, union membership began a steady decline in the mid-1950s. By 1970 organized labor represented only 27.4 percent of the nonagricultural workforce, and its percentage was headed ever downward. Labor was especially weak in the South.[13] This atrophy had significance beyond its consequences for individual workers, for as labor's membership shrank, so also did potential resources for Democratic candidates, and thus labor's influence within policy-making arenas.

Labor, however, was not the only segment of the economy experiencing troubles during this era. Despite the succession of economic booms, business suffered a deflation of prestige among both the mass public and the intellectual elite. The Depression was devastating to the image of business, especially big business. The probusiness bombast and flapdoodle by politicians and media in the 1920s had elevated capitalists to the status of demigods; when they proved helpless in the face of economic collapse, the evaporation of their glory was swift and decisive. Business leaders did not become pariahs; they had simply slipped down into the mortal mud where they had to argue and intrigue with everyone else. Moreover, the efforts of Roosevelt's New Deal to establish democratic control over the economy were hugely popular, as evidenced by a string of presidential and congressional elections. By the postwar years government direction, regulation, and taxation of capitalism were normal and expected in their general outlines, although controversial in their specific applications.

American citizens, by and large, had not turned from endorsement of free enterprise to allegiance to socialism. Instead, they had become ambivalent and self-contradictory. In a survey of citizen political attitudes in 1964, Lloyd Free and Hadley Cantril discovered that at the ideological level—that is, at the level of general statements about the respective roles of untrammeled private enterprise versus the regulatory and redistributive state, and citizen-versus-system responsibility for unemployment and poverty—half the American population scored as conservatives and only 16 percent as progressives. On the other hand, at the operational level—the level of support for or opposition to specific ongoing or proposed government programs—65 percent of the population was progressive and only 14 percent conservative. As nearly as Free and Cantril could determine from examining the methodologically unsatisfactory results of previous national surveys, the same public inconsistency had persisted since the 1930s.[14]

Public opinion was also undergoing a cultural change. Through the 1950s, the major economic questions revolved around how to make the national pie bigger and how to divide it. There was no questioning the assumption that the goal of an economy was to generate more. Beginning in the early 1960s, however, there began to be a shift in public attitudes toward valuing quality of life. This change in emphasis had several threads.

One was the dramatic rise in concern about the environment. Rachel Carson's 1962 book *Silent Spring*, an attack on the use of pesticides that opens with a tragic hypothetical portrait of a springtime without birds, struck a public nerve.[15] Some environmentalists had been criticizing the unconstrained nature of the American industrial machine for at least a decade, and especially its abuse and overuse of water in the West, but the success of Carson's book injected the movement as a whole into the public mind. The writings of Mary Austin, Wallace Stegner, Edward Abbey, and Aldo Leopold became major parts of the national conversation.[16] Just as important, small proenvironmental organizations, such as the Sierra Club and the Wilderness Society, found themselves growing, and growing more influential.[17] The Sierra Club's membership, for example, increased from 15,000 to 85,000 during the 1960s. By 1977 it had 180,000 members, and by the new millennium, 747,000, with a budget of $45 million.[18]

The second change in cultural emphasis was evident in the rise of the consumers' movement. When the New Deal had brought organized labor and minority ethnic organizations into its complex of represented interests, organized consumers had not been part of the coalition. Again, one book seemed to catalyze a nascent political upheaval, Ralph Nader's *Unsafe at Any Speed*. Nader's exposure of General Motors's cavalier disregard for driver and passenger safety, together with General Motors's clumsy attempts to discredit and blackmail him, duly exposed and excoriated by the media, turned him into a national institution. Not just Nader's group Public Citizen, but the Consumers' Union, Action for Children's Television, and a host of other consumer-oriented, politically active groups demanded, and got, access to policy making.

The changing economic and political emphasis that became evident during the 1960s was not the result of a few eloquent books and dedicated activists, although those provided leadership, but was the marker of a genuine cultural evolution. Ronald Inglehart has measured the movement in the values expressed by mass publics in several advanced industrial societies, including the United States. Inglehart chronicles a partial changeover from "materialist" to "postmaterialist" values in a large swath of the American population, beginning in the 1960s and continuing thereafter. Whereas citizens did not lose their interest in employment and inflation, the concerns of a significant fraction of the population became more complicated, emphasizing "quality of life" issues, such as environmentalism and consumerism, rather than focusing exclusively on production and distribution of goods.[19] Economic politics, like economic and political thought, became more complicated during the 1960s.

The politics of the 1960s witnessed two other upheavals, the civil rights movement and the New Left. But the civil rights movement, for all its economic implications and for all its political impact, was primarily a struggle to integrate the subjugated African American portion of the population into the American mainstream. It addressed the topic of legitimacy, but its rhetoric and emphasis were primarily moral, and were only secondarily addressed to politics and economics. It has been well chronicled elsewhere, and I will merely note its importance and move on. The New Left primarily addressed issues of alienation in a bureaucratized society, opposition to the Vietnam War, and personal alterations in lifestyle concerning sex and recreational drug use. All of those issues are interesting and potentially important, but they are not among the dominant concerns of this book. The New Left has also attracted much scholarly concern, and I will not add to it.

Elite intellectual opinion during this era also evolved. By the end of the Second World War it had taken a clear and decisive turn toward favoring governmental activism, at least in the arena of economic policy. Especially in the economics profession, but also in law, history, and the social sciences, the generation that came of age during the Depression and World War II was by and large favorably disposed toward state management of the economy and redistribution of wealth, contemptuous of traditional appeals to the virtues of the free market, and doubly contemptuous of those who were skeptical of concentrated public power. There was a consensus in this immediate postwar generation that government could identify and solve both social and economic problems, and that opinions to the contrary were the special pleadings of discredited interests.[20]

New Deal progressivism—what Robert Collins has termed "growth liberalism" —had thus achieved its own status as an orthodoxy by the end of World War II and for two decades afterward.[21] There was, further, one part of the orthodoxy that was beyond argument. By the postwar years it was accepted without question by both the elite and the mass that democracy was a good thing. Survey research confirmed that Americans were practically unanimous in embracing the concept of democracy and in endorsing such principles as majority rule, political equality, minority rights, and freedom of discussion, when these were stated in abstract terms.[22] Moreover, democracy appeared to be an ideal that had triumphed everywhere. In 1949, for example, the United Nations Educational, Scientific, and Cultural Organization (UNESCO) commissioned more than one hundred scholars to inquire into the acceptance of the concept around the world. They could not find a single person willing to criticize it. "Probably for the first time in history," read the report, "democracy is classed as the proper ideal description of all political and social organizations advocated by influential proponents."[23]

But ideals are one thing, and experience is another. The classic statements of democratic theory by John Locke in 1690 and Jean Jacques Rousseau in 1762 had enshrined the idea of citizen participation as the foundation of governmental legitimacy. Consequently, until well into the twentieth century social conflict over democratization had emphasized extension of the franchise. This struggle was not finally concluded in the United States until 1965, when Congress passed, and the Johnson administration and the federal courts began vigorously to enforce, the Voting Rights Act ensuring African Americans access to the ballot box. Even before that date, however, intellectuals had begun to become disillusioned with the way democracy was working out in practice among the large majority of adult Americans who already possessed the right to vote.

The problem was that American citizens were apparently proving themselves to be not up to the demands of democratic theory. The implicit assumptions of Locke and Rousseau had been that citizens, once given the chance to participate, would do so, would take their civic duties seriously enough to make sure that they became informed voters, and would learn the philosophy of the game well enough to support its basic rules, such as tolerance of unpopular viewpoints. By this standard, however, most Americans were unworthy of democracy. Only six out of ten bothered to vote in presidential elections, and fewer still in off years. Turnout was particularly abysmal in the southern states.[24] Moreover, the great majority of the population was sublimely uninformed on very many issues of national import, and even on such crucial facts as which party controlled Congress. Under such conditions it was impossible for most citizens to form opinions about many topics of relevance to governance, for they lacked sufficient information.[25] Worse, while ordinary people endorsed freedom of expression for those with minority views in the abstract, when asked to apply these generalizations to specific instances they proved alarmingly intolerant. In 1954, for example, 60 percent of Americans wished to deny an atheist the chance to make a speech in their community, and 58 percent were similarly willing to suspend a socialist's rights.[26] Given these facts, many scholars began to wonder what "democracy" meant in the modern world, and how a government allegedly based on the people's will could function.

The years from 1932 to 1974 therefore witnessed a great deal of creative and anxious thinking. The era produced novel paradigms in economics, law, and political science. Unlike the case in previous decades, however, when philosophies and theories, once adopted, tended to persist, the dominant theories of this era proved to be remarkably fragile. The entire public philosophy came under attack in the 1960s, and by the early 1970s virtually every new orthodoxy had either been discarded, or was crumbling, or was being vigorously challenged. The intellectual legacy of this period was thus one of destruction and discord.

PARADIGM SHIFT, I: ECONOMICS

Although neoclassical economics was replete with the usual scholarly controversies, schools, and eccentricities at the onset of the Depression, its practitioners very broadly shared a set of assumptions, values, beliefs, and methodologies. They viewed the national economy as a system of many small interacting units (plus, unfortunately, a few natural monopolies) in which, over the long run and in the absence of complicating factors, the invisible hand of market competition would force demand, supply, and prices into an optimum equilibrium. Explicitly or tacitly they endorsed Say's Law that supply creates its own demand. If government took measures to ensure that there was enough but not too much money in the system, they believed that prices would remain relatively stable. They tended to disapprove of factors that might disrupt the theoretically harmonious workings of the economy, such as collusive or government-sponsored private monopoly, labor unions, government regulation, or a departure from the gold standard.

Because economists thus thought they understood the general outlines of economic truth, during the prosperous decades preceding 1929 they contented themselves with elaborating details and participating in controversies within the general orthodoxy—within "normal science," in Thomas Kuhn's phrase.[27] But when the Depression inaugurated apparently permanent business stagnation and high unemployment, the crisis caused a loss of self-confidence in the profession, stimulated a reevaluation of the old verities, and spurred a burst of thinking outside the orthodox paradigm.

The general dissatisfaction with micro-oriented, neoclassical economics was never unanimous. Even before the Great Depression began in 1929, there were attacks on the standard model. At the height of the "Roaring Twenties," in *Business without a Buyer*, William Foster and Waddill Catchings argued that underconsumption would be the cause of future business downturns. Defending a position that in just a few years would be orthodoxy, they argued that "the reason we cannot sell the goods . . . is because the people who would like to buy them do not have sufficient incomes."[28] Their solution, also, would seem obvious a few years later: "if we increase the flow of money to consumers in proportion to increased productive activity, prosperity will continue."[29] Foster and Catchings fell just slightly short of elaborating the theory that would in 1936 make Keynes the most important economist of the century. But even if Keynes had come up with his own book in 1927, he would have been as uncelebrated as Foster and Catchings. The general prosperity had discouraged a search for new economic ideas.

The rapid descent of the Depression after the stock market crash of October 1929, however, acted as a spur to creative thought. Important attempts to break from traditional modes of thinking were made in the early 1930s by Joan Robinson at Cambridge and E. H. Chamberlin at Harvard, and in the mid-1930s by John Kenneth Galbraith, also of Harvard. These three rejected the image of an economy dominated, on the one hand, by many firms struggling within a system of perfect competition and, on the other, a few monopolies able to set their own prices. The theory of perfect competition, they pointed out, was based on the assumption that all the firms in an industry produce identical goods. But suppose that even though there are several or many companies, each one is able to persuade consumers, through advertising, that its products are different, unique—that is, that each firm is able to establish "product differentiation"? Then, up to the limit of consumer willingness to view one label of soap or one brand of automobile as superior to others, each firm becomes its own little monopoly. Up to that point, each firm could raise or maintain prices above the theoretical market-clearing rate; in particular, it could resist the downward price forces of a depression. If a large number of industries were dominated by such a situation of "monopolistic competition," then their interactions would be unable to lever prices in general down to an equilibrium level. The implication of this insight was that production under such circumstances would not be able to create its own demand, resulting in a suboptimum employment market, and many workers would be unable to find jobs.[30]

The theory of monopolistic competition had an important impact on economists in the 1930s and, in the 1950s, was a vital component of Galbraith's critique of the American economy. Nonetheless, it was not a revolution in thought. It was still based on the traditional assumptions and reasoning of neoclassical marginalism. The next exercise in creative thinking, however, departed entirely from the neoclassical mold, not only inaugurating an original methodology and heretical policy prescriptions but creating a new branch of social thought.

John Maynard Keynes was the insider's insider, a British aristocrat, a former cabinet minister, a well-known economist, a diplomat, an adviser to governments, a patron of the arts, and a famous wit. He was not, in other words, the sort of marginalized crank (Henry George, for example) whose ideas are apt to be ignored or ridiculed by the establishment. When *The General Theory of Employment, Interest, and Money* appeared in 1936, therefore, it was given a respectful hearing, reviewed in the best journals, and quickly set about converting economists to a new way of looking at the world.

Orthodox neoclassicism (except for the work of such mavericks as Foster and Catchings) viewed the economy as a series of micro interactions. To form a picture of the economy as a whole, it aggregated millions of buying and selling transactions. Other than its faith in a stable money supply, and its confidence in Say's Law, it had no vision of the economy as an independent totality. Keynes reversed the ends of the telescope, so to speak. He started from a vision of the economy as one organic entity, several aspects of which determined the nature of its individual transactions.

According to Say's Law, too much production, and therefore too few jobs, was not possible as long as the prices of commodities and wages were allowed to reach their natural level, because production would always employ enough people whose earnings would enable them to consume all the products. And conversely, as long as the people were employed, they would always buy enough to justify the production. Granted this law, Keynes asserted, "all the rest follows—the social advantages of private and national thrift . . . the classical theory of unemployment, the quantity theory of money, the unqualified advantages of *laissez-faire* in respect to foreign trade and much else."[31]

But, Keynes asked, what if people hoard some of their wages rather than spending them all? (He used the term "hoard" to reverse the presumably positive moral connotations of the word "save.") Under conditions of hoarding, there would not be enough total buying power ("effective demand") in an economy to purchase all the goods. With inventories piling up unsold, firms would be forced to cut back on employment. By taking purchasing power out of the economy, however, this action would further shrink effective demand, which would result in lower sales and therefore more layoffs, and so on in a downward spiral. This conceptualization of the possible malfunction of the economy as a whole, Keynes wrote, "supplies us with an explanation of the paradox of poverty in the midst of plenty. For the mere existence of an insufficiency of effective demand may, and often will, bring the increase of employment to a standstill *before* a level of full employment has been reached."[32]

In other words, the neoclassical economists were correct in foreseeing that an economy could achieve an equilibrium in which production, consumption, and employment were in some kind of enduring balance, but wrong in predicting that an economy would always have a tendency to arrive at that equilibrium position when the three factors were at a relative maximum. Instead, given various analytically understandable circumstances, an economy in a given era might stick at an equilibrium that featured high unemployment. Further, the rich in any community tend to consume less, relative to their total income, than their poorer compatriots. The more rich people there are in any community, therefore, the less likely it is to generate a satisfactory amount of total buying power. The paradoxical consequence must be that as a community becomes wealthier, it will be more vulnerable to the tendency to generate insufficient effective demand and therefore more likely to arrive at an equilibrium characterized by massive unemployment.

Once the problem of depression is characterized this way, the obvious solution to economic slowdown becomes one of finding means to stimulate effective demand. Keynes suggests three. First, he rejects the neoclassical opinion that wages should be allowed to drop until full employment is reached. This is a policy, he points out, of deliberately shriveling aggregate purchasing power. Instead, wages should be set as high as possible so that workers can buy as much as possible.[33] Second, he recommends "measures for the redistribution of incomes in a way likely to raise the propensity to consume."[34] Third, "[t]he State will have to exercise a guiding influence on the propensity to consume" by using its power to tax, spend, and regulate.[35] In particular, by spending on public works projects even past the point of a balanced budget, governments can move purchasing power into the hands of people who will spend it, thus spurring effective demand and causing the economy to spiral up instead of down.[36]

There is more to the *General Theory*, but those are the basics. Both as economics and as potential politics, it represented a paradigm shift. For Keynes had done more than to allow economists to think in macroeconomic terms. He had fired the final torpedo into the sinking ship of laissez-faire. Government activity, formerly a necessary evil to be used as sparingly as possible, was now not only frequently justified but mandatory. Further, Keynes turned several bedrock assumptions of moral superiority upside down: thrift was now bad and spending good, balanced governmental budgets (in times of sluggish business activity) were now bad and deficits good; low labor costs were now bad and union-induced high wages good; and leaving investment decisions to private individuals was bad and state direction good. In a large sense, Keynes legitimated democratic control over the economy.

Keynesian theory took a decade to seep into the official public policy of the United States. Nevertheless, Franklin Roosevelt, without ever embracing or even understanding Keynes's theory, followed Keynes's policy prescriptions in a vigorous, albeit ad hoc and inconsistent, manner. We can agree with Peter Temin that in ideological thrust, the New Deal is better described as "democratic socialism" rather than as Keynesianism, and still observe that, in effect, the overall direction of policy lurched in the direction Keynes advised.³⁷

By the end of the war, however, several important government officials and a platoon of rising young stars of the economics profession in the United States and Britain were fervent Keynesians. Over the next several decades Alvin Hansen, John Hicks, James Tobin, and others elaborated the theory; translated its vaguer parts into precise, often mathematical arguments; and endeavored to sell it to policy makers and the public at large.

Among the most important in developing Keynesianism, and certainly the most important in selling it, was Paul Samuelson. As a graduate student at Harvard in the 1930s, he later wrote, he had realized that the discipline of economics was a "sleeping princess" that had been awakened by the invigorating kisses of Keynesian theory and mathematical methods.³⁸ But though at last conscious, the princess still was not dancing, for Keynes had left many ideas undeveloped or inadequately explained, and his death in 1946 prevented him from expanding his new paradigm.

Samuelson, however, from his position as professor of economics at MIT, was the perfect chauffeur to drive the princess to the ball. His analytic and synthetic abilities were first rate; he was a lucid, even charming prose stylist; his mathematical skill was awesome; his energy seemed to be unlimited. Between 1937 and 1977 he published 293 articles in professional journals, expanding and refining Keynesian macroeconomic theory and melding it with neoclassical microeconomics. He made important contributions to the theories of welfare economics, general equilibrium, consumption, international trade, finance, public goods, monetarism, and capital flows. Before he and the others were finished, economists spoke of a "neoclassical synthesis" that combined a Keynesian short-run macro perspective with a neoclassical long-run micro perspective into a unified theory that explained almost everything.³⁹

Just as important were Samuelson's efforts to bring the new perspective to people outside the circle of professional scholars. His textbook, *Economics: An Introductory Analysis,* which first appeared in 1948, taught the subject to a generation of undergraduates. Written in an easy, almost conversational style that, despite its analytic rigor, made most of its arguments sound like common sense, by 1997 it had gone through fifteen editions, sold four million copies, and had been translated into forty-one languages. In the 1960s Samuelson began writing a column for every other issue of *Newsweek,* which introduced his ideas to thousands of noneconomists.⁴⁰

Although Keynesianism apparently offered a tool by which governments, employing fiscal policy (taxing and spending), could head off depressions, there was a flaw in the tool. Since 1936 Keynes's theory has been harshly criticized by many economists, not to mention politicians, journalists, and scholars in other disciplines. These criticisms are varied, but if one discards those that are true but basically trivial (some chapters of *The General Theory* are obscurely written) and those that are largely assertions of political preference rather than accusations of theoretical infirmity (Keynes advocates redistribution of wealth from the rich to the poor), the important points finally dissolve into just one: by advocating government deficit spending in order to raise the level of effective demand, Keynes is implicitly arguing that the state should tolerate inflation rather than unemployment.

Although nobody likes unemployment, it is a long-standing belief among economists that inflation is socially corrosive and economically ruinous. There is little empirical support for this belief; studies have been unable to find evidence that inflation rates below 20 percent have toxic consequences for the polity or the economy.[41] Nevertheless, it was and is the received wisdom that the Keynesian medicine, restorative in the correct amount, is poisonous if taken in too big a dose. Therefore in the three decades following the war, economists and government officials wanted to know how much inflation they had to tolerate in order to get unemployment down to acceptable levels, in order to be able to decide how large a budget deficit they could run before hyperinflation ruined them.

Although Samuelson was the bard of the new paradigm, this particular question seemed, for a while, to be answered by another scholar. Crucial to the acceptance of Keynesianism by both the academic and political worlds was an article published in 1958 by the British economist A. W. Phillips. Phillips noticed that over the course of the previous several centuries, there appeared to be a nonlinear but tight relationship between inflation and unemployment in Britain. Periods of higher unemployment coincided with lower inflation; periods of lower unemployment coincided with higher inflation. The relationship was so strong that Phillips graphed it, providing a theoretical tool by which government officials could calculate just how much unemployment they would have to endure in order to diminish inflation by a given amount, and how much inflation would rise if they lowered unemployment by a given amount. This "Phillips curve" apparently provided a practical methodology with which to flesh out Keynes's abstractions and permit government officials to "fine tune" the economy.[42] The curve's value as a policy tool, of course, would hold up only so long as politicians could count on the relationship between unemployment and inflation to continue in the future as it had in the past. During the 1950s and 1960s, this expectation held. After

1973, however, the correlation fell apart, and everyone's confidence in Keynesian fine-tuning collapsed.

Keynesianism was an ideological abomination for the right wing after the war. Keynes's endorsement of unbalanced budgets seemed to the conservatives to be an invitation to government irresponsibility, and his recommendation of wealth redistribution was, in their interpretation, a cry for class warfare. Readers of popular magazines that pedaled the conservative worldview—*Time* and *Readers' Digest*, for example—could easily get the idea, during the 1950s and 1960s, that Keynes was some sort of demon.

Nevertheless, policies to put money into the hands of people who would spend it were strongly endorsed not only by economists, and not only by labor unions, but also by important segments of the business community. Singed by the Depression, the American Main Street had tacitly decided that mass consumption must be encouraged as an economic policy and a cultural habit. In 1956, when William H. White, editor of *Fortune*, proclaimed that "thrift is now un-American," he expressed the zeitgeist.[43] The country had become, in Lizbeth Cohen's label, a "consumers' republic."[44]

Thus, although Keynesianism was officially excoriated by a large chunk of the Republican Party for decades after the war, it was implicitly endorsed by the Republican Eisenhower administration (1953–1961), and explicitly followed by the Democratic Kennedy (1961–1963) and Johnson (1963–1969) administrations.[45] When Republican president Nixon publicly avowed himself a Keynesian in 1971, the new paradigm received its official imprimatur as an orthodoxy.[46] And Keynes had not just triumphed in the United States. As political scientist Douglas Hibbs has shown, in most Western democracies during the postwar years, parties of the Right and parties of the Left played games with the Phillips curve. When progressive parties were elected to power, they adopted policies that raised inflation and lowered unemployment; the victory of conservative parties brought forth policies with the opposite effect.[47] The period from the end of the war to 1974 truly was, as Robert Lekachman dubbed it, the Age of Keynes.[48]

PARADIGM SHIFT, II: LAW

Just as the Great Depression knocked the pins out from under neoclassical economics, so also did it cause a great change of mind in the legal profession. The old verities of Field and Spencer, the doctrine of freedom of contract and the prejudice against government regulation of the economy, the assumption that labor unions were a conspiracy against the public—none of these survived the

1930s, at least as dominant ideologies. The Supreme Court fought a rear-guard action defending the old paradigm for a few years, but surrendered in 1937. In *West Coast Hotel Co. v. Parrish*, it upheld a Washington State minimum-wage law, thereby overruling the *Adkins* precedent and, in effect, repealing the doctrine of substantive due process. Speaking for the majority, Chief Justice Charles Evan Hughes read Herbert Spencer out of the Constitution:

> [T]he violation alleged by those attacking minimum wage regulation for women is deprivation of freedom of contract. What is this freedom? The Constitution does not speak of freedom of contract. . . . The legislature is entitled to adopt measures to reduce the evils of the "sweating system," the exploiting of workers at wages so low as to be insufficient to meet the bare cost of living. . . . Even if the wisdom of the policy be regarded as debatable and its effects uncertain, still the legislature is entitled to its judgment.[49]

The same year, in *National Labor Relations Board v. Jones and Laughlin Steel Corporation*, the Court ignored the doctrine it had upheld since the *E. C. Knight* decision of 1895 regarding national regulation of commerce. The majority decided that the National Labor Relations Act of 1935 was constitutional because labor relations indirectly affected the flow of traffic through interstate commerce, and the Constitution explicitly granted Congress the authority to regulate in that sphere. Justice James McReynolds, seeing the handwriting on the wall and not liking it, dissented with three other conservatives: "[The legislation] puts into the hands of a Board control over purely local industry beyond anything heretofore deemed permissible. . . . Manifestly that view of congressional power would extend it into almost every field of human industry."[50]

His complaint was perceptive, but it was irrelevant; the tide had turned. The Court did not invalidate another congressional statute under the commerce clause until 1997.

The Court propounded its new philosophy somewhat casually, in a footnote to an otherwise inconsequential case, *United States v. Carolene Products*, in 1938. Speaking for the majority, Justice Harlan Stone explained that he and his colleagues planned to be deferential toward legislative power in the general area of economic regulation. There were other topics of constitutional interest, however, that would draw "more exacting judicial scrutiny." If a legislature infringed on rights granted by the first ten amendments, or attempted to interfere with democratic processes (such as the right to vote), or made itself the instrument of majority tyranny against "discrete and insular minorities," it should not expect the same judicial deference that would apply to economic legislation. In other words, the Court would allow democracy to function, but not to undermine itself. And so, in the next several decades, the Court was noteworthy for its decisions in the areas of civil rights and liberties, representation in legislatures, and criminal law, rather than in economic regulation.[51]

The new paradigm had also become influential in legal philosophy—the ideas in law review articles and books that catch the attention of the profession, and the problems posed to students in law school classes—even before the Supreme Court adopted it. By about 1930 the American version of positivism, "legal realism," had a foothold in the discipline and enjoyed a dominant position by the end of the decade. Legal realists followed Oliver Wendell Holmes in believing that "the life of the law has not been logic: it has been experience," and Benjamin Cardozo (on the Supreme Court from 1932 to 1938, and before that a judge on the New York Court of Appeals) in holding that "law is not found, but made."[52] Like positivists everywhere, they ridiculed the notion that there was a "higher law" accessible to judges that allowed the judicial branch to inform the legislative branch what it could and could not do. There were no eternal verities, there was only the product of the legislature. The job of the judge was to apply statutes, not evaluate them.[53] Legal realism provided the philosophical foundation upon which the New Deal Court built a jurisprudence of judicial deference during the late 1930s.

But the 1940s were not kind to legal realism. Even before the end of World War II, the realization was sinking in that what the Nazis were doing to the Jews and other victims was perfectly legal. The legislature had passed enabling legislation, and the German courts, in accord with positivist principles, had ratified them. Nazi Germany, of course, was not a democracy, and the United States was. Still, by the end of the war the moral relativism of the realists seemed a good deal less refreshing and valuable than it had a few years previously. Now it looked like nihilism. The American legal community became suspicious that a nihilist philosophy had helped turn German democracy into tyranny, and might do so in the United States. Now it seemed that timeless principles, even natural law, might be a bulwark against totalitarianism.[54]

The evolution of legal thought during this period is well illustrated by the decline in the reputation of Oliver Wendell Holmes. In the 1930s, when realism reigned, Holmes was elevated to the status of an icon. He was, according to the positivists of the time, the one beacon of light during the darkness of the reign of Fieldism, the one man who had dared assert the relativism of law in an age of dogmatism. But as realism crumbled under the weight of history in the 1940s, Holmes's intellectual standing likewise plummeted. In 1950 Harold McKinnon denounced Holmes's philosophy as "a symbol of our intellectual wretchedness, a conspicuous example of our abandonment of those spiritual, philosophical and moral truths that have been the life of the western tradition." For the rest of the century Holmes's reputation waxed and waned, but was always several notches below the status of demigod.[55]

The swift decline of legal realism did not revive the fortunes of substantive due process or its associated jurisprudential regime. Those had acquired the reputation of being class warfare masquerading as constitutional truth, and neither attorneys nor judges were in a mood to revive them. Yet if nihilism was to be averted it would be necessary to come up with another defensible creed, one that would permit judges to rule on the appropriateness of laws but would still allow the people to govern themselves. In the 1950s the profession launched a quest for a new natural law.

This turned out to be very difficult to discover. Scholars are still looking for a new paradigm that will prove satisfactory to the American legal community. It was not that no one could come up with books and articles proposing standards of judgment for evaluating legislation—quite the contrary. But all the proposed substitutes for substantive due process seemed to suffer from one of two faults. Either they were so vague as to be impossible to apply in practice—such as "neutral principles"[56] or "reasoned elaboration."[57] Or they propounded clear standards that satisfied some scholars but aroused intense opposition in a significant proportion of the profession—such as the "law and economics" movement, the members of which advocated that the Constitution be interpreted so as to promote efficiency as defined by neoclassical theory.[58] By the 1970s the legal profession was rent with competing schools and philosophies. This was not the case of a dominant center against a critical periphery; there was no center.

In legal thinking, then, the period from 1932 to 1974 was one in which government regulation of the economy became an orthodoxy, but an orthodoxy that was not supported by an elaborated philosophy that commanded a consensus among lawyers and judges.

PARADIGM SHIFT, III: POLITICAL THOUGHT

The 1930s witnessed the most profound alteration of political discourse in American political history. Prior to the arrival of Franklin Roosevelt's New Deal in 1933, "liberalism" was defined in its classic European sense. A liberal valued individual liberty above all and consequently was highly skeptical of government meddling with the free market. An American liberal was thus apt to vote Republican, favor a strong judiciary that vigorously protected private property, and be skeptical of plans to apply democratic principles to important economic decisions. A liberal was antigovernment, at least on economic policy.

Progressives, however, had been growing restive for decades with the terms of political argument. They believed that government was not the only menace to liberty. Indeed, by the Depression a significant percentage of progressive intellectuals had come to the conclusion that it was the subjugation of the individual to business power that threatened liberty, and government that was a potential defender of the individual against private manipulation and abuse. The end of social life had not changed, they argued, but a different means had to be adopted to achieve the end. John Dewey, the most prestigious American philosopher of the first half of the century, stated the new attitude succinctly in 1935:

> The only form of enduring social organization that is now possible is one in which the new forces of productivity are cooperatively controlled and used in the interest of the effective liberty and the cultural development of the individuals that constitute society.... The idea that liberalism cannot maintain its ends and at the same time reverse its conception of the means by which they are to be attained is folly. The ends can now be achieved *only* by reversal of the means to which an early liberalism was committed.[59]

Henceforward in American public discourse, a "liberal" would be someone who favored government action on behalf of the less wealthy and powerful, which, in general, meant against business prerogative. Liberals were for graduated income taxes on individuals and corporations, state protection of labor unions, regulation of investment decisions, government ownership and operation of some large industries such as utilities, and, in general, the limiting of entrepreneurial freedom in the name of expanding freedom for everyone else. While they thus drained the classical liberal's devotion to personal freedom of economic definition, they endorsed it in a different context, translating it into a defense of personal expression. A modern liberal was progovernment on economic policy, although not necessarily on social policy. The "liberty" liberals defended was thus differently defined than the one early American liberals had enshrined as the ultimate ideal of government.

Post–New Deal liberalism had another side, also, one that pursued equalities of status and power as well as wealth. Thus liberals strongly supported overthrowing the South's system of apartheid and integrating African Americans fully into American society. As time and politics advanced, liberals came to emphasize liberty less and equality more, while retaining their faith in government action on behalf of the less favored and less successful. In general, by the end of this period an American liberal was someone who occupied approximately the same space on the political spectrum as a European socialist, although with less emphasis upon government ownership of industry and more emphasis upon regulation. Appropriately, therefore, Franklin Roosevelt was the first president to identify his own beliefs as "liberal" in its modern meaning.[60] An American conservative was someone who occupied approximately the same space as a European liberal.

Needless to say, modern American terminology is confusing to European visitors, to American undergraduate political philosophy students, and to readers of intellectual histories. To attempt to forestall perplexity in my readers without constantly having to remind them of the way I am using terms, for the rest of this book I will continue to use the word "liberal" in its classical sense: as someone who believes in individualism, private property, capitalism, competition, and democracy. A modern liberal is called a conservative, and is considered to be on the right of the political spectrum. I will occasionally employ these terms in that context. When speaking of people on the left of the political spectrum, I will use the word "progressive," not "liberal," except when quoting people who employ the conventional usage.

During the Great Depression, American progressives were not only in favor of expanding governmental power. An important segment of the political elite combined this new confidence in government activity with a dramatic loss of faith in the private enterprise system. An important case in point is President Roosevelt. The New Deal, at least in its early days, has been criticized by many scholars for its intellectual incoherence. Roosevelt seemed to be trying to put together a coalition of economic planners, Brandeisian trustbusters, capitalist rationalizers, advocates of enforced competition, socialist visionaries, big business, small business, labor, agriculture, consumer representatives, and sundry eccentric ideologues, without choosing among their incompatible intentions. One of Roosevelt's most important advisers, Raymond Moley, wrote that the administration's National Industrial Recovery Act (NIRA) was "a thorough hodge-podge" of contradictory recovery plans.[61] As a result, within two years of its establishment, the National Recovery Administration (NRA), the agency created to implement these contradictory visions, had become paralyzed, unable to proceed in any direction without alienating a significant segment of the coalition. When the Supreme Court, in one of the dying spasms of the old jurisprudence, declared the NIRA unconstitutional in 1935, it actually did the New Deal a favor by ridding it of an institution that was not working and was never going to work, while absolving it of the responsibility for failure.[62]

The fact that Roosevelt, the ultimate political animal, allowed his administration to reflect incoherent social forces, however, does not mean that he himself was without a consistent set of beliefs and values. As Sidney Milkis has explained, FDR intended to "challenge the core belief in the Anglo-American tradition that freedom was inherently *natural* and that the protection of natural rights required that a 'wall of separation,' as Jefferson put it, stand between society and the national government."[63] Roosevelt was the embodiment in action of thought articulated by John Dewey; he believed that it was time to hold on to the ends of liberalism, but reverse the means.

As early as 1912 Roosevelt had publicly expressed his view that "competition has been shown to be useful up to a point and no further,"[64] and during his tenure as New York governor during the 1920s he had elaborated on a philosophy with which a modern progressive would feel perfectly at home: "One of the duties of the State is that of caring for its citizens who find themselves the victims of such adverse circumstances as to make themselves unable to obtain even the necessities for mere existence without the aid of others. . . . To these unfortunate citizens aid must be extended by Government, not as a matter of charity, but as a matter of social duty."[65]

By 1932 Roosevelt was not only expressing explicitly progovernment ideas but was arguing that the historical impetus of free market capitalism was spent, necessitating a new era of national organization that he did not call, but clearly was, socialism:

> The day of the great promoter or the financial Titan, to whom we granted anything if only he would build or develop, is over. Our task now is not discovery or exploitation of natural resources, or necessarily producing more goods. It is the soberer, less dramatic business of administering resources and plants already in hand, of seeking to reestablish foreign markets for our surplus production, of meeting the problem of under consumption, of adjusting production to consumption, of distributing wealth and products more equitably, of adapting existing economic organizations to the service of the people. The day of enlightened administration has come.[66]

This speech could almost have been lifted from the pages of Bellamy's *Looking Backward*, published forty-three years earlier. It contains the same skepticism of the ability of independent private citizens to create new wealth, the same belief that the pie will never grow larger, the same confidence that only the national government will be able to distribute the pieces of the pie in an equitable manner, the same faith in the intelligence and public-spiritedness of bureaucratic administration. In its conviction that economic history has stopped and its rejection of private and advocacy of public activity, it could almost be a template for modern progressivism, except that it does not ascribe evil motives to capitalists. Roosevelt's policies, even after the demise of the NRA, were of necessity inconsistent, but his own values and intentions were always quite clear.

The American system coming out of the Depression and war years was partly a reflection of Roosevelt's ideology and partly a consequence of the compromises and expedients he adopted to retain his ability to govern. Ideologically, this system has been termed "embedded liberalism" by Mark Blyth, to emphasize the way workers were "embedded" in a social matrix rather than left at the mercy of market forces.[67] As he summarizes it, "This set of ideas centered on a passive fiscal policy with stable tax rates facilitating positive-sum outcomes for both business and labor."[68] Overall, this embedded liberal order rested on Keynesian justifications.[69]

Institutionally, this system featured a government structure that was divided horizontally—it was composed of many quasi-independent agencies—and vertically—although the federal government had much authority, so also did the states—interacting with an array of interest groups and party coalitions. Together, the structure and the array formed a political economy of almost preternatural complexity. The way this system worked can be illustrated by a brief sketch of its application to the biggest American industry, petroleum.

The American oil and gas industry was divided into hundreds of companies, ranging in size from some of the largest corporations in the world to one-man wildcatting operations, and including, in various combinations of all the sizes, production, distribution, refining, and retail sales.[70] The parts of the industry were traditionally hostile to one another. In particular, however, the smaller producers, carrying a collective memory of abuses by the Standard Oil monopoly during the previous century, were eternally suspicious of the intentions of the major companies. At the same time, all segments of the industry were wary of direction from Washington. Yet the Depression brought with it a collapse of prices so catastrophic as to overcome even their Jeffersonian hostility to government regulation.

The early 1930s thus witnessed a struggle in both the state capitals and in Washington, D.C., to fashion some system of industry governance that would preserve its essentially private nature, prevent the price of oil from rising too rapidly or too slowly, ensure everyone access to the market, and protect the small producers from the majors. By late 1935 the various political battles had put in place a system of marvelous intricacy. The federal government left to the states the details of how to "prorate" oil production within their own borders—that is, how to divide up the market among the various producers. In Texas, this effort took the form of detailed regulation by the state's railroad commission. In California, where the voters rejected a prorationing law in a referendum, the companies established their own private system and hired an arbitrator to allocate production quotas. Each state in turn fashioned its own system. Although investment decisions continued to be the responsibility of thousands of large and small private operators, they were made within state rules regulating where and how many wells could be drilled, how many barrels each could produce per month, and how the transportation of the oil was to be handled. Under the federal Connally Act of 1935, the Interior Department forbade shipments in interstate commerce of "hot oil" produced in defiance of these state regulations and authorized the states to establish an organization, the Interstate Oil Compact Commission (IOCC), to coordinate their prorationing efforts.

Within each state, individual producers lobbied the relevant agency to promulgate rules favoring themselves or their particular class of company. At the IOCC meetings, each state jostled with every other to procure a larger share of the pie for its own producers. At the same time, for various reasons of geology and politics, American production tended to be high cost, which made it advantageous to the majors to import oil from the Middle East, South America, and elsewhere. Major company lobbyists constantly attempted to persuade Congress and federal administrative agencies to support unlimited importation of oil. Meanwhile, domestic independent producers, aided by some other groups, such as the United Mine Workers of America, which feared competition from still cheaper oil, lobbied Congress and the current administration to forbid imports, and then, when that strategy failed, to place quotas on imported petroleum. While the various industry factions were engaging in running skirmishes, consumers' representatives threw their weight on the side of whichever policy alternative seemed to promise less expensive oil. When one group or another lost a major lobbying battle, it often sued; if it lost in the state courts, it would frequently take the issue to the federal level.

Amazingly, this system, resting on constant contention among many groups and individuals within all three branches of government at several tiers of federalism, managed to supply the nation with almost four decades of cheap, reliable energy. Various critics of the era blasted the system for its alleged irrationality and dismissal of the public interest.[71] In retrospect, however, the years 1935 to 1973 seem like the golden age of American petroleum.

The example of oil control illustrates the combination of state, federal, interstate, and private organizations that, by the mid-1940s, had so blended government and private industry at both the national and local levels that the American system was difficult to characterize. As noted, Blyth dubbed it "embedded liberalism." Sidney Milkis labeled it a new "economic constitutional order."[72] Michael Brown tagged it "commercial Keynesianism."[73] Other political scientists termed it "interest-group liberalism,"[74] "pluralism,"[75] or "polyarchy."[76] Economists called it a "mixed capitalistic enterprise system,"[77] or, more simply, a "mixed economy."[78] During the 1960s there was a great surge in numbers and types of interest groups—feminists, ethnic groups, environmentalists, consumers, and so on—as well as an increase in governmental agencies to accommodate President Johnson's Great Society programs. These changes, however, represented an expansion on the basic pattern rather than a difference of kind.

After the Second World War, political scientists specializing in the American system set about to solve two intellectual puzzles. First, they intended to fashion a dispassionate and, if possible, scientific analysis of the way the new political economy functioned. The quest for a science of politics had been launched much earlier, in 1908, by Arthur Bentley. Expressing disgust with the "barren formalism"—constitutional and descriptive studies—that marked the American political inquiry of his day, Bentley announced his intention of making political study scientific through the adoption of the technique of "quantitative comparison" of the "forces and pressures at work" on "great masses, groups, of men."[79] He argued that interest groups were the constituent elements of democratic politics, that "the governmental process is a group process."[80] Government at any given time is a function of the "complex of pressures" of groups impinging upon it.[81]

As Dorothy Ross has commented, Bentley's vision of politics "abandoned historical context, structure, and time" for a faux scientism that seemed to be modeled on the eternal natural laws of chemistry and physics.[82] Even if this ahistorical approach to studying politics might make sense, which is doubtful, it would only have worked if Bentley could have fashioned an operational methodology that would have allowed him to put into effect his dictum that "measure conquers chaos."[83] But his book was long on exhortation and short on, indeed, completely lacking in, empirical measures of interest-group influence.

Similarly, the other book of "scientific" advocacy memorable from the pre–World War II period, Harold Lasswell's *Politics: Who Gets What, When, How*, was presented as a tough-minded alternative to scholarly writing that concerned itself with legitimacy. The study of politics, wrote Lasswell, should examine the topics of interest to professional politicians, that is, "who gets what, when, how."[84] What mattered was the distribution of resources, and how that distribution was achieved.

The realism of Lasswell's approach commended itself to the discipline, and his book's subtitle became a frequently repeated mantra for determining relevance in political scholarship. Nevertheless, Lasswell's approach suffered from the same problems of operationalization as Bentley's: it was certainly possible to measure the distribution of resources, but how are we to measure the applications of influence that lead to that distribution? Quantitative or not, situated in historical context or not, it turned out to be extraordinarily difficult to measure "influence" and "power." Political scientists eventually gave up on the quest.

The second topic animating political scientists after the Second World War was the attempt to revise and update democratic theory in light of both the post–New Deal polity and the observed limitations of the mass public. If a democratic polity derived its governing legitimacy from the participation of the people, what interpretation could accommodate this democracy that seemed to feature hyperactive groups and an inactive public? Ideally, such an intellectual project would come up with a new interpretation that would both characterize the American system in a scientific sense and justify it according to the traditional values and theories of classical liberalism.

The efforts of mainstream political scientists along these lines tended to fall into two categories: those inspired by the vision, if not the absence of success, of Bentley, who emphasized the interest-group system, and those who emphasized party competition theories. During the 1950s the students of interest groups, whom I will call by their most-frequent appellation, "pluralists," continued the development of a theory of democracy in which organized groups at least supplemented, and perhaps supplanted, the individual citizen of the democratic ideal. According to David Truman in *The Governmental Process* (1950),

> the group experiences and affiliations of an individual are the primary, though not the exclusive, means by which the individual knows, interprets, and reacts to the society in which he exists. Their significance here is that they produce in their participants certain uniformities of behavior and attitude.... To identify and interpret these uniformities... is the most effective approach to understanding a society, "primitive" or complex, or a segment of it such as its political institutions.[85]

In the United States or elsewhere, when the "equilibrium" of the members of a group is disturbed—that is, something happens that is contrary to their interests or values—they react by forming a group or becoming more active in the groups to which they already belong.[86] They then interact with other groups within parties and governmental institutions to produce some sort of policy outcome.[87]

So far, Truman's formulation is just a refinement of Bentley's, but Truman then carries it into another realm by using it to justify the American system. There is no point, he argues, in wondering whether the interaction of groups produces the public interest, for that term is a fiction having no relevance to scientific inquiry.[88] Nevertheless, although there is no public interest there are unorganized groups, which is the same thing as saying that there are potentially organizable groups. Further, many people belong to more than one group, which is to say that their loyalties are divided. The potential for more organization plus the overlapping memberships of most of the public keeps the system from degenerating into tyranny, so that no one need worry about both "stability and peaceful change" in the United States.[89]

Although Truman's formulation was very influential, his reconceptualization of the American system did not much distinguish it from any other type of tolerable government. His characterization, in particular, lacked a forthright consideration of the democracy problem. That lack was supplied by Robert Dahl's *A Preface to Democratic Theory* in 1956. He considers the two previously dominant notions of democratic governance—the Madisonian and populist—and finds them both wanting in the present historical context. Madison's formulation is unsatisfactory because the founding statesman failed to fashion a compromise between his two conflicting goals of universally equal political rights and permanent limitations on the power of the majority.[90] Populist democracy's formulation is unsatisfactory because it assigns almost unlimited power to the majority. Since, as we now know, mass ignorance and abstention mean that there is no majority, in practice the doctrine rewards too much power to whatever minority happens to have maneuvered itself into power at the moment.[91] A new theory is needed.

Dahl's formulation, which he calls "polyarchal democracy," takes account of the different intensities of groups. Various possible policies excite various amounts of voting, campaign contributing, interest-group activity, and other forms of free participation. Therefore although "on matters of specific policy the majority rarely rules," "all other things being equal, the outcomes of a policy decision will be determined by the relative intensity of preference among the members of a group."[92] Because the United States has a political system "in which all the active and legitimate groups in the population can make themselves heard at some crucial stage in the process of decision," which "is no mean thing in a political system," there is no reason to worry about its justification.[93]

Into the 1960s this pluralist evaluation of the polity functioned as its paradigmatic description and defense. Marxists rejected it forcefully, but mainstream political scientists endorsed its broad outlines. In the mid-1960s, however, the myriad dissatisfactions of the decade reached the profession and inspired a series of attacks that were fatal to its theory of justification, if not to its descriptive accuracy.

The attack came from two directions. In the first place, critics argued that there were cumulative biases in regard to which interests were able to organize, and who, once organized, would be able to exert pressure on policy-making institutions. In elaborating this point they were greatly aided by economist Mancur Olson's 1965 *The Logic of Collective Action*. Assuming the rational, maximizing citizen of neoclassical theory, Olson demonstrated that large potential groups would be unlikely to establish "interactions" in response to a change of "equilibrium" because of a phenomenon called the "free rider problem." Because each person in a potential citizens' group (say, owners of Fords) would constitute a tiny percentage of the whole group, each could look forward to being unimportant for her participation. Because participation is costly, each would be likely to hang back, hoping to ride free on the exertions of the others. The consequence would be a failure to organize. On the other hand, each potential member of a producers' group (say, the Ford Motor Company) would constitute a large percentage of the whole group. As a result, each would see that success depended upon her participation and would therefore join. The same logic applied to contributing money, writing letters, or any other form of activity. There was thus a bias in the interest-group system in favor of producer trade associations and against consumer or public-interest groups, in favor of employers and against labor unions, and so on.[94] Although Olson's discussion clearly missed something in the formation of groups—it came just at the beginning of the explosion of environmental, consumer, and other organizations that should not have existed if his explanation was entirely accurate—it did provide a compelling reason to doubt that Dahl's "active and legitimate groups" would all be able to interact on equal terms. By introducing the suspicion of group inequality into the pluralist framework, Olson and those who elaborated his argument created a permanent doubt as to the framework's democratic justification.

In particular, critics of pluralist justification pointed out that the wealthy possessed resources and an organizational advantage that always biased the system in their favor. Education, control of economic institutions, and, often, personal acquaintance gave them automatic advantages in any organizing contest with the unwealthy, so that there was an insistent bias in favor of their cumulating power. As E. E. Schattschneider had observed in 1960, "The flaw in the pluralist heaven is that the heavenly chorus sings with a strong upper-class accent."[95] Critics of pluralism expanded on this theme throughout the 1960s.[96]

The second mainstream line of attack on pluralist theory arose from the suspicion that a government that produced policy only as a by-product of struggling interests was, in fact, incapable of governing. The best-known exponent of this view was Theodore Lowi, whose *The End of Liberalism* (1969) became one of the most-cited political books ever written.

The pluralists assume, argues Lowi, that their equilibrium between groups is actually the public interest.[97] It therefore "transforms logrolling from necessary evil to greater good."[98] But this is a pernicious illusion. When modern government leaves the process of decision making to bargaining among groups, it abdicates its rightful function, which is the identification and attainment of the common welfare. Lacking a moral justification, it suffers a crisis of authority, and becomes unable to govern effectively.[99]

The two streams of criticisms of 1950s pluralist theory, that it incorrectly assumes an equality of groups and that it has no conception of the public interest, were highly effective. By the end of this period the initial pluralist description of the way American politics actually worked was acknowledged to contain an important element of truth, but its moral defense of the system lay in tatters. Scholars in the subfield of interest groups continued to refine the portrait of their functioning, especially by showing, through theory and empirical research, how mass groups were created and maintained. They pointed out, for example, the importance of leadership entrepreneurs,[100] as well as outside funding sources,[101] in overcoming free-rider problems. But a defense of the American system as being wholesomely democratic because it supported a profusion of interest groups was not heard after the 1960s, at least not in such an unsophisticated manner.

Mainstream political science, however, was not about to give up on pluralism. Even in the early 1960s, before the explosion of criticism of his earliest theoretical efforts, Dahl had begun rethinking the American political system. In his study of power in New Haven, Connecticut, published as *Who Governs?* in 1961, he came to the conclusion that the most important component of governance in that city was not the interest-group system but the mayor. This elected official acted "at the center of intersecting circles" of influence. Around the mayor, patricians, entrepreneurs, ethnic spokespeople, the publisher of the city's two newspapers, labor leaders, other elected public officials, and, finally and indirectly, the people of the city all exerted some influence, depending on their interest and the circumstances.[102] Over the next several decades Dahl elaborated this view into a portrait of the United States as a roiling mass of political influence encompassing interest groups, government institutions, individual politicians, parties, the media, and the people, without one single central actor that could be termed decisive. Within this disorganized system, elites ruled, but they were forced by institutions and expectations to govern in a manner that was, most of the time and on most issues, relatively responsive to the public at large. Dahl's new pluralism theory became, if not the paradigm to which all political scientists assented, then at least the most widely acknowledged and influential interpretation of the way the system functioned.[103]

The second general defense of democracy within the context of a nonparticipant public originated, like Olson's critique of pluralism, in neoclassical economics. In 1942 Joseph Schumpeter published *Capitalism, Socialism and Democracy*, a wide-ranging examination of politics and economics that has since become an important influence in several areas of social thought. In one chapter, Schumpeter addressed the problem of the abstaining, ignorant, and intolerant democratic citizen, pointing out that "he is a member of an unworkable committee, the committee of the whole nation, and this is why he expends less disciplined effort on mastering a political problem than he expends on a game of bridge."[104] The solution to this conundrum, Schumpeter argues, is not to exhort citizens to behave better, or to give up hope for good government, but to reconceptualize democracy itself. Democracy should be understood as a system in which parties and individuals compete for the people's vote. As in the economic marketplace, in the political marketplace competition will ensure the closest possible approximation to the public interest. Individuals in the mass public do not have to be any more knowledgeable about the details of public policy than they are about the details of industry or agriculture; all they have to do is cast their vote for the candidate they find most appealing. The result of political competition is that "the social function is fulfilled, as it were, incidentally," or, in other words, that the invisible hand works in democratic politics as it works in a free market system.[105]

Schumpeter himself did not try to formalize his argument. Fifteen years later, however, Anthony Downs picked up Schumpeter's ball and ran with it for a touchdown in *An Economic Theory of Democracy* (1957). Assuming that voters and parties are rational maximizers of utility, Downs formally derived a variety of explanatory hypotheses about the democratic process. Adopting a well-known principle of economic competition in a linear space, for example, Downs predicted that parties in a two-party system would tend to converge in their policy promises, whereas those in a multiparty system would remain ideologically distinct.[106] As the parties in a dual system struggled for the political center until they became nearly identical in ideology, they would encourage voters to make decisions on some basis other than issues, such the personalities of candidates, or loyalty to past party heroes. Thus "[w]e are forced to conclude that rational behavior by political parties tends to discourage rational behavior by voters."[107] In a similar vein, Downs developed a gaggle of formal predictions and explanations, some of which are still occupying the subfield he and Schumpeter founded. Behind all the analysis, however, is the master assumption that rarely needs to be stated anymore: voters matter; therefore democracy works. Because parties (or candidates) compete for votes, the people govern. Despite the irrational tendencies of the electorate, competition creates a relatively rational system.

The economic theory of democracy, formalized into the "public choice" subfield of political science, attracted a great deal of persistent criticism. Some scholars pointed out, for example, that the idea that political competition takes place in a rigid, one-dimensional space is an extremely misleading description of what happens in American elections. Policy spaces, even if they are not complete reifications, are multidimensional and constantly evolving.[108] Others faulted the economic theory for describing electoral democracy as fully competitive when in fact it is oligopolistic. It has few sellers and many buyers, so that the economic dynamic, if it exists at all, is one of monopolistic rather than pure competition, which makes the invisible hand an inapt metaphor.[109] Further, as I develop in the next chapter, the Far Left argued that because the capitalist class finds ways either to manipulate voters or exercise power above the heads of public officials, elections are essentially a charade and studying them is a waste of time.

One criticism of Downsian approaches to electoral theory did not arise until much later, when public choice theorists themselves began to elaborate some of the implications of Olson's insight. When they began to apply the notion of the free-rider problem to voter turnout, they realized that if Olson was right, then Downs had to be wrong. Because the personal cost of voting would always be far below the possible benefits to a citizen, once the individual's probability of influencing an election was factored in, then no one should ever be motivated to vote, and turnout should be zero. If no one ever voted, then parties would have no incentive to alter their behavior—converge to the center—in order to attract votes.[110] In chapter 9 I discuss how this contradiction between Downs and Olson has threatened to derail the whole public choice project.

Nevertheless, the economic model survived and thrived. Termed either the "public choice" or "rational choice" approach to the study of politics, its appeal seems to lie in two distinct areas. First, it solves the moral problem of the relatively inactive and ignorant electorate. Public choice scholars have argued in a variety of contexts that democratic politics produces governments that act *as if* they were responding to the wishes of a rational and informed people. Democracy is thereby saved much embarrassment.[111] Second, the methodology appeals strongly to careerist scholars with a certain set of skills. If their calculus abilities are adequate, they are able to prove a variety of theorems for publication in the subfield's journals and take their place in a vigorous scholarly subculture. The public choice field has therefore grown until it has achieved nearly paradigmatic status, and is in fact threatening to cannibalize the rest of political science.

Besides those ideas coming out of the two disciplines dealing most directly with the subjects, late in this period the discipline of philosophy also contributed two important publications to American thinking about politics and economics. John Rawls, in *A Theory of Justice* (1971), and Robert Nozick, in *Anarchy, State, and Utopia* (1974), became widely influential across the range of social thought by returning to the by-now primal methodology of liberalism, reasoning from a hypothetical state of nature to conclusions about the moral principles and institutional foundations of modern society. Because Rawls belongs to the mainstream of social thought and Nozick belongs in some sense to the opposition to that mainstream, I discuss the former here and the latter in the next chapter.

Rawls's creative addition to the concept of the state of nature is the "veil of ignorance." Suppose, he posits, there was a state prior to society in which all "free and rational," if disembodied, people could design the society in which they would live, without knowing what position they would occupy in that society. This universal uncertainty would create a universal caution. All, seeking to minimize the worst that could befall them, would endorse as great an equality as could be possibly designed into that society. They would give everyone the same liberties, rights, and duties, and would endorse material inequalities only if these somehow created compensating benefits for the least-advantaged members of society.[112]

This "difference principle" may at first seem like a merely incremental advance over Locke, but Rawls follows it to its logical conclusion. Because the disembodied rational consciousnesses who are designing this utopia value equality above all, they must not only erase inequalities of result but also compensate for the "undeserved inequalities . . . of birth and natural endowments" that cause inequalities in the first place, in order to "redress the bias of contingencies." Having stated his "principle of redress," Rawls attempts to soften its implications by assuring his readers that "it does not require society to try to even out handicaps as if all were expected to compete on a fair basis in the same race." If the situation of society's worst off can be improved by helping those with superior natural endowments, fine. But if the disabled can only be raised in relative position by handicapping the able, then so be it. As a first step on the road to the realization of the principle of redress, Rawls suggests spending more money on the education of the less rather than the more intelligent.[113]

Although Rawls's prose style is measured and cautious, his argument provides the philosophical basis for a radical egalitarianism. Indeed, the implicit dynamic of the "principle of redress" must lead to the world portrayed in Kurt Vonnegut's 1961 anti-utopian short story, "Harrison Bergeron." In the society Vonnegut anticipates, governments devise ingenious handicaps to neutralize every human distinction—to redress the bias of contingencies. The intelligent are given helmets to wear that send piercing shrieks through to their ears at random intervals, thus distracting them so that they cannot concentrate. The graceful and strong are made to wear heavy weights to make them clumsy and weak. Those with acute eyesight are required to don spectacles with thick wavy lenses, so that they are half blind. And so on.[114] Vonnegut's mordant vision is intended to be a horrifying exaggeration, but it is no more than a plausible extension of Rawls's difference principle—although it anticipates the philosopher's work by a decade.

Rawls's omissions are as significant as his commissions. His vision of redistributive equality makes no provision for the productive capacity of an economy. Like Bellamy, like Veblen, like Franklin Roosevelt, he seems to think that the modern wealth machine is a given; it does not require maintenance from entrepreneurs (or even, apparently, from intelligent people who have been well schooled). There need be no incentives for risk-takers to create industries or for executives to run them once they are established, unless it can be established that such people increase the well-being of the worse-off. Rawls does talk vaguely of incentives, but never specifies to whom they are to be paid, or under what circumstances. Like his forerunners in the progressive tradition, he apparently believes that the economy will keep pumping out the goodies, and that the task of philosophy is to recommend the best way to distribute them.

Because of its apparently reasonable derivation of a firm philosophical foundation for government-mandated equality, Rawls's book became one of the great landmarks of the second half of the twentieth century. Political theorists refer to it constantly. As Nozick admits, they "must either work within Rawls' theory or explain why not."[115] Even outside of the confines of philosophy, no scholar is to be taken seriously in any discussion of justice unless she demonstrates a familiarity with Rawls's argument. Rawls's reasoning has even leaked into popular culture— one of the characters on the television show *The West Wing* employed the veil of ignorance, attributed to Rawls by name, to justify a policy proposal during the 2003 season. Rawls's book is, further, the inspiration for a major stream in modern jurisprudence, the advocates of "the New Equality," who want to establish the right to redistribution of wealth and power as a legal and constitutional principle.[116] It would be going too far to assert that *A Theory of Justice* has become a new paradigm. It would not, however, be an exaggeration to claim that it is the most important text of one of the most significant trends in modern social thought.

Nevertheless, Rawls's argument rests on fragile foundations. Its entire edifice is constructed on the assumption that free and rational people who were not subject to the corrupting effects of individual interests and perspectives would choose complete equality as the ultimate value; all else follows. As Nozick recognizes, however, there is no basis whatsoever for believing that Rawls correctly understands human nature, or that there is an ethical superiority to such a position even if it were chosen. Rawls's principles, he comments, "would reduce questions of evaluating social institutions to the issue of how the unhappiest depressive fares."[117] As we shall see, Nozick also posits a state of nature with history—free, disembodied, rational creatures designing their perfect society, but he assumes a people with different values.

During the period 1932 to 1974, traditional American values and expectations were turned upside down. At the beginning of the period, Americans had, by and large, been antigovernment and pro–free market. By the end of the period, at the elite if not entirely at the mass level, government activism had become the norm and laissez faire was considered an anachronism. The United States was still unquestionably a capitalist country, but its economic system was entwined with an aggressively activist federal government. Its public philosophy, composed of equal parts John Maynard Keynes and Franklin Roosevelt, could perhaps be termed twentieth-century Gallatinism, because it envisioned a private enterprise system that was democratically regulated, stimulated, and taxed for public purposes.

The new public philosophy, however, did not go unchallenged. From both the Right and the Left, dissent grew steadily throughout the era. Dissent swelled until, by the early 1970s, it had become the norm.

CHAPTER SEVEN

Dissent, 1932–1974

The American political economy that emerged from the New Deal was one that was still largely capitalist, yet regulated and subsidized by a fragmented state that introduced many sorts of considerations into the making of economic policy, including the interests and desires of large and small producers, workers, voters, and portions of the government itself. The new dominant public philosophy—government regulation within a capitalist system—that justified the New Deal order, however, did not go without challenge. On the left, some theorists became increasingly skeptical that a society in which most investment decisions remained in private hands could be democratically managed. The public interest, they argued, demanded a complete takeover or at least a more complete regulation of industrial direction by government. On the right, other theorists argued the opposite. In their view the increasing regulation of the economy was resulting, or would result, in both diminished economic efficiency and less justice. They maintained that if both prosperity and freedom were to be saved, America must reverse course and dismantle many of the changes introduced by the New Deal. By the early 1970s both streams of dissent had attracted so many adherents that their views could almost be said to have been absorbed within the mainstream paradigm. Once consisting of a dominant conservative ruling view and a weak but insistent progressive opposition, American public discourse had become to a large extent a series of rhetorical battles between dissidents.

CAPITALISM VERSUS DEMOCRACY

Since the beginning of the Republic it had been people on the right—broadly speaking, the commercial and landowning classes before the Civil War, and the representatives of industrial capitalism afterward—who had been suspicious of democracy. The tyranny of the majority over property had been the threat that haunted the possessing classes. The New Deal did not abolish this suspicion, but rather required conservatives to modify it in the light of experience. Conservatives had already abandoned the hope of denying the people the franchise; during the 1930s they were forced to give up the intention of using judicial interdictions to forbid democratic majorities to exercise power over property. In the place of these two strategies conservatives came to emphasize an antigovernment rhetoric that sought to discourage meddling with capitalism by minimizing the sphere of acceptable state activity. Ever since Herbert Spencer, conservatives had ridiculed and attacked governmental competence. During the 1930s and afterward this effort to encourage popular suspicion of state action became one of the two mainstays of conservative rhetoric (the other being the playing on popular noneconomic prejudices and fears, such as anticommunism, law and order, and prayer in schools). In the economic sphere, conservatism, and therefore Republicans, became the antigovernment party.

In approving an antistate line as the main component in their party's economic discourse, conservatives adopted public hypocrisy as their central rhetorical strategy. For American property owners were not antigovernment. Not only did they rely upon state power at home and abroad to protect, abet, and sponsor their investments, but they were deeply and enthusiastically involved in many New Deal programs to nurture private wealth. Farmers loved agricultural support programs, domestic oil producers reveled in market-demand prorationing, broadcasters delighted in the way the Federal Communications Commission assured them uncompetitive markets, the airlines doted on a paternalistic regulation by the Federal Aviation Administration, and so on. But to publicly endorse the concept of an active, benevolent government would have left conservatives vulnerable to requests for further state activity to aid the organization of unorganized workers, redistribute wealth, protect the environment, and adopt other such disagreeable policies. By the late 1930s, therefore, conservatives had settled into a pattern of reviling government in public and seeking to influence its activities on behalf of the interests they represented in private. A large portion of American political debate thus took place in a wonderland of hypocrisy and lies.

The evolution of rhetoric about democracy and capitalism on the American right was a means of accommodating conservative interests to political reality. The evolution of rhetoric on the left, however, was a genuine transformation of ideas.

Progressivism had always been the movement that endorsed democracy. From Gallatin, Jackson, and Lincoln through Brandeis and La Follette, the dream of the Left had been a democratized capitalism in which participation in the ballot box complemented, supplemented, and created participation in the economic growth of the country. Socialists, of course, had always denied the possibility that private property and democracy were compatible in theory or practice, but as a movement they were tiny and reviled. Now, however, as the Rooseveltian political economy established itself and functioned through the 1930s, 1940s, and beyond, many progressives began to worry that perhaps the socialists had been more perceptive than they had seemed before the Left had come to power.

The problem, as some progressives began to note, was that capitalism seemed to be able to defend itself and its interests quite well even within the ostensible progressivism of the New Deal. Not only were a variety of private interests looked after and nurtured by a Democratic government, but such evils as greatly unequal possession of wealth, and abuse and exploitation of employees, did not seem to be vanishing from American society. "Individual liberty in the political realm," wrote the historian Carl Becker in 1941, "proved inadequate because individual liberty in the economic realm failed to bring about even that minimum degree of equality of possessions and of opportunity without which political equality is scarcely more than an empty form." So what was needed? In order for democracy to survive, there must be "a sufficient equalization of possessions and opportunity to provide common men with what they will consent to regard as tolerable."[1] Becker's pessimistic assessment of American democracy appeared before postwar booms and tax policies had created a society that was much richer and in which the riches were more equally distributed. Nevertheless, his disenchantment with the possibility of reconciling private ownership with an acceptable life for common citizens became an ever-more-important thread of disillusionment in the thinking of the Left.

DISSENSION ON THE LEFT, I:
BETWEEN LIBERALISM AND SOCIALISM

The tradition of neoclassical economics, which at first seemed to face a mortal challenge from Keynesian theory, turned out to be remarkably adaptable and resilient. By the 1960s mainstream economists had combined the two theoretical perspectives into a "neoclassical synthesis" that regarded Keynesian policy measures as short-run expedients to correct undesirable perturbations in an economy that was still best analyzed, in its long-run aspects, with reference to models of free market equilibrium.

Yet dissenting traditions, never numerous or dominant, but quite tenacious and often eloquent, persisted. One of these, which I address later, was the Marxist tradition. Another was one that had acquired the somewhat misleading label "institutional economics," and which derived from Thorstein Veblen's work.

Following Veblen, institutionalists believed that neoclassical economics was an intellectual swindle based upon indefensible assumptions and an unrealistic methodology. Like their progenitor, they used whatever insights from anthropology, sociology, history, law, psychology, political science, or personal intuition served their needs in analyzing the political economy. Like him, they were quite critical of the arrangement of power and wealth within American society. Like him, they frequently employed satire to ridicule the defenders of the status quo. And like Veblen, but unlike neoclassicals, institutionalists shared no settled theory of human behavior or social evolution, so that their scholarship, however insightful, tended to be more noteworthy for ad hoc individualism than for systematic knowledge building. From the turn of the twentieth century to the 1950s such thinkers as John R. Commons, Robert Hoxie, Wesley Mitchell, Thurman Arnold, and C. E. Ayres contributed earnestly to critical scholarship on the American political economy without making much of a dent in mainstream thinking or public discourse.[2]

But the spirit of the times and the talents of one man were coming together. John Kenneth Galbraith, a Harvard economist, was thoroughly familiar with the neoclassical tradition, yet temperamentally resistant to its narrow methodology and uncritical acceptance of the market as the driving force of economic history, and sympathetic both to leftist dissatisfaction with the distribution of wealth and to leftist faith in the ability of government to plan better than uncoordinated individuals. Moreover, Galbraith was ahead of the curve on the postmaterial worldview, believing that the United States placed far too much emphasis on private consumption and far too little emphasis on public needs and on quality of life. In the early 1950s he began to put together a countertheory of the U.S. political economy that was simultaneously an attack on most of the assumptions underlying neoclassical economics, a critique of the way wealth and power were allocated in the new industrial state, and a merciless satire of American beliefs about the good society.

Galbraith has acknowledged Veblen's influence on his own views, and his expository approach is almost uncannily similar to Veblen's in the astringency of his attitude toward neoclassical economics, in the ferocity of his conviction as to the fundamental injustice of American society, in the hilarious savagery of his writing style, and in the indirect and sometimes obscure manner in which he develops his argument over several books.[3] He differs from the founder of institutional economics primarily in having mastered the ideas of economists who wrote after Veblen's death, primarily the theorists of "monopolistic competition," and Keynes.

He rejects "the theology of the market" and, in particular, one of its crucial but rarely discussed components, the assumption of consumer sovereignty.[4] In order for the market to work to create optima in supply, price, and social utility, consumers must have preferences that they act independently to maximize in a rational manner. If producers, however, are able to manipulate them so that they are unable to make independent decisions, then no rational choice is being exercised in the purchase of products, entrepreneurs are producing buyers along with their goods and services, and it is gibberish to speak of suppliers satisfying the needs of customers. Without consumer sovereignty, free markets have no theoretical justification; in fact, they do not exist. Galbraith bores in on this point, stressing the unarguable fact that American business spends billions every year on advertising. "[T]he institutions of modern advertising and salesmanship," he avers, ". . .cannot be reconciled with the notion of independently determined desires, for their central function is to create desires—to bring into being wants that previously did not exist."[5] "We live surrounded by a systematic appeal to a dream world which all mature, scientific reality would reject. We quite literally advertise our commitment to immaturity, mendacity, and profound gullibility. It is the hallmark of the culture."[6] Because industries are able to manage consumer wants, they are not the servants of market forces, the concepts of supply and demand are meaningless, and all neoclassical economics is rubbish.

Domination of the consumer is the basis for control of economic forces as a whole. Being able to manufacture consumer desires, firms are able to anticipate comfortable profits and proceed to plan a business strategy. With a secure source of ample revenue, they need not compete with each other, and so collude in various public and private venues. Not fearing a cost squeeze, they are able to grant generous wage concessions to unions, thus ensuring labor peace, and, incidentally, providing the economy with enough effective demand to keep it macroeconomically healthy. But it is necessary in order to avoid too much interference by government to keep up the pretense that the market, with its legitimating ideological function, rules. Therefore "[s]ince all the relevant groups affirm the importance of free markets in principle, while needing control in practice, the solution has been to impose control in practice while affirming the commitment to free markets in principle."[7] In order to ensure both the public affirmation of untruth and favorable government policies (research funds, lack of enforcement of antitrust laws, and so forth), industries maintain influential relationships with government bureaucracies and (this is not entirely clear—Galbraith is not much of a political scientist) underwrite the "cultivation of useful belief" in neoclassical economics.[8]

All is not well in the republic of economic fantasy, however. There are two fatal flaws in the American system. The first is that the "conventional wisdom," or public philosophy, is entirely focused on private goals. Because of their fabricated concentration on personal consumption, Americans are unable to deal with environmental degradation, urban poverty, sexism, racism, or any other social pathology. In the central passage from his 1958 best seller, *The Affluent Society*, Galbraith galvanized a generation of dissent with a vividly accurate portrait of life in a society with deranged values:

> The family which takes its mauve and cerise, air-conditioned, power-steered, and power-braked automobile out for a tour passes through cities that are badly paved, made hideous by litter, blighted buildings, billboards, and posts for wires that should long since have been put underground. They pass on into a countryside that has been rendered largely invisible by commercial art. . . . They picnic on exquisitely packaged food from a portable icebox by a polluted stream and go on to spend the night at a park which is a menace to public health and morals. Just before dozing off on an air mattress, beneath a nylon tent, amid the stench of decaying refuse, they may reflect vaguely on the curious unevenness of their blessings.[9]

The second difficulty with the American political economy is that only large firms in the "planning system" (automobiles, rubber, oil, soap, processed food, tobacco, and so on) are able to control their markets, cultivate governmental support, and thereby stabilize their environment.[10] These oligopolistic industries comprise about half the economy. The other half is comprised of small, numerous firms in industries (agriculture, construction, the arts, laundries) that are unable to control consumers and without the means to enlist government support. These make up the "market system," and to these the generalizations of neoclassical economics roughly apply. Nevertheless, the fact that the economy is made up of two systems introduces both instabilities and injustices. Inflation is endemic in the economy as a whole, because, since prices never go down in the planning system, their tendency is upward, which exerts overall inflationary pressure. Further, because of price rigidities in the planning system, it is subject to periodic deficiencies of effective demand, which result in recessions.[11] (It appears that there is something to neoclassical economics after all, as well as its Keynesian emendations.)

While it may be the planning system that sneezes, however, it is almost always the market system that catches cold. When the Federal Reserve Board tightens credit to combat inflation, the non-unionized workers in agriculture, construction, and related industries are thrown out of work.[12] Further, workers in the market system must pay the price, in frequent unemployment and wretched treatment by management when they do find a job, for the stability and wealth achieved by the firms and the lucky workers in the planning system. Therefore "the tendency of the economy is to one comparatively affluent, one comparatively impoverished working force. It is a conclusion that the circumstances of life in numerous urban ghettos, migrant camps and rural slums make real."[13]

The solution to the ills of the political economy is something Galbraith labels "The New Socialism," although it more closely resembles a very robust New Dealism.[14] Private property is not to be abolished, either at the personal or corporate level. The federal government is not to nationalize and manage the means of production, except in particular, narrowly defined cases (such as defense firms), because "[p]rivate bureaucracies rule in their own interest. So do public bureaucracies. Why exchange one bureaucracy for another?"[15] Instead, public policy must combine a much more vigorous regulation of the economy with a much more effective redistribution of wealth, the two activities to be informed by the ideal of advancing public needs rather than private profit. In order to achieve this goal, individuals will have to emancipate themselves from the false values that the advertising industry is attempting to inculcate, and they will in turn have to emancipate the state from the power of the planning system.[16]

Within the American thinking classes—not only professional intellectuals, but people who read op-ed articles in newspapers, watch public-policy talk shows on television, and discuss serious subjects at dinner parties—Galbraith's opinions had become, by the late 1950s, the very definition of respectable dissent. After *The Affluent Society*, all his books sold splendidly. He was constantly quoted by journalists, historians, sociologists, and political scientists. Paul Krugman may have been exaggerating when he termed Galbraith "the first celebrity economist" (the title more properly belongs to Veblen, or Henry Carey, or perhaps even Adam Smith), but there is no doubt that Galbraith loomed large in American thought from the 1950s through the 1990s.[17] He made it impossible to discuss private accumulation while ignoring public deficiency, and difficult to celebrate the advance of the "planning" section of the economy unless the "market" section was also doing well. Moreover, by focusing a spotlight on manipulation of consumers through advertising, he made it imperative that all further commentators on the economic scene at least consider the possibility that market forces were an illusion. Even those who execrated his ideas were forced to acknowledge them.

Galbraith has been treated well, however, neither by other professional economists nor by history. Neoclassicals noted the overall lack of specifics in Galbraith's indictment of the economy and pronounced themselves dissatisfied. How much spending on "private wants" was too much? How much more should the country spend on "public needs"? In the early 1970s George Stigler noted that "the non-defense budget of our nation-state and local, as well as federal government, has been growing at the rate of 10 percent per year since 1960."[18] Did this turnabout in public budgeting since the publication of *The Affluent Society* refute Galbraith's thesis? Was it possible that the United States was now spending the correct amount on public needs? How could we tell?

Moreover, economists during the 1960s and later were not impressed with Galbraith's description of the American economy as one dominated by large firms that had achieved immunity to market forces. Nothing in Galbraith's description of the new industrial state, Krugman observed in 1994, "was remotely on target. . . . The role of giant corporations in the U.S. economy has been shrinking, not rising. . . . Many of our biggest companies—from Sears to IBM—have been spectacularly unable to get consumers to buy their wares. . . . And nobody, least of all the auto companies, has been insulated from the market."[19]

In historical perspective, it seems possible that Galbraith's description of the American political economy of the 1950s and early 1960s did capture a transient reality. At the end of World War II the United States had no true competitors in economic might because the other industrial societies lay in ruins. In this artificial postwar world economy, it was possible for the American industries that lent themselves to oligopoly to administer prices without fear of consumers going to other producers. By the time *The New Industrial State* appeared in 1967, however, Germany and Japan were already becoming formidable competitors to the United States in a variety of sectors. "The planning system" had no reality in an arena of world competition, as a number of formerly dominant American industries have learned to their sorrow. Galbraith himself admitted as much, in the introduction to the fourth edition of the book in 1985: "I did not see the development of the foreign, most notably the Japanese, competition to which [the corporation] would be subject.... No one can doubt that in our older industries this competition has substantially impaired the certainty and effectiveness of the planning process."[20]

Galbraith's son, James Galbraith, has suggested that it might be the unstable globalized phase of the planning system that is transient, and that the future may see a reestablishment of market control on a multinational level.[21] If such an occurrence does come about, then John Kenneth Galbraith would certainly be remembered as a sage.

Before corporations established, or reestablished, an administered market on a global level, however, they would have to address the problem of consumer sovereignty. Neoclassical economists have never conceded that Galbraith's description of the new industrial state was ever even temporarily accurate, because they have never conceded that any corporation in any era has been able to manipulate consumers with advertising. Neoclassicals find Galbraith's assertions on this subject to be not only empirically falsified by everyday experience but symptomatic of a dangerous arrogance that permeates his work. Milton and Rose Friedman summed up the attitude of many when they wrote in 1979,

> What about the claim that consumers can be led by the nose by advertising? Our answer is that they can't—as numerous expensive advertising fiascos testify. One of the greatest duds of all time was the Edsel automobile, introduced by Ford Motor Company [in 1958] and promoted by a major advertising campaign [$250 million]. More basically, advertising is a cost of doing business, and the businessman wants to get the most for his money. Is it not more sensible to try to appeal to the real wants or desires of consumers than to try to manufacture artificial wants or desires? ... The real objection of most critics of advertising is not that advertising manipulates tastes but that the public at large has meretricious tastes—that is, tastes that do not agree with the critics'.[22]

The argument over consumer sovereignty is a profound one, perhaps the most important in economic controversy. For how is it possible to evaluate an economic system unless one can decide if it is producing enough of the right kind of goods and services and if they are being equitably distributed? And what are the right kind of goods and services, and how do we know? Neoclassical economists attempt to finesse these questions by assuming that consumers always choose what to buy according to their authentic, actual needs. This axiom, leftist dissenters point out, is entirely arbitrary—how do the neoclassicals know that people understand what is good for them? To this objection, the neoclassicals retort (in academic language, of course), "How do you know it isn't?"

The other great progressive dissenter of the postwar period was sociologist C. Wright Mills. Unquestionably a radical by temperament, Mills was almost as suspicious of leftist traditions of thought as he was of corporate capitalism. "The major developments of our time," he wrote in *The Sociological Imagination* in 1959, "can be understood neither in terms of the liberal [pluralist] nor the marxian interpretation of politics and culture. These ways of thought arose as guidelines to reflection about types of society that do not now exist. . . . Now we confront new kinds of social structure which, in terms of 'modern' ideals, resist analysis in the liberal and in the socialist terms we have inherited."[23]

Mills was respectful of some of Marx's insights, especially his early writings on alienation. Mills's 1951 book *White Collar* was an attempt to update the young Marx's concept of alienated labor and apply it to the new middle classes.[24] However, the work that established him as a major theorist among mainstream scholars was his attempt to portray the rulers in the United States in non-Marxist terms in his 1956 blockbuster *The Power Elite*.

In this landmark book, Mills tells us that "the American system" is one of "organized irresponsibility"—that is, it is irrational and immoral.[25] It functions not for the benefit of the citizens at large but for the aggrandizement of the holders of power, who constitute "an intricate series of overlapping circles."[26] And the members of this power elite (he uses the word "class," and even the phrase "upper class," but sparingly) are identifiable. They are the corporate rich and their subsidiary partners, the heads of institutional power in the media, the military, and the political structure. The members of the elite do not leave governance to chance, but actively organize to support their own prerogatives:

> The top corporations are not a set of splendidly isolated giants. They have been knit together by explicit associations, within their respective industries and regions and in supra-associations such as the NAM [National Association of Manufacturers]. These associations organize a unity among the managerial elite and other members of the corporate rich. They translate narrow economic powers into industry-wide and class-wide powers; and they use these powers, first, on the economic front, for example with reference to labor and its organizations; and, second, on the political front, for example in their large role in the political sphere.[27]

The method the rich in general and corporations in particular use to ensure their control over politicians is, of course, the systematic application of campaign contributions.[28] Meanwhile, they use their command over the media and educational institutions to manipulate the masses, distract them with celebrities, and, in general, instill a false consciousness that is favorable to their own interests.[29]

While his power elite sounds very much like a Marxist ruling class, Mills does not feel the compulsion of a Marxist to predict that its inherent contradictions will bring about the inevitable downfall of this system of unjust domination. His is the more traditionally American concern with legitimacy. "In economic and political institutions the corporate rich now wield enormous power, but they have never had to win the moral consent of those over whom they hold this power."[30] Although his analysis and his values have a Marxist tinge, therefore, his conclusion is more like Veblen's. He wants to help individual people (and particularly students) "turn personal troubles and concerns into social issues," and help the country "combat all those forces which are destroying genuine publics and creating a mass society."[31] He is, or aspires to be, a reformer rather than a prophet.

But if Mills made it clear that he was not a Marxist, he never cleared up the ambiguity about what he was. Whereas Marxists are unequivocal about where their ruling class comes from and where it is going, Mills is confusing on both subjects. Pluralist critics excoriated Mill's book for asserting that the power elite makes "the big decisions" without ever proving it, that is, without examining those decisions and demonstrating that his elite made decisions against opposition. In Robert Dahl's words, "I do not see how anyone can suppose that he has established the dominance of a specific group in a community or a nation without basing his analysis on the careful examination of a series of concrete decisions."[32] Meanwhile, Marxists were chiding Mills for not having the courage to follow his own analysis to its unarguable end. "It is not easy to criticize *The Power Elite* from a theoretical standpoint for the simple reason that the author often states or implies more than one theory on a given topic or range of topics," wrote Paul Sweezy. "[H]is work is strongly influenced by a straightforward class theory which, if he had stuck to it and consistently explored its implications, would have enabled him to avoid completely the superficialities and pitfalls of elitist thinking."[33]

Mills's blend of angry rejection of the legitimacy of the conventional wisdom, adroit use of masses of statistical evidence, vivid writing style, and theoretical ambiguity made him hugely influential from the 1950s into the 1970s. His impact on the New Left of the late 1960s was profound. Like Mills, New Leftists never developed a coherent critique of modern American society, but combined sensitivity to the alienating effects of capitalism with even greater sensitivity to the irresponsible power of those who seemed to run both the corporate economy and the polity. Among sociologists, Mills's aggressive use of elitist theory found many imitators, among students of American and other societies.[34] Even today, half a century later, it is almost obligatory that introductory textbooks in American government contain a discussion of "elite theories" of the polity.[35] The authors of some texts adopt an "elite theory" perspective, interpreting everything important that happens in the United States as the result of bargaining among elites or domination by one elite.[36] Coherent or not, accurate or not, Mills's dissension worked its way into the fabric of mainstream thought.

DISSENSION ON THE RIGHT: RENAISSANCE OF THE MARKET

By the end of World War II the market as an abstraction and as a functioning mechanism was suffering from a great deflation of esteem. Among the general thinking public, capitalism's apparent failure during the Depression, and prosperity's revival during the war-induced extension of state economic controls, had solidified the impression that market forces had to be tamed, coordinated, suppressed, redirected, enhanced, and governed. Among professional economists, theoretical advances in a number of areas had buttressed claims that markets must not be trusted to achieve the general good. There was, preeminently, the triumph of Keynesianism. In addition, economic theorists had identified a number of areas of actual or potential "market failure" that could prevent free exchanges from advancing the public weal. (Galbraith's characterization of the other members of his discipline as remaining stuck in admiration for the classical notion of the free market was quite misleading.) Economists had believed for many decades that monopolies were generally a bad thing. Now they identified broad areas of "externalities," in which economic activity conferred (usually) costs or (sometimes) benefits on outsiders. The only way payment for such disconnected activities could be rendered rationally seemed to be to resort to an overarching authority. Moreover, theorists began to model "collective goods problems," which prevented aggregates of individuals from realizing their goals (national defense, for example), because it was in nobody's interest to pay for such things voluntarily. Coming out of the war, it was a largely unspoken consensus within the discipline that market failures both necessitated and justified government intervention. And since such failures appeared to be pervasive, governmental direction of economic activity seemed almost always to be appropriate.[37]

Yet even as the progovernment, antimarket consensus built, the reaction was aborning. The first post-Keynesian defense of the market came from Austria, where economists had somehow managed over the preceding decades to adopt neoclassical ideas without embracing neoclassical methodologies. To the Austrians, of whom Ludwig von Mises and Friedrich Hayek were the leading examples, market forces did not need to be elaborated graphically or mathematically; their quest was to demonstrate the superiority of market to government activity in words.

The Austrians' argument, which commenced in the late 1930s shortly after Mises and Hayek moved to the United States, proceeded by simultaneously elaborating the wonders of the market and attacking the competence of government. The leftists assume, they argued, that the future can be known, but this is a grand conceit refuted by all human experience. As Mises put it, "The outstanding fact of history is that it is a succession of events that nobody anticipated before they occurred."[38] Because they cannot foretell the future, government bureaucracies are unable to use modern society's greatest resource, information, for they are so paralyzed by rules, procedures, and risk aversion that by the time they have overcome their own red tape, the knowledge they possess is out of date. On the other hand, decentralized market structures manned by risk-taking entrepreneurs and subject to competition are ideally suited to make quick and efficient use of information. Only markets, therefore, permit society to progress.[39]

Just as important, only free markets can protect freedom. The greatest illusion of the Left is that markets suppress individual liberty, while governments replace coercion with freedom of choice. The opposite is true. As Hayek expressed his theme,

> Economic activity provides the material means for all our ends. At the same time, most of our individual efforts are directed to providing means for the ends of others in order that they, in turn, may provide us with the means for our ends. It is only because we are free in the choice of our means that we are also free in the choice of our ends. Economic freedom is thus an indispensable condition of all other freedom, and free enterprise is both a necessary condition and a consequence of personal freedom.[40]

As a consequence, the headlong rush toward government planning and regulation is a transit into socialism, and "socialism means slavery."[41] The title of Hayek's most famous book, 1944's *The Road to Serfdom*, well captures the prophet-like tone of the Austrians' argument.

The Austrians had little impact either on the American thinking public or on the profession of economics as a whole for many years. They did, however, catch the eye of the few American economists who were not only dissatisfied with, but horrified by, the wholesale endorsement of government interference with market forces by the postwar professional mainstream. Of those, the earliest to adopt a sharply dissenting position, the most creative in his theoretical contributions to the discipline, and the one who ultimately came to be identified in the public mind as the chief gadfly of the Age of Keynes was Milton Friedman.

As a young scholar in 1946, Friedman coauthored with George Stigler, his friend and future colleague at the University of Chicago, a pamphlet attacking postwar rent control. The two argued that government controls, on the one hand, only created shortages and black markets. On the other hand, if rents were allowed to rise, the price mechanism would provide incentives for private builders to construct plenty of housing and the shortage would be eliminated. From the vantage point of the twenty-first century, this statement seems so simple and basic as to be almost self-evident. In the 1940s, however, it created indignation within the economics profession. Paul Samuelson later reported that the pamphlet "actually outraged the profession-that shows you where we were in our mentality in the immediate postwar period."[42]

This sort of professional reaction to arguments Friedman considered basic truth both reinforced his own free market ideology and turned him toward writing for a wider audience. After his appointment at Chicago in 1948, he produced not only a body of theoretical and empirical scholarship that established him as a superstar among economists but, increasingly, a wide assortment of popular publications intended to reacquaint the public with the virtues of the free market. He made a considerable impact with *Capitalism and Freedom* in 1962 and, with his wife, Rose, as coauthor, *Free to Choose* in 1979.[43] In the late 1960s he became a regular columnist for *Newsweek*, alternating with Paul Samuelson. These dueling columns provided public access to the opinions of the best the profession had to offer and contributed considerably to the graduate education of thinking Americans.[44]

Like the Austrians, Friedman always places a defense of the market as a moral imperative first and foremost in his popular writing. But he goes beyond Austrian generalities into detailed refutations of common criticisms of capitalist enterprise. Does the market create inequality? "Nothing could be further from the truth. Wherever the free market has been permitted to operate, wherever anything approaching equality of opportunity has existed, the ordinary man has been able to attain levels of living never dreamed of before."[45] Does capitalism discriminate on the basis of race, sex, religion, and so on? Absolutely not, because "there is an economic incentive in a free market to separate economic efficiency from other characteristics of the individual . . . the preserves of discrimination in any society are the areas that are most monopolistic in character, whereas discrimination against groups of particular color or religion is least in those areas where there is the greatest freedom of competition."[46] In the absence of government protections, will competition force businesses to sell shoddy or dangerous products or both? Not so, because "on the whole, market competition . . . protects the consumer better than do the alternative government mechanisms that have been increasingly superimposed on the market . . . a private firm that makes a serious blunder may go out of business. A government agency is likely to get a bigger budget."[47]

Not fearing to be thought old-fashioned, Friedman was quite willing to proclaim explicitly that Adam Smith had been right: the invisible hand operates to the benefit of society, and laissez-faire is the means to both justice and prosperity.[48] Without stopping there, he commiserates that Smith could not foresee the invention of the concept of market failure and its employment as a scythe to slash the props from under his structure of thought. Friedman charges that the modern critics of Smith's scheme, however, are disingenuous. While applying the notion of failure to the process of free exchange, they neglect to apply it to the activities of government itself. They seek to enforce a double standard, examining the imperfections of markets while assuming the competence of the state.[49] This is both a theoretical and a political failing, for it misleads economists as well as the attentive public.

Deducing policy prescriptions from his ideology, Friedman recommends that the state abandon a host of programs. Governments are to abolish occupational licensure (people would no longer need an M.D. degree to practice medicine), repeal minimum wage laws, eliminate farm price supports, pursue absolutely free trade, sell the national parks to private business, and so forth.[50] Further, he comes up with some creative proposals for solving social problems using the power of government, not to command and control, but to structure incentives so that market forces can be brought to bear. He invented the idea of school vouchers to replace the state educational bureaucracy, for example.[51]

While Friedman's celebrity as a public intellectual mainly rested on his defense of the market and criticism of government action, his fame among economists was based on his theoretical expansion of one of the facets of pre-Keynes neoclassical orthodoxy: monetarism. The pre-Keynesians believed that an appropriate amount of money in any economy would sponsor healthy growth while avoiding both inflation and recession (although they were more concerned about the former). Friedman elaborates this basic position into a single cause that explains everything. Too much money causes inflation; not enough money causes recession. When Keynes identified lack of effective demand as the problem that created deflation, he mistook the effect for the cause. The Great Depression was not the result of a lack of purchasing power; lack of purchasing power was the consequence of the Federal Reserve Board's high interest rates. Capitalism did not fail in the 1930s. It was strangled by government.[52]

The way to ensure steady prosperity without inflation is for the government to expand the national money supply by no less than 3 percent and no more than 5 percent annually. Among other things, this would mandate the end of Keynesian fiscal tinkering in general and the Phillips curve in particular, plus the rendering of deficit spending nearly impossible through the process of constitutional amendment. Both the federal and state governments would be required to spend no more than they collected in taxes, and taxation itself would be limited by constitutional boundaries. Both the federal and state governments would be forced, under most conditions, to balance their budgets annually.[53]

Friedman predicted, in 1968, that Keynesian attempts to trade off unemployment and inflation would lead to a condition of rising unemployment plus inflation—a condition Paul Samuelson dubbed "stagflation." When stagflation came about in the 1970s, Friedman's correct prognostication greatly enhanced his prestige within the profession.[54]

But Friedman has had his failures as well as his triumphs. His monetarist analysis of historical events has been sharply criticized for leaning on an unstable —that is, conveniently malleable—definition of "money."[55] Additionally, some historians have faulted his analysis of the causes of the Depression.[56] The adoption of monetarist policies by the Fed in the late 1960s and early 1970s, then again from 1979 to 1982, did not have the wholesome results he predicted. Instead, monetary restriction seemed to cause recessions rather than stable prosperity. Friedman and his disciples argued that the monetary medicine had not worked because it had not been tried long enough, but they failed to convince either most of the profession or much of the public, and the attempts were abandoned.[57] Furthermore, some of the important predictions of Friedman's kindred spirits in economics, such as Stigler, were refuted by empirical research during the 1950s, 1960s, and 1970s.[58]

Friedman and the other free market and monetarist economists had thus succeeded by 1974 in severely weakening the Keynesian paradigm, but had not managed to push through a counterrevolution. As a result, there was no more economic orthodoxy; all was contested terrain.

Friedman was not only the leader of free market, antigovernment economists in the postwar period, but also the model for thinkers in other disciplines who were attempting to revive and update conservatism. In *Anarchy, State, and Utopia* (1974), for example, philosopher Robert Nozick imagined, in effect, what political theory Locke would have fashioned if he had employed modern "Friedmanesque" concepts when considering the state of nature.[59]

Nozick's own account of the state of nature is odd and unsatisfying. Locke told us that God has given humankind three great natural rights—life, liberty, and property-which, because they are prior to the formation of civil society, must be the touchstones against which the moral rightness of governmental action is evaluated. In contrast, Nozick never lists the rights in his secular natural state or explains how humans came to acquire them, only asserting rather lamely at one point that "we have assumed that generally people will do what they are morally required to do."[60] Instead, he contents himself with conjecturing that from a state of anarchy, a "dominant protective agency" would arise through the exchange agreements between people attempting to shield their rights from the encroachments of others. While he never quite makes the point clearly, he concludes that the rights that would be protected are those involving physical safety, especially freedom from fear, although property rights seem to be included in the notion of safety. This protective agency is a minimalist state.[61] By assumption, this state is legitimate because it is the result of the "the invisible hand" operating through voluntary exchange by free people protecting their rights.[62]

Two considerations are important here. The first is that Nozick, unlike Smith, has no way to evaluate and therefore justify the product of the invisible hand. For Smith, the free market was superior to other economic forms because it was more efficient, that is, it produced more wealth for less social input. In contrast, Nozick has no measure of "rights efficiency" and therefore must simply assume that the people in the state of nature will make choices that result in their best interests, even though the final result is not the product of their conscious intention.

The second is that Nozick has no political theory per se; that is, he has no notion of what sort of institutions might be necessary to realize his theory of legitimacy. He has no such theory because, without actually rejecting Locke's argument that legitimacy is generated by the citizens participating in free elections, he ignores it. He does not consider what institutions might be necessary to formalize the voluntary exchanges that created the state. His attention is focused on determining what a state might legitimately do, not in deciding how that state might be constructed.

The final product of Nozick's assumptions, reasoning, and omissions is that while the minimalist state can be morally justified, anything more would be illegitimate. In particular, the redistributionist state (in other words, the New Deal plus the Great Society) is without moral foundation. Such a state rests upon the belief that civil society is a moral entity greater than the sum of its parts and that its governing body can therefore impose involuntary costs on some people in order to transfer part of their property to others, because such action is good for the public interest even if it is bad for the individuals who were coerced. But, Nozick contends, "no new rights 'emerge' at the group level"—there is no such thing as a sum greater than its parts.[63] Therefore all efforts at redistribution have no moral justification. In particular, "[t]axation of earnings from labor is on a par with forced labor," and consequently contradicts the root purpose for creating states in the first place.[64] Nozick's grand conclusion is that the minimalist state is utopia, and the grand implication must be that all the experiments of governmental activism of the twentieth century, all the dreams of progressives for equalization of wealth and power, and all the arguments in favor of legal rights against discrimination or for welfare are morally bogus.[65]

Although *Anarchy, State, and Utopia* caused a sensation when it was published, winning the 1975 National Book Award, and although it continues to be the inspiration for new generations of conservative thinkers, it has been surprisingly sterile in terms of generating a tradition of its own. Whereas Rawls's *A Theory of Justice* has been the inspiration for whole schools of leftist legal theorists and philosophers, Nozick's book stands as a unique prominence on the right, revered but unimitated. This lack of a Nozick school is probably caused by the methodological direction of modern social thought. Modern neoclassical academic conservatism has been strongly influenced by the mathematics of neoclassical economics. Conservative theorists now are nothing if they cannot prove a theorem. Because *Anarchy, State, and Utopia* consists entirely of words, it is out of methodological step with its own tradition. Contemporary conservatives therefore regularly cite and regularly praise Nozick, but turn away from him when looking for their own research projects.

The conservative renaissance that began in the 1950s did not, of course, consist entirely of scholarship. There was also a handful of journalists, of whom the most talented, and, ultimately, the most influential, was William F. Buckley Jr. In 1955 he founded *National Review*, a popular magazine devoted to excoriating liberal economic, social, and foreign policy; critiquing liberal assumptions; and articulating a conservative countervision of the good society. A person of remarkable energy, he also produced a corpus of polemical books and ideologically tinged secret-agent novels, and hosted a political talk show on public television. He and his publications became a rallying point for conservatives everywhere, and went from lonely voices during the 1950s to semiofficial spokesmen for the dominant ideology of the 1980s.

Like the Austrians and Friedman, Buckley's first assumption is the moral superiority of the free market over the governmental direction of society. As a polemicist rather than a scholar, however, he is much less restrained in his fervor. To Buckley, liberalism (in my usage, progressivism) is merely one of the masks worn by socialism, and socialism is merely one of the masks worn by communism. His job is to unmask the liberal surface to reveal the demonic face beneath. His writing style is a good deal more lively than that of the scholars; in fact, it is remarkably like Galbraith's in its merciless wit and fondness for compound sentences and allusive argument. Because of their pyramid of allusions, it is often impossible to summarize Buckley's jousts by compact quotation; one would have to reproduce many pages. In particular, it would be difficult to capture the overall impression left by his writing that, once one cuts through the euphemisms, red herrings, and irrelevancies, liberals are at heart just Communists, or at least fellow travelers. A small and merely suggestive sample of his style and substance from *Up from Liberalism* (1959) will have to suffice:

> The salient economic assumptions of liberalism are socialist. . . . The liberal sees no moral problem whatever in divesting the people of that portion of their property necessary to finance the projects certified by ideology as beneficial to the Whole. . . . The call by liberalism to conformity with its economic dispensations does not grow out of the economic requirements of modern life; but rather out of the liberal's total appetite for power . . . economically speaking, the people are merely gatherers of money which it is the right and duty of a central intelligence to distribute.[66]

Buckley's equation, that liberalism equals socialism equals communism, was part of a growing tendency in conservative discourse. Questioning the motives of one's ideological adversaries had a long tradition in America. Jefferson and Hamilton questioned each other's motives, as did Jackson and Clay, Lincoln and Douglas, Bryan and McKinley, Franklin Roosevelt and Hoover, and so on. There was even some precedent for intimating that one's adversary was secretly a partisan of a foreign power, as with Hamilton's alleged fondness for England and Jefferson's alleged allegiance to France. But in the late 1940s and 1950s conservatives launched an unprecedented campaign of innuendo that liberals were consciously disloyal to the United States and that they were secretly agents of the Soviet Union's foreign policy. In politics, Joseph McCarthy and Richard Nixon were the most noteworthy politicians to employ this rhetorical strategy. But Buckley, in his own more intelligent, less crude, finely indirect, and entertaining manner, insinuated the same message. If progressives want to deprive people of their liberty through collectivization, and Communists want to deprive people of their liberty through collectivization, what, in the end, is the difference? Buckley, therefore, for all his charm, contributed to the ongoing debasement of American political debate, a decline that culminated in the radio broadcasts of Rush Limbaugh a generation later.

DISSENSION ON THE LEFT, II:
MARX COMES TO AMERICA

The later Marx produced a prophecy with scientific pretensions. On average, the value of all commodities is a function of the amount of labor-time that they embody. By forcing workers to labor long past the number of hours that would equal the value they produce—by coercing surplus labor—capitalists create surplus value, or profit. But competition is always forcing capitalists to reduce the price of their products, which crimps their profit, which drives them to attempt to extract more surplus value as a compensation—that is, either to work their employees longer hours or pay them less. Technology helps somewhat in alleviating the problem, but because all capitalists sooner or later adopt labor-saving devices, the profit squeeze can only be ameliorated, not eliminated.

As capitalists are driven to exploit and cheat workers with ever-greater ingenuity and heartlessness, the working class as a whole slides into more intense misery. Its members do not revolt, however, because the ruling class has used its control of the ideology-creation apparatus—newspapers, pulpits, and so forth—to confuse and miseducate the working class into quiescence in the face of oppression. Nevertheless, some intellectuals and workers are not fooled by the pro-capitalist propaganda and work quietly as members of the Communist Party to bring others to awareness of the true nature of society.

At some point, there comes a crisis. Industry as a whole cannot function on a vanishing base of profit. There is a crash, a depression, the failure of many businesses, and then an industrial reorganization that replaces the smaller and weaker firms with larger, stronger corporations. The casualties of the crash, the failed entrepreneurs, fall into the proletariat. The new economy, dominated by larger firms controlled by fewer capitalists overseeing a more exploited working class, begins the cycle again. After several such upheavals, however, there are so few capitalists and so many abused proletarians that the ruling class loses control of society. The workers, led by the Communist Party, cast off their false consciousness, overthrow the tiny ruling class, and establish socialism, in which all people receive just compensation for their labors.[67]

Marxism was of no importance in the United States until the 1930s. During that decade, however, the evident collapse of capitalism seemed, to some, to fulfill the prophecy. Profits had vanished, and proletarianization was replacing traditional American upward mobility. Although the Communist Party was never a significant electoral force in the United States, during the Depression it did command the allegiance of a small percentage of workers and a somewhat larger percentage of intellectuals. There was no need for the intellectuals to do anything but follow the party line, for it seemed to be on the verge of triumph. During the Depression they therefore lent their talents to propaganda rather than independent thinking.

The trend of history beginning in the late 1930s, however, was devastating to Marxism. Such events as the Moscow purge trials, the Spanish civil war, and the nonaggression pact between the Soviet Union and Hitler's Germany, by exposing the murderous cynicism of the Communist state, created mass disillusionment among intellectuals.[68] After World War II the Depression turned into a series of economic booms, which seemed to discredit Marx as a genius who had foreseen the future. The anti-Communist investigations of the 1940s and 1950s in the United States, for all their excesses, succeeded in exposing the extent to which Marxist agents and sympathizers had attempted to capture some institutions—primarily the labor unions—and turn them into tools of Soviet foreign policy.[69] A wave of revulsion and fear swept the country in the late 1940s and 1950s, and "soft on communism" became an epithet of violent force. By the mid-1950s the number of practicing Marxists in the United States was vanishingly small.

But Marxism was not quite extinct. Through the 1950s and 1960s, a small number of Marxist intellectuals kept alive the spirit, if not the exact teachings, of the prophet. This was a task that required creative ingenuity. Profits were not vanishing. The masses were not sliding into misery. Revolutionary consciousness was not growing. The United States, the preeminent capitalist society, seemed to be among the freest, happiest, and most satisfied societies in history, not to mention the most powerful. It fell to Marxist intellectuals to explain why Marx, despite the superficial evidence to the contrary, had not been wrong about the direction of history, and why the United States was actually humming with injustice and on the verge of an economic catastrophe.

As with other intellectual traditions, Marxism contains schools, eccentrics, visionary crackpots, and definitional quibblers. Marxists disagree among themselves as much as neoclassical economists, or pluralists, or Christians. Nevertheless, it is possible to identify broad tendencies that are shared by most practitioners.

Marxists during this era generally followed one of, or a combination of, three strategies. In the first, they entered a state of intellectual denial, insisting that misery and decline were everywhere around them if only the evidence was interpreted correctly. "Capitalism had indeed raised the standard of living," wrote Michael Harrington in *The Twilight of Capitalism* in 1976, "but it had also enormously increased the requirements of living. People were eating better, living longer, but they had new needs, real or manipulated, and continued to exist on the very same margin even if at a higher level of consumption."[70] How dare those capitalists! They've learned how to exploit people by making their lives better and offering them new products! The nerve!

In the second strategy Marxists argued that the apparent failure of the historical predictions was an illusion because the drama was being played out on a larger stage, which naturally mandated more time to reach the climax. Capitalists had evolved new stratagems to postpone the inevitable, but the postponement was only temporary. The most popular variant of this argument was that the immiseration of the workers had been projected out into the undeveloped societies of the world. By learning how to proletarianize the people outside the industrial societies, capitalists had, in effect, turned everyone within the rich societies—even the poor—into real or de facto members of the ruling class. "When reviewed within the framework of the world marketplace," wrote William Appleman Williams in *The Great Evasion* in 1964, "the evidence concerning misery and proletarianization irrefutably supports Marx. The colonial or otherwise dependent segment of the capitalist marketplace continues to grow poorer while the Metropolitan sector increases in wealth. Between 1938 and 1958, the share of world income that went to the poor countries dropped from 9 to 6 percent. The United States increased its share by about 6 percent."[71] (The present book is not the place to get into a detailed evaluation of the evidence about economic advancement in industrialized and nonindustrialized countries. It is sufficient at the moment to point out that Williams's own figures do not support his contention. The rate at which a country or group of countries are gaining or losing percentages of the total world income tells us nothing about whether they are getting richer or poorer. If the pie is growing, a smaller slice may nonetheless constitute a larger overall portion of nourishment.) And so, as Paul Baran and Paul Sweezy wrote in 1966, "the class struggle in our time has been thoroughly internationalized."[72] In other words, Marxists implicitly conceded that the prophecy had failed in the societies for which it was intended, while they explicitly insisted that the failure was irrelevant, because a larger truth had superseded Marx's original insight.

In the third and most important strategy for dealing with the failure of prophecy, Marxists argued that the details of Marx's theory, and its application or irrelevance to empirical reality, did not matter. The heart of Marxism did not consist of compiling statistics about income shares, unemployment, monopoly, and the like, but in one empirical assumption and two moral axioms.

The empirical assumption was that the United States, like all capitalist countries, was run by a ruling class, variously described as being the rich, the owners of businesses, the owners of corporations, the owners plus the managers of corporations, or the owners and managers of corporations plus the various people who defend and service them at a high level, such as military generals.

The first moral axiom was that capitalism is inherently an irrational and unjust system. Thomas Weiskopf's 1978 statement that "the capitalist process of economic growth is characterized by a pervasive irrationality that seriously limits its ability to meet real human needs" nicely summarizes the thread that runs through all Marxist evaluation from the 1840s to the twenty-first century.[73]

Two of the major tasks of Marxist scholarship, therefore, were to identify and explain the irrationalities and injustices of capitalism, and identify the ways the members of the ruling class perpetuated their domination. If capitalist arrangements ever worked out for the general good, it was an unusual accident. If economic and social decisions ever benefited the noncorporate nonrich, it was the residuum of actions whose primary purpose was corporate benefit.

The second moral axiom was that while capitalist democracy was a sham, true democracy could be achieved through the installation of socialism. The first part of this axiom was (and is) the major area of agreement between various strands of the Left. It had been a well-established complaint of the non-Marxist Left for a century. Marxists simply reiterated the classic causal analysis of power in capitalist society. As Baran and Sweezy encapsulated it, "Votes are the nominal source of political power, and money is the real source: the system, in other words, is democratic in form and plutocratic in content.... And since in monopoly capitalism the big corporations are the source of big money, they are also the source of political power."[74]

Elaborating the second half of the moral axiom, however, forced Marxists to engage in an enterprise they have been generally reluctant to undertake: discussing the future. Marx himself devoted the overwhelming majority of his words to analyzing the system he despised and was notoriously reticent about what might happen after the working class had overthrown its oppressors and instituted the dictatorship of the proletariat, except to assure us that it would certainly be glorious. The record of Communist parties that had achieved power had not been reassuring to American audiences, and Marxists in the United States generally took some pains to insist that they, unlike the Leninists who had perverted the cause elsewhere, were committed democrats. American Marxists usually avoided attempts to characterize the functioning of a socialist democracy, but every now and then succumbed to the temptation to speculate.

When American Marxists did give in to entreaties to tell us what the country would look like after the revolution, they validated their initial reluctance, for their writing underwent a marked change. Normally affecting a style of hardheaded realism, when discussing the future socialist democracy they were overcome with romantic gush. All agreed, as Williams puts it, that

> the conception of meaningful or productive work would be very much different under socialism. . . . Work as the production of material goods for sustenance and convenience would occupy a marginal place in a socialist society. . . .
>
> Work would become transformed into any act which manifested the individual's or the group's urge and need to express its creative powers, and to extend and strengthen its relationships with nature and with other human beings.[75]

And what about government? That, too, would be transformed. As Gar Alperovitz assured us in 1974, " 'Planning' is obviously required here . . . but . . . the process of central 'planning' would be quite different from that of the rationalized state or the Soviet 'command economy.' It would be developed through local processes in each community, and then 'integrated' subsequently through regional and national politics generated out of local experience."[76]

In general, Marxists were not important to the intellectual life of the nation during the period 1932 to 1974. They achieved a certain prestige in the 1930s before the great disillusionment and influenced, and were influenced by, the New Left of the 1960s, but by and large were relegated to the margins of national life. However, by becoming employed in universities during this period, they were able to establish a base from which to contribute to American intellectual discourse. As progressives became more dissatisfied with the direction of politics and economics through the 1970s and beyond, Marxist ideas waxed influential. From a small beginning in the academy during the post–World War II period, they were able to have a significant impact on progressivism by the end of the century.

By 1974, dissent had entered the mainstream of American public discourse. Media representatives regularly sought John Kenneth Galbraith's views on economic policy. Milton Friedman alternated with Paul Samuelson in writing a column for *Newsweek*. Marxists were being hired by social science and humanities departments at most universities. The New Left was gone, but had imprinted itself on the values of a generation. There was a public philosophy of sorts, consisting of Keynesian economics and the attempt to fit every relevant group into the policy-making process, but it was the target of criticism from every side. Moreover, the American political economy was just beginning to experience a series of historical challenges. In other words, things would only get more interesting.

CHAPTER EIGHT

Democracy and Capitalism, 1974–2001

Things began to go wrong for the United States in late 1973. During the course of a brief war between Israel and its Arab neighbors, Saudi Arabia, the world's largest oil producer, shut down its wells. The consequences were tumult, chaos, unemployment, and inflation in the industrialized world. Under the auspices of the Organization of Petroleum Exporting Countries (OPEC), for six years afterward Saudi Arabia was able to stabilize the world's price of oil at about four times the 1973 price of $3 a barrel. During the Iranian revolution of 1979, there was another oil panic, with prices spiking at about $30 a barrel, causing the Consumer Price Index to rise 13.3 percent that year. The inflation ignited another round of unemployment.[1] With economic distress came political dissatisfaction.

The economy improved slowly after 1982, although the "Roaring Eighties," as some like to characterize the subsequent seven years, is a label more accurately attached to a small section of the population than to Americans as a group. On the one hand, inflation dropped sharply, not again topping 5.4 percent, unemployment fell gradually to just over 5 percent by 1990, and the annual growth in productivity averaged 3.6 percent. On the other hand, enormous federal budget deficits, resulting in a ballooning of the national debt from $994 billion at the end of fiscal 1981 to $4 trillion by the end of fiscal 1992, caused a number of long-term problems, including a rise in the national trade deficit to unprecedented heights. Further, the real wealth of average Americans stagnated while the real wealth of the richest fifth of the population increased rapidly. By 1991, in the midst of another recession, the typical family was enjoying a real income only about 5 percent higher than its 1973 counterpart, and the greater prosperity had been achieved by working longer hours. In other words, real wages were declining.[2]

Economic stagnation in the United States must always be understood in relative terms. Although the country did not boom in the two decades after 1974, it was hardly falling apart. Even its poor were quite comfortable when compared to ordinary people in almost any other country, or to Americans of only two generations earlier. Government welfare programs not only reduced the extent of officially measured poverty from 18 percent in 1960 to 7 percent in the late 1970s, but considerably cushioned the inconvenience of the remaining poverty.[3] By the late 1980s even the homeless, of whom there were several hundred thousand, could count on being given food, towels, blankets, soap, medicine, dental care, emergency hospital care, and shelter by public authorities.[4]

When the economy took off again in the 1990s, therefore, it zoomed not from rags to riches but from just so-so to fabulous. From the depths of the recession of 1991–1992, productivity growth surged forward to 2.8 percent in 1992, and continued strong afterward, hitting 4 percent late in the decade.[5] With the dramatically rising productivity came virtually full employment, unafflicted by inflation. The stock market leaped into the stratosphere, with the Dow Jones average hitting 4,000 in 1995, 6,000 in 1996, 8,000 in 1997, and passing 10,000 in 1999, by which time half of all American households owned stock directly or indirectly through mutual funds, individual retirement accounts (IRAs), or 401(k) plans.[6] By the late 1990s enthusiasts were writing of a "New Economy" that had transcended the business cycle and made recession impossible, that presaged "the second great age of global capitalism,"[7] "a global economic revolution,"[8] "an economy on Viagra, an economy that is rafting on white water, the best economy the world has ever seen."[9] The United States was giddy with riches in the late 1990s.

Curmudgeons and Cassandras warned that America was experiencing, not a liberation from the laws of work and want, but a speculative bubble.[10] There was wisdom in the caution, for the economy went into a recession in March 2001, a pause that was worsened by the fallout from the terrorist attacks of September.

Four aspects of the great bull market economy of the 1990s are important to emphasize. The first was the increasing internationalization of industry and the rising volume of world trade. In the late 1980s, as people began to discern a new sort of world order based on ever-easier international economic flows, observers started to speak of the process of "globalization" that would someday soon render national economies obsolete. The evidence to support use of the word—which quickly became a ubiquitous term—was easy to gather. From the middle to the end of the twentieth century, average tariff levels of the United States and other industrialized countries dropped from about 40 percent to about 6 percent. Stimulated by easier access, world trade increased from $57 billion in 1947 to $6 trillion in the 1990s. The volume of foreign exchange trading (buying and selling national currencies) reached $1.5 trillion *per day* by the late 1990s. By 1990, 40 percent of IBM's employees were not American, and a quarter of all exports from the United States bore the labels of foreign-owned companies. In 1991 Nike created the first worldwide television commercial to tout its athletic shoes. In 1996 the Coca-Cola corporation stopped dividing its markets into "domestic" and "foreign," placing the United States into a "North American" region that was not qualitatively different from any other.[11]

The second significant aspect of the economy of the 1990s was the increasing inequality of both income and wealth. Economists disagree sharply about the extent of the widening gap between the rich and everybody else, and even if there is such a growing disparity. On this topic it is easy for the nonspecialist to become entangled in dueling methodologies and esoteric assumptions. Nevertheless, most analysts agree that while the extent of economic inequality remained relatively stable from the end of World War II to 1970, it enlarged during the subsequent decade, then widened at an accelerated pace in the 1980s and 1990s.[12] While the income and wealth of the richest fifth of the population, and especially the richest 5 percent, shot upward from 1973 to the late 1990s, the income and wealth of the average American family stalled or increased only slightly. According to one estimate, the income of the lowest fifth of wage-earners stagnated and that of the median family grew by only 10 percent, while that of the top 5 percent enlarged by more than a third.[13] According to another, 85 percent of the increase in national wealth during the 1990s went to the top 1 percent of wealth holders, and the remaining 15 percent to the next-wealthiest 9 percent; 90 percent of the population advanced not at all.[14] According to another, the compensation of corporate chief executive officers went from 85 times the earnings of the average blue-collar employee in 1990 to 475 times those earnings in 1999.[15] As a consequence of these increasing disparities, by the middle 1990s the United States had the greatest gap between rich and poor of all the industrialized nations, and the greatest in its history.[16]

This growing inequality was not unrelated to the third important fact about the economy of the 1990s, the decline of the American labor union. Union membership peaked at 32.5 percent of the nonagricultural workforce in 1953, after which it deteriorated steadily. The decay accelerated in the 1980s and 1990s, so that by

2001 unions represented only 13.5 percent of workers. In the years 1996 to 2001 alone, the number of private-sector workers enrolled in unions fell by 252,000. Even adding the membership gains by public-sector unions, it dropped 68,000 during those five years.[17]

The unions' power to defend their members' wages has waned with the union membership. The "union premium," the average superiority of the compensation received by organized workers as opposed to the compensation received by unorganized workers for comparable jobs, is about 30 percent.[18] When union membership decays, income stagnates over most of the economy.[19] The workforce becomes divided in two: a small group of entrepreneurs, professionals, unionized workers, and assorted superstars in sports, entertainment, and science, whose incomes are rising rapidly, and a much larger group of nonunionized workers, mainly in service industries, who are being left behind. The decline of unions is therefore a consequence of other economic trends, but also a cause of growing inequality.

The fourth noteworthy aspect of the American boom of the late 1990s is that it was partly based on fraud. Although these things are hard to measure, the revelations that followed the bankruptcy of the corporate energy giant Enron in late 2001 made it clear that a significant portion of the apparently sterling profits of American business during the boom had been fictions. Corporate executives had collaborated with accounting firms to present imaginary profit figures to an investing public, and thereby jack up stock prices. As the Enron story unfolded, an enraged public demanded government action to more closely regulate business behavior. It appeared that 2001 marked the end of an era in American capitalism.

In politics, American society became noteworthy for a hyperindividualism that was even apparent in its interest groups. During the period 1974 to 2001, interest-group democracy took on a new cast as groups claiming to represent racial, religious, and sexual groupings made increasingly extreme demands for special treatment. Spokespeople for the "politics of difference," as it came to be called, heightened the allegedly unique qualities of members of any given group, denying that a common humanity or common citizenship bound them to others in society. As the logic of difference advanced, it caused people to notice ever-more dissimilarities, persuading groups to subdivide, then shred, then disintegrate, always moving toward the end point of complete social atomization.

The consequence of the politics of difference was most evident in the evolution —or dissolution—of the feminist movement. Beginning in the early 1970s with an emphasis on the differences between men and women, it advanced through ideological schism after schism until there was a valid question as to whether feminism was a movement or a collection of quarreling solipsists. As Anne Phillips summarized the problem in 1995,

> the question of who can best speak for or on behalf of another became a major source of tension, for once men were dislodged from their role of speaking for women, it seemed obvious enough that white women must also be dislodged from their role of speaking for black women, heterosexual women for lesbians, and middle-class women for those in the working class. The search for authenticity . . . then makes it difficult for anyone to represent an experience not identical to her own and, taken to this extreme, renders dialogue virtually impossible.[20]

The problems of unbridgeable differences of political identity were ironically dispiriting in view of the fact that, by the 1990s, American political, economic, and cultural values seemed to be prevailing nearly everywhere. The turn of China toward a market economy during the 1980s and the dissolution of the Soviet Union in 1991 merely culminated long-term historical trends that were making the United States preeminent in its wealth, power, and cultural influence.

The ascendancy of American values was most evident in the complete victory of "democracy" as the standard of legitimacy in all but backwater countries. Various observers pointed out that even dictators pretended to be democrats in order to borrow some legitimacy by association.[21] As Bhikhu Parekh summarized, "liberalism" (by which he meant the political side of liberalism, that is, democracy) had become a "metalanguage, enjoying the privileged status of being both a language like others and the arbiter of how other languages should be spoken."[22] Even more expansively, David Held described democracy as "the only 'grand' or 'meta' narrative that can legitimately frame and delimit the competing 'narratives' of the contemporary age."[23]

But if everyone was a democrat, "democracy" had become a useless indicator for identifying those with a specific set of interests and arguments. Because people and groups still held violently contradictory ideas about how politics and economics were to be structured, however, they still needed ideas and labels to differentiate their conflicting positions. As soon as democracy became a hegemonic value, therefore, everyone acquired an incentive to redefine it so that it would serve their own purposes by excluding their antagonists from the circle of legitimacy. Ideological battles, in all countries but particularly the United States, became struggles over whose set of principles and policies was truly democratic.

The competitive need to redefine democracy was not the only irony of the American metavictory. American citizens themselves seemed to hold contradictory attitudes about the concepts. Herbert McCloskey and John Zaller analyzed a series of public opinion surveys from the late 1950s to the late 1970s, presenting their findings in *The American Ethos* in 1984. They discussed a variety of responses that seemed to show that the public felt sincere ambivalence about the relationship of business and government. Large majorities, for example, endorsed "the free enterprise system," "private ownership of property," and "competition, whether in school, work, or business," yet majorities almost as large supported federal regulation of the drug, oil, food, chemical, and airline industries, as well as utilities, and similar majorities felt that "corporations and people with money" really ran the country and did not pay their fair share of taxes. McCloskey and Zaller concluded that "despite their [capitalism and democracy] central importance in American life, the values of the ethos are often in conflict."[24] Theirs was not the last survey to suggest such an interpretation. In a 2000 *Business Week*/Harris Poll, two-thirds of Americans gave business most of the credit for the prosperity of the 1990s, and opined that corporations were doing well in "making good products and competing in a global economy." On the other hand, 74 percent of the respondents believed that "big companies" had "too much power" in Washington.[25] Ambivalence about the twin pillars of liberalism was not something conjured up out of the imagination of disgruntled intellectuals; it was a mass phenomenon.

Ambivalence toward the American polity was evident in behavior as well as the expression of opinion. The 1960s inaugurated almost four decades of popular disillusionment with the political process that, by 2001, had reached alarming proportions. Alienation from the major institutions, as measured by various public opinion polls, rose steadily after the mid-1960s. For example, according to Gallup, 50 percent of the public professed to have "a great deal of confidence" in the Supreme Court in 1966, and 42 percent labeled themselves similarly happy with Congress. By 1999 the proportions were 20 percent and 9 percent, respectively.[26] Voting turnout drifted downward over the same period. In the 1960 election, slightly more than 60 percent of eligible adults went to the polls on election day. In 2000 barely half of the electorate made it into the voting booth. During the same period, turnout in off-year congressional elections decreased from about 45 percent of adults to only about 33 percent.[27] The voter turnout figures were particularly stark when the United States was compared to other countries that regularly consulted the opinions of their citizens. American turnout was considerably below that of most European democracies; well under Canada's, Japan's, and Israel's; and even worse than that of a Third World democracy such as India.

This sort of attitudinal and behavioral evidence gave much ammunition to those, especially on the left, who argued that there was something fundamentally askew in American politics. If democratic legitimacy rested on the participation of the citizens, but only half of the electorate, at best, were inspired to vote in national elections, what did that say about the legitimacy of the system? Leftists had a ready answer. "The U.S. political system is in deep decay, and ranks among the least democratic of those states holding reasonably regular and reasonably free elections," wrote Cohen and Rogers in 1983.[28] It was a refrain that would swell to a crescendo in the subsequent years.

Although there was much reason to be pleased with the course of American history from 1974 to 2001, therefore, the development of the economy and the polity provided many excuses for discontent. All during this period, the Right and the Left were attempting to frame arguments that would give their side an advantage. Their arguments involved a great deal of creative thinking and plenty of redefinition.

THE RIGHT REDEFINES CAPITALISM

When it comes to economic policy, the American Right has several segments, of which two are the scholars and the politicians. The scholars—neoclassical economists and their allies among the Austrian tradition—elaborate theoretical defenses of the market and theoretical attacks on government regulation. The politicians attempt to achieve or stay in office by serving the interests of capitalists.

Until the late 1970s there was no inconsistency between the intellectual appeals of these two wings. Scholars celebrated the market and denigrated government in academic language; politicians got elected through whatever rhetorical strategy seemed appropriate at the moment. Within the academy the decades after World War II witnessed a spirited argument between the at-first dominant Keynesians, ensconced at the Ivy League universities, the University of California, and Stanford, who recommended government management of the economy and were therefore Democrats, and the at-first discredited orthodox marketeers, dug in at the University of Chicago and George Mason University, who insisted on the accuracy of Adam Smith's original vision of "the principle of spontaneous order," in James Buchanan's words, and were therefore Republicans.[29] Politicians on the right simplified the conflict by trying to demonize Keynes and ridicule all government activity, meanwhile attempting, with the clear consciences common to hypocrites, to secure government largesse for their favored constituencies, such as farmers and the military-industrial complex. The economists and the politicians together deplored the great enlargement in social-service programs—especially those attempting to support the poor—that was one of the legacies of the Democratic administration of the 1960s. While the thinkers thought about these subjects, popularizers in journalism and within the academy itself spread simplified versions of academic doctrines to the general public and the politicians.

The troubles of the 1970s, however, stimulated a portion of the right-wingers within the academy to a rethinking. Without rejecting the touchstone of the market, they began to create additional theories to explain economic growth and discredit government regulation. Milton Friedman continued to decorate the edifice of monetarism—the contention that, while Keynesian fiscal experiments were foolish and counterproductive, government could perform a useful function by regulating (which in practice meant restraining the growth of) the national money supply. Robert Lucas (also at Chicago) became extremely influential by coming up with the theory of "rational expectations"—the argument that businesses, labor unions, and ordinary citizens anticipated and adjusted their behavior to counter the effects of government fiscal policy, thereby rendering that policy futile. Both monetarism and rational expectations theory declined in importance in the late 1980s.

The new theory that ultimately had the most powerful political impact, on the right and on the country as a whole, originated among scholars but swiftly came to dominate right-wing economic thinking among professional politicians, journalists, and the public at large. It was called "supply-side economics."

In the traditional view emerging from Smith's classic, the market is an institution and a process that, so to speak, has a life of its own. People exchange their goods, and the market marvelously raises and lowers prices to coordinate their efforts to the advantage of all. Although Smith also discussed investment, he tended to emphasize the market as a mechanism that ran, more or less, by itself. In like manner, the economic discourse that Smith founded tended to de-emphasize the study of investment, and therefore the behavior of entrepreneurs. As Joseph Schumpeter, the only major economist prior to the 1970s to take entrepreneurs seriously (and significantly, an Austrian), commented in 1946, "there is really no room for it [entrepreneurial behavior] in the economic system of the Smith-Ricardo-Mill-Marshall tradition."[30]

Until the 1970s most neoclassical economists gave lip service to investment but placed it theoretically in a sort of residual category, a more-or-less automatic result of other circumstances. Keynes, for example, while acknowledging the "animal spirits" that often lay behind investment, seemed to regard it as simply a function of the national interest rate; lower rates and investment will come forth.[31] Even right-wingers, lovers of capitalism, largely ignored capitalists. The cause was not ideological contempt but methodological negligence. Whether of the Right or Left, in the world of academic economics, "to be taken seriously," as Paul Krugman puts it, "an idea has to be *something you can model*," that is, something that can be deduced from the rational maximization axiom plus a few empirical assumptions, stated in the form of an equation, and proven as a mathematical theorem.[32] But no one had figured out a way to model human creativity. As a consequence, while right- and left-wing economists conceded the importance of entrepreneurial behavior, neither group had been able to model it, so it was a neglected topic.[33]

But what satisfied academics disappointed politicians, and more important, the politicians' business constituents. In the first place, even before the 1970s businesspeople thought that they were insufficiently appreciated within the public philosophy. In the second, during the decade, members of the business community were convinced that they were overregulated and overtaxed, and were additionally annoyed at the proportion of "their" taxes going to the nonproductive section of the population, that is, to the poor. In the third, economists didn't seem to be coming up with cures for stagflation. As a result, the nonacademic right wing turned to a barely respectable academic theory that fulfilled its needs better than mainstream orthodoxy.

In the 1970s American conservatives came to focus ever-more intently on "the crisis in capital formation" that was, they believed, at the root of every economic weakness.[34] Here the most important neoclassical thinker was Martin Feldstein. Through the 1970s, as the president of the National Bureau of Economic Research, which was largely funded by corporations, Feldstein wrote a series of papers in which he argued that the Keynesian "pursuit of easy money" had made the modern democratic state an engine of inflation.[35] Inflation, in turn, had "diverted the flow of capital away from investment in plant and equipment," with deleterious consequences for the economy as a whole.[36] The only solution was to restructure macroeconomic policy "to recognize the importance of fiscal incentives" and reduce inflation, thus increasing investment.[37] The federal budget must be balanced and taxes must be lowered, which, together, meant that spending must be cut.

Helping to sell these ideas to the public was a group of journalists sponsored by the editorial page of the *Wall Street Journal*, especially Jude Wanniski. Practically every day for years, Wanniski and his cadre wrote columns telling businesspeople that they were overregulated, undervalued, and, especially, overtaxed by the politicians running the federal and state governments. In 1978 Wanniski published *The Way the World Works*, a supply-side primer that prescribed tax and regulation relief for all the country's economic ills.[38] Neoclassical economists of every stripe, on the right and the left, believed that tax rates had *some* incentive effect on investment. Supply-siders went way beyond academic caution, preaching that even small changes in tax incidence, especially for potential investors, would have a very large impact on the growth rate of the economy.[39]

Helping to sell the ideas to government policy makers were a group of think tanks, particularly the Heritage Foundation and the American Enterprise Institute, that offered a mix of bona fide academic thought and policy propaganda that David Ricci has termed "research brokering."[40] Because professional scholars often present their ideas in dense jargon, and because they like to use mathematical models, their arguments and evidence are frequently inaccessible to politicians. The quasi-scholars at think tanks specialize in translating the ideas in academic literature into useful talking points for politicians, selecting, interpreting, and emphasizing as they proceed. There were, of course, liberal as well as conservative think tanks, most famously the Brookings Institution. As Ricci points out, however, "ideas, no matter how well founded in expert analysis, might lack persuasive force if detached from familiar values."[41] As it turned out, conservatives were much better than progressives in attaching their economic policy prescriptions to traditional American prejudices.

Before conservatives could present a convincing intellectual case for supply-side economics, however, they had to address a moral issue. During the 1970s, leftists opened a new conceptual battlefield in their war against capitalism. Under the influence of Jürgen Habermas, a German critical theorist, American leftists began to argue that capitalism generated governmental demands that democratic governments were not able to satisfy, that capitalist advertising created mass desires that could not be fulfilled, and that capitalism undermined the social institutions of family and character on which its own survival depended. As a result, Habermas argued, the entire institution of capitalism was facing a "legitimation crisis."[42] American leftists picked up the theme, and began to write books such as Alan Wolfe's *The Limits of Legitimacy* (1977), in which they combined analysis and prophecy to add a new twist to Marx's assertion that capitalism was inevitably doomed: "The emergence of late capitalism gives the political systems of Western Europe and the United States their stagnant character; societies become dominated by frustration, blockage, political opacity, exhaustion, rigidification, mystification, and overall lack of direction and confusion. The remaining political history of late capitalism will be a contest between the desperate need to do something and the inability to do anything."[43]

This left-wing argument became so important because it convinced many right-wingers. Procapitalist as they were, they nevertheless sensed that the system's moral foundations were being subverted, and they were astute enough to perceive that a system without mass belief could not survive no matter how much wealth it produced. As Irving Kristol, coeditor of the quasi-academic, quasi-popular journal the *Public Interest*, wrote in 1978,

> From having been a *capitalist, republican community* with shared values and a quite unambiguous claim to the title of a just order, the United States became a free democratic society where the will to success and privilege was severed from its moral moorings. . . . My reading of history is that, in the same way as men cannot for long tolerate a sense of spiritual meaninglessness in their individual lives, so they cannot for long accept a society in which power, privilege, and property are not distributed according to some morally meaningful criteria.[44]

Although Wolfe and the leftists were pleased with the prospect of social disintegration and Kristol and the conservatives were displeased, many of the conservatives thus conceded that the leftists had a point. If capitalism's legitimacy crisis was to be prevented, then something had to be done to provide the system with "morally meaningful criteria." Supply-side economics was not enough; somebody would have to come up with a new moral justification for the capitalist system.

In the late 1970s, then, American conservatives were searching for a coherent statement of a creed that would relegitimate capitalism while providing good policy reasons to cut taxes on the rich and eliminate government support for the poor. On the electoral front, the messenger arrived in 1980 in the person of Ronald Reagan, who managed to communicate faith in both capitalism's moral urgency and in its power to overcome all economic problems. Reagan, however, was no intellectual, and his policy statements constituted more a collection of aphorisms than a compelling treatise. The supply-siders still needed a readable statement of the entire creed.

In this as in other wishes the conservatives were lucky. *Wealth and Poverty*, authored by freelance journalist George Gilder, arrived the same year as Reagan's election. Vibrantly written, this book satisfied all the needs of the new capitalism as an explanation, a justification, a polemic, and an anthem. Although Gilder had no credentials as a scholar, he was able to synthesize a great deal of academic research from neoclassical and Austrian economics, anthropology, sociology, history, and even criminology in an intelligent and compelling manner, add some earnest preaching, sprinkle the whole with witty scorn of the Left, and present the result as though it was merely common sense.

Were some doubting capitalism's legitimacy? The result of an abject misunderstanding, asserted Gilder. Capitalists do not invest because they are greedily attempting to make themselves rich; they do it as a selfless offering to other people. In investing, they give of themselves as a contribution to the community.[45]

Is the inequality generated by capitalist success a problem? Absolutely not. The riches of successful capitalists are a good thing for society.[46]

But if capitalism is such a good thing, why does it create resentment? Because, explains Gilder, of the envy of intellectuals who can manipulate words but not produce anything tangible, and thus are both resentful of "society's . . . greatest benefactors, the producers of wealth," and equipped with the intellectual weapons with which to denigrate their betters.[47] Intellectuals, themselves devoid of useful skills, come to believe that the entrepreneurial talents are vulgar and harmful, a belief they then pass on to their impressionable young students. Thus "[t]he idea that all wealth is acquired through stealing is popular in prisons and at Harvard."[48] From the universities, the poison of class envy diffuses through important sectors of society.

While defending capitalism's legitimacy and disparaging its critics, Gilder was at the same time able to provide a one-word answer to the fundamental question of who creates wealth: entrepreneurs. It followed that government should do everything possible to provide incentives to entrepreneurs, and everything possible to avoid getting in their way. Taxes should be lowered and regulations ruthlessly pruned. Keynes was not only wrong, but irrelevant; economists and politicians should give up their fascination with demand management and focus on the supply side.[49]

Slightly shifting his use of the paradigm of incentive, Gilder was similarly able to provide a one-word answer to the question of what causes poverty: government. If people are rewarded for sober, industrious behavior, they will work; if they are rewarded for inactivity, they will not work. By supporting the poor in their idleness through welfare, unemployment compensation, food stamps, public housing, Medicaid, and so forth, governments remove the motivation for the impoverished to escape their situation, because "[i]n order to succeed, the poor need most of all the spur of their poverty."[50] Although they might seem compassionate in the short run, in the long run all government efforts to cushion the unpleasantness of poverty simply make the problem more intractable. The most compassionate long-run solution is to eliminate such programs and allow people to fend for themselves.

It was easy for progressive scholars and journalists to find fault with the argument of *Wealth and Poverty*. Gilder's focus on entrepreneurs caused him to miss the fact that the economy was dominated by big corporations whose behavior was not entrepreneurial. Nothing in supply-side economics addressed the problem of market failure, especially as it was manifested in externalities and monopoly. The conservatives' enthusiasm for cutting welfare contradicted their professed concern for the institution of the family, because forcing single mothers to find jobs could not be good for their children. Poverty is not caused by governments paying people to be idle, but by governments failing to take the necessary steps to establish full employment. There is no relationship, among the countries of the industrialized world, between tax ratios and the growth rate of economies. And on and on.[51] Paul Krugman, heir to Paul Samuelson's mantle of chief interpreter of the left side of neoclassical economics through newspaper columns, continually assailed the theory, asserting that "the supply-siders are cranks,"[52] and that it is a doctrine "without a shred of logic or evidence in its favor."[53]

Supply-side economics and its associated moral preachings, however, were immune to all the criticism, for they had evolved past economic theorizing and become a political creed. They provided the Republican Party with a set of policy prescriptions that were intensely agreeable to a formidable coalition of interests and that could be sold as being grounded on both a scientific analysis and a moral truth. Under Reagan, the Republican-dominated Congress in 1981 adopted the Economic Recovery Tax Act (ERTA), slashing income-tax rates for everyone, but mainly the rich, and proceeded to cut welfare benefits, while the administration was trying to eliminate or hamstring as many regulations as possible.[54]

When Reagan smashed his Democratic challenger, Walter Mondale, who had promised to raise taxes in order to combat the ballooning federal deficits, in the 1984 election, supply-side economics became the tent pole of Republican ideology. Henceforth Republican candidates in both national and state races recommended tax cuts for the rich as the solution to every conceivable social problem. They were the main component of George H. W. Bush's domestic policy agenda during his presidency. When his son, George W. Bush, was running for the presidency in 2000, the candidate suggested that taxes should be cut because the economy was booming. In 2001, after his election, when the economy had gone into recession, George W. Bush argued that taxes should be cut because the economy was flagging. A belief in supply-side economics had become one of the litmus tests for political conservatism in the United States. It was not the subject of rational consideration, but an article of faith.

If he had been a traditional neoclassical theorist, President Reagan would have been shocked by the size of the federal deficits he was creating, because, traditionally, the budget gap would have been expected to generate inflation. But the Reagan administration, instead of covering the deficit by printing dollars, cheated. It issued bonds that were largely purchased by foreigners. Thus it allowed the Japanese, Europeans, and Arabs to cover the American budget deficit, and was spared the need to put more money into the economy. Inflation was avoided, and the consequences of deficit financing could be put off onto generations who would arrive long after Reagan and his advisers had left the scene. In the meantime, Republicans could luxuriate in the popularity of their supply-side president.

The new-time religion was spread throughout the population by a previously unknown ideological huckster employing an old medium. Rush Limbaugh made his first radio broadcast on July 4, 1988.[55] Almost instantly, his combination of confidently conservative economic doctrine and aggressively conservative social beliefs, delivered in a highly intelligent, well-considered manner, and mixed with personal attack, misinformation, imaginative satire, and shameless egotism, proved hugely popular. By the mid-1990s he could be heard on more than eleven hundred stations. He was playing to an estimated audience of more than twenty million each day, and, according to surveys, was the main source of political news and analysis for 26 percent of the population, or almost seventy million people.[56] After the tremendous Republican victory in the congressional races of 1994, many in the party gave him at least partial credit for their success.

In many ways Limbaugh's own ideas were a standard compendium of traditional American individualism, faith in the market, and hostility to government, allied with a few social positions such as antagonism to abortion. As he wrote in a best-selling book published in 1992,

> I believe in the individual, in less government so as to allow the individual maximum freedom to create and achieve; that societies which are founded on restricting the government rather than the individual are optimum . . . that my belief in individuality and limited government does not preclude me from advocating the requisite amount of governmental authority to ensure law and order in our society . . . that political and economic freedom are inextricably intertwined; that society owes its citizens equality of opportunity but cannot guarantee them equality of outcome.[57]

In his radio broadcasts, however, Limbaugh gave much more attention to supply-side economics than this passage suggests he would. Taxes were his obsession, turning up in some discussion almost every week. All economic problems could be solved by cutting taxes; any plan to raise taxes on anybody (but especially, of course, the rich) was a recipe for disaster. When President George H. W. Bush, facing titanic budget deficits, reluctantly acquiesced in a Democratic plan to raise the top personal income tax rate from 28 percent to 31 percent in 1990, Limbaugh virtually read him out of the party, devoting every broadcast for weeks to vituperative excommunication. In 1992, on the November morning after Bill Clinton was elected president and the Democrats retained both houses of Congress, Limbaugh rhetorically offered to bet national Democratic chairman Ron Brown $1 million that by election day 1996, both unemployment and inflation would have skyrocketed, so sure was he that non-supply-side policies would wreck the economy. In November 1996 the voters returned Clinton to the White House within a context of strong and rising prosperity and an utter lack of inflation. In his postelection broadcasts, Limbaugh never mentioned his previously tendered wager with the now-deceased Brown. Perhaps he was showing respect for the dead, or perhaps he forgot.

Limbaugh also did his bit to relegitimate capitalism in general and being rich in particular. "Whether you are a businessman or someone earning a salary," he wrote to his audience in his first book, "you should never apologize for trying to earn more money. . . . If anything, you are morally SUPERIOR to those liberal compassion fascists who claim you are greedy. You have a real job; they just beg for a living."[58]

For a while during the 1990s, bona fide journalists published articles detailing Limbaugh's "errors of fact, errors of interpretation, errors of exaggeration," but after a while, when the revelations did nothing to contract the size of his audience, they gave up.[59] No doubt, also, Limbaugh garnered support with uncompromisingly impolite attacks on groups who were unpopular on the right side of the spectrum, on "feminazis," "environmentalist wackos," the "arts and croissant crowd" (supporters of the National Endowment for the Arts), and similar rhetorical targets.

Whatever the reason for his success, it spawned a host of imitators, and the airwaves of the 1990s were full of Limbaugh clones. American talk radio was crammed with rude right-wing ideologues who generally managed to reproduce his incivility while failing to duplicate his intelligence. With the rise of the Fox News television network, the Limbaugh combination of invective-laced ideological expression and misinformation migrated to the more powerful medium, where it enjoyed great success. Limbaugh is not single-handedly responsible for lowering the tone of American public discourse, but he has been the most important single contributor to its decline.

Besides Limbaugh, right-wing ideologues offered a few improvements of detail to supply-side economics in the years after the ascent of Reagan. They countered leftist claims that capitalism and democracy were incompatible by pointing out the indisputable historical fact that the two social systems had been born together and always existed together. This was no coincidence, argued the conservatives, for only in a society with free markets could other freedoms flourish.[60]

Conservatives also confronted the charge that increasing economic inequality canceled out the achievements of capitalism. Some, like Gilder, dealt with this accusation by turning it back on the progressives, asserting that it was government, not private enterprise, that caused inequality by causing poverty.[61] Some maintained that continuing globalization and the New Economy would create such a boom that all inequality would be eliminated.[62] Mainly, however, conservatives simply insisted that inequality was the result of market forces that were good for everybody, and that the people who were becoming fabulously rich deserved their fortunes because they were designing the wonderful world of tomorrow. In Dinesh D'Souza's words, "the prime culprit in causing contemporary social inequality seems to be merit. . . . Inequality is not a virtue in and of itself, but it is an inevitable by-product of a free society that seeks to reward citizens in proportion to their productive worth."[63]

By and large, conservatives were in power after 1981. They held the presidency for thirteen of the twenty-one years, 1981 to 2001; the Senate for twelve, not entirely overlapping, years; and the House for six. To a large extent they were successful in their project of "dismantling embedded liberalism," as Mark Blyth put it.[64] Whereas the New Deal and the Great Society had regulated business, the conservative regime largely deregulated it. Whereas the New Deal had established the National Labor Relations Board in 1935 as the unions' institutional protector, the Reagan administration turned it into a tool of management domination.[65] By the 1990s, in Blyth's words, "a new neoliberal institutional order," more complicated but similar to the pre-1930s regime of political economy, and featuring a privileged position for capital and the subordination of labor to the market, had been put in place and ratified twice by the voters.[66]

In the long perspective of American history, this new order can be seen as the contemporary iteration of the Hamiltonian insistence that capitalism must be as insulated as much as possible from democratic interference. Its electoral triumph was the result, not just of the economic troubles of the 1970s, which the public blamed on the Democrats; not just on the more clever conservative use of economic ideas; and not just on the vastly greater resources the conservatives were able to marshal in order to spread their ideas. Within the sphere of elections it was mainly the result of the coalition Reagan built between capitalism and Christian social conservatism.[67] Exploration of the politics of that alliance would take us far beyond the subject matter of this book.

THE LEFT REDEFINES DEMOCRACY

If the strongholds of the Right were talk radio, capitalism itself, and evangelical Christianity, one of the major strongholds of the Left was in the academy. Although some progressive intellectuals were employed as journalists, the center of gravity of the post-1981 Left was located in the universities. Whereas the target audience of the Right consisted of average people, therefore, the target audience of the Left consisted of college professors. These different audiences gave rise to a profound difference of style between communications in the two arenas. Being strongly influenced by talk radio, conservative discourse, even on the campaign trail, was frequently vulgar, personal, brutal, clear to the point of simple-mindedness, and repetitive. Being strongly influenced by academic theorizing, progressive discourse was often elevated, abstract, impersonal, and erudite to the point of obscurity, although progressive political candidates had to simplify and clarify their ideas in order to reach potential voters. In particular, as the period wore on, academic leftists became ever-more-strongly influenced by European social theory, especially the tradition flowing from French poststructuralist thought. Unfortunately, the French intelligentsia had decided after World War II that, to be respectable, social thought must be expressed in a highly recondite style. As a consequence, American progressives tended to adopt a pretentious and, at times, almost comically abstruse mode of expression. Gone were the days when C. Wright Mills wrote leftist polemics that any intelligent person could understand.

The habitually obscure mode of expression is very frequently paired, in progressive writing, with a profound and overly dramatic pessimism. The first words of the first chapter of *On Democracy* (1983) by Joshua Cohen and Joel Rogers, "These are dark times,"[68] could just as easily have been placed at the beginning of much leftist writing. To the Left, it is always dark times. The economy is always getting worse for ordinary people, no matter how prosperous its overall performance. Government, under the sway of capitalists, is always passing new measures to facilitate exploitation of workers. The actual level of economic activity and the actual intent of government measures are both irrelevant. Thus in 1971 Frances Fox Piven and Richard Cloward published *Regulating the Poor*, in which they argued, in essence, that welfare was a capitalist plot to keep the poor in their place.[69] In 1982 they published *The New Class War*, in which they argued that the

Reagan administration's efforts to cut welfare constituted a capitalist plot to keep the poor in their place.[70] The tone of a typical leftist publication is thus similar to the tone of a typical short story by Edgar Allan Poe, only not so cheerful.

Stylistic considerations aside, there was a conceptual evolution in progressive thought after the 1970s. Through that decade even non-Marxist progressives were strongly influenced by Marxist assumptions. Although non-Marxist leftists might reject the notion that capitalism was hurtling toward its inevitable destruction, and although they might be leery of the idea that the United States was under the suzerainty of a ruling class, they did tend to focus on class conflict as the fundamental fact of economic and political life. During the 1980s and 1990s, however, three historical forces tended to undermine the Marxist, or quasi-Marxist, paradigm. First, New Left notions of alienation rather than working-class exploitation as the defining problem of modern capitalist society, and of participatory democracy as the solution to the problem, steadily gained acceptance. Second, the refusal of working-class Americans to behave as the leftists thought they should, and, in particular, their frequent tendency to vote for conservative candidates, assumed ever greater importance in the progressive catalog of paradoxes to be overcome, or at least explained. Third, communism's rapid loss of self-confidence in the late 1980s, and its almost total collapse in the early 1990s, combined with the stellar performance of national and international capitalism during that decade, convinced most leftists that the system they hated really was much better at sustaining prosperity, and more politically stable, than they had previously admitted. Through the 1970s it was common for leftists to speak of "late capitalism," as if to emphasize their belief in its imminent collapse.[71] By the 1990s they were using the noun without the modifier, or inventing some alternate term, such as "neoliberal democracy," to characterize their subject.[72]

If there was one progressive assumption that did not change during this era, it was the moral axiom that the market, although it might generate wealth, was essentially and inevitably unjust. Leftists elaborated this moral critique with great thoroughness. They argued that entrepreneurs, contrary to the celebratory assertions of the Right, do not deserve to control great wealth. Entrepreneurial skill is the result of environmental or genetic factors, which do not confer any moral superiority. The same logic apples to a willingness to take risks.[73]

Furthermore, leftists attacked the neoclassical argument that an "optimum" generation of wealth would be the result of unregulated market decisions. Even neoclassical economics, they pointed out, admitted that externalities such as pollution, which allowed a business to shunt its costs onto other people, might require government intervention to ensure that the costs were appropriately allocated. As Andrew Schmookler summarized in 1993, however, "externalities are everywhere ... externalities are so pervasive that, like so much rock salt sprinkled liberally across the landscape, they rust out the iron-clad logic of the market ideology."[74]

Additionally, leftists rejected the conservative assumption that consumers are competent to make informed judgments in the marketplace, not because progressives believed that people are stupid, but because they thought that consumers never had adequate information. In theoretical terms, firms and industries have an incentive to produce deceptive and manipulative information about their products, so even motivated consumers are always too ignorant to make rational choices.[75]

The progressive critique of the market even had its socially conservative side. Progressive conservatives—if that is what they should be called—maintained that market forces, with their impersonal emphasis on profit, destroy community.[76]

For all these reasons, progressives as a group were deeply skeptical of globalization, which seemed to them to be a scheme to allow the capitalist market to grow out of reach of whatever weak restraints national governments had been able to place on it.[77] In Thomas Frank's words, the logic of both national and international market forces sums up to "coercion, monopoly, and the destruction of the weak, not ... universal affluence."[78]

The major empirical evidence for the market's indefensibility, discussed by virtually every progressive, is the growing inequality of wealth. Indeed, reliance on inequality as the trump card against capitalism is almost the defining characteristic of the modern Left. Unequal wealth alone, they believe, is bad enough. A surprisingly large percentage of leftists do not even bother to make the point explicitly, simply presenting the facts on inequality as if they were enough of a condemnation of the system. Others draw the moral, asserting that it is "the single most serious economic problem we have,"[79] or that "we need a rebellion against the idea that people are actually paid in proportion to the value of what they produce."[80]

But however bad it is in itself, to the Left the truly horrific aspect of growing inequality is not the economic reality per se. It is the fact that *"an unequal distribution of wealth means an unequal distribution of power."*[81] The economic problem is thus really a legitimacy problem. For if wealth translates into power, then the ideal that all people are created equal, one of the foundational principles of the polity, is being violated systematically and with increasing success by the rich. No amount of prosperity can compensate for this moral abomination. The fundamental conflict of American politics, the new struggle between darkness and righteousness, is not the rich against the poor, or the middle class against the working class, but "Capitalism Against Democracy."[82]

Progressives have given a great deal of time and attention to the mechanisms by which the rich, and particularly the corporate rich, translate their wealth into power. Progressive analysis generally concentrates on the crucial position of the media in modern American society. Newspapers and television stations are capitalist enterprises whose so-called information is actually a combination of conservative propaganda and celebrity-driven fluff intended to distract citizens from serious discussion of public affairs. Media advertising is expensive, and so in order to attract campaign contributions from business, candidates in both major parties are forced to avoid discussion of any issues, and especially the distribution of wealth and income, that would discomfit the source of those contributions. Real issues therefore never make it into public discourse. Through their sponsorship of think tanks, corporations generate a blizzard of phony academic research that crowds out actual scholarly debate from the public arena. Spokespeople for the powers that be are handsomely sponsored and promoted; spokespeople for labor, or for the poor, are generally denied access to the mass media. Corporations spend many millions on public affairs "advocacy advertising" that is every bit as mendacious as their commercial advertising.[83] The grand consequence of this strenuous and largely successful campaign of propaganda and manipulation is "a consensus in which massive abuse of the language of popular consent" masks "a repugnant politics of enrichment for some and degradation of millions of others."[84] What appears to be a robust, even raucous, culture of political discussion in the United States is actually a carefully constructed illusion: "It is often the case that different producer groups take turns bombarding the public with misleading information. This is called 'national debate.' "[85]

Since the beginning of the Republic, capitalism and democracy have existed intertwined and mutually dependent as ideals, albeit in practical tension. Now the Left is attempting to resolve the practical tension by redefining the democratic ideal. The message of the Left is frequently that the United States has only a sham democracy, because authentic democracy is not possible under a capitalist economy. As long as private enterprise controls the media and candidates for public office rely upon campaign contributions from the rich, the polity is actually a plutocracy buttressed by a gigantically expensive public relations campaign.[86] If this redefinition becomes generally accepted, a capitalist society will be, by definition, politically illegitimate. The progressive metaproject over the last generation has thus been to split apart the two pillars of classical liberalism, preserving the idea that citizen participation legitimates government while casting aside the idea that individual freedom of economic activity creates prosperity and virtue.

Even theorists of the "politics of difference," who generally downplay economic questions in their preoccupation with ethnicity or sex, take it as a given that, whatever they want, it cannot be attained under capitalism. The source of injustice might be phallocentrism and capitalism, or Eurocentrism and capitalism, or homophobia and capitalism, or logocentrism and capitalism, but in any case it is always capitalism. As Iris Marion Young summarizes with a typically breezy dismissal of most of Western culture, "The politics of difference insists on liberation of the whole group of Blacks, women, American Indians, and that this can be accomplished only through basic institutional changes ... absent from the calculating individualism of white professional capitalist society."[87]

The true democracy envisioned by leftists goes by a variety of names, "liberal socialism,"[88] "radical democracy,"[89] "strong democracy,"[90] "associative democracy,"[91] even "participatory democracy."[92] Sometimes it consists of an emphasis on workers' control of their jobs; sometimes it favors a more old-fashioned centralization of power; often it is vaguely rhetorical rather than specifically programmatical. But whatever its nuances of content, and however it is labeled, it is socialism. In theory, leftists want to take control over investment and economic organization away from private owners and lodge them in some sort of public assembly, whether of a local, regional, or national scope, although in practice this change would inevitably have to be administered by government bureaucracies. The "empowered" citizens will then make economic decisions with an eye toward public interest and community values rather than private greed.

The Left has come in for a great deal of cogent criticism, some from the Right or the center, some from within the Left itself. As a tendency, although of course not in every individual case, the Left is guilty of all of the intellectual crimes of which it is accused. This makes a great deal of progressive theory quite depressing to read and perhaps explains the general lack of influence of the Left in American society outside of a few fairly small bastions like the university.

First, leftist writings tend to combine fervent millenarianism with a maddening unwillingness to confront hard issues. Progressives have a tendency to be very well versed in the writings of other progressives but surprisingly ignorant of conservative thinking. As a group they fail to grapple seriously with arguments about the capacity of decentralized systems to deal with information more efficiently than centralized bureaucracies, or with considerations of the ability of the market to assimilate and respond to unpredictability better than the "command system" of government, or with assertions about the greater protection for personal liberty in a society with plural power centers, or with arguments about the greater talent of individuals to know what is good for themselves than for outside authorities to either know or care, or with the functional utility of an entrepreneurial class. Moreover, leftists sometimes display an unconcern with sketching the details of how, for example, the workers in control of a factory would raise investment, analyze business opportunity, determine investment strategies, handle personnel decisions, deal with economic losses, or engage in any of the activities that private firms conduct as a matter of course. Progressive writers often seem to think that once people are given back control over their lives, or some such banality, the economic problem will be solved. As Eugene Genovese, a former leftist, has written, they "have a strategy for social change, but they never outline the content of the desired change itself. They invoke 'participatory democracy' and 'equality' as if these code words speak for themselves."[93]

Second, progressives tend to hide the coercive potential of their ideas behind comfortably evasive assumptions. They pretend, for example, that the problem of democratic apathy will disappear as soon as participation becomes authentic with the elimination of capitalism. Then, because participation means something, ordinary citizens will be delighted to spend their nonworking time in meetings during which they debate public policy. One of the most perceptive of the progressives, Michael Walzer, has attempted to confront the problem of participation by admitting the probable reality: "Participatory democracy means the sharing of power among the activists. Socialism means the rule of men with the most evenings to spare . . . participatory democracy has to be paralleled by representative democracy. I am not sure precisely how to adjust the two; I am sure they have to be adjusted."[94]

Despite his frankness, neither Walzer nor any leftist has specified how to prevent participatory democracy from succumbing to the activists' temptation to engage in manipulation and coercion. It happened in the past. It would happen in the future.

Their assumptions about noncapitalist democracy leads to the third serious problem with progressive thought. Much of their intellectual method consists of two assertions. They first contrast a shining ideal of democracy with the tarnished reality of modern government and find that the reality falls distressingly short of the ideal. They then describe the ideal of their socialist vision as if the reality would match the ideal. The reality of the present under capitalism is contrasted with the ideal of the socialist future. Not surprisingly, the ideal looks better.

Few progressives bother to confront the conservative charge that government activity also has its imperfections. The tendency of government administrative agencies to become a class unto themselves with interests and purposes divergent from the ones for which they were created is a phenomenon long studied and deplored. In the English-speaking world, this tendency is called "bureaupathology"; in Russia, the word is *"vedomstvennost"*; in China, it is *"pen-wei chu-yi."*[95] Bureaucracies become irrational and incompetent; they waste money, persist in absurd enterprises, and ignore citizens' rights. Moreover, government activity, like all human action, generates unintended consequences. Policies honestly adopted to solve social problems not infrequently make them worse. If there is one truth the political science and public administration scholarship of the twentieth century established beyond doubt, it is that government is always expensive, frequently incompetent, and sometimes dangerous. Yet most progressive theorizing ignores the potential of government abuse. Apparently, leftists believe that all the negative aspects of government action are caused by its corruption by capitalism. They seem to think that after capitalist democracy is replaced with "strong democracy" or the equivalent, bureaupathology will cease to be a problem.

Finally, progressives base their analysis of the polity on dubious empirical foundations. Their portrait of the American media as given over to procapitalist propaganda may have some foundation in fact, but it also contains a large serving of wishful thinking. Leftist research into both the news[96] and the entertainment[97] media is noteworthy for reliance on anecdotal evidence, subjectively analyzed. More mainstream scholarly investigations of the news media, using quantitative data, find that the question of bias is complicated and subtle. Some projects have found Democratic bias, and some Republican. Some have concluded that there is bias against incumbents. Some have detected a media hostility against all candidates.[98] Leftists might claim that since there is very little prosocialist advocacy to be found in mainstream media, that this lacuna is evidence of conscious suppression of one point of view. Perhaps, but it is more likely that the media are responding to a lack of public interest.

Whereas the evidence allows no very strong judgment about news bias, research on the entertainment media is much more conclusive. The best, most systematic studies on the content of motion picture and television stories establish without a doubt that American entertainment tends to portray business and business executives in a hostile manner.[99] Moreover, Hollywood tends to cast the rich in general as villains.[100] American entertainment, produced by capitalist corporations, tends to be anticapitalist.

The attempt of the Left to redefine democracy, therefore, has thus far failed as theory, as empirical research, as history, as philosophy, and as polemic. The Left badly needs a new Marx, or at least a new Mills, to inject some life into its appeals.

THE CENTER MUDDLES THROUGH

Between the equally unsatisfactory visions of the Right and Left, the modern American center has attempted to take a sensible and humane stand on slippery ground. The essential characteristic of centrists is that they see flaws in all analyses, positions, utopias, realities, and prescriptions. As a result, their worldview consists of pervasive ambiguity, and their ideological position is one of sustained ambivalence.

When they are confronted with criticisms of the American economy and polity, the centrist strategy is to concede all the points except the conclusion that the systems should be radically altered. Is democracy vitiated by mass apathy, corrupted by the power of wealth, and demoralized by the guerrilla warfare of selfish groups? Does the necessity for constant compromise dissipate the possibility of pursuing coherent, responsible policy? Does the loud propaganda and demagoguery of the public arena drown out the calm, disinterested interchange of public discourse? Yes. But then, life is hard; nothing is gained by whining about it. "Democracy is for the stout of heart who know that there are things worth fighting for in a world of paradox, ambiguity, and irony," as Jean Bethke Elshtain put it in 1995.[101] What would those things be? Pretty much what we have already: a constitutional democracy in which argument and compromise substitute for violence.[102] Does she mean that American society cannot be improved? No, there is great room for improvement. We need a "new social covenant" in which Americans would retreat from the current "politics of displacement" in which "private identity takes place over public ends or purposes."[103] But these improvements should be urged on citizens without losing heart and without succumbing to the temptations of radical posturing.

Similarly, the centrists concede much of the Left's analysis of capitalism's corruption of democracy. As Charles Lindblom observed, also in 1995, "advertising and public relations drown us in unilateral communication . . . we still mindlessly discuss free speech largely as though the concept refers to discourse among persons all capable of voicing or writing."[104] But this admission does not convince Lindblom to endorse the progressives' conclusion that socialism must be adopted if genuine democracy is to have a chance. No: "I suspect that we are more in the infancy of process control through democracy than in its maturity or senility."[105] Give democracy time; things will work out; the present is not so intolerable.

In the same vein, in 1999 John Mueller acknowledged that capitalism is an "unlovable system" and that there is a "mismatch between the democratic ideal" and "its grim, grimy, and unavoidable reality."[106] The solution to the mismatch, however, is not to junk the system but to adjust the ideal. In the long run, it is better to "trust the market."[107] Further, by thinking of democracy as a system of "popular veto" rather than "popular rule," the ideal can be brought much more in line with reality.[108]

Underlying the centrists' toleration for the admitted imperfections of the modern American political economy is a historically grounded conviction that there is no such thing as perfection in this world. As Robert Dahl wrote in 1989, "ideal political systems, and ideal states in particular, have never existed, do not exist, and almost surely never will exist." Nevertheless, "[a] hardheaded look at human experience, historical and contemporary, shows that among political societies that have actually existed, or now exist, those that most nearly satisfy the criteria of the democratic idea are, taken all around, better than the rest."[109] It turns out that the United States satisfies these criteria fairly well.[110] (In other contexts, Dahl makes recommendations that are decidedly leftist.[111] In the present context, he is best described as a centrist because he does not question the legitimacy of the pluralist, or "polyarchical," reality of the contemporary American polity.)

As contributors to modern arguments over politics and economics, the centrists offer an unusual tone. They are reasonable. They make no untenable assumptions, assert no absolute moral claims, and abstain from demonizing people who disagree with them. They apotheosize no system and cast no class as heroes. Their method is long-run empiricism combined with cautious analysis. Their style is fair-minded equivocation. Within the context of recent developments in the history of ideas, they are surprisingly persuasive.

GRUNDLOSIGKEIT

The unraveling of the scholarly consensus on methodologies and philosophical assumptions that commenced during the 1960s advanced so rapidly that during the final two decades of the century, American social thought was in complete disarray. In economics, Irving Kristol wrote in 1980 that "the body of *undisputed* theory is shrinking before our very eyes, not growing."[112] In political science, as Lawrence Dodd and Calvin Jillson summarized in 1994, "we find a vast assortment of differing schools of thought and scholarly approaches, scholars of differing traditions who seldom converse with one another or listen to competing interpretations, and an incoherent body of knowledge that often appears in fundamental contradiction."[113] In history, J. Daryle Charles reports that the discipline was by 1999 enduring an "extended epistemological crisis" that was resulting in collective demoralization.[114] In political theory, according to Bhikhu Parekh in 2000, philosophers "are deeply divided about the nature, task, and state of their discipline."[115]

The disintegration of shared intellectual assumptions was at least as evident in legal thought as in other disciplines. Drucilla Cornell observed in 1995 that legal scholarship was succumbing to "the post-modern problem of *Grundlosigkeit*—the loss of grounding of legal rules in fundamental principles."[116] Bernard Schwartz laments: "Legal thought has become as fragmented as modern life itself. . . . Contempt for the very notion of certainty and rational coherence has increasingly become the accent of jurisprudence."[117] And Cass Sunstein agrees that we now live in a "postcanonical legal universe."[118]

Postcanonical it might be, but legal thought, like American social thought generally, has tended to sort itself into streams of right, left, and center. Thinkers in each stream tend to share general methodological assumptions and political values even while they differ in the details of their arguments.

On the right, the two most important thinkers have been Richard Posner and Richard Epstein. Posner is noteworthy for his attempt to apply the conceptual apparatus of neoclassical economics to legal thinking. I discuss his ideas in chapter 9. Here, I examine Epstein.

Epstein is in a sense a man out of his time, a classical liberal and republican who would have felt comfortable discussing philosophy with John Adams and James Madison. In his view, the fundamental social problem is government encroachment on individual rights, and the solution is enshrinement of private property as an unassailable bulwark against state power. As he wrote in 1987, "I am persuaded that the dangers of faction demonstrate the wisdom of entrenching individual rights against the state."[119] This was the purpose of the Constitution fashioned by the founders, and when the Supreme Court abandoned this meta-understanding of the document's political function in 1937, it opened the door to the tyranny of the majority working through the faux legitimacy of democratic procedures. American jurisprudence must return to the pre–New Deal theory of the Constitution, for "[t]o allow a theory of an evolving constitution to undermine the text is to substitute naked value preferences for law."[120]

Epstein's particular favorite candidate for a constitutional passage that will shield individual rights from naked value preferences wielded by tyrants is the takings clause of the Fifth Amendment, which provides that "nor shall private property be taken for public use, without just compensation." For two generations after the 1930s, the courts interpreted this clause to mean that while the power of eminent domain was a justifiable adjunct of governance, any direct confiscation of property must be compensated. It did not apply to indirect effects on the value of property because literally any decision by government might have such an incidental impact. If all the indirect consequences of any governmental decision—declarations of war, environmental protection, legislation protecting the right for workers to unionize, zoning regulations, property taxes, and limitless other possibilities—called for calculation of losses to everyone affected, and payment to them, then government would be paralyzed. Desiring to allow government to regulate the economic life of the country, the courts interpreted the takings clause narrowly.

But governmental paralysis—or at least a radical diminution of its activity—is exactly what Epstein would like to bring about. In his 1985 book, *Takings*, he argues that "*all* regulations, *all* taxes, and *all* modifications of liability are takings of private property prima facie compensable by the state."[121] "It will be said that my position invalidates much of the twentieth century legislation, and so it does.... The New Deal *is* inconsistent with the principles of limited government and with the constitutional principles designed to secure that end."[122] And so welfare programs are unconstitutional, as are rent control laws, zoning, most environmental protection regulation, the National Labor Relations Act, graduated income taxes, and, in general, most of the activities of federal and state governments since the 1930s.

Taking Epstein as indicative of the economic side of contemporary right-wing jurisprudence (there is a social side also, which proceeds from different premises and arrives at different conclusions about governmental power, and which I will not discuss), it is clear that the alienation of contemporary conservatives from democracy is so intense that they have almost become anarchists. Indeed, although Epstein quibbles slightly with Robert Nozick's methodology in *Anarchy, State, and Utopia*, he concurs most heartily with Nozick's conclusion that only the most minimal state can be ethically justified.[123]

But Nozick is a philosopher attempting to persuade his readers to agree with his principles. It would violate his purpose to attempt to impose his vision on others. Epstein, on the other hand, would like to inspire a small coterie of unelected judges to force the rest of the population to live with his views of the Constitution. While his argument is couched in the language of judicial restraint, therefore, his actual message is that the dictatorship of judges should replace the free participation of citizens. Whereas conservative jurists after the Civil War employed the due process clause of the Fourteenth Amendment to substitute elite preferences for democratic government, Epstein wants to use the takings clause for exactly the same purpose. Like his exemplars in the late nineteenth century, he hopes to exploit the language of rights to conceal the coercion of the few against the many.

Epstein's influence continued to grow on the right through the 1980s and 1990s, and into the new millennium. By 2005 *Takings* had been in print for two decades, and Epstein was being touted as a leading candidate for a Supreme Court appointment, when one became available.[124]

On the left, the practitioners of critical legal studies have decided that what Epstein wants to do is what law already does. That is, they believe that American law, New Deal or no New Deal, is simply the formally coercive part of the "the ideology of the ruling class,"[125] or the ruling gender, or the ruling sexual preference, or the ruling race, which is always either composed of, or dependent on, capitalists or capitalism. There is no single identifiable group of dominant thinkers on the left because legal progressives, like progressivism in general, have splintered into a plethora of intellectual fiefdoms. Nevertheless, progressive legal scholars share basic assumptions with leftists outside law schools.

To the Crits, as they are called, "legal doctrine helps perpetuate injustice by providing justifications for it."[126] All jurisprudence except theirs is merely the rationalization of domination. It follows that all thinkers outside the Left are fundamentally, although not necessarily consciously, dishonest, engaged in the practice of serving power while pretending to pursue truth.

Like their comrades in the other disciplines, leftist legal theorists have been strongly influenced by Marx, Nietzsche, Derrida, Habermas, Lévi-Strauss, Marcuse, and Lacan, but especially by Foucault, whose belief that there is no truth but only power constructed by discourse is mightily appealing to people whose work lives consist of manipulating discourse.[127] Like other leftists, they have tended to separate into tribes and subtribes, the members of each believing that their task is to intervene "in the historical and social intelligibility of *reality* in a world in which 'reality' appears ('makes sense') quite differently depending upon the subject's position along the material social matrices of race, gender, sexuality, and class."[128] Nevertheless, as with the rest of the Left, whatever reality the progressives settle on, it rejects capitalism.

The general leftist method for intervening in the social intelligibility of legal reality is to trace a given law or constitutional interpretation back to a dominant interest—to males, or whites, or property owners, or heterosexuals, or all of these—and attempt to demonstrate that the statute or decision is merely an elaborate justification for the continued hegemony of the interest. They always conclude that it is. The logical inference must be that only people of a given category could either legislate or interpret for people in that category. Although Crits generally do not make this point explicitly, it would be necessary under their ideal regime for African Americans to make laws for African Americans, women for women, and then African American women for African American women, and on and on until everyone had their own personal statutes and constitution. In practice, of course, it would never come to this. Presumably after being elevated to the Supreme Court, leftist legal scholars, having liberated themselves from oppressive discourse, would interpret the Constitution on everyone's behalf.

Progressive legal thought is subject to the same criticisms as progressive social thought generally. As a group, progressive legal writers tend to evade difficult issues, elide the coercive potential of their ideas, implicitly compare a present reality to a future ideal, treat empirical evidence sloppily, and so on.[129] In addition, however, they seem to have been even more seriously infected with the postmodern disease: the belief that there is no ultimate truth except theirs. If this position is "true" (at this point, leftist writers begin to put that word, as well as "reality," in quotation marks), it must also be true that all nonleftists are consciously or unconsciously insincere. Progressives would have us believe that everybody outside the confines of the Left is, in effect, a flack for the ruling powers. As a logical extension, if we disagree with them, we have not liberated ourselves from the status of intellectual lackeys. Critical legal theorists are sometimes accused of nihilism,[130] but they actually believe in nihilism for everybody else and truth for themselves.

Flanked by the coercive dreams of the Right and the Left, centrist legal theorists struggle with the familiar problems of ambiguity and ambivalence. The influential centrist theorists have been antipositivists; that is, they think that all statutes must be evaluated according to some higher standard outside the law itself. Centrists have been influenced by Rawls, and would like to implement his idea that justice should be defined as fairness or, in practice, an equality of rights and even, perhaps, of economic outcomes. In this sense they are on the left of the political spectrum. But they are not anticapitalist; they might best be described as having a New Deal ethos, albeit one that has been educated by decades of experience since the 1930s. Furthermore, because they are antipositivists, they know that an important purpose of a constitution is to restrain all power, whether or not it originates in the people. Their task, then, is to articulate principles of deliberation that will guide judges in deciding which laws realize acceptable democratic impulses and which laws would institute unacceptable impulses.

This project turns out to be difficult to realize. Centrist legal theory is a mass of equivocation and generally turns out to enunciate "principles" of jurisprudence that are too vague to guide anyone.

In 1985, for example, Rogers Smith recommended that judges should read the Constitution "as expressing the precepts of rational liberty."[131] Here is his explanation of the concept:

> [R]ational liberty is not only an instrumental but also a substantive standard for human conduct. It does espouse a certain process for determining our actions, namely reflective deliberation on our circumstances and on the various commitments, ideals, desires, opportunities, and constraints that those circumstances present to us. But it also includes a substantive requirement for the outcome of such deliberation: . . . we must always strive to maintain in ourselves, and to respect in others, those very capacities for deliberative self-guidance and self-control.[132]
>
> [T]here is a justification for intervention by the relatively insulated judiciary when the community has unnecessarily infringed on conduct generally conceded to be essential to the rational self-government of some persons. Barring such extreme instances, changes in disliked policies must be sought through the electoral branches.[133]

If judges already know what our various "commitments, ideals, desires, opportunities, and constraints" are, and if they agree about what is "conduct generally conceded to be essential to the rational self-government of some persons," then they should have no trouble applying this principle to actual law. The problem is that all the hard cases deal with issues in which people do not agree on such ideals and conduct. If everyone already agreed on basic principles, there would be no need for jurisprudence.

Similarly, in 1986 Ronald Dworkin suggested that the "interpretive concept" of "law as integrity" should be the guiding light for American judges.[134] This approach "asks judges to assume, so far as this is possible, that the law is structured by a coherent set of principles about justice and fairness and procedural due process, and asks them to enforce these in the fresh cases that come before them . . . the ambition [informing this method] is to be a community of principle."[135]

Unless one assumes that Rawls wrote the Constitution, and that therefore his notion of distributive justice is its overarching interpretive principle, there is nothing in this earnest blob of opacity, nestled in a 470-page book, to guide a judge in evaluating anything. It is noteworthy that Dworkin is frequently mentioned as one of the most influential modern legal theorists.[136]

Similarly, Cass Sunstein has attempted in a string of publications to enunciate some "metaprinciples" of constitutional interpretation.[137] Although these are complicated and subtle, they all derive from Sunstein's understanding of the document as an attempt "to encourage and profit from deliberation. . . . The system of checks and balances—the cornerstone of the system—was designed to encourage discussion among different government entities."[138] Political accountability and deliberation are therefore metaprinciples, as are protections of disadvantaged groups, prohibition of procedural unfairness, and so forth.[139] In sum, the Constitution should be construed so as to encourage democratic discussion.

This is a clear and admirable principle as far as it goes. It advises a judge, for example, that laws forbidding flag burning are unconstitutional because the prohibited act is a contribution to political discussion. But the principle of democratic deliberation is relevant to only a small percentage of the cases judges are expected to decide. In the areas of jurisprudence that occupy the attention of conservatives, economic regulations, for example, Sunstein's metaprinciples give less understandable guidelines. He believes, on the one hand, that "a system based exclusively on private orderings and private markets is undesirable in light of the multiple breakdowns of markets, the existence of public aspirations, the injustice of current distribution."[140] Therefore the conservative principle that government should not regulate is wrong. He admits, on the other hand, that sometimes regulation produces "benefits that are dwarfed by the costs," and that there are "paradoxes of regulation: regulatory strategies that . . . bring about results precisely opposite to those that are intended."[141] It would be helpful if we could declare the good regulations constitutional and the bad regulations unconstitutional, but, alas, "[a] claim of failure must depend on some view about the nature of a well-functioning regulatory regime, and such views are controversial."[142] Since the purpose of jurisprudence is to resolve such controversy, this statement represents an abandonment of the point of the exercise.

In the end, Sunstein admits that his principles of deliberation do not tell us how to interpret the Constitution in the area of regulation. The best we can hope for is that legal theorists will be helpful to the executive and legislative branches in suggesting more intelligent policies.[143]

As a group, centrist legal theorists are far less satisfying than centrist political theorists. This is probably because the nature of the task is different in the two areas. Centrist political theorist such as Dahl and Elshtain only have to make a plausible argument that, for all its faults, the democratic capitalist system is too good to inspire revolutionary overthrow. Centrist legal theorists have to articulate a set of principles by which to interpret the Constitution. The former goal is much easier, and political theorists succeed. The latter goal is supremely difficult, and legal theorists fail. As a consequence, as of the turn of the twenty-first century, there was no satisfying, plausible American jurisprudence from the Right, the Left, or the center.

By the first year of the twenty-first century, American social thought was fraying along a variety of dimensions. The classical liberal consensus that the good society consisted of a capitalist economic system and a democratic political system was being subjected to intellectual shear, as the Right was redefining capitalism to lessen its traditional emphasis upon market forces and enhance its formerly implicit endorsement of class struggle, and the Left was seeking to redefine democracy to exclude the possibility that it could coexist with a capitalist economy. Meanwhile, intellectual schools were multiplying as scholarly disciplines divided according to philosophical and methodological preferences, until the ideal of a community of discourse whose members were devoted to the disinterested considerations of social problems seemed to be receding. The terrorist attacks of September 2001 imposed a consensus over national political discussion, but the fundamental disagreements remaining under the surface suggested that the new restraint and comity were temporary.

And so history does not end when the story is brought to a close. The question remains as to whether the insights provided by a survey of the several centuries of American thought will allow us to say something worthwhile about the present and the future.

CHAPTER NINE

Present and Future

No one can foretell the future. But because anticipations of the future are based on knowledge of the present and past, it might be useful to speculate about the ways that traditional American approaches to thinking about politics and economics will work themselves out over the next few decades.

NATURAL LAW SWALLOWS EVERYTHING

The approach to economic analysis inaugurated by Adam Smith two and a quarter centuries ago and refined into modern economics by combining quantifiable methodology with the normative concept "efficiency" during the 1870s has by now become an almost irresistible force in social thought. Its steady advance to domination of not only specifically economic thinking but also of much of jurisprudence and political science is one of the obvious trends of the age. It has become the modern equivalent of natural law—a system of normative prescriptions resting on factual premises—as ubiquitous in contemporary discussions of politics and economics as the old natural law Smith sought to displace. If we are to grasp the essence of social debate in the future, we will have to understand the underpinnings of this contemporary natural law.

When Hugo Grotius asserted in the seventeenth century that natural law would be applicable even if God did not exist, he meant that we can reason from human nature and human circumstances to the rules that are necessary to the achievement of thriving societies. Because "Man" is "a Nature endowed with Reason," the law of reason must rule over his actions.[1] Neoclassical economists have discovered a way to impose this dictum on modern thought. The device of the "theorem," a mathematical formula that, given some enabling assumptions, allows anyone with the requisite knowledge of calculus to reason to conclusions about the rules of efficient behavior, turns economic methodology into an engine of irresistible intellectual power.

Jeremy Taylor, another seventeenth-century natural lawyer, also had some relevant advice about the practical application of reason to God's rules. Humans, having free will, were always at liberty to ignore natural law. But "God has annexed punishments to breaches of the law of nature, and the prospect of those punishments constitutes its obligatory force."[2] In the same way, humans are always free to violate the efficiency recommended by neoclassical economics. Uneducated or irrational people can refuse to endorse actions that lead to a greater overall ratio of benefits to costs as defined by the methodology of economics. But economists do not hesitate to warn that the consequences of such disobedience, in poverty and misery, will be so self-evidently objectionable that they constitute an obligatory force. Because most economists cannot imagine that anyone would want to be poorer rather than richer, they feel confident in assuming that their analyses carry implicit but self-evident moral obligations. When many economists see other people willfully disregarding their advice, therefore, they are powerfully tempted to judge those people as both dimwitted and depraved.

Since the arrival of neoclassical economics, various critics in and out of the academy have directed fusillades of criticism at its methodological assumptions. Observers have rejected economists' use of the postulate of perfect information; their assumption of instantaneous communication; their use of the concept of homogeneous goods in each category of goods; their belief in the perfect mobility of factors, especially labor; and so on. At its most fundamental, this criticism is directed against the foundational assumption of the methodology, the postulate that human beings act rationally to maximize their expected utility.

Some of the dissatisfaction with the assumption of rationality rests on the fact that, in David Braybrooke's words, "though it can itself be saved from tautology, [it] offers the feeblest resistance to being converted into one."[3] Braybrooke means that although the assumption is an empirical assertion about how real people actually behave, and therefore contingent upon empirical verification, economists are always tempted to regard the outer evidence (behavior) as completely indicative of the inner truth (rational maximization), thus rendering verification moot. They rely on observed behavior as "revealed preference," absolutely isomorphic with psychological imperative.[4] Their research rests on an empirical foundation that is beyond empirical test.

Other scholars have not permitted neoclassicals to assume human rationality so cavalierly. For many years psychologists and the small number of experimental economists have tested the fundamental assumption in a variety of experiments using human volunteers. They have also done case studies of business firms to see if such organizations can be described as engaging in maximizing behavior. Most of these studies have concluded that the assumption is mistaken. As Tversky and Kahneman summarize, psychological studies demonstrate that "the deviations of actual behavior from the . . . model are too widespread to be ignored, too systematic to be dismissed as random error, and too fundamental to be accommodated by relaxing the . . . system."[5] In its application to the behavior of firms, also, the primal assumption is, as Mark Blaug reports, "as frequently contradicted as confirmed" by the available evidence.[6]

Further, a few prominent mainstream economists have occasionally questioned the value of the maximization assumption. In France, Maurice Allais, a future Nobel Prize winner, rejected it as early as the 1950s.[7] In Britain, Graham Loomes has contributed much of the empirical testing that has shown it to be at variance with reality.[8] In the United States, Herbert Simon, another Nobel Prize winner, chided the orthodox members of his discipline for forty years for stubbornly "ignoring the boundedness of human rationality."[9] Simon preferred that humans be seen as "satisficers," not maximizers, that is, that they be understood as choosing among multiple goals, providing themselves a minimum level of satisfaction of one, then moving on to another.[10] Yet these three, however much their work is respected, and however much empirical and conceptual value they have added to the teachings of the profession, are virtually without followers. Apparently the discipline's enormous accumulated investment in rational maximizing creates an inertia too heavy to overcome.

But surely neoclassical economists cannot have been knowingly foisting a bogus paradigm on the rest of us for lo these many years? Of course not. The position of the discipline as a whole is that *it doesn't matter* if the maximizing assumption is unrepresentative of reality, because all that matters is the predictive power of the theorems they generate using it.

In making this point, economists always refer to a 1953 article by Milton Friedman entitled "The Methodology of Positive Economics." This essay is virtually the methodological gospel of the discipline. When Daniel Hausman called it, in 1994, "the most influential work on economic methodology of this century," he was actually understating the case.[11] In terms of articulating the argument with which the discipline justifies its own existence, it is the *only* work on methodology that counts. Whenever economists address the issue of unrealistic assumptions, they refer to this article as having obviated the need for further discussion. If, therefore, Friedman is persuasive in his defense of the use of empirically unrealistic assumptions, noneconomists should be cautious about doubting the foundations of the enterprise, If, however, he is seriously mistaken in his thesis, skepticism is warranted.

The purpose of a social or other science, states Friedman, is to predict. "Viewed as a body of substantive hypotheses, theory is to be judged by its predictive power for the class of phenomena which it is intended to 'explain' . . . the only relevant test of the *validity* of a hypothesis is comparison of its predictions with experience."[12] In order to generate such predictive hypotheses, it will often be necessary

> to have "assumptions" that are wildly inaccurate descriptive representations of reality, and, in general, the more significant the theory, the more unrealistic the assumptions (in this sense). The reason is simple. A hypothesis is important if it "explains" much by little, that is, if it abstracts the common and crucial elements from the mass of complex and detailed circumstances surrounding the phenomena to be explained and permits valid predictions on the basis of them alone. To be important, therefore, a hypothesis must be descriptively false in its assumptions; it takes account of, and accounts for, none of the many other attendant circumstances, since its very success shows them to be irrelevant for the phenomena to be explained.[13]

Institutional economists, Marxists, some philosophers of science, an occasional historian or sociologist, and even a few maverick neoclassicals have taken Friedman to task, over the past half century, for a variety of epistemological, philosophical, or logical sins he allegedly commits in this article. It contains, however, a powerful argument. Many scholars would accept the premise that the purpose of a social science is to predict behavior, and the conclusion that any theory that generates hypotheses that consistently succeed at this task is at least provisionally valid, no matter how outlandish its assumptions. The appropriate response to Friedman, then, is to judge economic science on its own terms: how well do economists predict behavior?

Poorly, as it turns out. In the first place, economists as a group avoid empirical work. Various studies have come to the conclusion that only a half to two-thirds of the ten thousand articles published in economics journals each year contain data of any kind. This is a ratio that falls very short of that found in the journals of the two disciplines to which economists like to compare theirs, physics and chemistry. Moreover, those empirical studies that are published contain evidence that is seldom replicated, and when it is, the statistical controls in common use in other social sciences are frequently ignored or violated.[14]

In the second place, and more important, when economists do make serious efforts to subject their theories to empirical tests, the theories are very frequently disconfirmed. That economic theories have a weak record when subjected to actual evidence may seem startling to those not in the discipline, who are likely to be familiar with its great prestige but not its lackluster performance. Yet the long-run record of the failure of even the most influential theories to live up to Friedman's standard is unambiguous:

1. The Law of Demand. If there is one central theory in the discipline since Smith, it must be that when prices for any product rise, demand falls, and conversely. This is an easy relationship to observe. When economists have tried to observe it systematically, "it receives only very weak confirmation, both statistically, and experimentally," reported Deirdre McCloskey in 1998, "and in either case the results depend on various untested assumptions."[15]

2. Economic growth. In 1956 Robert Solow published an article offering a model of economic growth for a generic economy. He posited that growth in any given economy was a function of the relative sizes of its capital stock and its labor force, and technological progress, which was a constant. This article spawned a huge industry of application to various real economies; in fact, it virtually founded a whole subfield. For this pioneering work, Solow received the Nobel Prize in 1987. For three decades after its publication, however, the economists who employed his model of growth did not test it against actual economies. They assumed that it applied, and derived predictions about those economies' future states accordingly.

   In the mid-1980s a number of economists set about empirical application and began to test Solow's model against the historical growth of actual countries. When they did so, they discovered that its major predictions (for example, that standards of living in developed societies would converge, and that investors in all economies would receive diminishing returns to capital investment over time) were decisively disconfirmed by the evidence.[16]

3. Oil prices. After the second oil crisis of 1979, predicting future prices and demand became a hot subject among econometric modelers. In 1982 scholars at the Economic Modeling Forum of Stanford University ran ten statistical models of the international oil market, each employing slightly different assumptions. Although some of the models correctly predicted that prices

would fall in the mid-1980s, none of them predicted that prices in 2000 would be lower than in 1980. Most of them predicted a rise around 1990, to very high levels by 2000.[17] Yet by the late 1990s real oil prices were considerably lower than they had been in 1980.[18]

4. OPEC. A related branch of the oil prediction industry was the effort by economists to model, and thus foresee, the behavior of the Organization of Petroleum Exporting Countries (OPEC). Various members of the profession tried their hand at modeling the organization's behavior in the years immediately after 1979. The controlling assumption of all the predictions was that the member states of OPEC would attempt to maximize their national wealth. None of these models managed to generate predictions that came anywhere near OPEC's actual behavior. As Theodore Moran complained in 1982, "[T]he idea of economic rationality and the pursuit of economic self-interest have not been able to play the role of precise guide to, or constraint on, the determination of OPEC oil policy."[19]

5. Short-run economic forecasting. Few economists are bold enough to claim that they can predict economic activity decades ahead of the fact. Short-run forecasting, however, is a thriving business. Both governments and private organizations in the developed countries issue predictions about how their economies will fare a year hence. These forecasts depend upon the usual computer-assisted econometric models and pay particular attention to predictions of inflation and unemployment. They are all equally useless. As Paul Ormerod summarized in 1998, "The problems of forecasting are not confined to official bodies, nor to any particular theory of how the economy operates. All approaches, whether governmental or private, Keynesian or monetarist, have done equally badly."[20]

6. Movements in asset prices. Economists try to explain changes in the prices of currencies, equities, and government bonds with reference to the "efficient markets" hypothesis. For this purpose, they sometimes assume, first, that the price of an asset reflects its "fundamental" value, and second, that information about fundamentals is available to all potential buyers. One of the implications of this theory is that movements in asset prices will be fairly small over short periods of time. The actual empirical experience, however, is that prices are much more volatile than the theory allows. Kenneth Arrow, a Nobel Prize winner, describes this fact as an "empirical falsification" of the theory.[21]

7. Crime. Economists have attempted to put their conceptual apparatus to use in noneconomic areas, such as crime. The sociological perspective on crim-

inals is, in general, that they are basically irrational, that they rarely think through the possible consequences of their behavior and are therefore creatures of impulse rather than calculation. The economic perspective is that criminals are just as calculating as the average business entrepreneur, and that therefore their behavior can be changed by modifying the probability that they will be caught and punished. Although a large number of economists have attempted to fashion critical tests between these two theories of criminal behavior, their efforts have come to nothing. There is at least as much evidence that "good character" (that is, a moral conscience) determines law abidingness as there is that rational calculation does so.[22]

8. "Rational expectations." The most influential neoclassical innovation over the last three decades of the twentieth century was the theory of rational expectations. As propounded by Robert Lucas (who was awarded the Nobel Prize in 1995) and others, it led to models of the economy that incorporated assumptions about the way business and workers respond to government policy. Citizens learn to anticipate policies that will either produce or suppress inflation, and modify their behavior accordingly. Businesses raise prices, and unions increase their wage demands, in anticipation of inflation. Therefore, virtually all government economic policy is canceled out by counteracting actions in the population.[23] Rational expectations theorists argue for the "policy irrelevance proposition:" nothing the federal government can do could make the economy better, so the correct policy strategy is to stop meddling and let capitalism take its course.[24]

Despite the heavy impact on the profession by the rational expectations paradigm, summarized Jonathan Kershner in 1999, "The problem was that its enormous theoretical promise did not yield significant practical applications."[25] In the words of the author of one empirical test, "the weight of the evidence is sufficiently strong to compel us to suspend belief in the hypothesis of rational expectations."[26] By the dawn of the new millennium, the consensus in the discipline had shifted away from the rational expectations approach and back toward a modified Keynesianism that took more account of monetarism than had Keynes's original formulation.[27] The viability of that hybrid remained to be tested.

Neoclassical economics, therefore, frequently fails the one test it accepts as decisive. Time and again, theories based upon the maximizing assumption are either unable to produce clear empirical conclusions or are refuted outright. If the theories do not predict accurately, then, according to Friedman's dictum, the erroneous assumptions cannot be justified. And if the maximizing assumption cannot be justified, noneconomists are entitled to be highly skeptical of the pronouncements of the discipline.

The fact that it is methodologically dubious has not stopped economics, however, from becoming the queen of the social sciences. Because its mathematical models offer the illusion of knowledge to a world drowning in ambiguity, that world has embraced it with incautious ardor. It is the only social science whose practitioners are awarded Nobel prizes. Nearly half of all National Science Foundation grants to social scientists, and more than half of the grants from other federal funding agencies, go to economists.[28] And its methodology and philosophical perspective are slowly but surely colonizing other disciplines, bringing the maximization paradigm to law and political science. It appears to be the wave of the future in social thought.

If there is one person who embodies that wave in jurisprudence, it is Richard Posner, formerly of the University of Chicago law school, and now a judge on the U.S. Court of Appeals for the Seventh Circuit. His mission since the 1960s has been to imbue American law with the assumptions and reasoning style of neoclassical economics. His remarkable productivity and clear prose style, when combined with the general popularity of the subject, have combined to make him one of the most influential legal thinkers in the country.[29]

Although his assertions are phrased with scholarly caution, Posner is explicitly attempting to persuade Americans to adopt neoclassical economic theory as natural law, and then use that natural law as a standard by which to judge the positive law. His first book, *Economic Analysis of Law* (first edition 1972), is partly a textbook and partly an essay in persuasion for his particular perspective. Legal scholars cite it regularly. Its theses are that "it may be possible to deduce the basic formal character of law itself from economic theory" and further, that "economic theory . . . has ethical implications. It provides unexpected support to those who believe that not all commands backed by state force are entitled to claim obedience as law."[30] Market forces are to assume the status of a constitutional principle, not to be subverted by the popular branch of government.

Over the last three decades Posner has elaborated the argument that actual law is to be held to the standard of neoclassical natural law. He is not a mathematician and only rarely provides a formal structure to an argument; instead, he borrows the formalized conclusions of economists in regard to the social value of markets. He endorses the assumption that "man is a rational maximizer of his ends in life,"[31] and, through a process of reasoning sometimes straightforward and sometimes surreptitious, turns it into the ethical command that governments are morally obligated to pursue the ideal of efficient wealth maximization. He slides from neutral analysis to moral command by presuming that everyone must want to be richer and that they must therefore assent to his plan for achieving riches. Thus "[i]n measuring economic costs and benefits, the economist *qua* economist is not engaged in the separate task of telling policymakers how much weight to assign to economic factors."[32] Nevertheless, "I have defended . . . the ethical principle known as 'wealth maximization,' which I consider to be an attractive principle to guide political choice, especially by courts formulating and applying common law rules such as those governing tort, contract, property, and criminal law. . . . 'Wealth maximization' holds that a transaction or other change in the use of ownership of resources is good if it increases the wealth of the society."[33]

"Wealth maximization," of course, is in practice the same thing as "efficiency" as defined by the methods and concepts of neoclassical economics. Posner claims that although the law and the neoclassicals employ a different vocabulary, American judges have always been economists at heart. "The common law exhibits a deep unity that is economic in character," a unity that is often hidden because much of the economic reasoning of judges has been implicit.[34] But while judges, for hundreds of years, have been pursuing economic efficiency, the same cannot be said of legislators. As a consequence, "statutes exhibit a less pervasive concern with efficiency and a much greater concern with wealth distribution. . . . There is abundant evidence that legislative regulation of the economy frequently, perhaps typically, brings about less efficient results than the market–common law system of resource allocation."[35] Therefore, although Posner always leaves the conclusion implicit, his ultimate recommendation is that judges should strive to impose their enlightened understanding on the people's representatives through interpretation of the Constitution and statutory law. Thus he praises the Supreme Court from the Civil War to the 1930s for protecting "liberty of contract" and elevating classical economic theory to the status of a constitutional principle.[36] Although he always attempts to sound like a disinterested scholar, the impartial style and the implicit conclusions are insufficient to conceal the determinedly antidemocratic nature of his body of work.

Posner's application of neoclassicism, with all of its barely hidden moralizing and contempt for empirical evidence, is well illustrated by his analysis of labor law in a 1984 edition of the *University of Chicago Law Review*. His thesis is that the National Labor Relations Act and subsequent actions by the federal government are part of a general strategy of cartelizing the labor market so that unions may raise the aggregate quantity of their members' income at the expense of everyone else in society. Posner goes through his usual exercise of denying that he is engaged in a moral exegesis, while making plain that he is in fact doing just that. "I emphasize that I am using the word 'cartelization' in a nonpejorative, technical sense.... My analysis is positive, not normative," he asserts.[37] This claim might have been more convincing if he had not just finished claiming that "labor law is ... founded on a policy that is the opposite of the policies of competition and economic efficiency that most economists support."[38] Having thus explained his normative purpose with a wink and a nod, he goes on to apply a standard neoclassical analysis to labor unions, describing them simply as "worker cartels designed to raise the price of labor above the competitive level," with all the mischievous consequences that implies.[39]

This analysis derives from the assumptions of neoclassical methodology and relieves Posner of the obligation of supporting his discussion with evidence. He notices that some empirical research has concluded that labor unions, by raising the productivity of their members, actually add to the wealth of society and thus make the workforce and the firm more efficient than they would be otherwise. An author in another discipline might conclude from this finding that more research was needed to establish if the empirical relationship between unions and productivity was real or spurious. But Posner has no need of research: "Although some empirical support has been marshaled for this productivity—enhancement theory of unionization, the theory is extremely hard to accept. It is inconsistent with the fundamental assumption of economics: that people, in this case employers, are rational profit or utility maximizers."[40]

Thus do the assumptions of the methodology, in Posner's world, trump the empirical findings that run contrary to the conclusions dictated by the assumptions. Perhaps sensing the weakness of this position, in the next paragraph Posner makes another stab at dealing with the problem of empirical findings contradicting his favored conclusions. "The proposition that unions enhance productivity," he writes, "also flies in the face of massive, if unsystematic, evidence pointing to the opposite conclusion."[41] The reader anticipates a few footnotes documenting this massive accumulation of evidence, but Posner does not provide a single citation, there or anywhere else in his article, to support the claim.

It is for good reasons, therefore, that Richard Posner is the famous representative of neoclassical economics in jurisprudence. He has learned his modern economics well. He denies normative intent while smuggling in moral reasoning everywhere. He adopts an empirically false master assumption, and afterward ignores or declines to accept empirical research pertaining to his subject. He nevertheless argues that this methodology should have greater stature in determining public policy than the results of the democratic process. And he is winning.

Neoclassical economics has become at least as influential in political science as it has in jurisprudence. Applied to political phenomena, its methodology forms the "public choice" or "rational choice" subfield of the discipline. Unlike law, its manifestation in political science is not dominated by a single theorist but has inspired dozens of practitioners. The public choice approach is closer to academic economics than is Posner's work because almost all of it is formalized, the great majority of its published research consisting of theorem proving.

Public choice theorists trace their tradition back to two pioneering projects by economists. In 1951 Kenneth Arrow published *Social Choice and Individual Values*, in which he demonstrated that a variety of formalized assumptions about democracy were logically inconsistent with one another. In practical terms, the implication of this conclusion was that given a certain type of democratic procedure (voting on policy alternatives in pairs) and given some hypothetical distributions of preferences in the electorate, it might be impossible for the polity to arrive at a logically intelligible decision. Alternative A might beat alternative B, and B might beat C, but C would, irrationally, beat A.[42] Arrow's work raised the question of whether it was at all possible for democratic institutions to translate preferences into policy, and if so, under what conditions. The second founding text of the public choice movement was Anthony Downs's *An Economic Theory of Democracy* in 1957, which I discussed in chapter 6. Building on the issues raised in these two works, public choice theory has grown to the position it now occupies as the single largest subfield in the discipline. By the mid-1990s two out of any five articles in a typical issue of the *American Political Science Review* employed public choice methodology to address public choice questions.[43]

Despite its great popularity, public choice, being merely the redirection of neoclassical economics toward political questions, rests on the same questionable epistemology. Although there are differing schools within the general subfield, almost all public choice theorists almost all the time adopt the assumption that the entities they are studying, be it voters, parties, employees of an administrative agency, or whatever, are rational maximizers.[44] This position is usually justified with reference to Friedman's 1953 argument about unrealistic assumptions being acceptable as long as the theories predict empirical reality, although there does seem to be more disquiet about this premise within public choice theory than there is within economics per se.[45] When challenged as to the validity of their methodology, public choice theorists have been known to say, "At least we have a theory of human behavior!" meaning that other approaches to the study of politics do not have a microtheory on which they can base macroresearch. The fact that the microtheory is wrong is less important than that it exists.

As disciples of Friedman, however, public choice theorists, like their neoclassical mentors, are bound to maintain that the realism of their assumptions is irrelevant. What matters is the extent to which their theories adequately predict empirical reality. And again, as with orthodox economics, the record of public choice in this regard is seriously wanting. In a hostile review of the subfield in 1994, Green and Shapiro concluded that its theory "fares best in environments that are evidence poor."[46] And the fact is that most of the work in the subfield has consisted of exploring the implications of various hypothetical scenarios, or, in other words, in the avoidance of empirical research.

The avoidance is perhaps wise, because when public choice theory has confronted empirical reality the result has often been ugly. The classic example is the decades of time, reams of paper, and gallons of ink the theorists expended while attempting to model voter turnout. According to the rational-maximizer paradigm, citizens in a mass society should weigh the costs of their participation against the value to themselves of the policies that will be pursued if their favored party or candidate wins, factor in the chance that their one vote will decide the election, then decide not to go to the polls. The cost of voting, in time and mental effort, must be larger than the possibility of one person deciding an election, unless the value to the individual citizen of a policy victory is astronomically high. Public choice theory therefore nicely predicts the behavior of the half the population that abstains in presidential elections, and the three-fifths that stays home in off-year congressional elections. The problem is the millions of people who do vote. All public choice theories predict zero, or close to zero, turnout, and are therefore failures by Friedman's criteria. The only way that the theorists managed to get their theorems to predict actual citizen behavior was to embellish them with ad hoc assumptions about citizens' sense of civic duty, the value of maintaining democracy, and the like, all of which were empirically unmeasured by the researchers and, anyway, introduced theoretical elements that violated the basic assumptions of the model.[47] By 2001 public choice theorists had tacitly admitted defeat and abandoned the project of modeling voter turnout.

Like neoclassical economics, however, the public choice subfield is a vast enterprise comprising many dozens of practitioners, with its own journals (as well as access to the general political science journals), domination of several highly ranked departments at major universities, and a growing prestige within the discipline. Surely all this success could not be based on the deceptively intimidating rigor of mathematical modeling? Surely there must be some examples of important public choice projects that generated testable propositions and then actually passed empirical muster?

To answer these questions, it will be useful to consult a 1997 textbook, *Analytical Politics*, by Melvin Hinich and Michael Munger, two eminent scholars in the subfield. This book possesses the two great virtues of coupling clear word explanations of all the topics with the math theorems that prove the conclusions, and surveying the major topics of the subfield in a thorough, organized manner. If public choice passes the empirical test, it will be evident in this book.

In the first, introductory chapter, the authors whet our appetite by promising to present to their readers the public choice questions that have been subjected to "extensive and rigorous empirical testing."[48] Of the next five chapters, four offer no empirical data, and one contains an at-best casual reference to voting behavior during the Jacksonian era. In chapter 7, the authors discuss the development of the voter turnout literature in the face of successive failures of versions of the theory to predict the actual behavior of citizens. Their summary statement tells us that "though the *levels* of behavior are hard to explain, voters respond to costs of voting, opportunity costs of time, and other factors the 'rational' model predicts, by being less likely to vote."[49] This is an honest reference to actual empirical research and does provide some interesting and useful information to students of mass behavior. However, it leaves the central mystery unsolved: why does a large percentage of the population perform the irrational act of voting? Neither Hinich and Munger, nor any other public choice theorist, can answer.

In chapter 8 the authors discuss a variety of theoretical and empirical studies of voting choice (rather than turnout) within committees. Although much of the discussion is abstruse, the bottom line is that the empirical evidence has not turned out to be as the theories predicted. In response to the repeated failure of their models of the power of an agenda-setter in committees, theorists have added a variety of assumptions, each of which "makes the analytical model more realistic and general. These extensions are accomplished, however, only with a significant increase in the complexity of the model." Because of this increase in complexity, "we are no longer able to make clear predictions about the outcome of majority rule processes with an agenda setter."[50] In summary, reality has disconfirmed public choice theories on this topic.

In their ninth and final chapter, the authors address "the nature of issues in mass elections." They first contrast Downs's "spatial" theory of candidate selection with more recent "directional" theories that construct ideological spaces that differ from Downs's straight-line continuum (circular spaces, for example). They report that "a significant body of empirical work supports the view of political competition found in directional theory," but neither cite nor analyze examples of such work. The reader is therefore unable to evaluate their contention, and the effect of this inability is to make their discussion entirely dependent on theory, without empirical content. The authors then turn to a discussion of ideological voting in Congress, and here, at last, report on a series of studies by Poole and Rosenthal that generated testable propositions and matched them against congressional voting in the generation prior to the Civil War.[51] This is a report of an unambiguously genuine empirical contribution. Hinich and Munger then examine various theories of ideological formation in the mass public, referring to some empirical studies along the way, but not testing any propositions with evidence. They close their book with the "hope that knowing the limitations of institutions and rules will make making good [democratic] choices a little easier."[52]

From the evidence of this textbook, then, the majority of public choice work ignores empirical reality altogether, and of the theories that have been subjected to empirical tests, most have been disconfirmed. There does appear to be a small number of research projects in which public choice theories generated empirical testing and in which the theories have been supported by the evidence. This contribution should not be deprecated. But the ratio of reliable material within the massive accumulation of public choice publications is exceedingly small and produces very little confidence in the enterprise as a whole. It is a weak record with which to justify the takeover of a discipline.

If neoclassical methodology in economics, law, and political science is the wave of future, what conclusions can scholars, politicians, and ordinary citizens draw about its value? The only conclusion that seems defensible is that intense skepticism is the best strategy. No argument from neoclassical premises should be rejected out of hand. But neoclassicals should always be required to produce and explain the evidence justifying their theoretical claims. Entirely theoretical arguments, or those not clearly supported by empirical data, should be considered voodoo. This strategy would almost certainly cause us to reject the entire argument of Posner and those influenced by him. It would admit a few—but only a few—arguments in economics and political science. It would certainly deflate the pretensions to preeminence of neoclassical methodology. It would also recast the arguments over a variety of public policy issues, including globalization.

GLOBALIZATION

Globalization is a political fact and an economic ideal. However, given the varieties of market failure in domestic economies discovered over the twentieth century, it is remarkable that at the beginning of the twenty-first economists' worship of the international market is undiminished. One would think that they would have found various theoretical problems with the market between countries, also. It has not happened. Neoclassical economists on the left and the right disagree vigorously about how much government regulation is justified in domestic economies, but on the international economy they are all as pro–free trade as David Ricardo. Paul Samuelson, doyen of the neoclassical Left, has stated that the doctrine of comparative advantage, upon which the formal model of free trade is founded, is "the most beautiful idea in economics."[53] A survey of economists' opinions during the 1980s revealed that only 3 percent of the respondents disagreed with the assertion that "tariffs and import quotas reduce general economic welfare."[54] Crauford Goodwin has observed that "if there is the equivalent of anti-Christ in economics, it is the proponent of trade restraint."[55] As globalization expands and accelerates, therefore, economists are ever-more pleased.

Given the limitations of the neoclassical worldview discussed in the previous section, however, perhaps it would be prudent for the rest of us to restrain our enthusiasm. The maximization assumption alone should make us reluctant to endorse economists' models that portray free trade is a utopian ideal. In addition, there is another methodological aspect of neoclassical economics with direct relevance to the free trade controversy. This is the practitioners' refusal to measure "cardinal utility." It is difficult to find straightforward discussions of this topic in the economic literature. It seems to have been shoved into the collective unconscious of the discipline. Dragging it out, however, will demonstrate just how tenuous the doctrine of free trade actually is.

In the late nineteenth and early twentieth centuries, economists engaged in an internal debate about the measurement of utility. The details of this discussion do not concern us, but the outcome was important. Most economists decided that it was impossible to measure each individual's utility on a continuous, "cardinal" scale. The most that anyone could hope for would be measurement on an "ordinal" scale—one in which it could be discovered that a consumer preferred alternative A to alternative B, but not by how much. In practice, ordinal utility would be inferred from willingness to pay for various alternatives. An automobile is more highly valued than a watch, because people are willing to pay more for it. An implication of the rejection of cardinal utility (I am eliding a long dispute here) is that interpersonal measurements of utility are invalid, except those gauged by the amount people are willing to pay. Although some economists will acknowledge that, yes, there are valued things that are not measured by our techniques, and yes, some subjective losses can be far more intense than objectively measurable gains, in practice the neoclassicals only admit as reality those differences of utility that can be measured by money transactions. By methodological alchemy, therefore, a large portion of the human experience of costs and benefits became invisible to them.[56]

Take a hypothetical case of a hundred steelworkers at a plant in Pittsburgh. They each garner wages of $50,000 per year, for a total earnings of $5 million. The plant makes steel at a certain price. Suppose, then, that a more efficient Swedish firm begins importing less expensive steel into the United States. Suppose further that U.S. manufacturing firms begin using the cheaper imported steel, to the extent that every one of the 280 million Americans saves $.25 a year. Unable to compete, the Pittsburgh plant closes, and the American steelworkers lose their jobs. To an economist, the value to the country is glaringly obvious. Consumers have saved a total of $70 million, while the steelworkers have only lost $5 million. What could be clearer than that the imported steel is a good deal for the United States, and that a tariff to keep out imported steel, advocated by the steelworkers' union, is a conspiracy against the public? The "value" of the workers' jobs in self-esteem and camaraderie, their anguish at becoming unemployed, the stress on their families, the devastation to their communities—all of this is invisible to economists. Meanwhile, the fact that consumers will never even notice the individual "value" of $.25 is also disregarded. Economists, having proven the public interest, are free to regard those who protest the imported steel as special pleaders, Luddites, or victims of "Globaphobia," as one economics screed is titled.[57]

Lest this hypothetical example be thought an exaggeration, consider an actual instance from a recent textbook. In the mid-1980s domestic timber and lumber producers complained that Canada was subsidizing its lumber exports to the United States. In 1986 the U.S. International Trade Commission was on the verge of leveling a 15 percent import tax on Canadian lumber. Canada objected strenuously and threatened economic warfare. The Reagan administration negotiated with the Canadian government, and reached a compromise: the proposed duty, which would have been collected by the U.S. government, was replaced by a 15 percent export tax, to be collected and retained by Canada. Here is how that episode is analyzed in *Modern Industrial Organization* (2000) by Dennis Carlton and Jeffrey Perloff:

> [U]nder either a 15 percent U.S. tariff or a 15 percent Canadian export tax, U.S. lumber producers gained $416.8 million and U.S. lumber users lost $556.9 million. . . . The combined loss to the United States and Canada combined from either the tariff or the tax was $22.5 million. With the tariff, the United States would have gained $200.4 million and Canada would have lost $223 million. Instead, with the export tax, Canada gained $117.6 million and the United States lost $140.1 million.[58]

There is not a peep in this discussion about the costs—emotional or monetary—to lumberjacks, their families, or their communities of losing their jobs because of Canadian imports. Having been prevented by their epistemology from considering these costs, the authors can then report that the Reagan administration's policy was simply a "way to benefit foreigners."[59]

Similarly, orthodox economists can have no sympathy with the plight of the rural inhabitants of Guatemala, El Salvador, Honduras, and Nicaragua. Until 1989 jobs in those countries were protected by the International Coffee Agreement, which assigned production quotas to each country. With the collapse of the agreement that year, coffee prices have spiraled downward as unrestrained competition has encouraged each country to produce more, thus glutting the market. Increased competition and production, and falling prices, of course, are exactly what economists like about globalization. No doubt they can prove with their calculations that the period since 1989 has been the best in history for coffee drinkers. Meanwhile, however, Central American coffee farmers, unable to anticipate a profit, have abandoned cultivation. "The result," according to Marc Edelman, "has been evictions from plantation housing, increased migration to teeming slums and severe hunger among unemployed coffee workers.... Unregulated markets are a large part of the reason why 700,000 Central Americans face starvation and nearly 1 million more suffer serious food shortages." Tens of thousands of the unemployed have headed north, hoping to sneak across the southern border of the United States, where they might be able to find a job.[60] The chickens of globalization are coming home to roost, unforeseen by the economists' models.

This sort of incomprehension drives nonneoclassical scholars to distraction. One can almost hear Herman Daly and John Cobb Jr. quivering with indignation when they survey the direction of modern free trade with its blithe disregard for everything except the objective monetary gains to traders and consumers:

> Once community is devalued in the name of free trade, there will be a generalized competing away of community standards. Social security, Medicare, and unemployment benefits all raise the cost of production, just like high wages, and they too will not survive a general standards—lowering competition. Likewise, environmental protection and conservation standards of the community also raise costs of production and will be competed down to the level that rules in overpopulated Third World countries. Free trade, as a way of erasing the effect of national boundaries, is simultaneously an invitation to the tragedy of the commons.[61]

My point here is not that trade is bad; it is very often good. Nor is it that those who advocate tariffs and import quotas cannot be selfish special interests; frequently they are. My point is that neoclassical economists, apparently the purest, most disinterested advocates of globalization, are incapable of engaging in a genuine discussion about its true costs and benefits. The ideological spectacles they wear prevent them from seeing anything but its benefits. They could not engage in a real debate with Daly and Cobb, for topics discussed by the those critics are not part of the neoclassical universe of discourse. They are unable even to consider the possibility that special interests and classes may be the chief beneficiaries of trade, or that appeals to trade restraint on behalf of the public interest may, in some circumstances, be valid. "The most beautiful idea in economics" has become a dogma that prevents genuine discussion of policy alternatives.

Economists, however, are not the only advocates of globalization in American public life. A number of journalists, professors, and politicians have weighed in, most of them assuring the public that everything is going to be wonderful; they should just hang on and enjoy the ride. These advocates make a number of optimistic prophecies. Globalization will penalize corruption; it will advance democratization; it will raise living standards everywhere; it will lead to the decline of interstate violence; it will prevent the clash of civilizations; it will decrease inequality; and so on.[62] Not every globalizer would go as far as President George W. Bush, who has declared publicly that free trade is "a moral imperative," but his assertion is only slightly farther down the road than that of a host of commentators.[63]

Although the globalizers have been dedicated and prolific in touting the economic benefits of world trade, they have been surprisingly lax in addressing the political problems it raises. As the locus of economic activity shifts inexorably away from more-or-less self-contained national entities toward the world market as a whole, questions must naturally arise about what authority will make the rules, adjudicate the disputes, and enforce the decisions governing the arguments that will naturally arise in the new system. The history of capitalist development is full of conflict, between producers and other producers, between producers and consumers, between employers and employees, between business and government, between business and environmentalists, between regions, between sectors, and more. The story of the United States is partially the record of the working out of these conflicts within a system of national authority. In the international arena, however, where there is no overarching authority, how will the inevitable disputes be resolved?

This is no hypothetical question. Attacks on unrestrained globalism, coming mainly but not exclusively from the Left, grew to a crescendo during the 1990s, culminating in a series of violent demonstrations during various meetings of national trade ministers late in the decade. Many opponents of globalization go well beyond Daly and Cobb, charging that the process is bad for the environment, bad for workers, bad for the distribution of wealth, bad for domestic political stability, and bad for democracy. Moreover, there is some serious scholarly work that supports all the charges.[64] Opponents of globalization raise the issue of whether capitalists should be allowed to pursue their private interests, on the blind faith that everything will work out for the best, or whether some world authority representing noncapitalists, also, is a moral necessity.

Globalizer theorists acknowledge the need for some sort of international governance to handle future economic conflict, but they are strangely insensitive to the moral problems raised by the question of authority. Virtually all acknowledge that we have reached a stage in world history in which the nation-state is no longer satisfactory. Thus Kenichi Ohmae states baldly that "traditional nation states have become unnatural, even impossible, business units in a global economy."[65] (Ohmae is Japanese, but he has lived and worked in the United States, and his publications are cited by American and European scholars. I therefore consider his work to be a contribution to American thought.)

> So long as nation states continue to view themselves as the essential prime movers in economic affairs, so long as they resist—in the name of national interest—any erosion of central control as a threat to sovereignty, neither they nor their people will be able to harness the full resources of the global economy.... In the long sweep of history, nation states have been a transitional form of organization for managing economic affairs.[66]

Besides exhorting national states to admit their own obsolescence, however, Ohmae has few suggestions as to how a new world economic order might be governed. Similarly, Richard Rosecrance prophecies *"the rise of the virtual state,"* but his opinions about how a virtual world might handle its conflicts are restricted to platitudes:

> The virtualization process requires an effective regulatory state....
> This means that essentially Western commercial codes, legal systems, and relatively incorruptible political practices should be emulated in other regions of the world ... the market and the state must work together to achieve favorable economic outcomes.[67]

Others are more willing to explain that global coordination requires international authorities, and these, by definition, must be able to override parochial governments. Jeffrey Garten tells us that "in the economic realm, where global markets can influence the dollar and American interest rates, or when 30 percent of U.S. growth is reliant on open markets abroad, hang-ups about economic sovereignty are an anachronism."[68] Robert Wright is even more blunt. The subtitle to one of his articles in the *New Republic* is "World Government Is Coming. Deal with It."[69]

Other globalizers have sought to elude the necessity of endorsing world government by concocting fantasies of the way the forces of free trade will solve the problems they create. Thus, for example, in a national best seller entitled *The Lexus and the Olive Tree* (2000), Thomas Friedman acknowledges that "one of the biggest questions to arise in the age of globalization is how we deal with the important issues of workers' rights and sweatshops in the developing world."[70] This is a good start, for the issue Friedman addresses is, in fact, important. His comments on the topic, however, are remarkable for their fatuity:

> In the face of such a challenge the human rights community needs to retool in this post–Cold War world, every bit as much as the old arms makers have to learn how to make subway cars and toasters instead of tanks.... In such a world, activists have to learn how to use globalization to their advantage. They have to learn how to compel companies to behave better by mobilizing global consumers through the Internet. I call this the "network solution for human rights," and it's the future of social advocacy. It is bottom up regulation, or side-by-side regulation—not top-down regulation. You empower the bottom, instead of waiting for the top, by shaping a coalition that produces better governance without global government.[71]

While there is a certain charm to his vision of world government by a wired and aroused citizenry, Friedman, like Ohmae, Rosecrance, Garten, and many others, misses the point made continuously by the protestors in the streets. The political issue of globalization is not essentially the problem of coordination among business firms, or the problem of subjecting businesses to oversight by activist consumers, or the problem of protecting workers from competition from overseas peasants willing to labor for pennies an hour, or the problem of protecting the environment from firms that are pressured by the competitive necessity of cutting costs, although all these are important. At its core, the political issue of globalization is the problem of legitimacy. For if governments derive their just powers from the consent of the governed, and the only government worth supporting is one of the people, by the people, and for the people, by what moral right would an unelected international body exercise authority over anyone? Globalizers have been curiously obtuse in regard to this issue, discussing international political problems as though they consisted entirely of coordination difficulties and lacked any moral dimension.

Leftist critics of globalization, in contrast, have been intensely aware of the legitimacy problem, constantly reminding anyone who will listen that such newly created international quasi-political institutions as the North American Free Trade Agreement (NAFTA), the World Trade Organization (WTO), and the International Monetary Fund (IMF) lack any but the most tenuous connection to citizen participation. And indeed, these organizations almost appear to have been designed by Alexander Hamilton, so insulated are they from mass influence.

For example, Chapter 11 of NAFTA virtually elevates business firms to the status of sovereign nations. It allows investors to sue governments for any regulation that causes a loss of profits. Such suits are heard in a special NAFTA court consisting, at present, of two U.S. and three Canadian judges. When California sought to ban the gasoline additive MTBE, a possible human carcinogen, the chemical's maker, a Canadian corporation named Methanex, sued under the Chapter 11 provisions. Although the case has not yet been decided, an adverse decisions would mean that the state would have to pay the firm more than $1 billion if it wanted to ban the chemical.[72] Even if the state wins, its own democratically elected government will have been submitted to the judgment of an international body several layers removed from popular control and at any rate dominated by officials from another country.

The principle is similar in regard to the WTO, which in 1998 invalidated an American law designed to protect sea turtles because it interfered with the international movement of seafood.[73] By what moral theory does the WTO exercise authority over an elected government? So far, only the Left has asked the question, and none of the globalizers have been able to supply an even marginally plausible answer.

If globalizers ever do face the legitimacy question frankly, they will have to resolve a gigantic version of the dilemma that almost aborted the new Constitution in 1787. In that distant but relevant era, the large states preferred that representation in the new democracy be based on population; the small states preferred some sort of equal representation. Representatives of the poor, and debtors, wanted to give any new government as much democratic authority as possible. Representatives of the rich, and creditors, who dominated at the convention, wanted a government whose powers were hemmed in with many restrictions, and subject to the oversight of an independent judiciary. The resulting Constitution was difficult and awkward to use, and in some important respects antidemocratic, but it created a polity that survived. American society in 1787, however, was a lovefest compared to the world today. A world democracy, even one structured along the lines of the U.S. government, would contain a Senate dominated by relatively unpopulated but internally undemocratic countries, and a House of Representatives dominated by large, desperately poor countries such as China, India, Brazil, and Nigeria, most of which are also internally undemocratic. Moreover, many of these populous countries have cultures that are actively hostile to free market capitalism. If, in other words, globalizing capitalists try to ignore their legitimacy problem by strengthening undemocratic organizations such as the WTO, they will face mounting opposition from the world's populations, including those in the capitalist countries. If they attempt to avoid accusations of illegitimacy by creating a truly democratic world government, they will put anticapitalists into power. The dilemma can only grow worse as the global economy increases in importance. It will, furthermore, be made much worse by the linking of the Arab conflict with Israel to the fundamentalist Islamic hostility to all the West's institutions, a linkage that grows stronger and more threatening before our eyes.

The advocates of globalization have thus failed to address the legitimacy problem. The professional political theorists have not done much better. Academic scholars—people who mostly write articles in professional journals for each other, but always retain the hope that their ideas will be influential in the wider world, à la Rawls—disagree as to whether there is really a new world aborning, and, therefore, if social thought requires a fresh legitimacy theory. Those who do believe that globalization is creating an unprecedented social reality necessitating a new political theory have so far only advocated that thinkers move toward such a philosophy; they have not actually come up with one themselves.[74] While the world awaits the new Locke, the WTO, NAFTA, and the IMF extend their unlegitimated power, and the mobs rage in the streets.

In summary, American political thought—in fact, Western thought in general—is not dealing adequately with the problems created by the success of American economic institutions. The official, scholarly approach to economic problems, the neoclassical paradigm, is unable even to consider most of the pertinent issues. The semiofficial globalization boosterism has failed to understand the profound issue at the heart of the antiglobalization movement. Academic theorists understand the problem, but so far have been unable to solve it. The future looks to be ambiguous, confused, and dangerous.

THE FUTURE OF LIBERALISM

For two and a quarter centuries, liberalism, meaning the fusion of capitalism and democracy, has been the dominant system of beliefs, values, and institutions in the United States. The economic and political wings of the ideology have been inseparable because they shared the core principles of individualism, personal liberty, moral equality, and competition. Despite some variations introduced by other ideologies, individual eccentricity, or group interest, the twin liberalisms have, as Louis Hartz famously argued in 1955, permeated American thought. Hartz was mistaken, however, in describing the liberal tradition as being one of all-encompassing consensus. The truth is quite the contrary, and many of the interesting features of American ideological conflict have derived from the fact that the two portions of liberalism have always been in tension. Typically, on the right, partisans of capitalism have been wary of the potential of democracy to threaten property, and have devised a variety of restraints, including the Constitution, to keep the people's power within bounds. Especially, they have advocated a strong judiciary charged with the task of protecting the rights to accumulation, possession, and transfer from the tyranny of the majority. Similarly, on the left, partisans of democracy have been skeptical of the ability of the people to govern themselves without there being some restraints on the power of capitalism. Progressives have argued, with plausibility, that inequalities of wealth inevitably translate into inequalities of power, and have therefore advocated redistribution of wealth in order to achieve a greater equality of power. Because of the irrepressible tension between democracy and capitalism, much of the interest in watching American political arguments through various eras comes from observing the way that the two principles have both reinforced and opposed one another.

Beginning in the 1960s, however, the dissonant alliance between capitalism and democracy began to decay. In particular, the American Left began to redefine democracy so as to make it incompatible with capitalism. This attempted liberal divorce proceeded slowly and has not yet reached the mainstream of American politics. It is still largely confined to academic thinking. But scholars have influence beyond the university, and the new way (for America, not new for Europe) of thinking about democracy has become more influential. Meanwhile, various thinkers on the right, especially such legal theorists as Epstein and Posner, have been attempting to move American jurisprudence back toward its pre–New Deal position of bulwark against majority tyranny. It is not impossible to imagine a future American political dialogue in which the Right has moved so far from accepting democracy, and the Left has moved so far from accepting capitalism, that the liberal consensus at the center of American politics dissolves.

What would ideological conflict under such conditions look like? An easy answer would be, "It would look like post–World War II Europe," featuring strong socialist parties and a much larger welfare state, though with a more powerful business party than in any European country. But the United States, as usual, would probably be distinctive even as it became less like its old self. An American postliberalism would not simply mimic European politics. Although I cannot divine what the future holds, I can extrapolate from the tendencies of the present Right and Left, and make an educated guess about what their relations might produce as history unfolds. I would also like to evaluate the strengths and weaknesses of each side of the spectrum in terms of the public interest as I understand it.

Partisans of the American Right share an assumption that the invisible hand, working through the price system, is usually capable of coordinating private decisions to reach a socially desirable outcome. They further assume that the state is almost always incompetent, frequently irrational, and often evil. The great value in this approach to politics is that it establishes a presumption against state action that requires advocates of new government activities to justify them. They will frequently not be able to convince conservatives but at least they have been forced to make rational arguments to the public at large. Moreover, the Right is correct in its second assumption. State action is often a gigantic waste of social resources and not uncommonly pernicious. There are many worse political principles than the one that says that government should not do anything more and should cease many of its present activities. Additionally, as a companion to their respect for the market and their disrespect for government, American conservatives value the contribution that businesspeople in general and entrepreneurs in particular make to the economy. And because the private enterprise economy is, in fact, the marvelous wealth machine that the Right proclaims it to be, they are wise in attempting to nurture its creators.

The weaknesses of the Right's approach, however, are threefold. First, the Right does not really believe its own diatribe against government. Conservatives are all in favor of some kinds of government activity: always military and police action, and often regulation of sexual and religious activities; in addition, they rather grumpily endorse a host of social programs such as public schooling (financed, if not necessarily administered, by government), building infrastructure, and more. American conservatives have never dedicated themselves to answering the question: under what conditions is government activity justified? As a consequence, the odor of hypocrisy hangs over all conservative discussion.

Second, while solicitude for the welfare of entrepreneurs is a good thing, the American Right has often morphed that wholesome attitude into simple errand-running on behalf of the rich. In embracing supply-side economics with witless enthusiasm, conservatives have again avoided questions of distinction: when is a tax cut for the wealthy a good thing? As far as the contemporary American Right is concerned, it is always a good thing. This habit leaves the Right vulnerable to the Left's charge that it is not actually recommending public-regarding policies but simply pursuing class warfare.

Third, American conservatives, with a few exceptions, have failed to take seriously the issue of material inequality. By and large they either ignore it or toss off some banality about higher rewards going to merit. But ever-increasing inequality is a serious, socially debilitating, and morally corrosive fact of American society. By its cavalier disregard for this crucial problem, the Right once again raises the suspicion that its only concern is the protection of the haves from the have-nots. Such a stance may garner Republican candidates all the campaign contributions they could ever desire in the short run, but it will do little to protect the public repute of conservative ideology in the long run. The Right's refusal to take the issue of material inequality seriously enhances the intellectual and moral stature of the Left.

Partisans of the American Left turn the assumptions of the Right on their heads. Progressives believe that there is no such thing as the invisible hand; uncoordinated private decisions do not work out for the public good except accidentally. On the other hand, the state, if democratically accountable, is able to act competently and rationally to reach socially desirable outcomes. As a corollary, the rich in general and entrepreneurs in particular have no just claim to moral superiority or unusual social utility. The wealthy have either acquired their riches through cheating, manipulation, and speculation, or they have inherited them, directly as money, or indirectly as brains and character. Wealth equals political power, but shouldn't; the dependence of governance on the class able to contribute campaign funds and hire lobbyists raises serious questions about the legitimacy of the system.

The Left has two great virtues. Its insight into the causal nexus of wealth and power is profound and poses the crucial question of the legitimacy of an ostensibly democratic system. The force of the progressive critique of the power of wealth is illustrated by the controversy over (ultimately successful) efforts in 2001 and 2002 to pass a bill to control campaign contributions in federal elections. In support of this bill, progressives pointed to the undeniable connection between the ability to contribute to candidates and those candidates' subsequent policy decisions. Opposing the bill, conservatives could only offer the lame argument that to prevent the rich from dominating campaigns would be to deny them freedom of speech. Although the passage of this bill into law was greatly helped by the Enron scandal, unfolding at the same time, the scandal only served as a convenient illustration of the problem. The greater reason the progressive critique of the system carried the day is that it was based on a valid analysis of the problem. Whether the McCain-Feingold Act will actually suppress the domination of elections by money is problematic. Nevertheless, whether it succeeds or fails, it illustrates the sensitivity of the Left, and the insensitivity of the Right, to a serious democratic problem.

The second progressive strength is based on the fact that government, under some conditions, is both necessary and capable. As mentioned, this point is not even contested at the practical level by conservatives. At the rhetorical level, conservatives vilify government action, but when they want something done they are willing to violate their own ideological principles. Only progressives can have a frank discussion of whether government action is necessary, and if so, what kind would be appropriate, because only progressives are ideologically capable of accepting such action as a fact of life. Conservatives often accuse progressives of being too quick to run to government for solutions to social problems, and much of their criticism is justified. As long as conservatives are unable to offer a set of principled rules for appropriate government action, however, they exile themselves from a serious discussion of alternatives to progressive proposals. In this sense, when it comes to governance, progressives are the only game in town.

The Left, however, has its own serious weaknesses. As a group, progressives are as unreasonably hostile to private enterprise as conservatives are as unreasonably hostile to government. It is as though leftists do not want to give capitalists credit for the achievements of capitalism. They sometimes seem to reverse the formula of Gilder's *Wealth and Poverty*: whatever the situation, they advocate higher taxes and more regulation. The leftward politics of anti-supply-side economics are as irrational as the rightward politics of the supply side. They are irrational because it is, in fact, private individuals who create almost all the wealth of our astounding society, a wealth that supports scientific progress, sponsors medical and public health advancements that are responsible for a steadily lengthening life expectancy, brings forth a steady stream of interesting and useful new products and services, and, directly or indirectly, pays the salaries of the leftist scholars who are attempting to bring capitalism into disrepute. The Left's hostility to those responsible for such achievement raises justified questions about whether its representatives should be trusted to direct the political economy.

Second, the Left has taken the "principle of redress," which Rawls invented to argue that society should attempt to compensate for inequalities of natural endowment, and enshrined it unreflectively as a moral absolute.[75] Progressive authors are astonishingly quick to assert that people do not deserve the above-average income they have garnered through above-average achievement. Whether it is

Paul Samuelson claiming that "there is only the most tenuous connection between rewards and deservingness";[76] or John Roemer assuring us that entrepreneurs do not merit great wealth because entrepreneurial skill and the willingness to take risks are only the result of environmental or genetic factors;[77] or Cass Sunstein arguing that market outcomes, including personal incomes, are "morally arbitrary," because they depend upon the accidents of history;[78] or Robert Kuttner maintaining that "the market reflects nothing more than luck,"[79] progressives display an increasing reluctance to concede the moral right to superior rewards for superior performance.

The major problem with the Left's increasing willingness to deny higher compensation for any achievement is not that, if adopted as a principle, it would make all wages and salaries the subject of interest-group pressure, rearranging every person's income on the basis of a politically determined "deservingness" that would inevitably reward victims more than achievers—although it would do that. The major problem is that it is impossible to accept the sincerity of those making the argument. It is appropriate, when discussing this issue, to apply the principle of self-application: is it plausible that those advocating severing compensation from market forces would endorse the application of the principle to their own lives? Would Paul Samuelson be in favor of the state redistributing his Nobel Prize money to someone else? Would Cass Sunstein acquiesce in having his law professor's salary given to a person outside of the university? Would Robert Kuttner gladly relinquish his positions as columnist for *Business Week* and co-editor of the *American Prospect* to a tyro with no accomplishments in journalism? Do they think that their own achievements, being the result of accidentally inherited genetic factors and historical good fortune, do not deserve to be recognized? Or do they think that government should redistribute the rewards of capitalists but not of intellectuals? To ask these questions is to expose the absurdity of the difference principle and the leftist posturing it has inspired. But whether or not they would agree to have the principle applied to themselves, progressives are advocating that it be applied to everyone else. Conservatives are right to view this development with contempt.

Third, the Left is vulnerable to the charge that in its eagerness to apply democratic authority to every problem, it is both wildly overestimating what government can do and greatly underestimating the potential menace of coercive power. A great many progressive writers seem to assume that power will cease to be dangerous as soon as it is cleansed of capitalist disinformation. A branch of the Right is disquieting because it is blithely willing to transfer power to unelected judges. The entire Left, however, is at least as alarming in its faith in the trustworthiness of an unrestrained people, or, worse, those who act in the people's name. Reading progressive literature, one acquires an ever-greater respect for Adams's, Madison's, and Hamilton's insistence that all institutions must be hindered and enfeebled because no one can be trusted with unconstrained power.

If the liberalism that underlies American political argument disintegrates into progressive and conservative ideologies that are plausible projections of present trends, therefore, the resulting public discourse is unlikely to improve on the one available now. Both the probable future Right and Left will have serious liabilities. This gross imperfection in both ideological trends is a major problem because somebody has to govern. If the conceptual apparatus of each side is deeply flawed, it will not matter who that somebody is. Progressives and conservatives will make different decisions, based upon incompatible premises, but all equally reckless. Clearly, some rethinking is necessary if the Republic is to manage the future as well as it has the past.

Beginning in the 1990s there have been some attempts to either recast liberalism or provide some alternative premises for a new ideology. Of these, the most interesting are the various attempts to revive something like the old republicanism of the eighteenth century. The new republican theorists would not attempt to retract personal freedoms but fashion an alternative ideal of society that emphasized the act of creating shared values through common deliberation. "Despite its appeal, the liberal vision of freedom lacks the civic resources to sustain self-government," wrote Michael Sandel, in a much-cited book, in 1996. "The republican tradition, with its emphasis on community and self-government, may offer a corrective to our impoverished civic life."[80] Although Sandel's idea is short on specifics, his is an appealing first effort to rethink the future. Similarly, James Fishkin has not just imagined but implemented a new institution for American society, a "deliberative convention" in which randomly chosen citizens meet and discuss public issues in an atmosphere that maximizes information and dispassionate analysis while minimizing partisan spin.[81]

Neither of these efforts is likely to inspire radical changes in the polity. Their importance consists in their status as beginning efforts to transcend what appear to be the dangers looming ahead: a politics of identity that fractures the polity, a class struggle unrestrained by notions of shared citizenship, and an out-of-control economy that is increasingly disconnected from democratic legitimacy. It is the obligation of the rest of us to supplement their contributions. The purpose of thinking on this subject should be neither to retain, nor destroy, nor reform liberalism, but to create a system of ideas and values that could ensure prosperity while guaranteeing legitimacy as the nation progresses.

Notes

PREFACE

1. Hartz, *Liberal Tradition*.
2. R. McCloskey, *American Conservatism*; Schattschneider, *Semi-Sovereign People*, 119.
3. C. Lloyd, *Structures of History*, 17, 47, 164.
4. Ibid., 24–25; Litowitz, *Postmodern Philosophy*, 1, 12–13, 18, passim.
5. Foucault, *Archaeology of Knowledge*, 76.
6. Ibid., 185, 186.
7. C. Lloyd, *Structures of History*, 24–25, 142–143.
8. Clower, "Ideas of Economists," in Klamer, McCloskey, and Solow, *Consequences of Economic Rhetoric*.
9. C. Lloyd, *Structures of History*, 38; Boyd, "Scientific Realism," in Boyd, Gasper, and Trout, *Philosophy of Science*, 195.
10. C. Lloyd, *Structures of History*, xvi; see also Hempel, "Empiricist Criteria," in Boyd, Gasper, and Trout, *Philosophy of Science*, 71–84.
11. C. Lloyd, *Structures of History*, 46, 52, 93–95.
12. R. Smith, "If Politics Matters," 5.
13. Marx, "Eighteenth Brumaire," in Feuer, *Marx and Engels*, 320.
14. Morone, "Other's America," 186; McWilliams, "Le Guru Returns," 22.

CHAPTER 1. ORIGINS, 1690–1776

1. Ellis, *American Political Cultures*, viii.
2. Carr, *Time, Narrative, and History*, 115, 155–156, 177.
3. Locke, *Second Treatise of Government*, 13.
4. Becker, *Declaration of Independence*, 27.
5. Lutz, "Influence of European Writers," 191–193.
6. Franklin, "Direct Taxes," in Koch, *American Enlightenment*, 81.
7. Otis, "Rights of the British Colonies," in Jensen, *Tracts of the American Revolution*, 28.
8. Goddard, editorial in the *Constitutional Courant*, in Jensen, *Tracts of the American Revolution*, 89.
9. Adams, "Rights of the Colonists," in Jensen, *Tracts of the American Revolution*, 235.
10. Hamilton, "The Farmer Refuted," in Koch, *American Enlightenment*, 594.

11. Virginia constitution of 1776, quoted in F. G. Wilson, *American Political Mind*, 94.
12. Massachusetts constitution of 1780, reproduced in John Adams, *Political Writing*, 96–98.
13. Kendall, *John Locke*, 70.
14. Hartz, *Liberal Tradition*, 62.
15. Ibid., 15, 226, 271.
16. Wilentz, *Chants Democratic*, 219, 387–388.
17. Foner, "Socialism in the United States," 59, 74–75.
18. Kloppenberg, "From Hartz to Tocqueville," in Jacobs, Novak, and Zelizer, *Democratic Experiment*, 364–365.
19. R. Smith, *Civic Ideals*, 470.
20. The phrases are from Morone, "Other's America," 186–187.
21. Ibid., 192.
22. Smith, in Skinner, *System of Social Science*, 9.
23. A. Smith, *Lectures on Jurisprudence*, 316–317.
24. Ibid., 318–321; Rothschild, *Economic Sentiments*, 233.
25. A. Smith, *Wealth of Nations*, 14.
26. Ibid., 485.
27. Winch, *Adam Smith's Politics*, 98, 112.
28. Rothschild, *Economic Sentiments*, 61, 64, 67, 71.
29. A. Smith, *Theory of Moral Sentiments*; A. Smith, *Lectures on Jurisprudence*, 344, 363, 365, 378, 384, 388, 514, 527.
30. Rothschild, *Economic Sentiments*, 231.
31. Gide and Rist, *Economic Doctrines*, 103.
32. Shalhope, *Roots of Democracy*, 160.
33. Henretta, *American Capitalism*, xvii–xxi.
34. Kramnick, "'Great National Discussion,'" 4–5.
35. Bailyn, *Ideological Origins*; G. Wood, *Creation*; Pocock, *Machiavellian Moment*.
36. Bolingbroke, quoted in G. Wood, *Creation*, 21.
37. Hamilton's speech at the constitutional convention, June 18, 1787, as recorded by James Madison, in Hamilton, *Writings*, 156.
38. J. Harrington, *Commonwealth of Oceana*, 19–20.
39. Thomas Jefferson to Thomas Mann Randolph, May 30, 1790, in Koch and Peden, *Writings of Thomas Jefferson*; Shalhope, *Roots of Democracy*, 48.
40. Pangle and Pangle, *Learning of Liberty*, 168–169; Banning, *Jeffersonian Persuasion*, 36–37.
41. Lutz, "European Writers," 194; Banning, *Jeffersonian Persuasion*, 55–57.
42. Appleby, "Republicanism," 21.
43. Appleby, *Capitalism*, 62–63.
44. Ibid., 15; Kramnick, "'Great National Discussion,'" 16–17.
45. Goebel, "American Populism," 112.
46. Sandel, *Democracy's Discontent*.
47. Kloppenberg, *Virtues of Liberalism*, 41.
48. Morone, *Hellfire Nation*, 41–51; Kuehn, *Congregationalist Political Thought*, 93, 94,

126; Innes, *Creating the Commonwealth*, 204–207; Breen, *Good Ruler*, xii, 161–162, 167, 273; Morgan, *Puritan Political Ideas*; Schneider, *Puritan Mind*, 157, 197.
49. R. McCloskey, *American Conservatism*.
50. Greenstone, *Lincoln Persuasion*, xxi, 6.
51. Morone, *Democratic Wish*, 1, 22.
52. Eisenach, "American Political Thought," 170.
53. Ellis, *American Political Cultures*, 151.

CHAPTER 2. THE FOUNDING, 1776–1819

1. Faulkner, *American Economic History*, 210–211, 296, 299; Atack and Passell, *New Economic View*, 113, 240.
2. Henretta, *American Capitalism*, 249; Faulkner, *American Economic History*, 161.
3. Atack and Passell, *New Economic View*, 181.
4. Lee, quoted in J. Ely, *Guardian*, 26.
5. M. Horwitz, *Transformation of American Law, 1780–1860*, 31.
6. F. G. Wilson, *American Political Mind*, 177–179; Williamson, *American Suffrage*, 38.
7. Jefferson and Pendleton, quoted in G. Wood, *Creation*, 530.
8. Baumol, "Eight Laws," 265–281; Blaug, *Economic Theory*, 160–162.
9. Baumol, "Eight Laws"; Dorfman, *Economic Mind*, vol. 2, 513; A. Perry, *Political Economy*, 42, 155.
10. Pocock, *Machiavellian Moment*, 448, 484; Spengler, "Political Economy," 25, 58.
11. Hammond, *Banks and Politics*, 35–37.
12. Nelson, *Liberty and Property*, 89–90, 94, 111; T. Ferguson, "Party Realignment," 31–34.
13. Faulkner, *American Economic History*, 207–209.
14. Bailyn, *Ideological Origins*, 236–246; J. Miller, *Federalist Era*, 104.
15. Washington, quoted in Faulkner, *American Economic History*, 210–211; Jefferson to Edward Coles, August 25, 1814, in Koch and Peden, *Writings of Thomas Jefferson*, 641; Adair, "James Madison," in *Founding Fathers*, 185, 199.
16. Lovejoy, *Reflections*, 52.
17. Wills, *Explaining America*, 264.
18. M. White, *Philosophy*, 162.
19. Hofstadter, *American Political Tradition*, 9.
20. G. Wood, *Creation*, 505.
21. Rakove, *Original Meanings*, 190.
22. Abbott, "*Federalist Papers*," 525.
23. Hamilton, Jay, and Madison, *Federalist*, 337.
24. Ibid., 61.
25. Ibid., 59.
26. Peterson, *James Madison*, 106.
27. Sheldon, *Philosophy of James Madison*, 13–14.
28. Wills, *Explaining America*, 20.
29. Quoted in Spengler, "Political Economy," 15.

30. Fleischacker, "Adam Smith's Reception," 898.
31. Ibid., 897.
32. A. Smith, *Wealth of Nations*, 850.
33. Ibid., 851.
34. Ibid., 851–852.
35. Hamilton, Jay, and Madison, *Federalist*, 339–340.
36. Ibid., 54.
37. Ibid., 57, 337.
38. Ibid., 60.
39. Ibid., 59.
40. Ibid., 337.
41. Ketcham, *Anti-Federalist Papers*, 231.
42. Dahl, *Preface*, 22; Hofstadter, *American Political Tradition*, 7, 17; B. Barber, "Compromised Republic," in R. Horwitz, *Moral Foundations*, 24–27, 30–31.
43. Mason, "Split Personality," in Roche, *American Political Thought*, 165.
44. Hamilton, quoted in J. Miller, *Alexander Hamilton*, 124.
45. Hamilton, "Speech," in Hamilton, *Writings*, 493.
46. J. Miller, *Federalist Era*, 80.
47. The first part of the quotation is from Letwin, "Economic Policy of the Constitution," in Dickman, *American Constitution*, 130; second part from Dorfman, *Economic Mind*, vol. 1, 416.
48. Bowers, "Hamilton," in Cooke, *Alexander Hamilton*, 11.
49. J. Miller, *Alexander Hamilton*, 230, 235.
50. Hamilton, quoted in J. Miller, *Federalist Era*, 40.
51. Hamilton, "Report on Public Credit," in Koch, *American Enlightenment*, 625.
52. Hume, quoted in J. Miller, *Alexander Hamilton*, 233.
53. Hamilton, "Report on Public Credit," 626.
54. Hamilton to Robert Morris, April 30, 1781, in Koch, *American Enlightenment*, 573–574.
55. Banning, *Jeffersonian Persuasion*, 139.
56. Hamilton, "Report on a National Bank," in Koch, *American Enlightenment*, 628.
57. Ibid.
58. McDonald, *Alexander Hamilton*, 194–195.
59. Hamilton, "Report on Manufactures," in Koch, *American Enlightenment*, 632.
60. Ibid., 637.
61. Ibid.
62. Nelson, *Liberty and Property*, 40–48.
63. Cooke, "Reports of Alexander Hamilton," in Cooke, *Hamilton*, 82; J. Miller, *Federalist Era*, 65; Faulkner, *American Economic History*, 169.
64. Nelson, *Liberty and Property*, 49, 50.
65. Hamilton, Jay, and Madison, *Federalist*, 503, 509.
66. Ibid., 506.
67. Ibid., 505.

68. Hamilton to Edward Carrington, May 26, 1792, in Hamilton, *Writings*, 749.
69. Knott, *Alexander Hamilton*, 73–75.
70. Ibid., 26.
71. Skowronek, *New American State*, 22.
72. Hamilton to Theodore Sedgwick, July 10, 1804, in Hamilton, *Writings*, 1022.
73. Jefferson to Thomas Mann Randolph, May 30, 1790, in Koch and Peden, *Writings of Thomas Jefferson*, 496.
74. Appleby, "Republicanism," 33.
75. Jefferson, "Notes on Virginia," in Koch and Peden, *Writings of Jefferson*, 280.
76. Maclay, quoted in Banning, *Jeffersonian Persuasion*, 148.
77. Jefferson, "The Anas," in Koch and Peden, *Writings of Jefferson*, 127.
78. Jefferson, quoted in Hofstadter, *American Political Tradition*, 35.
79. Madison, quoted in Peterson, *James Madison*, 188–189.
80. Jackson, quoted in Hammond, *Banks and Politics*, 116.
81. Jefferson to John Taylor, May 28, 1816, in James Adams, *Jeffersonian Principles*, 23.
82. Hammond, *Banks and Politics*, 219–220, 240; Peterson, *James Madison*, 291–292; Walters, *Albert Gallatin*, 254–255; Agar, *Price of Union*, 193.
83. Madison, quoted in Hobson, "Republicanism," in Paul and Dickman, *Liberty*, 89.
84. Agar, *Price of Union*, 161–162.
85. Taylor, quoted in F. G. Wilson, *American Political Mind*, 170.
86. Taylor from *Principles and Policy* and *Tyranny Unmasked*, both quoted in Parkes, *American Experience*, 150–151.
87. Randolph, quoted in Kirk, *John Randolph*, 149.
88. Ibid., 44, 47, 53.
89. Taylor, *Arator*, 180.
90. Randolph, quoted in Coit, *John C. Calhoun*, 166.
91. Randolph, "Roads and Canals," in Kirk, *John Randolph*, 433.
92. Taylor, quoted in Bradford, introduction to *Arator*, 30.
93. Kirk, *John Randolph*, 165; Bradford, introduction to *Arator*, 31.
94. Bayard, quoted in J. Miller, *Federalist Era*, 107.
95. Freeman, *Affairs of Honor*, 203.
96. McCullough, *John Adams*.
97. Dorfman, "Regal Republic," in Roche, *Origins*, 128.
98. Adams, quoted in Koch, *Founding Fathers*, 89, 92.
99. Adams, quoted in P. Smith, *John Adams*, vol. 1, 243.
100. Adams, quoted in McCullough, *John Adams*, 377.
101. Adams, quoted in P. Smith, *John Adams*, vol. 2, 755.
102. P. Smith, *John Adams*, vol. 2, 1130.
103. Adams, quoted in McCoy, *Elusive Republic*, 213.
104. Adams to Benjamin Rush, August 28, 1811, in Koch, *American Enlightenment*, 211.
105. Ibid.
106. P. Smith, *John Adams*, vol. 2, 843; Adams, quoted in Malone, *Ordeal of Liberty*, 29.
107. Adams, quoted in McCullough, *John Adams*, 428.

108. Randolph, quoted in Walters, *Albert Gallatin*, 191.
109. Gallatin, "Finances of the United States," in E. J. Ferguson, *Writings of Albert Gallatin*, 40.
110. Ibid.
111. Gallatin, quoted in Walters, *Albert Gallatin*, 48, see also 95.
112. Gallatin, "Report to a Committee of Congress," January 2, 1804, in E. J. Ferguson, *Writings of Albert Gallatin*, 222–227.
113. Jefferson to Gallatin, July 12, 1803, in Nelson, *Liberty and Property*, 128.
114. Gallatin, quoted in Nelson, *Liberty and Property*, 128.
115. E. J. Ferguson, introductory material in *Writings of Albert Gallatin*, 264.
116. Gallatin, "Report on the Bank," in E. J. Ferguson, *Writings of Albert Gallatin*, 264–274.
117. Gallatin to William H. Crawford, chairman of the Senate, January 30, 1811, in E. J. Ferguson, *Writings of Albert Gallatin*, 275–280.
118. Gallatin, "Report on Roads and Canals," April 6, 1808, in E. J. Ferguson, *Writings of Albert Gallatin*, 228–239.
119. Gallatin, "Report on Manufactures," April 19, 1810, in E. J. Ferguson, *Writings of Albert Gallatin*, 240–263.
120. Franklin, quoted in Eckes, *Opening America's Market*, 2.
121. Peterson, *James Madison*, vol. 1, 97.
122. P. Smith, *John Adams*, vol. 2, 765–766; Faulkner, *American Economic History*, 159; J. Miller, *Federalist Era*, 15.
123. Nelson, *Liberty and Property*, 59–60.
124. Atack and Passell, *New Economic View*, 121.
125. Quoted in ibid., 130.
126. Madison, quoted in Nelson, *Liberty and Property*, 135.
127. Faulkner, *American Economic History*, 169.
128. Quincy, quoted in Hofstadter, *American Political Tradition*, 42.
129. Jefferson, quoted in Hofstadter, *American Political Tradition*, 41.

CHAPTER 3. DEMOCRACY AND CAPITALISM, 1819–1862

1. Brunner, *Time Almanac*, 795, 796; North, *Structure and Change*, 191; Fogel and Engerman, *Time on the Cross*, 250; Henretta, *American Capitalism*, 177–178; Scott, *Pursuit of Happiness*, 75.
2. Atack and Passell, *New Economic View*, 191, 194.
3. Faulkner, *American Economic History*, 299.
4. Temin, *Jacksonian Economy*, 91; Faulkner, *American Economic History*, 209–211.
5. Appleby, "Popular Sources," 440–441, 444; Welter, *Mind of America*, 180–181; Boorstin, *National Experience*, 30, 110.
6. Grund, quoted in Hofstadter, *American Political Tradition*, 57.
7. Tomlins, *Law, Labor, and Ideology*, 128–131, 149; Rayback, *American Labor*, 56–57, 59, 60, 67, 81–82; Lipset, Trow, and Coleman, *Union Democracy*, 18.
8. Faulkner, *American Economic History*, 205–206.

9. Fogel and Engerman, *Time on the Cross*, 73, 77, 129; Fogel and Engerman, *Without Consent*; Wright, *Cotton South*, 12–15, 24, 35, 139–142.
10. Quoted in Boorstin, *National Experience*, 147.
11. Faulkner, *American Economic History*, 266; Brunner, *Time Almanac*, 795–96.
12. Dorfman, *Economic Mind*, vol. 2, 596.
13. Fetter, "Early History of Political Economy," in Gherity, *Economic Thought*, 477.
14. Conkin, *Prophets of Prosperity*, 30, 313.
15. Ricardo, *Principles of Political Economy*, 61–62.
16. Dorfman, *Economic Mind*, vol. 2, 710.
17. Mill, *Principles of Political Economy*, 1, 553.
18. Ibid., 123.
19. Fetter, "Early History," 485; Boorstin, *National Experience*, 106–107.
20. Dorfman, *Economic Mind*, vol. 2, 567; Kaufman, *Capitalism*, 45–66.
21. Carey, *Harmony of Interests*; Larson, *Internal Improvement*, 136.
22. List, *National System*. It should be noted that List denied he was a mercantilist because he does not define wealth as the amount of bullion in a country; the point is well taken, but his emphasis on the seamlessness of national power and wealth is clearly mercantilist. See also Fetter, "Early History," 477–481.
23. McVickar, quoted in Dorfman, *Economic Mind*, vol. 2, 519.
24. McVickar, quoted in Conkin, *Prophets of Prosperity*, 114.
25. Conkin, *Prophets of Prosperity*, 87, 203, 204, 237–238.
26. Ibid., 211.
27. Leggett, *Democratick Editorials*, 5.
28. Brownson, "Laboring Classes," in Levy, *Political Thought in America*, 243.
29. Whitman, " 'Editorials' in the *Brooklyn Daily Eagle*," in Levy, *Political Thought in America*, 200.
30. Novak, *Peoples' Welfare*, 53–54, 58, 63, 79–80, 120, 163–186, 194, 204.
31. Larson, *Internal Improvement*, 93, 105, 190.
32. Ibid., 236, 238; Gunn, *Decline of Authority*, 1, 169, 184, 256–257.
33. Larson, *Internal Improvement*, 238–239.
34. Atack and Passell, *New Economic View*, 652.
35. Calculated from tables available at www.economagic.com.
36. John, *Spreading the News*, 3–5, 223, 236, 238.
37. Sedgewick, quoted in Kelley, *Cultural Pattern*, 158.
38. Nagel, *John Quincy Adams*, 357, 367, 374–375; Van Deusen *Jacksonian Era*, 91.
39. Speech by Josiah Quincy on suffrage, in Peterson, *Democracy*, 66.
40. Speech by James Kent on suffrage, in Peterson, *Democracy*, 194, 197.
41. Speech by Philip Nicholas on suffrage, in Peterson, *Democracy*, 394–395.
42. "City of Richmond," in Peterson, *Democracy*, 383–384.
43. Speech by John Cooke on suffrage, in Peterson, *Democracy*, 303–304.
44. Williamson, *American Suffrage*, 204–205, 206–207, 225, 267–268, 280; Degler, *Out of Our Past*, 136.
45. McCormick, "New Perspectives on Jacksonian Politics," in Bonadio, *Political Parties*, vol. 2, 543–549.

46. Warren, *Bankruptcy*, 52.

47. Emerson, journal entry in Gilman, *Ralph Waldo Emerson*, 63; Emerson, quoted in Parrington, *Main Currents*, vol. 2, 392.

48. "Declaration of Sentiments" and introductory material in S. Davis, *American Political Thought*, 157, 170.

49. Rowan, quoted in Welter, *Mind of America*, 80–81.

50. Alabama "Remonstrance," February 4, 1828, in Goodrich, *Government and the Economy*, 233, 234.

51. Calhoun, quoted in Hofstadter, *American Political Tradition*, 71.

52. Carey, *Harmony of Interests*, 23, 45.

53. Ibid., 41–55.

54. Ibid., 55.

55. Carey, quoted in Fetter, "Early History," 482; see also Van Deusen, *Jacksonian Era*, 19–20.

56. Carey, *Financial Crises*, 8.

57. Ibid.

58. Webster, "Speech in Defense of the Tariff," in Levy, *Political Thought in America*, 178–179.

59. Rayback, *American Labor*, 86–89; Fox, *Decline of Aristocracy*, 58.

60. List, *National System*, 351.

61. Ibid., 351, 347.

62. Ibid., 166.

63. Ibid., 123.

64. Ibid., 126.

65. Ibid., 42–43, 324.

66. List, "Letter II," July 12, 1827, in Goodrich, *Government and the Economy*, 208.

67. Hamilton, quoted in Dangerfield, *Awakening of American Nationalism*, 277.

68. Attack and Passell, *New Economic View*, 130–141.

69. Schlesinger, *Age of Jackson*, 45.

70. Hallett, quoted in Welter, *Mind of America*, 169.

71. Jackson, quoted in Coit, *John C. Calhoun*, 261.

72. Jackson's veto message, July 10, 1832, in Goodrich, *Government and the Economy*, 316–317.

73. Webster's speech to Senate, July 11, 1832, in Goodrich, *Government and the Economy*, 326, 329.

74. Hammond, *Banks and Politics*, 572, 614; Rayback, *American Labor*, 90; Atack and Passell, *New Economic View*, 91, 104; Faulkner, *American Economic History*, 166.

75. Rayback, *American Labor*, 90–91.

76. For arguments and evidence that Jackson's actions were peripheral to the panic of 1837, see Temin, *Jacksonian Economy*, 23, 119, 141, 151–154; for a discussion of the evidence that Jackson was significantly responsible, see Atack and Passell, *New Economic View*, 96–102.

77. Van Buren, quoted in Van Deusen, *Jacksonian Era*, 121–122; see also Faulkner, *American Economic History*, 165.

78. Leggett, *Democratick Editorials*, 185–186; Blair, quoted in Kelley, *Cultural Pattern*, 156; Wood, quoted in Schlesinger, *Age of Jackson*, 112.

79. *Boston Atlas*, quoted in Schlesinger, *Age of Jackson*, 112; Webster, quoted in Van Deusen, *Jacksonian Era*, 122; Clay, quoted in Remini, *Henry Clay*, 558.

80. Atack and Passell, *New Economic View*, 85.

81. Ibid., 103–107.

82. Degler, *Out of Our Past*, 162; W. Miller, *Arguing about Slavery*, 10–11.

83. Hammond, quoted in W. Miller, *Arguing about Slavery*, 10.

84. Atack and Passell, *New Economic History*, 362.

85. Eaton, *Growth of Southern Civilization*, 305.

86. Wirt, quoted in Brown, "Missouri Crisis," in Bonadio, *Political Parties*, 564.

87. Stern, introduction to Stowe, *Uncle Tom's Cabin*, 7, 25, 33.

88. Douglass, "Fourth of July?" July 5, 1852, in S. Davis, *American Political Thought*, 220–221.

89. Quoted in W. Miller, *Arguing about Slavery*, 349.

90. Leach, quoted in Welter, *Mind of America*, 355.

91. Lincoln, "Speech in Independence Hall," February 22, 1861, in T. H. Williams, *Abraham Lincoln*, 137; W. Miller, *Arguing about Slavery*, 501.

92. Foner, *Free Soil*, 9, 54, 97.

93. Scott, *Pursuit of Happiness*, 98.

94. Dew, "Dew on Slavery," in *Political Register*, 822.

95. Lincoln, "Fragment on Slavery," in T. H. Williams, *Abraham Lincoln*, 39.

96. Grampp, "John Taylor," 260; Coit, *John C. Calhoun*, 331; Pickens, quoted in Coit, *John C. Calhoun*, 334.

97. Ruffin, excerpted in McKitrick, *Slavery Defended*, 84–85.

98. Fitzhugh, *Cannibals All!* 73, 79.

99. Brownson, "Laboring Classes," 239–240.

100. Lincoln, "Speech at Kalamazoo, Michigan," August 27, 1856, in T. H. Williams, *Abraham Lincoln*, 65.

101. Foner, *Free Soil*, 16.

102. Coit, *John C. Calhoun*, 334; Hofstadter, *American Political Tradition*, 89.

103. Sundquist, *Dynamics of the Party System*, 80–81.

104. Meister, "Legacy of *Dred Scott*," 204, 242.

105. *Dred Scott v. Sandford*, 19 Howard 393, 15 L.Ed. 691 (1857).

106. Warren, *Bankruptcy*, 28, 60–61, 64–65, 76–79, 85; Baxter. *Daniel Webster*, 119.

107. J. Ely, *Guardian*, 66–67; Baxter, *Daniel Webster*, 119.

108. M. Horwitz, *Transformation of American Law, 1780–1860*, 140, 154–155.

109. Swift, *A System of the Laws of the State of Connecticut*, quoted in M. Horwitz, *Transformation of American Law, 1780–1860*, 142, also 141–143, 180–185, passim.

110. Baxter, *Daniel Webster*, 154.

111. M. Horwitz, *Transformation of American Law, 1780–1860*, 37–40.

112. Rayback, *American Labor*, 56–59, 81–82, 91–92; Tomlins, *Law, Labor, and Ideology*, 209–215.

113. *Dartmouth College v. Woodward*, 4 Wheat. 518, 4 L.Ed. 629 (1819).

114. J. Ely, *Guardian*, 65–66.
115. *Charles River Bridge v. Warren Bridge*, 11 Pet. 420, 9 L.Ed. 773 (1837).
116. Kent, quoted in Baxter, *Daniel Webster*, 134–135.
117. Lincoln, message to Congress, July 4, 1861, in T. H. Williams, *Abraham Lincoln*, 162.

CHAPTER 4. INDUSTRIALISM AND ITS DISCONTENTS I, 1862–1898

1. North, *Structure and Change*, 191; Landes, *Poverty of Nations*, 307.
2. Faulkner, *American Economic History*, 411.
3. Atack and Passell, *New Economic View*, 458.
4. Garraty, *New Commonwealth*, 33, 34.
5. H. Adams, *Education of Henry Adams*, 298.
6. Garraty, *New Commonwealth*, 17, 231–233; Hofstadter, *American Political Tradition*, 171.
7. North, *Structure and Change*, 191; Ginger, *Age of Excess*, 93; Faulkner, *Politics*, 91.
8. Faulkner, *American Economic History*, 476.
9. Atack and Passell, *New Economic View*, 378–393.
10. Hays, *Response to Industrialism*, 127–128.
11. Atack and Passell, *New Economic View*, 243.
12. Hobsbawm, *Age of Capital*, 149.
13. Glaab and Brown, *Urban America*, 111.
14. Garraty, *New Commonwealth*, 191–192.
15. Faulkner, *American Economic History*, 482, 483; Hays, *Response to Industrialism*, 95.
16. *New York Herald*, quoted in Higham, *Strangers in the Land*, 31.
17. Parkman, quoted in Benedict, "Laisser-Faire and Liberty," 307.
18. Garfield, quoted in Benedict, "Laisser-Faire and Liberty," 307.
19. Rayback, *American Labor*, 134–135.
20. Ibid., 166–167; Paul, *Conservative Crisis*, 20.
21. Rayback, *American Labor*, 196–197.
22. Faulkner, *Politics*, 88.
23. Kleppner, *Third Electoral System*, 56, 185, 190, 328, 360, 371; McSeveney, *Politics of Depression*, 113; Sundquist, *Dynamics of the Party System*, 107–108; T. Ferguson, "Party Realignment," 49.
24. For Mill's influence, see Blaug, *Economic Theory*, 187; Gide and Rist, *Economic Doctrines*, 352–353.
25. Mill, quoted in Blaug, *Economic Theory*, 225.
26. Sabine, *Political Theory*, 706–707.
27. Blaug, *Economic Theory*, 309–312; Hovenkamp, "Substantive Due Process," 409.
28. Hovenkamp, "Substantive Due Process," 409, 436.
29. Walker, quoted in Hofstadter, *Social Darwinism*, 144.
30. Commager, *American Mind*, 231.
31. A. Perry, *Political Economy*, 129, 134–135.

32. Ibid., 31.
33. Ibid., 35.
34. Ibid., 40, 155.
35. Ibid., 184.
36. Ibid., 204.
37. Ibid., 478.
38. H. Wood, *Natural Law*, 15.
39. Ibid., 76, 138, 139.
40. Ibid., 181–182.
41. Ibid., 193.
42. Walker, quoted in Dorfman, *Thorstein Veblen*, 72–73.
43. Gould, "Two Work Sites," 256–257.
44. Darwin, *Origin of Species*, 76.
45. Spencer, *First Principles*, 280–297, 318, 324, 369; Sabine, *Political Theory*, 722.
46. Kirkman, quoted in Hofstadter, *Social Darwinism*, 129.
47. Carnegie, "Wealth," in Levy, *Political Thought in America*, 332.
48. Spencer, quoted in Gould, "Two Work Sites," 261.
49. Spencer, *On Social Evolution*, 235–236.
50. Hofstadter, *Social Darwinism*, 41; Schwartz, *Main Currents*, 302.
51. Hofstadter, *Social Darwinism*, 34.
52. Actual phrases from tributes to Spencer, compiled by Commager, *American Mind*, 85.
53. Sumner, *Social Classes*, 14, 65, 113–114.
54. Ibid., 9.
55. Sumner, "Democracy and Plutocracy," in *On Liberty*, 140.
56. Sumner, *Social Classes*, 15.
57. Sumner, "Republican Government," in *On Liberty*, 83.
58. Hofstadter, *Social Darwinism*, 63.
59. Magoc, *Yellowstone*, 9, 14–17; Schullery, *Searching for Yellowstone*, 59–61, 64–65.
60. Bensel, *American Industrialization*, xxi.
61. Skocpol, *Protecting Soldiers*, 103, 106, 110, 115, 127, 149.
62. 25 Atl. 718 (N.H. 1889), discussed in Schwartz, *Main Currents*, 333.
63. K. Hall, *Magic Mirror*, 193; Scheiber, "Property Law," in Friedman and Scheiber, *American Law*, 133–134, 138–139.
64. Hovenkamp, "Substantive Due Process," 399; Twiss, *Lawyers and the Constitution*, 97, 145.
65. Hovenkamp, "Substantive Due Process," 379–380; Twiss, *Lawyers and the Constitution*, 104, 106, 115, 153, 155–156; Schwarz, *Legal Thought*, 304, 305, 342–343, 363–364.
66. Tiedeman, quoted in Paul, *Conservative Crisis*, 16–17.
67. Appleton, quoted in Schwartz, *Main Currents*, 323; from *Allen v. Inhabitants of Jay*, 60 Me. 124 (1872).
68. Marshall, quoted in Paul, *Conservative Crisis*, 69.
69. Judson, quoted in Paul, *Conservative Crisis*, 67.
70. Dillon, quoted in Paul, *Conservative Crisis*, 80.

71. Cooley, *Constitutional Limitations*, 45–46.
72. Ibid., 356.
73. Benedict, "Laisser-Faire and Liberty," 293.
74. Cooley, quoted in Benedict, "Laisser-Faire and Liberty," 331.
75. M. Horwitz, *Transformation of American Law, 1870–1960*, 21.
76. Hovenkamp, "Substantive Due Process," 387–388, 391.
77. Ibid., 439.
78. Schwartz, *Main Currents*, 308.
79. 16 Wall. 36, 21 L.Ed. (1873).
80. *Munn v. Illinois*, 94 U.S. 113, 24 L.Ed. 77 (1877).
81. *Santa Clara County v. Southern Pacific Railroad Company*, 118 U.S. 394 (1886).
82. *Chicago, Milwaukee, and St. Paul Railway C. v. Minnesota*, 134 U.S. 418, 10 S.Ct. 462, 702, 33 L.Ed. 970 (1890).
83. *Allgeyer v. Louisiana*, 165 U.S. 578 (1897).
84. *In Re Jacobs*, 98 N.Y. 98 (1885), quoted in K. Hall, *Magic Mirror*, 230.
85. *Ritchie v. People*, 155 Ill. 111 (1893).
86. Paul, *Conservative Crisis*, 105–106; M. Horwitz, *Transformation of American Law, 1870–1960*, 151, 162.
87. Summarized and quoted in Paul, "Legal Progressivism," in Friedman and Scheiber, *American Law*, 285.
88. M. Horwitz, *Transformation of American Law, 1870–1960*, 16, 17, 155; Schwartz, *Main Currents*, 374.
89. G. E. White, "Path," 35.
90. K. Hall, *Magic Mirror*, 220.
91. Choate, quoted in Twiss, *Lawyers and the Constitution*, 110–116.
92. *Pollock v. Farmers Loan and Trust Company*, 158 U.S. 601, 15 S.Ct. 673, 39 L.Ed. 1108 (1895); *United States v. E. C. Knight*, 156 U.S. 1, S.Ct. 249, 39 L.Ed. 325 (1895).
93. Taft, quoted in Paul, *Conservative Crisis*, 113.
94. Debs injunction, July 2, 1894, reprinted in Wayne, *Pullman Boycott*, 31–32.
95. *In Re Debs*, 158 U.S. 564 (1895).
96. Debs speech reported in Debs, *Writings and Speeches*, 7; facts on the crowd from Salvatore, "Debs," in Dubofsky and Van Tine, *Labor Leaders*, 93.
97. Debs, quoted in Salvatore, "Debs," 94.
98. Gillman, "Use the Courts," 512, 516–518, 521; Bensel, *American Industrialization*, 7.
99. Thompson, quoted in Paul, "Legal Progressivism," 285.
100. Ibid., 286.
101. Holmes, *Common Law*, 1.
102. See Hicks, *Populist Revolt*; Goodwyn, *Populist Moment*; Ritter, *Goldbugs and Greenbacks*.
103. See Hofstadter, *Age of Reform*, 62–65; Atack and Passell, *New Economic View*, 419–424.
104. Hicks, *Populist Revolt*, 88; Ritter, *Goldbugs and Greenbacks*, 24, 62–78.
105. Bensel, *American Industrialization*, 8, 88–90.

106. Goodwyn, *Populist Moment*, 12.
107. Allen, quoted in Sundquist, *Dynamics*, 140.
108. Davis, quoted in Argersinger, *Agrarian Radicalism*, 72–73.
109. "National People's Party Platform," in Tindall, *Populist Reader*, 90–91.
110. Goebel, "American Populism," 112.
111. Appleby, "Republicanism," 21; Appleby, *Capitalism*, 15, 62–63.
112. Lewelling, "Speech at Huron Place," in Tindall, *Populist Reader*, 149.
113. *Farmers' Almanac*, quoted in Pollack, *Populist Response*, 26–27.
114. *Farmers' Alliance*, quoted in Pollack, *Populist Response*, 15.
115. "National People's Party Platform," 90–96.
116. Goodwyn, *Populist Moment*, 122; Ginger, *Age of Excess*, 127–128.
117. Argersinger, *Agrarian Radicalism*, 205.
118. Gompers, "Organized Labor," in Tindall, *Populist Reader*, 187–188.
119. Ritter, *Goldbugs and Greenbacks*, 211, 232–233, 240.
120. Roberts, introduction to George, *Progress and Poverty*, ix, xi; Aaron, *Men of Good Hope*, 62.
121. George, *Progress and Poverty*, 126.
122. Ibid., 171–172.
123. Sumner, quoted in Aaron, *Men of Good Hope*, 56.
124. Fromm, foreword to Bellamy, *Looking Backward*, v; Newman, *Economic Thought*, 158.
125. Newman, *Economic Thought*, 188.
126. Ibid., 78.
127. Reed, "Protective Tariff," in Scull, *Great Leaders*, 93.
128. Crisp, quoted in Trubowitz, *Defining the National Interest*, 90.
129. Ibid., 75–80.
130. Ibid., 73.
131. Ibid., 76.
132. Bryan, "Cross of Gold" speech, in Scull, *Great Leaders*, 644.
133. Democratic Party platform, in Scull, *Great Leaders*, 586–595.
134. Bryan, quoted in Hofstadter, *American Political Tradition*, 193.
135. Kleppner, *Cross of Culture*, 324, 333, 335, 338.
136. McSeveney, *Politics of Depression*, 179.
137. Hoar, quoted in Ritter, *Goldbugs and Greenbacks*, 171.
138. Guild, quoted in Ritter, *Goldbugs and Greenbacks*, 170.
139. McKinley, quoted in McSeveney, *Politics of Depression*, 178.
140. Republican Party platform, in Scull, *Great Leaders*, 501–512.
141. Burnham, "Changing Shape."
142. Faulkner, *Politics*, 210.
143. Burnham, *Critical Elections*, 71–90; T. Ferguson, "Party Realignment," 49–57.
144. Faulkner, *American Economic History*, 539.
145. Warren, *Bankruptcy*, 140–143.
146. Atack and Passell, *New Economic View*, 501.

CHAPTER 5. INDUSTRIALISM AND ITS DISCONTENTS II, 1898–1932

1. Faulkner, *American Economic History*, 459.
2. Heilbroner and Singer, *Economic Transformation*, 177; Faulkner, *American Economic History*, 476.
3. Heilbroner and Singer, *Economic Transformation*, 112.
4. Brandeis, quoted in Mason, *Brandeis*, 417.
5. Ibid., 420.
6. Atack and Passell, *New Economic View*, 458; Mowry, *Theodore Roosevelt*, 149–155; T. Ferguson, "Normalcy to New Deal," 53–68; Anderson, *Economics*, 100–101.
7. Lipset and Bendix, *Social Mobility*, 83; Hofstadter, *Age of Reform*, 217.
8. All quotes from Schlesinger, *Crisis*, 61.
9. Lewis, *Main Street*, 258.
10. Atack and Passell, *New Economic View*, 548–549; Mowry, *Theodore Roosevelt*, 75–76.
11. Atack and Passell, *New Economic View*, 536–537, 540; Rayback, *American Labor*, 212–213, 279; Forbath, *American Labor Movement*, 110.
12. Weinstein, *Corporate Ideal*, 7–8, 13, 15; Forbath, *American Labor Movement*, 64; Posner, "Economics of Labor Law," 991.
13. Skowronek, *New American State*, 24, 283.
14. Ibid., 284, 286–288.
15. Carpenter, *Bureaucratic Autonomy*; Kloppenberg, *Uncertain Victory*, 385, 386; Morone, *Democratic Wish*, 98–126; Skocpol, *Social Policy*, 19–24; Kernell, "Rural Free Delivery," 103–112; Carpenter, "Political Foundations," 113–122.
16. Atack and Passell, *New Economic View*, 652.
17. W. Barber, *Economic Thought*, 171–172; R. Frank, *Microeconomics*, 87–91, 344–345.
18. W. Barber, *Economic Thought*, 170; Blaug, *Economic Theory*, 311–312, 345, 347; Coleman, "Economics and the Law," 649.
19. R. Frank, *Microeconomics*, 351.
20. Marshall, "General View of Distribution," excerpt from *Principles of Economics*, in Newman, Gayer, and Spencer, *Source Readings*, 431.
21. Cannan, quoted in Hutt, *Keynesian Episode*, 60.
22. Marshall, quoted in W. Barber, *Economic Thought*, 193; on Say's Law: Lekachman, *Age of Keynes*, 83–85; W. Barber, *Economic Thought*, 187–189; on the quantity theory and the gold standard: W. Barber, *Economic Thought*, 187; Lekachman, *Age of Keynes*, 66; Blaug, *Economic Theory*, 645–646; on opposition to government subsidies, labor unions, etc.: Hutt, *Keynesian Episode*, 54–55.
23. Hovenkamp, "Substantive Due Process," 438.
24. Clark, quoted in Mason and Leach, *In Quest of Freedom*, 366–367.
25. Clark, *Distribution of Wealth*, excerpted in Newman, Gayer, and Spencer, *Source Readings*, 412.
26. Clark, quoted in Blaug, *Economic Theory*, 450.
27. Clark, *Distribution of Wealth*, 422.

28. Blaug, *Economic Theory*, 460–461; Posner, "Economics of Labor Law," 1000–1001; Brown and Medoff, "Trade Unions," 355.

29. Pigou, *Economics of Welfare*, excerpted in Newman, Gayer, and Spencer, *Source Readings*, 664.

30. Hovenkamp, "Substantive Due Process," 441; Blaug, *Economic Theory*, 409, 636–637; Coleman, "Economics and the Law," 655.

31. Newman, *Economic Thought*, 304; Shove, "Marshall's *Principles*," in Gherity, *Economic Thought*, 453–454; Lekachman, *Age of Keynes*, 86.

32. *Smyth v. Ames*, 168 U.S. 466 (1898), 725.

33. Hadley, quoted in Mason and Leach, *In Quest of Freedom*, 411.

34. *Lochner v. New York*, 198 U.S. 45, 25 S.Ct. 539, 49 L.Ed. 937 (1905).

35. *Bakers Journal*, quoted in Kens, *Judicial Power*, 129.

36. *Adair v. U.S.*, 208 U.S. 161, 190 (1908); *Coppage v. Kansas*, 236 U.S. 1, 28 (1915).

37. *Hammer v. Dagenhart*, 247 U.S. 251, 38 S.Ct. 529, 62 L.Ed. 1101 (1918).

38. *Adkins v. Children's Hospital*, 261 U.S. 525, 43 S.Ct. 394, 67 L.Ed. 785 (1923).

39. Prohibition: *Rhode Island v. Palmer*, 253 U.S. 350 (1920); lottery tickets: *Murphy v. California*, 225 U.S. 623, 629 (1912); pool halls: *Clark v. Deckebach*, 274 U.S. 392 (1927); motion pictures: *Mutual Film Corp. v. Industrial Commission of Ohio*, 236 U.S. 239 (1915).

40. Burner, "Election of 1924," in Murphy, *Political Parties*, 1079; J. Ely, *Guardian*, 116.

41. J. Hall, "Integrative Jurisprudence," 21–23, 27; Curtis, *Law as Large as Life*, 3, 8–9, 19; Rommen, *Natural Law*, 111–113, 115, 116, 143, 199.

42. *Lochner* dissent.

43. *Coppage* dissent.

44. *Dagenhart* dissent.

45. *Adkins* dissent.

46. *Abrams v. U.S.*, 250 U.S. 616, 624 (1919).

47. Mason, *Brandeis*, 35, 86, 92–93.

48. Brandeis, quoted in Mason, *Brandeis*, 101, 103.

49. Brandeis, *Curse of Bigness*, 105, 107.

50. Curtis, *Law as Large as Life*, 59.

51. Baer, quoted in Schultz and Coleman, *Labor Problems*, 115.

52. Coolidge, quoted in Schlesinger, *Crisis*, 57.

53. Hoover, *Challenge to Liberty*, 32–33.

54. Ibid., 27–28.

55. Hoover, quoted in Hofstadter, *American Political Tradition*, 297.

56. Hoover, *Challenge to Liberty*, 52–53.

57. Hoover, statement to the press in defense of "Mutual Self-Help," in Levy, *Political Thought in America*, 395–396.

58. Arnold, "Ambivalent Leviathan," in Greenstone, *Public Values*, 115.

59. Schlesinger, *Crisis*, 237; Anderson, *Economics*, 271.

60. On the social background, education, etc. of the Progressives, see Hofstadter, *Age of Reform*, 217–218; Weinstein, *Corporate Ideal*, 168; Mowry, *Theodore Roosevelt*, 86–87.

61. W. Wilson, "Freemen Need No Guardians," in Levy, *Political Thought in America*,

351; T. Roosevelt, *Autobiography*, 328; La Follette, "Have Faith in the People," in Leopold, Link, and Cobs, *Problems in American History*, 183.

62. Smith, quoted in Boorstin, *Democratic Experience*, 409.

63. Morone, *Democratic Wish*, 126.

64. On Veblen being viewed as a satirist: Dorfman, *Thorstein Veblen*, 506; on Veblen's influence on modern economists: K. Arrow, "Thorstein Veblen," 5–9; Hofstadter, *Social Darwinism*, 156.

65. Veblen, "Evolutionary Science?" in Gherity, *Economic Thought*, 526–544; Veblen, "Marginal Utility," in Newman, Gayer, and Spencer, *Source Readings*, 524–529.

66. Veblen, *Instinct of Workmanship*, 187, 189.

67. A. Smith, *Wealth of Nations*, 128.

68. Veblen, *Engineers*, 108.

69. Veblen, *Instinct of Workmanship*, 194–200.

70. Veblen, *Leisure Class*, 35, 38, 70.

71. Ibid., 87.

72. Veblen, *Theory of Business Enterprise*, excerpted in Newman, Gayer, and Spencer, *Source Readings*, 533–539; Dorfman, *Thorstein Veblen*, 216; K. Arrow, "Thorstein Veblen," 7.

73. Veblen, *Engineers*, 58.

74. The first three quotations are from Veblen, *Instinct of Workmanship*, 187, 217, 334; the final quotation is from Veblen, *Engineers*, 40–41.

75. Agar, *Price of Union*, 657–661; Link, *Woodrow Wilson*, 4–5, 55; Taft, "Judicial Decisions," in Leopold, Link, and Cobs, *Problems in American History*, 90–91; Taft, quoted in Mowry, *Theodore Roosevelt*, 237, see also 271.

76. Roosevelt, quoted in Weinstein, *Corporate Ideal*, 71.

77. Roosevelt, speech to Progressive Party convention, in Leopold, Link, and Cobs, *Problems in American History*, 194–196.

78. Roosevelt, "Nationalism," in T. Roosevelt, *Writings*, 174.

79. W. Wilson, *Crossroads of Freedom*, 77.

80. Ibid., 79.

81. Wilson, quoted in Thorsen, *Woodrow Wilson*, 158.

82. Link, *Woodrow Wilson*, 63–65; Schickel, *D. W. Griffith*, 268–270; Prindle, *Risky Business*, 149.

83. Morgan, "Eugene V. Debs," in Roche, *American Political Thought*, 240.

84. Debs, "Acceptance Speech," in Levy, *Political Thought in America*, 388–390.

85. On the elimination of racism: Debs, "The Negro," in Debs, *Writings and Speeches*, 65; on the elimination of sexism: "Unionism and Socialism" in Debs, *Writings and Speeches*, 123; the quotation (1908) is from Roche, *American Political Thought*, 239.

86. On freedom of speech: Debs, "Plea for Solidarity," in Debs, *Writings and Speeches*, 372; Debs quotation from 1918 in Roche, *American Political Thought*, 246.

87. Debs, "Acceptance Speech," 390.

88. *Information Please Almanac*, 614.

89. Abel and Bernanke, *Macroeconomics*, 485; Atack and Passell, *New Economic View*, 517–520; Temin, *Great Depression*, 8–9; Chernow, *House of Morgan*, 122, 128.

90. Anderson, *Economics*, 100–101.

91. Atack and Passell, *New Economic View*, 574; Anderson, *Economics*, 269.
92. Anderson, *Economics*, 210–211.
93. Atack and Passell, *New Economic View*, 584–585, 632; T. Ferguson, "Normalcy to New Deal," 85.
94. J. R. Davis, *New Economics*, 12–13, 24.
95. Hoover, quoted in Atack and Passell, *New Economic View*, 614.
96. Epstein and Ferguson, "Monetary Policy," 965; Temin, *Great Depression*, 28–29.
97. Atack and Passell, *New Economic View*, 600–601.
98. Temin, *Great Depression*, 95.
99. Hoover, quoted in J. K. Galbraith, *Great Crash*, 190.
100. Atack and Passell, *New Economic View*, 601.

CHAPTER 6. NEW PARADIGMS, 1932–1974

1. Atack and Passell, *New Economic View*, 628, 630–631; Patterson, *Grand Expectations*, 56.
2. *Information Please Almanac*, 53.
3. Patterson, *Grand Expectations*, 11, 451.
4. M. Harrington, *Other America*, 176–178; Heilbroner and Singer, *Economic Transformation*, 213.
5. Patterson, *Grand Expectations*, 381–382.
6. Ibid., 312, 639; Heilbroner and Singer, *Economic Transformation*, 212–213; R. Samuelson, "Age of Inflation," 32.
7. Calleo and Rowland, *America*, 162–163.
8. Abel and Bernanke, *Macroeconomics*, 419–420, 485; Calleo and Rowland, *America*, 88–90.
9. L. Friedman, *American Law*, 575; Rayback, *American Labor*, 319, 345; Posner, "Economics of Labor Law," 988–1011; Leuchtenburg, *New Deal*, 150–151.
10. Rayback, *American Labor*, 315, 383; Patterson, *Grand Expectations*, 322.
11. Greenstone, *Labor in American Politics*, 10–11, 51, passim.
12. Rayback, *American Labor*, 366, 406–407; Patterson, *Grand Expectations*, 50–51, 326; Rees, *Economics of Trade Unions*, 18, 22, 124–125, 175–177.
13. Patterson, *Grand Expectations*, 325; Rees, *Economics of Trade Unions*, 22.
14. Free and Cantril, *Political Beliefs*, 1–32.
15. Carson, *Silent Spring*.
16. Austin, *Land of Little Rain*; Stegner, *Beyond the Hundredth Meridian*; Stegner, "Wilderness Letter," in Stegner, *Marking the Sparrow's Fall*, 111–117; Abbey, *Desert Solitaire*; Leopold, *Sand County Almanac*.
17. Reisner, *Cadillac Desert*, 144, 283, 286–289.
18. Ornstein and Elder, *Interest Groups*, 161; Sierra Club documents on membership and budget in 2002.
19. Ingelhart, *Silent Revolution*; Ingelhart, "Post-Materialism."
20. Silk, *Economists*, 65; Lekachman, *Age of Keynes*, 266–301.
21. Collins, *More*, 61, 97.

22. Prothro and Grigg, "What Do Americans Really Believe?" in Shafritz and Weinberg, *Classics in American Government*.
23. UNESCO report, quoted in Pickles, *Democracy*, 11.
24. Burnham, "Changing Shape," table 1.
25. Key, *Public Opinion*, 79, 82, 85, 90–91.
26. Stouffer, *Civil Liberties*, 29–34, passim.
27. Kuhn, *Scientific Revolutions*, 35–42.
28. Foster and Catchings, *Business without a Buyer*, 19.
29. Ibid., 35.
30. Silk, *Economists*, 92–95, 96; Blaug, *Economic Theory*, 412–417; W. Barber, *Economic Thought*, 224–225.
31. Keynes, *General Theory*, 21.
32. Ibid., 30–31.
33. Ibid., 12–13, 267.
34. Ibid., 373.
35. Ibid., 378.
36. Ibid., 129.
37. Temin, *Great Depression*, 108–109, 111, 134.
38. P. Samuelson, "Economics in a Golden Age," in Brown and Solow, *Paul Samuelson*, 6.
39. Merton, "Financial Economics," 137; Tobin, "Macroeconomics and Fiscal Policy," in Brown and Solow, *Paul Samuelson*, 197–200, passim.
40. Skouson, "Welcome Back," 198.
41. Kirshner, "Inflation," 609–618; Barro, "Inflation and Economic Growth," 166–176.
42. Trevithick, *Inflation*, 55–56.
43. White, quoted in Cohen, *Consumers' Republic*, 211.
44. Ibid.
45. J. K. Galbraith, *Economics, Peace, and Laughter*, 55; Weir, "Acceptance of Keynesianism," in P. Hall, *Political Power*, 85–86; Patterson, *Grand Expectations*, 464.
46. P. Hall, "Conclusion," in P. Hall, *Political Power*, 377 n.34; Krugman, *Peddling Prosperity*, 15.
47. Hibbs, "Macroeconomic Policy," 1467–1487; see also Cameron, "Public Economy," 1243–1261 (Cameron conducted a study similar to that of Hibbs; his main purpose was to explain variations in the growth of public sectors over time. He supports Hibbs's main argument regarding Left versus Right parties, but points out that there are also other important variables, such as openness to international trade); and Beck, "American Macroeconomic Outcomes," 83–93 (Using different data and methods than Hibbs employed, Beck concludes that, in the United States, variations among presidential administrations, rather than party control of Congress, explain macroeconomic outcomes. His data do support the general picture of governments engaging in Keynesian manipulation, however).
48. Lekachman, *Age of Keynes*, passim.
49. *West Coast Hotel v. Parrish*, 300 U.S. 379, 57 S.Ct. 578, 81 L.Ed. 703 (1937).

50. *National Labor Relations Board v. Jones and Laughlin Steel Corporation*, 301 U.S. 1, 57 S.Ct. 615, 81 L.Ed. 893 (1937).
51. *United States v. Carolene Products*, 304 U.S. 144 (1938), n.4.
52. Holmes, *Common Law*, 1; Cardozo, quoted in M. Horwitz, *Transformation of American Law, 1870–1960*, 190.
53. Schwartz, *Main Currents*, 488–489.
54. Rommen, *Natural Law*, 133–136; G. E. White, *Patterns*, 132, 140.
55. McKinnon, quoted in G. E. White, *Patterns*, 215–216.
56. M. Horwitz, *Transformation of American Law, 1870–1960*, 265–267.
57. G. E. White, *Patterns*, 146–148, 152.
58. Foundation texts of the "law and economics" movement are Coase, "Problem of Social Cost," 1–30; and Posner, "Economic Approach," 399.
59. Dewey, "Liberalism and Social Action," in Levy, *Political Thought in America*, 418.
60. Judis, "Structural Flaw," 20.
61. Moley, quoted in Irons, *New Deal Lawyers*, 23.
62. Hawley, *New Deal*, 12–50, 102–124, 130–131; Leuchtenburg, *New Deal*, 66–69; Schlesinger, *Coming of the New Deal*, 119–135.
63. Milkis, "Economic Constitutional Order," in Milkis and Milheur, *Triumph of Liberalism*, 32.
64. Roosevelt, quoted in Mason and Leach, *In Quest of Freedom*, 465.
65. Ibid.
66. F. D. Roosevelt, "Commonwealth Club Address," in Levy, *Political Thought in America*, 424.
67. Blyth, *Great Transformations*, 4, 5.
68. Ibid., 94.
69. Ibid., 5.
70. The information in this discussion comes from Prindle, *Texas Railroad Commission*, 19–94; Yergin, *Prize*, 223–228, 248–259, 535–540; Hawley, *New Deal*, 218; Blair, *Control of Oil*, 161–164.
71. Blair, *Control of Oil*, passim; Engler, *Politics of Oil*, 483–498.
72. Milkis, *Political Parties*, 81.
73. Brown, "State Capacity," 199.
74. Lowi, *End of Liberalism*, 71.
75. Connolly, "Challenge to Pluralist Theory," in Connolly, *Bias of Pluralism*, 3–34.
76. Dahl, *Preface*, 84.
77. P. Samuelson, *Economics*, 35.
78. Heilbroner and Singer, *Economic Transformation*, 209.
79. Bentley, *Process of Government*, 162, 197, 354.
80. Ibid., 354.
81. Ibid., 464.
82. Ross, *American Social Science*, 303.
83. Bentley, *Process of Government*, 200.
84. Lasswell, *Politics*.

85. Truman, *Governmental Process*, 21.
86. Ibid., 26, 30–31, 36, 44.
87. Ibid., 43, 45–66.
88. Ibid., 50–51.
89. Ibid., 515, 535.
90. Dahl, *Preface*, 31.
91. Ibid., 54.
92. Ibid., 124, 135.
93. Ibid., 137, 150.
94. Olson, *Logic of Collective Action*, 28, 35, 48, 71, 86, 143.
95. Schattschneider, *Semi-Sovereign People*, 35.
96. Connolly, *Bias of Pluralism*.
97. Lowi, *End of Liberalism*, 47.
98. Ibid., 76.
99. Ibid., 292–293.
100. Salisbury, "Exchange Theory," in Salisbury, *Interest Group Politics*, 32–70.
101. Walker, "Origins and Maintenance," 390–406.
102. Dahl, *Who Governs?* 204, passim.
103. For a summary and evaluation of Dahl's work, see Von Der Muhle, "Robert A. Dahl," 1070–1096.
104. Schumpeter, *Capitalism, Socialism and Democracy*, 261.
105. Ibid., 282.
106. Downs, *Economic Theory*, 115.
107. Ibid., 136.
108. Stokes, "Spatial Models," in Campbell et al., *Political Order*, 164–170.
109. Held, *Models of Democracy*, 196–197.
110. Green and Shapiro, *Rational Choice Theory*, 3, 47, 50, 68, 74; Hinich and Munger, *Analytical Politics*, 136–153.
111. Two examples of arguments, based upon public choice concepts, that the political system functions as though the public is rational and informed are Arnold, "Inattentive Citizens," in Dodd and Oppenheimer, *Congress Reconsidered*, 401–416; and Fiorina, *Retrospective Voting*, 194–200.
112. Rawls, *Theory of Justice*, 11–12, 14–15, 76–80.
113. Ibid., 100–101.
114. Vonnegut, *Welcome to the Monkey House*, 7–14.
115. Nozick, *Anarchy*, 183.
116. Schwartz, *Main Currents*, 586–587.
117. Nozick, *Anarchy*, 190.

CHAPTER 7. DISSENT, 1932–1974

1. Becker, *Modern Democracy*, 48, 85.
2. Commons, "Institutional Economics," in Newman, Gayer, and Spencer, *Source Readings*, 557–574; Mitchell, "Role of Money," in Newman, Gayer, and Spencer, *Source*

Readings, 543–547; Arnold, *Folklore of Capitalism*; Ayres, *Theory of Economic Progress*; Ross, *American Social Science*, 371–386.

3. Parker, *John Kenneth Galbraith*, 39.
4. J. K. Galbraith, *New Industrial State*, 200.
5. J. K. Galbraith, *Affluent Society*, 126.
6. J. K. Galbraith, *Economics, Peace, and Laughter*, 30.
7. J. K. Galbraith, *New Industrial State*, 265.
8. J. K. Galbraith, *Economics, Peace, and Laughter*, 6, 152–153, 155.
9. J. K. Galbraith, *Affluent Society*, 199–200.
10. J. K. Galbraith, *Economics, Peace, and Laughter*, 43–44, 115, 152.
11. J. K. Galbraith, *Economics and the Public Purpose*, 173–174.
12. Ibid., 187.
13. Ibid., 195.
14. Ibid., 213.
15. Ibid., 266, see also 212, 273.
16. Ibid., 207–313.
17. Krugman, *Peddling Prosperity*, 14.
18. Stigler, *Citizen and the State*, 118.
19. Krugman, *Peddling Prosperity*, 14.
20. J. K. Galbraith, *New Industrial State*, xxxi–xxxii.
21. James Galbraith, "Planning System," in Bowles, Edwards, and Shepherd, *Unconventional Wisdom*, 253.
22. Friedman and Friedman, *Free to Choose*, 214.
23. Mills, *Sociological Imagination*, 167.
24. Mills, *White Collar*, passim.
25. Mills, *Power Elite*, 350, 357, 361.
26. Ibid., 283.
27. Ibid., 122.
28. Ibid., 166.
29. Ibid., 71–93, 302–305, 316.
30. Ibid., 344.
31. Mills, *Sociological Imagination*, 186.
32. Dahl, "Ruling Elite Model," in Domhoff and Ballard, *C. Wright Mills*, 30–31.
33. Sweezy, "Ruling Class?" in Domhoff and Ballard, *C. Wright Mills*, 122, 127.
34. Porter, *Vertical Mosaic*, 522, 523.
35. Three recent examples are Dye, Gibson, and Robison, *Politics in America*, 16–17, 20; Bardes, Shelley, and Schmidt, *Government and Politics Today*, 13–14, 241; and O'Connor and Sabato, *Essentials of American Government*, 12–13.
36. Dye and Ziegler, *Irony of Democracy*.
37. Silk, *Economists*; Stigler, "Intellectual and the Marketplace," in Klaasen, *Invisible Hand*, 31–42; Brennan and Tollison, preface to J. Buchanan, *What Should Economists Do?* xi–xv; Blaug, *Economic Theory*, 633–635; Asch and Seneca, *Government and the Marketplace*, 51–124, 137–141, 473–478.
38. Von Mises, *Theory and History*, 378.

39. Hayek, "Use of Knowledge," in Klaasen, *Invisible Hand*, 121–135.
40. Ibid.
41. Hayek, *Road to Serfdom*, 13.
42. Samuelson, quoted in Silk, *Economists*, 65.
43. M. Friedman, *Capitalism and Freedom*; Friedman and Friedman, *Free to Choose*.
44. Silk, *Economists*, 81.
45. Friedman and Friedman, *Free to Choose*, 137.
46. M. Friedman, *Capitalism and Freedom*, 109.
47. Friedman and Friedman, *Free to Choose*, 212–213.
48. M. Friedman, *Adam Smith's Relevance*, 6, 15.
49. Ibid., 12.
50. M. Friedman, *Capitalism and Freedom*, 31, 57, 180, 181; Friedman and Friedman, *Free to Choose*, 188.
51. Friedman and Friedman, *Free to Choose*, 148–172.
52. M. Friedman, "Demand For Money"; Friedman and Friedman, *Free to Choose*, 239–252; M. Friedman, *Capitalism and Freedom*, 78; Silk, *Economists*, 80–81; Friedman and Schwartz, *Great Contraction*, 111–113.
53. Friedman and Friedman, *Free to Choose*, 296.
54. Krugman, *Peddling Prosperity*, 43–45.
55. Ibid., 38.
56. Silk, *Economists*, 80.
57. Ibid., 82–83; Krugman, *Peddling Prosperity*, 53–54.
58. Shepherd, "Monopoly," in Bowles, Edwards, and Shepherd, *Unconventional Wisdom*, 170.
59. Nozick, *Anarchy*, 26.
60. Ibid., 119.
61. Ibid., 24–25, 66–67, 69, 70, 112–114, 118, 170.
62. Ibid., xi, 18–19, 118.
63. Ibid., 90.
64. Ibid., 169.
65. Ibid., 333.
66. Buckley, *Up from Liberalism*, 121–122, 126.
67. Marx, *Capital*; Marx and Engels, "Communist Manifesto," in Mendel, *Essential Works of Marxism*, 13–44.
68. Crossman, *God That Failed*; Orwell, *Homage to Catalonia*; Koestler, *Darkness at Noon*.
69. Prindle, *Politics of Glamour*, 39–50; Rayback, *American Labor*, 316–317, 366, 406–408.
70. M. Harrington, *Twilight of Capitalism*, 326.
71. W. A. Williams, *Great Evasion*, 57.
72. Baran and Sweezy, *Monopoly Capital*, 9.
73. Weisskopf, "Capitalist Economic Growth," in Edwards, Reich, and Weisskopf, *Capitalist System*, 396.
74. Baran and Sweezy, *Monopoly Capital*, 155.

75. W. A. Williams, *Great Evasion*, 104–105.
76. Alperovitz, "Pluralist Commonwealth," in Brenner, Borosage, and Weidner, *Exploring Contradictions*, 221.

CHAPTER 8. DEMOCRACY AND CAPITALISM, 1974–2001

1. Patterson, *Grand Expectations*, 783–785; R. Samuelson, "Age of Inflation," 32.
2. Krugman, *Peddling Prosperity*, 4, 111, 159; Rosecrance, *Virtual State*, 143; *American Almanac*, 424; Gilpin, *Global Capitalism*, 228–229; Abel and Bernanke, *Macroeconomics*, 6; T. Frank, *One Market*, 6.
3. Schwarz, *America's Hidden Success*, 24–27.
4. Olasky, *Tragedy of American Compassion*, 208–209.
5. Krugman, *Peddling Prosperity*, 129; Rosecrance, *Virtual State*, 145.
6. Gilpin, *World Capitalism*, 4; T. Frank, *One Market*, 128, 155; D'Souza, *Virtue of Prosperity*, 5.
7. Hale, quoted in Gilpin, *World Capitalism*, 15, see also 5.
8. Rosecrance, *Virtual State*, 210.
9. D'Souza, *Virtue of Prosperity*, 3.
10. Gilpin, *Global Capitalism*, 4, 5.
11. Ibid., 20–22; Reich, *Work of Nations*, 3, 8, 77, 128–129; LaFeber, *Michael Jordan*, 56, 67.
12. James Galbraith, *Created Unequal*, 87–88; T. Frank, *One Market*, 6.
13. Gilpin, *Global Capitalism*, 307–308.
14. D'Souza, *Virtue of Prosperity*, 64.
15. T. Frank, *One Market*, 7.
16. Dolbeare and Hubbell, *U.S.A. 2012*, 38.
17. Judis, "Love's Labor Lost," 18.
18. Ferguson and Rogers, *Right Turn*, 84.
19. Rodrik, *Globalization*, 24–25, 36.
20. Phillips, "Politics of Presence," in Blaug and Schwarzmantel, *Democracy*, 164.
21. Dahl, *Democracy and Its Critics*, 2, 239; Sen, "Democracy as a Universal," in Blaug and Schwarzmantel, *Democracy*, 420–423; Blaug and Schwarzmantel, "Participation Introduction," in Blaug and Schwarzmantel, *Democracy*, 440.
22. Parekh, "Theorizing Political Theory," in O'Sullivan, *Political Theory*, 253.
23. Held, *Models of Democracy*, 297–298.
24. McClosky and Zaller, *American Ethos*, 1, 120, 122, 140, 146, 176.
25. A. Bernstein, "Too Much Corporate Power?" 144–149.
26. Gallup polls for relevant years.
27. My thanks to Walter Dean Burnham for providing me with turnout figures.
28. Cohen and Rogers, *On Democracy*, 32–33.
29. J. Buchanan, *What Should Economists Do?* 84.
30. Swedburg, *Joseph A. Schumpeter*, 407.
31. Keynes, *General Theory*, 162–164.
32. Krugman, *Development*, 5.

33. J. Buchanan, *What Should Economists Do?* 281; Buchanan and Vanberg, "Creative Process," in Hausman, *Philosophy of Economics*, 320.
34. Drucker, "Toward the Next Economics," 9.
35. Feldstein, *Capital Formation*, 13; Blyth, *Great Transformations*, 158.
36. Feldstein, *Inflation*, 14.
37. Ibid.
38. Wanniski, *Way the World Works*, 97, passim.
39. Abel and Bernanke, *Macroeconomics*, 588–589.
40. Ricci, *Transformation of American Politics*, 163.
41. Ibid., 207.
42. Habermas, *Legitimation Crisis*, 23, 49, 73, 75.
43. Wolfe, *Limits of Legitimacy*, 252.
44. Kristol, "Virtue Loses," in Levy, *Political Thought in America*, 487.
45. Gilder, *Wealth and Poverty*, 26–27, 30, 37.
46. Ibid., 31.
47. Ibid., 119.
48. Ibid., 120.
49. Ibid., 43–63.
50. Ibid., 144.
51. Lekachman, *Greed Is Not Enough*, passim; Slemrod and Bakija, *Taxing Ourselves*, 99–102; Piven and Cloward, *New Class War*, 52–55; Kuttner, *Economic Illusion*, 187, 227, 256–258.
52. Krugman, *Peddling Prosperity*, 90.
53. Krugman, *Accidental Theorist*, 51.
54. Slemrod and Bakija, *Taxing Ourselves*, 27–28.
55. Limbaugh, *Way Things Ought to Be*, 11.
56. St. George, "Talk Radio"; Bart, "Talkradio Titans," 39.
57. Limbaugh, *Way Things Ought to Be*, 2.
58. Ibid., 78.
59. Ibid., 9; see also *Extra!*, "The Way Things Aren't," 17; *Extra!*, "More Limbicilic Statements," 3.
60. T. Frank, *One Market*, xiv, 179; Friedman and Friedman, *Free to Choose*.
61. Gilder, *Wealth and Poverty*, 13, 88.
62. Rosecrance, *Virtual State*, 65.
63. D'Souza, *Virtue of Prosperity*, 82, 109.
64. Blyth, *Great Transformations*, 180.
65. Ibid., 182.
66. Ibid., 6.
67. Martin, *God on Our Side*, 214–218, 221–225; Hodgson, *Turned Right Side Up*, 160–177.
68. Cohen and Rogers, *On Democracy*, 15.
69. Piven and Cloward, *Regulating the Poor*, xiii, passim.
70. Piven and Cloward, *New Class War*, 7, 23, 31, passim.
71. Wolfe, *Limits of Legitimacy*, 252, 259.

72. McChesney, *Rich Media*, 113.
73. Roemer, *Free to Lose*, 64, 66; P. Samuelson, *Economics from the Heart*, 4, 5; Sunstein, *After the Rights Revolution*, 39.
74. Schmookler, *Illusion of Choice*, 56, 58.
75. Adams and Brock, *Bigness Complex*, 251.
76. Daly and Cobb, *Common Good*; Berry, *Unsettling of America*, 7, 21; Berry, *What Are People For?* 111, 113, 116, 128, 131, 134–135.
77. Dolbeare and Hubbell, *U.S.A. 2012*, 37, 43, 87; Daly and Cobb, *Common Good*, 438.
78. T. Frank, *One Market*, 86–87.
79. Dolbeare and Hubbell, *U.S.A. 2012*, 38.
80. James Galbraith, *Created Unequal*, 265.
81. Kuttner, *Economic Illusion*, 207.
82. Piven and Cloward, *New Class War*, 1.
83. McChesney, *Rich Media*, passim; Parenti, *Inventing Reality*, passim; Dolbeare and Hubbell, *U.S.A. 2012*, 64, 117, 118; Ferguson and Rogers, *Right Turn*, 88.
84. T. Frank, *One Market*, 274.
85. Cohen and Rogers, *On Democracy*, 63.
86. Ibid., 147; McChesney, *Rich Media*, 30, 283, 285; Dolbeare and Hubbell, *U.S.A. 2012*, 34–137, 151–155; Held, *Models of Democracy*, 308, 316.
87. Young, "Politics of Difference," in Blaug and Schwarzmantel, *Democracy*, 411.
88. Held, *Models of Democracy*, 323, 329, 331, 334.
89. Mouffe, "Radical Democracy?" in Blaug and Schwarzmantel, *Democracy*, 527.
90. B. Barber, "Strong Democracy," in S. Davis, *American Political Thought*, 472.
91. Hirst, "Associative Principles," in Blaug and Schwarzmantel, *Democracy*, 487.
92. Kymlicka and Norman, "Return of the Citizen," in Blaug and Schwarzmantel, *Democracy*, 220–221.
93. Genovese, "Critical Legal Studies," in Leonard, *Legal Studies*, 270.
94. Walzer, "Day in the Life," in Blaug and Schwarzmantel, *Democracy*, 459–460.
95. Lindblom, *Politics and Markets*, 67.
96. Parenti, *Inventing Reality*; McChesney, *Rich Media*.
97. Parenti, *Make-Believe Media*; Ryan and Kellner, *Camera Politica*.
98. B. Buchanan, *Renewing Presidential Politics*, 148, 150; Fiorina and Peterson, *New American Democracy*, 281–283.
99. Powers, Rothman, and Rothman, "Hollywood Movies," 563–581; Lichter, Lichter, and Rothman, "Show Business," 20–24.
100. Powers, Rothman, and Rothman, *Hollywood's America*, 139.
101. Elshtain, *Democracy on Trial*, 89.
102. Ibid., 22, 61.
103. Ibid., 30–31, 52.
104. Lindblom, "Market and Democracy," 686–687; see also Lindblom, *Politics and Markets*, for the author's earlier discussion of this and related points.
105. Lindblom, "Market and Democracy," 688.
106. Mueller, *Ralph's Pretty Good Grocery*, 68, 165.
107. Ibid., 120.

108. Ibid., 157.
109. Dahl, *Democracy and Its Critics*, 83–84.
110. Ibid., 220–222.
111. Dahl, *Preface*.
112. Kristol, "Rationalism in Economics," 202.
113. Dodd and Jillson, "Study of American Politics," in Dodd and Jillson, *Dynamics of American Politics*, 1.
114. Charles, review of *In Defense of History*, by Evans, 93.
115. Parekh, "Theorizing Political Theory," 243.
116. Cornell, "Challenge to Legal Positivism," in Leonard, *Legal Studies*, 234.
117. Schwartz, *Main Currents*, 554.
118. Sunstein, *After the Rights Revolution*, 191.
119. Epstein, foreword to Macedo, *New Right*, xii.
120. Ibid., xiv.
121. Epstein, *Takings*, 95.
122. Ibid., 281.
123. Ibid., 334–338.
124. Rosen, "Unregulated Offensive," 42, 48.
125. Lehman, *Signs of the Times*, 38, quoted in Schwartz, *Main Currents*, 607.
126. Binder, "Critical Legal Studies," 1–36.
127. Leonard, "Introduction," in Leonard, *Legal Studies*, 2, 6, 11; see also Caudill, "Freud," in Leonard, *Legal Studies*, 49.
128. Leonard, "Introduction," 3.
129. Genovese, "Critical Legal Studies," 269–298; Posner, *Overcoming Law*, 272; Schwartz, *Main Currents*, 610–614; D. Arrow, " 'Rich,' " 149–171, esp. 165.
130. Schwartz, *Main Currents*, 609, 610.
131. Smith, *Liberalism*, 227.
132. Ibid., 200.
133. Ibid., 236.
134. Dworkin, *Law's Empire*, 87, 225.
135. Ibid., 243.
136. Schwartz, *Main Currents*, 594.
137. Sunstein, *After the Rights Revolution*, 238.
138. Sunstein, *Partial Constitution*, 23.
139. Sunstein, *After the Rights Revolution*, 238.
140. Ibid., 228.
141. Ibid., 74.
142. Ibid., 84.
143. Ibid., 232.

CHAPTER 9. PRESENT AND FUTURE

1. Grotius, quoted in Tuck, *Natural Rights Theories*, 76.
2. Taylor, quoted in Tuck, *Natural Rights Theories*, 112.

3. Braybrooke, "Economic Thinking," 19.
4. Ibid., 28–41.
5. Tversky and Kahneman, "Rational Choice," in Cook and Levi, *Limits of Rationality*, 60; see also Hausman and McPherson, "Economics," in Hausman, *Philosophy of Economics*, 259.
6. Blaug, *Methodology of Economics*, 151; see also Cyert and March, *Behavioral Theory*, 117, 297; Plott, "Rational Choice," in Cook and Levi, *Limits of Rationality*, 146.
7. Ormerod, *Butterfly Economics*, 72.
8. Ibid.
9. Simon, "Methodological Foundations of Economics," in *Models of Bounded Rationality*, vol. 3, 320.
10. Simon, "Satisficing," in *Models of Bounded Rationality*, vol. 3, 295–298.
11. Hausman, introduction to "Methodology of Positive Economics," by M. Friedman, in Hausman, *Philosophy of Economics*, 180.
12. M. Friedman, "Methodology of Positive Economics," in Hausman, *Philosophy of Economics*, 184.
13. Ibid., 188.
14. Ziliak and McCloskey, "Size Matters," 331–355; Blaug, *Methodology of Economics*, xxi–xxii; Klamer and McCloskey, "Human Conversation," in Klamer, McCloskey, and Solow, *Consequences of Economic Rhetoric*, 7.
15. Deirdre McCloskey, *Rhetoric of Economics*, 24–25.
16. Ormerod, *Butterfly Economics*, 152–154, 156–158, 160, 162, 164.
17. Gately, "Prospects for Oil Prices," 528.
18. Abel and Bernanke, *Macroeconomics*, 85.
19. Moran, quoted in Gately, "Ten-Year Retrospective," 1110.
20. Ormerod, *Butterfly Economics*, 78–80.
21. Arrow, quoted in Ormerod, *Butterfly Economics*, 15–16.
22. Ibid., 36–37; Rhoads, *Economist's View*, 190.
23. Lucas, "Expectations," 103–122; Sargent and Wallace, "'Rational' Expectations," 241–254.
24. The phrase is from Blyth, *Great Transformations*, 143.
25. Kirshner, "Inflation," 610.
26. Lovell, "Tests of Rational Expectations," 110–124.
27. Kirshner, "Inflation," 613.
28. M. Bernstein, *Perilous Progress*, 101.
29. Schwartz, *Main Currents*, 566.
30. Posner, *Economic Analysis of Law* (1972), 393, 394.
31. Ibid., 1–2.
32. Posner, "Economics in Law," in Parisi, *Economic Structure of Law*, 107.
33. Ibid., 129.
34. Posner, *Economic Analysis of Law* (1972), 98, 320–327.
35. Ibid., 327, 329.
36. Ibid., 266.
37. Posner, "Economics of Labor Law," 990.

38. Ibid.
39. Ibid., 991.
40. Ibid., 1000.
41. Ibid., 1001.
42. K. Arrow, *Social Choice*.
43. Green and Shapiro, *Rational Choice Theory*, 3.
44. Aldrich, "Rational Choice Theory," in Dodd and Jillson, *Dynamics of American Politics*, 211.
45. Green and Shapiro, *Rational Choice Theory*, 30–32.
46. Ibid., 195.
47. Ibid., 47, 50, 68, 74; Hinich and Munger, *Analytical Politics*, 136–153.
48. Hinich and Munger, *Analytical Politics*, 5.
49. Ibid., 149.
50. Ibid., 177.
51. Ibid., 195–197.
52. Ibid., 211.
53. Samuelson, quoted in Gilpin, *Global Capitalism*, 50.
54. Donald McCloskey, "Rhetoric of Economics," in Hausman, *Philosophy of Economics*, 411.
55. Goodwin, "Economists' Discourse," in Klamer, McCloskey, and Solow, *Consequences of Economic Rhetoric*, 211.
56. Blaug, *Economic Theory*, 347, 358–359, 369, 618; Pearce, *Dictionary of Modern Economics*, 556.
57. Burtless et al., *Globaphobia*.
58. Carlton and Perloff, *Modern Industrial Organization*, 583.
59. Ibid.
60. Edelman, "Price of Free Trade."
61. Daly and Cobb, *Common Good*, 220–221.
62. T. Friedman, *Lexus*, 180, 187, 189, 227; Rosecrance, *Virtual State*, 15, 62–64, 65.
63. Bush, quoted in Weisbrot, "Tricks of Free Trade," 64.
64. Rodrik, *Globalization*, passim; Hirst, "Globalization," in O'Sullivan, *Political Theory*, 180.
65. Ohmae, *End of the Nation State*, 5.
66. Ibid., 136, 141.
67. Rosecrance, *Virtual State*, 90, 95.
68. Garten, *Big Ten*, 150.
69. Wright, "Continental Drift," 18.
70. T. Friedman, *Lexus*, 206.
71. Ibid., 207.
72. Weisbrot, "Tricks of Free Trade," 63, 67.
73. Gilpin, *Global Capitalism*, 104.
74. Hirst, "Globalization," 177–178.
75. Rawls, *Theory of Justice*, 100–101.
76. P. Samuelson, *Economics from the Heart*, 4.

77. Roemer, *Free to Lose*, 64, 66.
78. Sunstein, *After the Rights Revolution*, 39.
79. Kuttner, *Economic Illusion*, 16.
80. Sandel, *Democracy's Discontent*, 6.
81. Fishkin, *Democracy and Deliberation*; Fishkin *Voice of the People*.

Bibliography

Aaron, Daniel. *Men of Good Hope: A Story of American Progressives*. London: Oxford University Press, 1951.
Abbey, Edward. *Desert Solitaire: A Season in the Wilderness*. New York: McGraw-Hill, 1965.
Abbott, Philip. "What's New in the *Federalist Papers?*" *Political Research Quarterly* 49 (September 1996): 525–545.
Abel, Andrew S., and Ben S. Bernanke. *Macroeconomics*. 3rd ed. Reading, Mass.: Addison-Wesley, 1998.
Abrams, Richard M., ed. *Issues of the Populist and Progressive Eras, 1892–1912*. New York: Harper and Row, 1969.
Adair, Douglass. *Fame and the Founding Fathers: Essays by Douglass Adair*. Indianapolis: Liberty Fund, 1974.
Adams, Henry. *The Education of Henry Adams*. Cambridge, Mass.: Houghton, Mifflin, 1961.
Adams, James Truslow. *Jeffersonian Principles and Hamiltonian Principles*. Boston: Little, Brown, 1932.
Adams, John. *The Political Writings of John Adams*. Indianapolis: Bobbs-Merrill, 1954.
Adams, Walter, and James W. Brock. *The Bigness Complex: Industry, Labor, and Government in the American Economy*. New York: Pantheon, 1986.
Agar, Herbert. *The Price of Union*. Boston: Houghton, Mifflin, 1966.
Aldrich, John. "Rational Choice Theory and the Study of American Politics." In Lawrence C. Dodd and Calvin Jillson, eds., *The Dynamics of American Politics: Approaches and Interpretations*. Boulder, Colo.: Westview Press, 1994.
Alperovitz, Gar and Jeff Faux. *Rebuilding America: A Blueprint for the New Economy*. New York: Pantheon, 1984.
American Almanac 1996–1997. Washington, D.C.: U.S. Bureau of the Census, 1996.
Anderson, Benjamin M. *Economics and the Public Welfare: A Financial and Economic History of the United States, 1914–1946*. 2nd ed. Indianapolis: Liberty Press, 1979.
Appleby, Joyce. *Capitalism and a New Social Order: The Republican Vision of the 1790s*. New York: NYU Press, 1984.
———. "The Popular Sources of American Capitalism." *Studies in American Political Development* 9 (Fall 1995): 440–460.
———. "Republicanism in Old and New Contexts." *William and Mary Quarterly* 43, no. 1 (January 1986): 21–34.

Argersinger, Peter H. *The Limits of Agrarian Radicalism: Western Populism and American Politics.* Lawrence: University Press of Kansas, 1995.

Arnold, Peri E. "Ambivalent Leviathan: Herbert Hoover and the Positive State." In J. David Greenstone, ed., *Labor in American Politics.* New York: Random House, 1969.

Arnold, R. Douglas. "Can Inattentive Citizens Control Their Elected Representatives?" In Lawrence C. Dodd and Bruce I. Oppenheimer, eds., *Congress Reconsidered.* 5th ed. Washington, D.C.: Congressional Quarterly Press, 1998.

Arnold, Thurman. *The Folklore of Capitalism.* New Haven, Conn.: Yale University Press, 1937.

Arrow, Dennis W. "'Rich,' 'Textured,' and 'Nuanced': Constitutional 'Scholarship' and Constitutional Messianism at the Millennium." *Texas Law Review* 78, no. 1 (November 1999): 149–172.

Arrow, Kenneth J. *Social Choice and Individual Values.* 2nd ed. New Haven, Conn.: Yale University Press, 1963.

———. "Thorstein Veblen as an Economic Theorist." *American Economist* 19, no. 1 (Spring 1975): 5–9.

Asch, Peter, and Rosalind Seneca. *Government and the Marketplace.* Chicago: Dryden, 1985.

Atack, Jeremy, and Peter Passell, eds. *A New Economic View of American History from Colonial Times to 1940.* 2nd ed. New York: W. W. Norton, 1994.

Austin, Mary. *The Land of Little Rain.* 1903. Reprint, New York: Penguin, 1988.

Ayres, C. E. *The Theory of Economic Progress: A Study of the Fundamentals of Economic Development and Cultural Change.* 2nd ed. 1944. New York: Schocken, 1962.

Bailyn, Bernard. *The Ideological Origins of the American Revolution.* Cambridge, Mass.: Harvard University Press, 1967.

———. *The Origins of American Politics.* New York: Random House, 1965.

Balinsky, Alexander *Albert Gallatin: Fiscal Theories and Policies.* New Brunswick, N.J.: Rutgers University Press, 1958.

Banning, Lance. "Jeffersonian Ideology Revisited: Liberal and Classical Ideas in the New American Republic." *William and Mary Quarterly* (January 1986): 3–20.

———. *The Jeffersonian Persuasion: Evolution of a Party Ideology.* Ithaca, N.Y.: Cornell University Press, 1978.

Baran, Paul, and Paul M. Sweezy. *Monopoly Capital: An Essay on the American Economic and Social Order.* New York: Modern Reader, 1966.

Barber, Benjamin R. "The Compromised Republic: Public Purposeless in America." In Robert H. Horwitz, ed., *The Moral Foundations of the American Republic.* 2nd ed. Charlottesville: University of Virginia Press, 1979.

———. "Strong Democracy: Participation Politics for a New Age." In Sue Davis, ed., *American Political Thought: Four Hundred Years of Ideas and Ideologies.* Englewood Cliffs, N.J.: Prentice-Hall, 1996.

Barber, William J. *A History of Economic Thought.* New York: Penguin, 1967.

Bardes, Barbara A., Mack C. Shelley, and Steffen W. Schmidt. *American Government and Politics Today.* 4th ed. Stamford, Conn.: Wadsworth/Thomson, 2002.

Barro, Robert J. "Inflation and Economic Growth." *Bank of England Quarterly Bulletin* 35, no. 2 (May 1995): 166–176.

Bart, Peter. "Talkradio Titans See Validation in Newt's Rise." *Daily Variety*, January 1995, 39.
Baumol, William J. "Say's (at Least) Eight Laws, or What Say and James Mill May Really Have Meant." In *Microtheory: Applications and Origins*. Cambridge, Mass.: MIT Press, 1986.
Baxter, Maurice G. *Daniel Webster and the Supreme Court*. Amherst: University of Massachusetts Press, 1966.
Beck, Nathaniel, "Parties, Administrations, and American Macroeconomic Outcomes." *American Political Science Review* 76, no. 1 (March 1982): 83–93.
Becker, Carl L. *The Declaration of Independence: A Study in the History of Political Ideas*. New York: Random House, 1922.
———. *Modern Democracy*. New Haven, Conn.: Yale University Press, 1941.
Bellah, Robert N., Richard Madsen, William M. Sullivan, Ann Swidler, and Steven M. Tipton. *Habits of the Heart: Individualism and Commitment in American Life*. New York: Harper and Row, 1985.
Bellamy, Edward. *Looking Backward 2000–1887*. 1888. Reprint, New York: New American Library, 1960.
Benedict, Michael Les. "Laisser-Faire and Liberty: A Re-Evaluation of the Meaning and Origin of Laisser-Faire Constitutionalism." *Law and History Review* 3, no. 2 (Fall 1985): 293–332.
Bensel, Richard Franklin. *The Political Economy of American Industrialization, 1877–1900*. Cambridge: Cambridge University Press, 2000.
Bentley, Arthur F. *The Process of Government*. 1908. Reprint, Cambridge, Mass.: Harvard University Press, 1967.
Bernstein, Aaron. "Too Much Corporate Power?" *Business Week*, September 11, 2000, 144–149.
Bernstein, Michael A. *A Perilous Progress: Economists and Public Purpose in Twentieth-Century America*. Princeton, N.J.: Princeton University Press, 2001.
Berry, Wendell. *The Unsettling of America: Culture and Agriculture*. San Francisco: Sierra Club, 1977.
———. *What Are People For? Essays by Wendell Berry*. San Francisco: North Point, 1990.
Binder, Guyora. "On Critical Legal Studies As Guerrilla Warfare." *Georgetown Law Journal* 76, no. 1 (October 1987): 1–36.
Blair, John M. *The Control of Oil*. New York: Pantheon, 1976.
Blaug, Mark. *Economic Theory in Retrospect*. 3rd ed. Cambridge: Cambridge University Press, 1978.
———. *The Methodology of Economics, or How Economists Explain*. 2nd ed. Cambridge: Cambridge University Press, 1992.
Blaug, Ricardo, and John Schwarzmantel. "Participation Introduction." In Ricardo Blaug and John Schwarzmantel, eds., *Democracy: A Reader*. New York: Columbia University Press, 2000.
———, eds. *Democracy: A Reader*. New York: Columbia University Press, 2000.
Blyth, Mark. *Great Transformations: Economic Ideas and Institutional Change in the Twentieth Century*. Cambridge: Cambridge University Press, 2002.

Bonadio, Felice A., ed. *Political Parties in American History.* 2 vols. New York: G. P. Putnam's Sons, 1974.
Boorstin, Daniel J. *The Americans: The Democratic Experience.* New York: Random House, 1973.
———. *The Americans: The National Experience.* New York: Random House, 1965.
Bowers, Claude G. "Hamilton: A Portrait." In Jacob E. Cooke, ed., *Alexander Hamilton: A Profile.* New York: Hill and Wang, 1967.
Bowles, Samuel, Richard C. Edwards, and William G. Shepherd, eds. *Unconventional Wisdom: Essays on Economics in Honor of John Kenneth Galbraith.* Boston: Houghton Mifflin, 1989.
Boyd, Richard. "On The Current Status of Scientific Realism." In Richard Boyd, Philip Gasper, and J. D. Trout, eds., *The Philosophy of Science.* Cambridge, Mass.: MIT Press, 1991.
Boyd, Richard, Philip Gasper, and J. D. Trout, eds. *The Philosophy of Science.* Cambridge, Mass.: MIT Press, 1991.
Bradford, M. E. Introduction to *Arator: Being a Series of Agricultural Essays, Practical and Political, in Sixty-Four Numbers,* by John Taylor. 1818. Reprint, Indianapolis: Liberty Fund, 1978.
Brandeis, Louis D. *The Curse of Bigness: Miscellaneous Papers of Louis D. Brandeis.* New York: Viking, 1935.
———. *Other People's Money, and How the Bankers Use It.* Washington, D.C.: National Home Library Foundation, 1933.
———. *The Social and Economic Views of Mr. Justice Brandeis.* New York: Vanguard, 1930.
Braybrooke, David. "Economic Thinking in Political Science: Maximizing on the Way to Tautology." *Manuscrito* 10, no. 2 (1987): 2.
———. *Natural Law Modernized.* Toronto: University of Toronto Press, 2001.
Breen, T. H. *The Character of the Good Ruler: A Study of Puritan Ideas in New England, 1630–1730.* New Haven, Conn.: Yale University Press, 1970.
Brennan, H. Geoffrey, and Robert D. Tollison. Preface to *What Should Economists Do?* by James M. Buchanan. Indianapolis: Liberty Fund, 1979.
Brenner, Philip, Robert Borosage, and Bethany Weidner. *Exploring Contradictions: Political Economy in the Corporate State.* New York: David McKay, 1974.
Brown, Charles, and James Medoff. "Trade Unions in the Production Process." *Journal of Political Economy* 86, no. 3 (June 1978): 355–378.
Brown, E. Cary, and Robert M. Solow, eds. *Paul Samuelson and Modern Economic Theory.* New York: McGraw-Hill, 1983.
Brown, Michael K. "State Capacity and Political Choice: Interpreting the Failure of the Third New Deal." *Studies in American Political Development* 9 (Spring 1995): 187–212.
Brown, Richard H. "The Missouri Crisis, Slavery, and the Politics of Jacksonianism." In Felice A. Bonadio, ed., *Political Parties in American History.* 2 vols. New York: G. P. Putnam's Sons, 1974.
Brownson, Orestes. "The Laboring Classes." In Michael B. Levy, ed., *Political Thought in America: An Anthology.* Chicago: Dorsey, 1988.
Brunner, Borgna, ed. *Time Almanac 1999.* Boston: Information Please LLC, 1998.

Buchanan, Bruce. *Renewing Presidential Politics: Campaigns, Media, and the Public Interest.* New York: Rowman and Littlefield, 1996.

Buchanan, James M. *What Should Economists Do?* Indianapolis: Liberty Fund, 1979.

Buchanan, James M., and Viktor J. Vanberg. "The Market as a Creative Process." In Daniel M. Hausman, ed., *The Philosophy of Economics: An Anthology.* 2nd ed. Cambridge: Cambridge University Press, 1994.

Buckley, William F., Jr. *Up from Liberalism.* New York: Bantam, 1968.

Burnham, Walter Dean. "The Changing Shape of the American Political Universe." *American Political Science Review* 59, no. 1 (March 1965): 7–28.

———. *Critical Elections and the Mainsprings of American Politics.* New York: W. W. Norton, 1970.

Burtless, Gary, Robert Z. Lawrence, Robert E. Litan, and Robert J. Shapiro. *Globaphobia: Confronting Fears about Open Trade.* Washington, D.C.: Brookings Institution, 1998.

Burton, David H. *Political Ideas of Justice Holmes.* London: Fairleigh Dickenson University Press, 1992.

Calhoun, John C. *A Disquisition on Government and Selections From the Discourse.* 1853. Reprint, Indianapolis: Bobbs-Merrill, 1953.

Calleo, David P., and Benjamin M. Rowland. *America and the World Political Economy: Atlantic Dreams and National Realities.* Bloomington: Indiana University Press, 1973.

Cameron, David R. "The Expansion of the Public Economy: A Comparative Analysis." *American Political Science Review* 72, no. 4 (December 1978): 1243–1261.

Carey, Henry C. *Financial Crises: Their Causes and Effects.* Philadelphia: Henry Carey Baird, 1864.

———. *The Harmony of Interests, Agricultural, Manufacturing, and Commercial.* 2nd ed. New York: Myron Finch, 1852.

Carlton, Dennis W., and Jeffrey M. Perloff. *Modern Industrial Organization.* 3rd ed. Reading, Mass.: Addison-Wesley, 2000.

Carnegie, Andrew. "Wealth." In Michael B. Levy, ed., *Political Thought in America: An Anthology.* Chicago: Dorsey, 1988.

Carpenter, Daniel P. *The Forging of Bureaucratic Autonomy: Reputations, Networks, and Policy Innovation in Executive Agencies, 1862–1928.* Princeton, N.J.: Princeton University Press, 2001.

———. "The Political Foundations of Bureaucratic Autonomy: A Response to Kernell." *Studies in American Political Development* 15 (Spring 2001): 113–122.

Carr, David. *Time, Narrative, and History.* Bloomington: University of Indiana Press, 1986.

Carson, Rachel. *Silent Spring.* Boston: Houghton Mifflin, 1962.

Caudill, David S. "Freud and Critical Legal Studies: Contours of a Radical Socio-Legal Psychoanalysis." In Jerry Leonard, ed., *Legal Studies as Cultural Studies: A Reader in (Post)Modern Critical Legal Theory.* Albany: State University of New York Press, 1995.

Charles, J. Daryle. Review of *In Defense of History*, by Richard J. Evans. *Academic Questions* (Winter 1999/2000): 92–94.

Chernow, Ron. *The House of Morgan: An American Banking Dynasty and the Rise of Modern Finance.* New York: Simon and Schuster, 1990.

Cleaver, Harry. *Reading Capital Politically.* 1979. Reprint, Leeds, England: Anti-Thesis, 2000.
Clower, Robert W. "The Ideas of Economists." In Arjo Klamer, Donald M. McCloskey, and Robert M. Solow, eds., *The Consequences of Economic Rhetoric.* Cambridge: Cambridge University Press, 1988.
Coase, Ronald. "The Problem of Social Cost." *Journal of Law and Economics* 3 (1960): 1–30.
Cohen, Joshua, and Joel Rogers. *On Democracy: Toward a Transformation of American Society.* New York: Penguin, 1983.
Cohen, Lizbeth. *A Consumers' Republic: The Politics of Mass Consumption in Postwar America.* New York: Knopf, 2003.
Coit, Margaret L. *John C. Calhoun: American Portrait.* Boston: Houghton Mifflin, 1950.
Coleman, Jules L. "Economics and the Law: A Critical Review of the Foundations of the Economic Approach to Law." *Ethics* 94, no. 4 (July 1984): 649–679.
Collier, Charles. "Henry George's System of Political Economy." *History of Political Economy* 11 (Spring 1979): 64–93.
Collins, Robert. *More: The Politics of Economic Growth in Postwar America.* Oxford: Oxford University Press, 2000.
Commager, Henry Steele. *The American Mind: An Interpretation of American Thought and Character since the 1880's.* New Haven, Conn.: Yale University Press, 1950.
Commons, John R. "Institutional Economics." In Philip C. Newman, Arthur D. Gaye, and Milton D. Spencer, eds., *Source Readings in Economic Thought.* New York: W. W. Norton, 1954.
Conkin, Paul K. *Prophets of Prosperity: America's First Political Economists.* Bloomington: Indiana University Press, 1980.
Connolly, William E., ed. *The Bias of Pluralism.* New York: Atherton, 1971.
Cook, Karen Schneer, and Margaret Levi, eds. *The Limits of Rationality.* Chicago: University of Chicago Press, 1990.
Cooke, Jacob E., ed. *Alexander Hamilton: A Profile.* New York: Hill and Wang, 1967.
Cooley, Thomas M. *A Treatise on the Constitutional Limitations Which Rest Upon the Legislative Power of the States of the American Union.* Boston: Little, Brown, 1868.
Cornell, Drucilla. "Time, Deconstruction, and the Challenge to Legal Positivism: The Call For Judicial Responsibility." In Jerry Leonard, ed., *Legal Studies as Cultural Studies: A Reader in (Post)Modern Critical Legal Theory.* Albany: State University of New York Press, 1995.
Croly, Herbert. *The Promise of American Life.* 1909. Reprint, New York: E. P. Dutton, 1963.
Crossman, Richard, ed. *The God That Failed.* New York: Bantam, 1965.
Curtis, Charles P. *Law as Large as Life: A Natural Law for Today and the Supreme Court as Its Prophet.* New York: Simon and Schuster, 1959.
Cyert, Richard M. and James G. March. *A Behavioral Theory of the Firm.* Englewood Cliffs, N.J.: Prentice-Hall, 1963.
Dahl, Robert A. "A Critique of the Ruling Elite Model." In G. William Domhoff and Hoyt Ballard, eds., *C. Wright Mills and the Power Elite.* Boston: Beacon Press, 1968.
———. *Democracy and Its Critics.* New Haven, Conn.: Yale University Press, 1989.
———. *A Preface to Democratic Theory.* Chicago: University of Chicago Press, 1956.

———. *A Preface to Economic Democracy.* Berkeley: University of California Press, 1985.
———. *Who Governs? Democracy and Power in an American City.* New Haven, Conn.: Yale University Press, 1961.
Daly, Herman E., and John B. Cobb Jr. *For the Common Good: Redirecting the Economy toward Community, the Environment, and a Sustainable Future.* Boston: Beacon, 1994.
Dangerfield, George. *The Awakening of American Nationalism 1815–1828.* New York: Harper and Row, 1965.
Darwin, Charles. *The Origin of Species.* 1st edition originally published 1859; 5th edition originally published 1872. 5th ed. New York: Collier Macmillan, 1962.
Davis, J. Ronnie. *The New Economics and the Old Economists.* Ames: Iowa State University Press, 1971.
Davis, Sue, ed. *American Political Thought: Four Hundred Years of Ideas and Ideologies.* Englewood Cliffs, N.J.: Prentice-Hall, 1996.
Debs, Eugene V. "Acceptance Speech." In Michael B. Levy, ed., *Political Thought in America: An Anthology.* Chicago: Dorsey, 1988.
———. *Writings and Speeches of Eugene V. Debs.* New York: Hermitage 1948.
Degler, Carl N. *Out of Our Past: The Forces That Shaped Modern America.* Rev. ed. New York: Harper and Row, 1970.
d'Entreves, A. P. *Natural Law.* London: Hutchinson University Press, 1951.
Destler, Chester McArthur. *American Radicalism, 1865–1901.* Chicago: Quadrangle, 1946.
Dew, Thomas Roderick. "Dew on Slavery." *Political Register* 2, no. 25 (October 16, 1833): 771–823.
Dewey, John. "Liberalism and Social Action." In Michael B. Levy, ed., *Political Thought in America: An Anthology.* Chicago: Dorsey, 1988.
Dodd, Lawrence C., and Calvin Jillson. "Conversations on the Study of American Politics: An Introduction." In Lawrence C. Dodd and Calvin Jillson, eds., *The Dynamics of American Politics: Approaches and Interpretations.* Boulder, Colo.: Westview Press, 1994.
Dodd, Lawrence C., and Bruce I. Oppenheimer, eds. *Congress Reconsidered.* 5th ed. Washington, D.C.: Congressional Quarterly Press, 1993.
Dolbeare, Kenneth M., and Janette Kay Hubbell. *U.S.A. 2012: After the Middle-Class Revolution.* Chatham, N.J.: Chatham House, 1996.
Domhoff, G. William. "State and Ruling Class in Corporate America." In Richard C. Edwards, Michael Reich, and Thomas E. Weisskopf, eds., *The Capitalist System.* 2nd ed. Englewood Cliffs, N.J.: Prentice-Hall, 1978.
———. *Who Rules America?* Englewood Cliffs, N.J.: Prentice-Hall, 1967.
Domhoff, G. William, and Hoyt Ballard. *C. Wright Mills and the Power Elite.* Boston: Beacon, 1968.
Dorfman, Joseph. *The Economic Mind in American Civilization.* 2 vols. New York: Viking, 1946.
———. "The Regal Republic of John Adams." In John P. Roche, ed., *Origins of American Political Thought.* New York: Harper and Row, 1967.
———. *Thorstein Veblen and His America.* New York: Viking, 1934.
Downs, Anthony. *An Economic Theory of Democracy.* New York: Harper and Row, 1957.
Drucker, Peter F. "Toward the Next Economics." *Public Interest,* special issue (1980): 4–18.

D'Souza, Dinesh. *The Virtue of Prosperity: Finding Values in an Age of Techno-Affluence*. New York: Simon and Schuster, 2000.

Dubofsky, Melvyn, and Warren Van Tyne, eds. *Labor Leaders in America*. Urbana: University of Illinois Press, 1987.

Dworkin, Ronald. *Law's Empire*. Cambridge, Mass.: Harvard University Press, 1986.

Dye, Thomas R., L. Tucker Gibson, and Clay Robinson. *Politics in America*. 6th ed. Upper Saddle River, N.J.: Prentice-Hall, 2005.

Dye, Thomas R., and Harmon Ziegler. *The Irony of Democracy: An Uncommon Introduction to American Politics*. Belmont, Calif.: Wadsworth, 1970.

Eaton, Clement. *The Growth of Southern Civilization 1790–1860*. New York: Harper and Row, 1961.

Eckes, Alfred E., Jr. *Opening America's Market: U.S. Foreign Trade Policy since 1776*. Chapel Hill: University of North Carolina Press, 1995.

Edelman, Marc. "Price of Free Trade: Famine." *Los Angeles Times*, March 22, 2002.

Edwards, Richard C., Michael Reich, and Thomas E. Weisskopf, eds. *The Capitalist System*. 2nd ed. Englewood Cliffs, N.J.: Prentice-Hall, 1978.

Eisenach, Eldon J. "Reconstituting the Study of American Political Thought in a Regime-Change Perspective." *Studies in American Political Development* 4 (1990): 169–230.

Elkins, Stanley M. *Slavery: A Problem in American Institutional and Intellectual Life*. New York: Grosset and Dunlap, 1963.

Ellis, Richard J. *American Political Cultures*. New York: Oxford University Press, 1995.

———. "Radical Lockeanism in American Political Culture." *Western Political Quarterly* 45 (December 1992): 825–850.

Elshtain, Jean Bethke. *Democracy on Trial*. New York: Basic Books, 1995.

Ely, James W., Jr. *The Guardian of Every Other Right: A Constitutional History of Property Rights*. 2nd ed. New York: Oxford University Press, 1998.

Ely, Richard T. *Socialism: Examination of Its Nature, Its Strength and Its Weakness with Suggestions for Reform*. New York: Thomas Y. Crowell, 1894.

Engler, Robert. *The Politics of Oil: A Study of Private Power and Democratic Directions*. Chicago: University of Chicago Press, 1961.

Epstein, Richard A. Foreword to *The New Right v. the Constitution*, by Stephen Macedo. Washington, D.C.: Cato Institute, 1987.

———. *Takings: Private Property and the Power of Eminent Domain*. Cambridge, Mass.: Harvard University Press, 1985.

Epstein, Gerald, and Thomas Ferguson. "Monetary Policy, Loan Liquidation, and Industrial Conflict: The Federal Reserve and the Open Market Operations of 1932." *Journal of Economic History* 44, no. 4 (December 1984): 957–983.

Erickson, David F., and Louisa Bertch Green, eds. *The Liberal Tradition in American Politics: Reassessing the Legacy of American Liberalism*. New York: Routledge, 1999.

Extra! "The Way Things Aren't: Rush Limbaugh Debates Reality." July/August 1994, 17.

———. "Yet More Limbicilic Statements." June 1995, 3.

Faulkner, Harold U. *American Economic History*. 6th ed. New York: Harper and Brothers, 1949.

———, ed. *Politics, Reform, and Expansion 1890–1900*. New York: Harper and Row, 1959.

Feldstein, Martin. *Inflation, Tax Rules, and Capital Formation.* Chicago: University of Chicago Press, 1983.
Ferguson, E. James, ed. *Selected Writings of Albert Gallatin.* Indianapolis: Bobbs-Merrill, 1967.
Ferguson, Thomas. "From Normalcy to New Deal: Industrial Structure, Party Competition, and American Public Policy in the New Deal." *International Organization* 38, no. 1 (Winter 1984): 41–94.
———. "Party Realignment and American Industrial Structure: The Investment Theory of Political Parties in Historical Perspective." In P. Zavemlka, ed., *Research in Political Economy.* Greenwich, Conn.: JAI, 1983.
Ferguson, Thomas, and Joel Rogers. *Right Turn: The Decline of the Democrats and the Future of American Politics.* New York: Hill and Wang, 1986.
Fetter, Frank A. "Early History of Political Economy in the United States." In James A. Gherity, ed., *Economic Thought: A Historical Anthology.* New York: Random House, 1965.
Fiorina, Morris, P. *Retrospective Voting in American National Elections.* New Haven, Conn.: Yale University Press, 1981.
Fiorina, Morris P., and Paul E. Peterson. *The New American Democracy.* Boston: Allyn and Bacon, 1998.
Fishkin, James S. *Democracy and Deliberation: New Directions for Democratic Reform.* New Haven, Conn.: Yale University Press, 1991.
———. *The Voice of the People: Public Opinion and Democracy.* New Haven, Conn.: Yale University Press, 1995.
Fitzhugh, George. *Cannibals All! Or Slaves without Masters.* 1857. Reprint, Cambridge, Mass.: Harvard University Press, 1960.
Fleischacker, Samuel. "Adam Smith's Reception among the American Founders, 1776–1790." *William and Mary Quarterly* (October 2002): 897–924.
Fogel, Robert W. *The Fourth Great Awakening and the Future of Egalitarianism.* Chicago: University of Chicago Press, 2000.
Fogel, Robert W., and Stanley L. Engerman, *Time on the Cross.* Boston: Little, Brown, 1974.
———, eds. *Without Consent or Contract: The Rise and Fall of American Slavery.* Vol. 2. New York: W. W. Norton, 1992.
Foner, Eric. *Free Soil, Free Labor, Free Men: The Ideology of the Republican Party before the Civil War.* New York: Oxford University Press, 1970.
———. "Why Is There No Socialism in the United States?" *History Workshop* 17 (Spring 1984): 57–80.
Forbath, William E. *Law and the Shaping of the American Labor Movement.* Cambridge, Mass.: Harvard University Press, 1991.
Foster, William Trufant, and Waddill Catchings. *Business without a Buyer.* Boston: Houghton Mifflin, 1927.
Foucault, Michel. *The Archaeology of Knowledge and the Discourse of Language.* New York: Pantheon, 1972.
Fox, Dixon Ryan. *The Decline of Aristocracy in the Politics of New York 1801–1840.* 1919. Reprint, New York: Harper and Row, 1965.
Frank, Robert H. *Microeconomics and Behavior.* 3rd ed. New York: McGraw-Hill, 1997.

Frank, Thomas. *One Market under God: Extreme Capitalism, Market Populism, and the End of Economic Democracy*. New York: Doubleday, 2000.

Franklin, Benjamin. "On the Imposition of Direct Taxes upon the Colonies without Their Consent." In Adrienne Koch, ed., *The American Enlightenment: The Shaping of the American Experiment in a Free Society*. New York: George Braziller, 1965.

Free, Lloyd A., and Hadley Cantril. *The Political Beliefs of Americans: A Study of Public Opinion*. New Brunswick, N.J.: Rutgers University Press, 1967.

Freeman, Joanne B. *Affairs of Honor: National Politics in the New Republic*. New Haven, Conn.: Yale University Press, 2001.

Frieden, Jeffrey A. "Monetary Populism in Nineteenth-Century America: An Open Economy Interpretation." *Journal of Economic History* 57 (June 1997): 367–395.

Friedman, Lawrence M. *American Law in the 20th Century*. New Haven, Conn.: Yale University Press, 2002.

———. *A History of American Law*. New York: Simon and Schuster, 1973.

Friedman, Lawrence M., and Harry Scheiber, eds. *American Law and the Constitutional Order: Historical Perspectives*. Cambridge, Mass.: Harvard University Press, 1978.

Friedman, Milton. *Adam Smith's Relevance for 1976*. Los Angeles: International Institute for Economic Research, 1976.

———. *Capitalism and Freedom*. Chicago: University of Chicago Press, 1962.

———. "The Demand for Money: Some Theoretical and Empirical Results." *Journal of Political Economy* 67, no. 4 (August 1959): 327–351.

———. "The Methodology of Positive Economics." In Daniel M. Hausman, ed., *The Philosophy of Economics: An Anthology*. 2nd ed. Cambridge: Cambridge University Press, 1994.

Friedman, Milton, and Rose Friedman. *Free to Choose: A Personal Statement*. New York: Avon, 1979.

Friedman, Milton, and Anna Jacobson Schwartz. *The Great Contraction, 1929–1933*. Princeton, N.J.: Princeton University Press, 1965.

Friedman, Thomas L. *The Lexus and the Olive Tree*. Updated ed. New York: Random House, 2000.

Frisch, Morton J. *Alexander Hamilton and the Political Order: An Interpretation of His Political Thought and Practice*. New York: University Press of America, 1991.

Fry, Michael, ed. *Adam Smith's Legacy: His Place in the Development of Modern Economics*. New York: Routledge, 1992.

Galbraith, James K. *Created Unequal*. Chicago: University of Chicago Press, 2000.

———. "Trade and the Planning System." In Samuel Bowles, Richard C. Edwards, and William G. Shepherd, eds., *Unconventional Wisdom: Essays on Economics in Honor of John Kenneth Galbraith*. Boston: Houghton Mifflin, 1989.

Galbraith, John Kenneth. *The Affluent Society*. New York: New American Library, 1958.

———. *Economics, Peace and Laughter*. New York: New American Library, 1971.

———. *Economics and the Public Purpose: How We Can Head Off the Mounting Economic Crisis*. New York: New American Library, 1973.

———. *The Great Crash*. Boston: Houghton-Mifflin, 1954.

———. *The New Industrial State*. New York: New American Library, 1967.

Garraty, John A. *The New Commonwealth 1877–1890*. New York: Harper and Row, 1968.

Garten, Jeffrey E. *The Big Ten: The Big Emerging Markets and How They Will Change Our Lives*. New York: Basic Books, 1997.
Gately, Dermot. "The Prospects for Oil Prices, Revisited." *Annual Review of Energy* 11 (1986): 513–538.
———. "A Ten-Year Retrospective: OPEC and the World Oil Market." *Journal of Economic Literature* 22, no. 3 (September 1984): 1100–1114.
Genovese, Eugene D. "Critical Legal Studies as Radical Politics and World View." In Jerry Leonard, ed., *Legal Studies as Cultural Studies: A Reader in (Post)Modern Critical Legal Theory*. Albany: State University of New York Press, 1995.
George, Henry. *Progress and Poverty*. 1879. Reprint, New York: Robert Schalkenbach Foundation, 1980.
Gherity, James A., ed. *Economic Thought: A Historical Anthology*. New York: Random House, 1965.
Gide, Charles, and Charles Rist. *A History of Economic Doctrines*. Boston: D. C. Heath, 1948.
Gilder, George. *Wealth and Poverty*. New York: Bantam, 1981.
Gilje, Paul A., ed. *Wages of Independence: Capitalism in the Early American Republic*. Madison, Wis.: Madison House, 1997.
Gillman, Howard. "How Political Parties Can Use the Courts to Advance Their Agendas: Federal Courts in the United States, 1875–1891." *American Political Science Review* 96, no. 3 (September 2002): 511–524.
Gilman, William H., ed. *Selected Writings of Ralph Waldo Emerson*. New York: New American Library, 1965.
Gilpin, Robert. *The Challenge of Global Capitalism: The World Economy in the 21st Century*. Princeton, N.J.: Princeton University Press, 2000.
Ginger, Ray. *Age of Excess: The United States from 1877 to 1914*. New York: Macmillan, 1965.
Glaab, Charles N., and A. Theodore Brown. *A History of Urban America*. London: Macmillan, 1967.
Glad, Paul W. *McKinley, Bryan, and the People*. Philadelphia: J. B. Lippincott, 1964.
Goebel, Thomas. "The Political Economy of American Populism: From Jackson to the New Deal." *Studies in American Political Development* 11 (Spring 1997): 109–148.
Goodrich, Carter, ed. *The Government and the Economy*. Indianapolis: Bobbs-Merrill, 1967.
Goodwin, Crauford. "The Heterogeneity of the Economists' Discourse: Philosopher, Priest, and Hired Gun." In Arjo Klamer, Donald M. McCloskey, and Robert M. Solow, eds., *The Consequences of Economic Rhetoric*. Cambridge: Cambridge University Press, 1988.
Goodwyn, Lawrence. *The Populist Moment: A Short History of the Agrarian Revolt in America*. Oxford: Oxford University Press, 1978.
Gordon, Robert W., ed. *The Legacy of Oliver Wendell Holmes, Jr.* Stanford, Calif.: Stanford University Press, 1992.
Gordon, Wendell, and John Adams. *Economics as Social Science: An Evolutionary Approach*. Riverdale, Md.: Riverdale, 1989.
Gould, Stephen Jay. *The Lying Stones of Marrakech: Penultimate Reflections in Natural History*. New York: Harmony, 2000.
———. "A Tale of Two Work Sites." In *The Lying Stones of Marrakech: Penultimate Reflections on Natural History*. New York: Harmony Books, 2000.

Grampp, William D. "Adam Smith and the American Revolutionists." *History of Political Economy* 11 (Summer 1979): 179–191.

———. "John Taylor: Economist of Southern Agrarianism." *Southern Economic Journal* 11, no. 3 (January 1945): 255–268.

Green, Donald P., and Ian Shapiro. *Pathologies of Rational Choice Theory: A Critique of Applications in Political Science.* New Haven, Conn.: Yale University Press, 1994.

Green, James R. *The Lincoln Persuasion: Remaking American Liberalism.* Princeton, N.J.: Princeton University Press, 1993.

———. *The World of the Worker: Labor in Twentieth-Century America.* New York: Hill and Wang, 1980.

Greenstone, J. David, ed. *Labor in American Politics.* New York: Random House, 1969.

———. *Public Values and Private Power in American Politics.* Chicago: University of Chicago Press, 1982.

Griswold, Charles L., Jr. *Adam Smith and the Virtues of Enlightenment.* New York: Cambridge University Press, 1999.

Grofman, Bernard, and Donald Wittman, eds. *The Federalist Papers and the New Institutionalism.* New York: Agathon, 1989.

Gunn, L. Ray. *The Decline of Authority: Public Economic Policy and Political Development in New York, 1800–1860.* Ithaca, N.Y.: Cornell University Press, 1983.

Gutman, Herbert G. *Slavery and the Numbers Game: A Critique of* Time on the Cross. Chicago: University of Illinois Press, 1975.

Haakonssen, Knud. *Natural Law and Moral Philosophy: From Grotius to the Scottish Enlightenment.* Cambridge: Cambridge University Press, 1996.

Habermas, Jurgen. *Legitimation Crisis.* Boston: Beacon, 1973.

Haines, Aubrey L. *The Yellowstone Story: A History of Our First National Park.* Yellowstone Park, Wy.: Yellowstone Library and Museum Association, 1977.

Hall, Jerome. "From Legal Theory to Integrative Jurisprudence." *University of Cincinnati Law Review* 33, no. 2 (Spring 1964): 153–206.

Hall, Kermit L. *The Magic Mirror: Law in American History.* New York: Oxford University Press, 1989.

Hall, Peter A. "Conclusion: The Politics of Keynesian." In Peter A. Hall, ed., *The Political Power of Economic Ideas: Keynesianism across Nations.* Princeton, N.J.: Princeton University Press, 1989.

———, ed. *The Political Power of Economic Ideas: Keynesianism across Nations.* Princeton, N.J.: Princeton University Press, 1989.

Hamilton, Alexander. "The Farmer Refuted." In Adrienne Koch, ed., *The American Enlightenment: The Shaping of the American Experiment in a Free Society.* New York: George Braziller, 1965.

———. *Writings.* Edited by Joanne Freeman. New York: Classics of the United States, 2001.

Hamilton, Alexander, John Jay, and James Madison. *The Federalist.* 1787. Reprint, New York: Random House, 1937.

Hammond, Bray. *Banks and Politics in America from the Revolution to the Civil War.* Princeton, N.J.: Princeton University Press, 1957.

Harrington, James. *The Commonwealth of Oceana*. 1656. Reprint, Cambridge: Cambridge University Press, 1992.
Harrington, Michael. *The Other America: Poverty in the United States*. Baltimore: Penguin, 1962.
———. *The Twilight of Capitalism*. New York: Simon and Schuster, 1976.
Hartz, Louis. *The Liberal Tradition in America: An Interpretation of American Political Thought since the Revolution*. New York: Harcourt, Brace and World, 1955.
Hattam, Victoria. "Economic Visions and Political Strategies: American Labor and the State, 1865–1896." *Studies in American Political Development* 4 (1990): 82–129.
Hausman, Daniel M., ed. *The Philosophy of Economics: An Anthology*. 2nd ed. Cambridge: Cambridge University Press, 1994.
Hausman, Daniel M., and Michael S. McPherson. "Economics, Rationality, and Ethics." In Daniel M. Hausman, ed., *The Philosophy of Economics: An Anthology*. 2nd ed. Cambridge: Cambridge University Press, 1994.
Hawley, Ellis W. *The New Deal and the Problem of Monopoly*. Princeton, N.J.: Princeton University Press, 1966.
Hayek, Friedrich A. *The Road to Serfdom*. Chicago: University of Chicago Press, 1944.
———. "The Use of Knowledge in Society." In Adrian Klaasen, ed., *The Invisible Hand: Essays in Classical Economics*. Chicago: Henry Regnery, 1965.
Hays, Samuel P. *The Response to Industrialism, 1885–1914*. New York: Harper and Row, 1957.
Heilbroner, Robert L. *The Worldly Philosophers: The Lives, Times and Ideas of the Great Economic Thinkers*. 1953. Reprint, New York: Simon and Schuster, 1980.
Heilbroner, Robert L., and Aaron Singer. *The Economic Transformation of America*. New York: Harcourt Brace Jovanovich, 1977.
Held, David. *Models of Democracy*. 2nd ed. Stanford, Calif.: Stanford University Press, 1996.
Hempel, Carl. "Empiricist Criteria of Cognitive Significance: Problems and Changes." In Richard Boyd, Philip Gasper, and J. D. Trout, eds., *The Philosophy of Science*. Cambridge, Mass.: MIT Press, 1991
Henretta, James A. *The Origins of American Capitalism*. Boston: Northeastern University Press, 1991.
Hibbs, Douglas A. "Political Parties and Macroeconomic Policy." *American Political Science Review* 71, no. 4 (December 1977): 1467–1487.
Hicks, John D. *The Populist Revolt: A History of the Farmers' Alliance and the People's Party*. 1931. Reprint, Lincoln: University of Nebraska Press, 1961.
Higham, John. *Strangers in the Land: Patterns of American Nativism, 1860–1925*. New York: Atheneum, 1968.
Hinich, Melvin, and Michael C. Munger. *Analytical Politics*. Cambridge: Cambridge University Press, 1997.
Hirst, Paul. "Associative Principles and Democratic Reform." In Ricardo Blaug and John Schwarzmantel, eds., *Democracy: A Reader*. New York: Columbia University Press, 2000.
———. "Globalization, the Nation State, and Political Theory." In Noel O'Sullivan, ed., *Political Theory in Transition*. New York: Routledge, 2000.

Hobsbawm, E. J. *The Age of Capital: 1848–1875.* New York: New American Library, 1979.

Hodgson, Godfrey. *More Equal Than Others: America from Nixon to the New Century.* Princeton, N.J.: Princeton University Press, 2004.

———. *The World Turned Right Side Up: A History of the Conservative Ascendancy in America.* New York: Houghton Mifflin, 1996.

Hofstadter, Richard. *The Age of Reform: From Bryan to F.D.R.* New York: Random House, 1955.

———. *The American Political Tradition and the Men Who Made It.* New York: Random House, 1948.

———. *Social Darwinism in American Thought.* Rev. ed. Boston: Beacon, 1955.

Holmes, Oliver Wendell, Jr. *The Common Law.* Boston: Little, Brown, 1881.

Holt, Michael F. *The Political Crisis of the 1850s.* New York: John Wiley, 1978.

Hoover, Herbert. *The Challenge to Liberty.* New York: Charles Scribner's Sons, 1934.

———. *Further Addresses upon the American Road 1938–1940.* New York: Charles Scribner's Sons, 1940.

———. "Mutual Self Help." In Michael B. Levy, ed., *Political Thought in America: An Anthology.* Chicago: Dorsey, 1988.

Horwitz, Morton J. *The Transformation of American Law, 1780–1860.* 1977. Reprint, New York: Oxford University Press, 1992.

———. *The Transformation of American Law, 1870–1960: The Crisis of Legal Orthodoxy.* New York: Oxford University Press, 1992.

Horwitz, Robert H., ed. *The Moral Foundations of the American Republic.* 2nd ed. Charlottesville: University of Virginia Press, 1979.

Hovenkamp, Herbert. "The Political Economy of Substantive Due Process." *Stanford Law Review* 40 (January 1988): 379–448.

Hurst, James Willard. *Law and Social Order in the United States.* Ithaca, N.Y.: Cornell University Press, 1977.

Hutchinson, John. *The Imperfect Union: A History of Corruption in American Trade Unions.* New York: E. P. Dutton, 1970.

Huthmacher, J. Joseph, and Warren I. Susman, eds. *Herbert Hoover and the Crisis of American Capitalism.* Cambridge, Mass.: Schenkman, 1973.

Hutt, W. H. *The Keynesian Episode: A Reassessment.* Indianapolis: Liberty Fund, 1979.

Information Please Almanac 1988. Boston: Houghton Mifflin, 1988.

Inglehart, Ronald. "Post-Materialism in an Environment of Insecurity." *American Political Science Review* 75, no. 4 (December 1981): 880–900.

———. *The Silent Revolution: Changing Values and Political Styles among Western Publics.* Princeton, N.J.: Princeton University Press, 1977.

Innes, Stephen. *Creating the Commonwealth: The Economic Culture of Puritan New England.* New York: Norton, 1995.

Irons, Peter H. *The New Deal Lawyers.* Princeton, N.J.: Princeton University Press, 1982.

Jacobs, Meg, William J. Novak, and Julian E. Zelizer, eds. *The Democratic Experiment: New Directions in American Political History.* Princeton, N.J.: Princeton University Press, 2003.

Jensen, Merrill, ed. *Tracts of the American Revolution 1763–1776*. Indianapolis: Bobbs-Merrill, 1967.

Johansen, Robert W., ed. *The Lincoln-Douglas Debates of 1858*. New York: Oxford University Press, 1965.

John, Richard R. *Spreading the News: The American Postal System from Franklin to Morse*. Cambridge, Mass.: Harvard University Press, 1995.

Judis, John B. "Love's Labor Lost." *New Republic*, June 25, 2001, 11.

———. "Structural Flaw." *New Republic*, February 28, 2005, 20–23.

Kaufman, Allen. *Capitalism, Slavery, and Republican Values: American Political Economists, 1819–1848*. Austin: University of Texas Press, 1982.

Kelley, Robert. *The Cultural Pattern in American Politics: The First Century*. New York: Random House, 1979.

Kendall, Willmoore. *John Locke and the Doctrine of Majority Rule*. Urbana: University of Illinois Press, 1959.

Kens, Paul. *Judicial Power and Reform Politics: The Anatomy of* Lochner v. New York. Lawrence: University Press of Kansas, 1990.

Kernell, Samuel, ed. *James Madison: The Theory and Practice of Republican Government*. Stanford, Calif.: Stanford University Press, 2003.

———. "Rural Free Delivery as a Critical Test of Alternative Models of American Political Development." *Studies in American Political Development* 15 (Spring 2001): 103–112.

Ketcham, Ralph, ed. *The Anti-Federalist Papers and the Constitutional Convention Debates*. New York: Penguin, 1986.

Key, V. O., Jr. *Public Opinion and American Democracy*. New York: Alfred A. Knopf, 1961.

Keynes, John Maynard. *The General Theory of Employment, Interest, and Money*. 1936. Reprint, New York: Harcourt Brace Jovanovich, 1964.

Kirk, Russell. *The Conservative Mind from Burke to Eliot*. New York: Avon, 1953.

———. *John Randolph of Roanoke: A Study in American Politics*. 4th ed. Indianapolis: Liberty Fund, 1997.

Kirschner, Jonathan. "Inflation: Paper Dragon Or Trojan Horse?" *Review of International Political Economy* 6 (Winter 1999): 609–618.

Klaasen, Adrian, ed. *The Invisible Hand: Essays in Classical Economics*. Chicago: Henry Regnery, 1965.

Klamer, Arjo, and Donald N. McCloskey. "Economics in the Human Conversation." In Arjo Klamer, Donald M. McCloskey, and Robert M. Solow, eds., *The Consequences of Economic Rhetoric*. Cambridge: Cambridge University Press, 1988.

Klamer, Arjo, Donald M. McCloskey, and Robert M. Solow, eds. *The Consequences of Economic Rhetoric*. Cambridge: Cambridge University Press, 1988.

Kleppner, Paul. *The Cross of Culture: A Social Analysis of Midwestern Politics, 1850–1900*. New York: Free Press, 1970.

———. *The Third Electoral System, 1853–1892*. Chapel Hill: University of North Carolina Press, 1979.

Kloppenberg, James T. "From Hartz to Tocqueville: Shifting the Focus from Liberalism to Democracy in America." In Meg Jacobs, William J. Novak, and Julian E. Zelizer, eds.,

The Democratic Experiment: New Directions in American Political History. Princeton, N.J.: Princeton University Press, 2003.

———. *Uncertain Victory: Social Democracy and Progressivism in European and American Thought, 1870–1920*. New York: Oxford University Press, 1986.

———. *The Virtues of Liberalism*. Oxford: Oxford University Press, 1998.

Knott, Stephen F. *Alexander Hamilton and the Persistence of Myth*. Lawrence: University Press of Kansas, 2002.

Koch, Adrienne, ed. *The American Enlightenment: The Shaping of the American Experiment in a Free Society*. New York: George Braziller, 1965.

———. *Power, Morals, and the Founding Fathers: Essays in Interpretation of the American Enlightenment*. Ithaca, N.Y.: Cornell University Press, 1961.

Koch, Adrienne, and William Peden, eds. *The Life and Selected Writings of Thomas Jefferson*. New York: Modern Library, 1944.

Koester, Arthur. *Darkness at Noon*. New York: New American Library, 1961.

Kramnick, Isaac. "The 'Great National Discussion': The Discourse of Politics in 1787." *William and Mary Quarterly* (January 1988): 3–32.

———. *Republicanism and Bourgeois Radicalism: Political Ideology in Late Eighteenth-Century England and America*. Ithaca, N.Y.: Cornell University Press, 1990.

Kristol, Irving. "When Virtue Loses All Her Loveliness: Some Reflections on Capitalism and the Free Society." In Michael B. Levy, ed., *Political Thought in America: An Anthology*. Chicago: Dorsey, 1988.

———. "Rationalism in Economics." *Public Interest*, special issue (1980): 201–218.

Krugman, Paul. *The Accidental Theorist and Other Dispatches from the Dismal Science*. New York: W. W. Norton, 1998.

———. *Currencies and Crises*. Cambridge, Mass.: MIT Press, 1992.

———. *Development, Geography, and Economic Theory*. Cambridge, Mass.: MIT Press, 1995.

———. *Peddling Prosperity: Economic Sense and Nonsense in the Age of Diminished Expectations*. New York: W. W. Norton, 1994.

Kuehn, Dale S. *Massachusetts Congregationalist Political Thought, 1760–1790: The Design of Heaven*. Columbia: University of Missouri Press, 1996.

Kuhn, Thomas. *The Structure of Scientific Revolutions*. Chicago: University of Chicago, 1962.

Kuppenheimer, L. B. *Albert Gallatin's Vision of Democratic Stability*. Westport, Conn.: Praeger, 1996.

Kuttner, Robert. *The Economic Illusion: False Choices between Prosperity and Social Justice*. New York: Harcourt Brace Jovanovich, 1984.

Kymlicka, Will, and Wayne Norman. "The Return of the Citizen." In Ricardo Blaug and John Schwarzmantel, eds., *Democracy: A Reader*. New York: Columbia University Press, 2000.

LaFeber, Walter. *Michael Jordan and the New Global Capitalism*. New York: W. W. Norton, 1999.

La Follette, Robert. "Have Faith in the People." In Richard W. Leopold, Arthur S. Link, and Stanley Cobs, eds., *Problems in American History*. 3rd ed. Englewood Cliffs, N.J.: Prentice-Hall, 1966.

Landes, David S. *The Wealth and Poverty of Nations: Why Some Are So Rich and Some So Poor.* New York: W. W. Norton, 1998.
Larson, John Lauritz. *Internal Improvement: National Public Works and the Promise of Popular Government in the Early United States.* Chapel Hill: University of North Carolina Press, 2001.
Laski, Harold J. "The Political Philosophy of Mr. Justice Holmes." *Yale Law Journal* 40, no. 5 (March 1931): 683–703.
Lasswell, Harold J. *Politics: Who Gets What, When, How.* New York: Times/Mirror, 1958.
Leggett, William. *Democratick Editorials: Essays in Jacksonian Political Economy.* Indianapolis: Liberty Fund, 1984.
Lekachman, Robert. *The Age of Keynes.* New York: McGraw-Hill, 1966.
———. *Greed Is Not Enough: Reaganomics.* New York: Pantheon, 1982.
Leonard, Jerry D. "Introduction: (Post)Modern Legal Studies as (Critical) Legal Studies." In Jerry D. Leonard, ed., *Legal Studies as Cultural Studies: A Reader in (Post)Modern Critical Theory.* Albany: State University of New York Press, 1995.
———, ed. *Legal Studies as Cultural Studies: A Reader in (Post)Modern Critical Theory.* Albany: State University of New York Press, 1995.
Leopold, Aldo. *A Sand County Almanac.* London: Oxford University Press, 1949.
Leopold, Richard W., Arthur S. Link, and Stanley Cobs, eds. *Problems in American History.* 3rd ed. Englewood Cliffs, N.J.: Prentice-Hall, 1966.
Lerner, Max, ed. *The Mind and Faith of Justice Holmes: His Speeches, Essays, Letters, and Judicial Opinions.* New York: Modern Library, 1954.
Letwin, William. "Economic Policy of the Constitution." In Ellen Frankel Paul and Howard Dickman, eds., *Liberty, Property and the Foundations of the American Constitution.* Albany: State University of New York Press, 1989.
———. *The Origins of Scientific Economics: English Economic Thought 1660–1776.* London: Methuen, 1963.
Leuchtenburg, William E. *Franklin D. Roosevelt and the New Deal.* New York: Harper and Row, 1963.
Levy, Michael B., ed. *Political Thought in America: An Anthology.* Chicago: Dorsey, 1988.
Lewis, Sinclair. *Main Street.* New York: Harcourt, Brace, and World, 1920.
Lichter, Linda S., S. Robert Lichter, and Stanley Rothman. "How Show Business Shows Business." *Public Opinion* (October/November 1982): 10–12.
Limbaugh, Rush H., III. *The Way Things Ought to Be.* New York: Pocket Books, 1992.
Lindberg, Leon N., and Charles S. Maier, eds. *The Politics of Inflation and Economic Stagnation: Theoretical Approaches and International Case Studies.* Washington, D.C.: Brookings Institution, 1985.
Lindblom, Charles E. "Market and Democracy: Obliquely." *PS: Political Science and Politics* 28, no. 4 (December 1995): 684–688.
———. *Politics and Markets: The World's Political Economic Systems.* New York: Basic Books, 1977.
Link, Arthur S. *Woodrow Wilson and the Progressive Era, 1910–1917.* New York: Harper and Row, 1954.

Lipset, Seymour Martin. *The First New Nation: The United States in Historical and Comparative Perspective.* Garden City, N.Y.: Doubleday, 1967.

Lipset, Seymour Martin, and Reinhard Bendix. *Social Mobility in Industrial Society.* New Brunswick, N.J.: Transaction, 1992.

Lipset, Seymour Martin, Martin Trow, and James Coleman. *Union Democracy.* Garden City, N.Y.: Doubleday, 1956.

List, Freidrich. *The National System of Political Economy.* 1841. Reprint, New York: Augustus M. Kelley, 1966.

Litowitz, Douglas E. *Postmodern Philosophy and Law.* Lawrence: University Press of Kansas, 1997.

Lloyd, Christopher. *The Structures of History.* Oxford: Blackwell, 1993.

Lloyd, Henry Demarest. *Wealth against Commonwealth.* 1894. Reprint, New York: Harper and Brothers, 1902.

Locke, John. *Second Treatise of Government.* 1690. Reprint, Indianapolis: Hackett, 1980.

Lovejoy, Arthur O. *Reflections on Human Nature.* Baltimore: Johns Hopkins University Press, 1961.

Lovell, Michael. "Tests of Rational Expectations Hypotheses." *American Economic Review* 76 (1986): 110–124.

Lowi, Theodore J. *The End of Liberalism: Ideology, Policy, and the Crisis of Public Authority.* New York: W. W. Norton, 1969.

Lucas, Robert E., Jr. "Expectations and the Neutrality of Money." *Journal of Economic Theory* 4 (1972): 103–124.

Lumsden, Keith, Richard Attiyeh, and George Leland Bach, *Microeconomics.* Englewood Cliffs, N.J.: Prentice-Hall, 1966.

Lutz, Donald S. "The Relative Influence of European Writers on Late Eighteenth-Century American Political Thought." *American Political Science Review* 78 (March 1984): 189–197.

Lyotard, Jean-Francois. *The Postmodern Explained.* Minneapolis: University of Minnesota Press, 1992.

Magoc, Chris J. *Yellowstone: The Creation and Selling of an American Landscape 1870–1903.* Albuquerque: University of New Mexico Press, 1999.

Malone, Dumas. *Jefferson and the Ordeal of Liberty.* Boston: Little, Brown, 1962.

———. *Jefferson and the Rights of Man.* Boston: Little, Brown, 1951.

———. *Jefferson the President: First Term 1801–1805.* Boston: Little, Brown, 1970.

———. *Jefferson the President: Second Term 1805–1809.* Boston: Little, Brown, 1974.

———. *Jefferson the Virginian.* Boston: Little, Brown, 1948.

Malthus. T. R. *Principles of Political Economy: Considered with a View to Their Practical Application.* 1st edition originally published 1820; 2nd edition originally published 1836. New York: Augustus M. Kelley, 1951.

Marshall, Alfred. "General View of Distribution." In Philip C. Newman, Arthur D. Gayer, and Milton H. Spencer, eds., *Source Readings in Economic Thought.* New York: W. W. Norton, 1954.

Martin, William. *With God on Our Side: The Rise of the Religious Right in America.* New York: Broadway, 1996.

Marx, Karl. *Capital: A Critique of Political Economy*. New York: Modern Library, 1906.
——. *Capital and Other Writings*. New York: Modern Library, 1932.
——. "The Eighteenth Brumaire of Louis Bonaparte" (1871). In Lewis S. Feuer, ed., *Marx and Engels: Basic Writings On Politics and Philosophy*. Garden City, N.Y.: Doubleday, 1966.
Marx, Karl, and Friedrich Engels. "The Communist Manifesto" (1848). In Arthur P. Mendel, ed., *Essential Works of Marxism*. New York: Bantam, 1961.
Mason, Alpheus Thomas. *Brandeis: A Free Man's Life*. New York: Viking, 1946.
——. "The Federalist—A Split Personality." In John P. Roche, ed., *American Political Thought: From Jefferson to Progressivism*. New York: Harper and Row, 1967.
Mason, Alpheus Thomas, and Richard H. Leach. *In Quest of Freedom: American Political Thought and Practice*. Englewood Cliffs, N.J.: Prentice-Hall, 1959.
McChesney, Robert W. *Rich Media, Poor Democracy: Communication Politics in Dubious Times*. Urbana: University of Chicago Press, 1999.
McCloskey, Deirdre N. *The Rhetoric of Economics*. 2nd ed. Madison: University of Wisconsin Press, 1998.
McCloskey, Donald N. "The Rhetoric of Economics." In Daniel M. Hausman, ed., *The Philosophy of Economics: An Anthology*. 2nd ed. Cambridge: Cambridge University Press, 1994.
McClosky, Herbert, and John Zaller. *The American Ethos: Public Attitudes toward Capitalism and Democracy*. Cambridge, Mass.: Harvard University Press, 1984.
McCloskey, Robert Green. *American Conservatism in the Age of Enterprise, 1865–1910*. New York: Harper and Row, 1951.
McCormick, Richard P. "New Perspectives On Jacksonian Politics." In Felice A. Bonadio, ed., *Political Parties in American History*. 2 vols. New York: G. P. Putnam's Sons, 1974.
McCoy, Drew R. *The Elusive Republic: Political Economy in Jeffersonian America*. Chapel Hill: University of North Carolina Press, 1980.
McCullough, David. *John Adams*. New York: Simon and Schuster, 2001.
McDonald, Forrest. *Alexander Hamilton: A Biography*. New York: W. W. Norton, 1982.
——. *Norvus Ordo Seclorum: The Intellectual Origins of the Constitution*. Lawrence: University Press of Kansas, 1985.
——. *We the People: The Economic Origins of the Constitution*. Chicago: University of Chicago Press, 1958.
McKitrick, Eric L., ed. *Slavery Defended: The Views of the Old South*. Englewood Cliffs, N.J.: Prentice-Hall, 1963.
McSeveny, Samuel. *The Politics of Depression: Political Behavior in the Northeast, 1893–1896*. New York: Oxford University Press, 1972.
McWilliams, James E. "Le Guru Returns." *Texas Observer* May 21, 2004, 22.
Meister, Robert. "The Logic and Legacy of *Dred Scott*: Marshall, Taney, and the Sublimation of Republican Thought." *Studies in American Political Development* 3 (1989): 199–262.
Mendel, Arthur P., ed. *Essential Works of Marxism*. New York: Bantam, 1965.
Merriam, C. Edward. *A History of American Political Theory*. New York: Macmillan, 1910.
Merrill, Horace Samuel. *Bourbon Leader: Grover Cleveland and the Democratic Party*. Boston: Little, Brown, 1957.

Merton, Robert C. "Financial Economics." In E. Cary Brown and Robert M. Solow, eds., *Paul Samuelson and Modern Economic Theory*. New York: McGraw-Hill, 1983.

Mettler, Suzanne. *Dividing Citizens: Gender and Federalism in New Deal Public Policy*. Ithaca, N.Y.: Cornell University Press, 1993.

Milkis, Sidney M. *Political Parties and Constitutional Government: Remaking American Democracy*. Baltimore: Johns Hopkins University Press, 1999.

Milkis, Sidney M., and Jerome M. Mileur, eds. *The New Deal and the Triumph of Liberalism*. Boston: University of Massachusetts Press, 2002.

Mill, John Stuart. *Principles of Political Economy*. Boston: Lee and Shepard, 1872.

Miller, John C. *Alexander Hamilton and the Growth of the New Nation*. New York: Harper and Row, 1959.

——. *The Federalist Era, 1789–1801*. New York: Harper and Row, 1960.

Miller, William Lee. *Arguing about Slavery: The Great Battle in the United States Congress*. New York: Alfred A. Knopf, 1996.

Mills, C. Wright. *The Power Elite*. 1956. Reprint, New York: Oxford University Press, 1959.

——. *The Sociological Imagination*. London: Oxford University Press, 1959.

——. *White Collar: The American Middle Classes*. 1951. Reprint, New York: Oxford University Press, 1956.

Minowitz, Peter. *Profits, Priests, and Princes: Adam Smith's Emancipation of Economics from Politics and Religion*. Stanford, Calif.: Stanford University Press, 1993.

Mitchell, Wesley C. "The Role of Money in Economic Theory." In Philip C. Newman, Arthur D. Gayer, and Milton H. Spencer, eds., *Source Readings in Economic Thought*. New York: W. W. Norton, 1954.

Modigliani, Franco. "On the Wealth of Nations." In Michael Fry, ed., *Adam Smith's Legacy: His Place in the Development of Modern Economics*. New York: Routledge, 1992.

Morgan, Edmund S., ed. *Puritan Political Ideas 1558–1794*. Indianapolis: Bobbs-Merrill, 1965.

Morone, James A. *The Democratic Wish: Popular Participation and the Limits of American Government*. New York: Basic Books, 1990.

——. *Hellfire Nation: The Politics of Sin in American History*. New Haven, Conn.: Yale University Press, 2003.

——. "The Others' America: Notes on Rogers Smith's *Civic Ideals*." *Studies in American Political Development* 13 (Spring 1999): 186–197.

Mouffe, Chantal. "Radical Democracy: Modern or Post-Modern?" In Ricardo Blaug and John Schwarzmantel, eds., *Democracy: A Reader*. New York: Columbia University Press, 2000.

Mowry, George E. *The Era of Theodore Roosevelt and the Birth of Modern America, 1900–1912*. New York: Harper and Row, 1958.

Mueller, John. *Democracy, Capitalism, and Ralph's Pretty Good Grocery*. Princeton, N.J.: Princeton University Press, 1999.

Murphy, Paul L. *Political Parties in American History, 1890–Present*. New York: G. P. Putnam's Sons, 1974.

Nagel, Paul C. *John Quincy Adams: A Public Life, a Private Life*. New York: Alfred A. Knopf, 1998.

Nelson, John R. *Liberty and Property: Political Economy and Policymaking in the New Nation, 1789–1812.* Baltimore: Johns Hopkins University Press, 1987.
Newman, Philip C. *The Development of Economic Thought.* New York: Prentice-Hall, 1952.
Newman, Philip C., Arthur D. Gayer, and Milton H. Spencer, eds. *Source Readings in Economic Thought.* New York: W. W. Norton, 1954.
North, Douglass C. *Structure and Change in Economic History.* New York: W. W. Norton, 1981.
Novak, William J. *The People's Welfare: Law and Regulation in Nineteenth-Century America.* Chapel Hill: University of North Carolina Press, 1996.
Novick, Sheldon M., ed. *The Collected Works of Justice Holmes: Complete Public Writings and Selected Judicial Opinions of Oliver Wendell Holmes.* Vol. 3. Chicago: University of Chicago Press, 1995.
Nozick, Robert. *Anarchy, State, and Utopia.* New York: Basic Books, 1974.
Oates, Stephen B. *With Malice toward None: A Life of Abraham Lincoln.* New York: Harper Collins, 1994.
O'Connor, Karen, and Larry Sabato. *Essentials of American Government: Continuity and Change.* New York: Pearson/Longman, 2004.
Ohmae, Kenichi. *The End of the Nation State: The Rise of Regional Economies.* New York: Free Press, 1995.
Olasky, Marvin. *The Tragedy of American Compassion.* Washington, D.C.: Regnery Gateway, 1992.
Olson, Mancur, Jr. *The Logic of Collective Action: Public Goods and the Theory of Groups.* 1965. Reprint, New York: Schocken, 1970.
Ormerod, Paul. *Butterfly Economics: A New General Theory of Social and Economic Behavior.* New York: Pantheon, 1998.
Ornstein, Norman, and Shirley Elder. *Interest Groups, Lobbying, and Policymaking.* Washington, D.C.: Congressional Quarterly Press, 1978.
Orren, Karen. *Belated Feudalism: Labor, the Law, and Liberal Development in the United States.* New York: Cambridge University Press, 1991.
Orwell, George. *Homage to Catalonia.* Boston: Beacon, 1952.
Pangle, Lorraine Smith, and Thomas L. Pangle. *The Learning of Liberty.* Lawrence: University Press of Kansas, 1992.
Parekh, Bhikhu. "Theorizing Political Theory." In Noel O'Sullivan, ed., *Political Theory in Transition.* New York: Routledge, 2000.
Parenti, Michael. *Inventing Reality: The Politics of News Media.* 2nd ed. New York: St. Martin's, 1993.
———. *Make-Believe Media: The Politics of Entertainment.* New York: St. Martin's, 1992.
Parker, Richard. *John Kenneth Galbraith: His Life, His Politics, His Economics.* New York: Farrar, Straus, and Giroux, 2005.
Parkes, Harry Bamford. *The American Experience: An Interpretation of the History and Civilization of the American People.* New York: Vintage, 1959.
Parrington, Vernon Louis. *Main Currents in American Thought.* Vol. 3, *The Beginnings of Critical Realism in America 1860–1920.* Norman: University of Oklahoma Press, 1930.
———. *Main Currents in American Thought.* Vol. 2, *The Romantic Revolution in America 1800–1860.* Norman: University of Oklahoma Press, 1927.

Patterson, James T. *Grand Expectations: The United States, 1945–1974.* New York: Oxford University Press, 1996.
Paul, Arnold M. *Conservative Crisis and the Rule of Law: Attitudes of Bar and Bench, 1887–1895.* Ithaca, N.Y.: Cornell University Press, 1960.
———. "Legal Progressivism, the Courts, and the Crisis of the 1890s." In Lawrence M. Friedman and Harry Scheiber, eds., *American Law and the Constitutional Order: Historical Perspectives.* Cambridge, Mass.: Harvard University Press, 1978.
Paul, Ellen Frankel, and Howard Dickman, eds. *Liberty, Property and the Foundations of the American Constitution.* Albany: State University of New York Press, 1989.
Pearce, David W., ed. *The MIT Dictionary of Modern Economics.* 4th ed. Cambridge, Mass.: MIT Press, 1992.
Peek, George A., Jr., ed. *The Political Writings of John Adams.* Indianapolis: Bobbs-Merrill, 1954.
Perry, Arthur Latham. *Elements of Political Economy.* New York: Charles Scribner's Sons, 1878.
Perry, Ralph Barton. *Puritanism and Democracy.* New York: Vanguard, 1944.
Peterson, Merrill, ed. *Democracy, Liberty, and Property: The State Constitutional Conventions of the 1820s.* Indianapolis: Bobbs-Merrill, 1966.
———. *James Madison: A Biography in His Own Words.* 2 vols. New York: Newsweek, 1974.
———. *The Portable Thomas Jefferson.* New York: Penguin, 1975.
Phillips, Anne. "The Politics of Presence." In Ricardo Blaug and John Schwarzmantel, eds., *Democracy: A Reader.* New York: Columbia University Press, 2000.
Pickles, Dorothy. *Democracy.* Baltimore: Penguin, 1972.
Piven, Frances Fox, and Richard A. Cloward. *The New Class War: Reagan's Attack on the Welfare State and Its Consequences.* New York: Pantheon, 1982.
———. *Regulating the Poor: The Functions of Public Welfare.* New York: Random House, 1971.
Plott, Charles R. "Rational Choice in Experimental Markets." In Karen Schneer Cook and Margaret Levi, eds., *The Limits of Rationality.* Chicago: University of Chicago Press, 1990.
Pocock, John G. A. *The Machiavellian Moment: Florentine Political Thought and the Atlantic Republican Tradition.* Princeton, N.J.: Princeton University Press, 1973.
Pole, J. R. *The Pursuit of Equality in American History.* Berkeley: University of California Press, 1978.
Pollack, Norman. *The Populist Response to Industrial America: Midwestern Populist Thought.* New York: W. W. Norton, 1962.
Porter, John. *The Vertical Mosaic: An Analysis of Social Class and Power in Canada.* Toronto: University of Toronto Press, 1965.
Posner, Richard A. *Economic Analysis of Law.* 1st ed. Boston: Little, Brown, 1972.
———. *Economic Analysis of Law.* 3rd ed. Boston: Little, Brown, 1986.
———. "An Economic Approach to Legal Procedure and Judicial Administration." *Journal of Legal Studies* 2 (1973): 399.
———. *Overcoming Law.* Cambridge, Mass.: Harvard University Press, 1995.
———. "Some Economics of Labor Law." *University of Chicago Law Review* 51, no. 4 (Fall 1984): 988–1011.

———. "Some Uses and Abuses of Economics in Law." In Francesco Parisi, ed., *The Economic Structure of Law: The Collected Economic Essays of Richard A. Posner*, Vol. 1. Northampton, Mass.: Edward Elgar, 2000.

Pound, Rosco. *The Formative Era of American Law*. Boston: Little, Brown, 1938.

Powers, Stephen, David J. Rothman, and Stanley Rothman. "Hollywood Movies, Society, and Political Criticism." *The World and I* (April 1991): 563–581.

———. *Hollywood's America: Social and Political Themes in Motion Pictures*. Boulder, Colo.: Westview Press, 1996.

Prindle, David F. *Petroleum Politics and the Texas Railroad Commission*. Austin: University of Texas Press, 1981.

———. *The Politics of Glamour: Ideology and Democracy in the Screen Actors Guild*. Madison: University of Wisconsin Press, 1988.

———. *Risky Business: The Political Economy of Hollywood*. Boulder, Colo.: Westview Press, 1993.

Pringle, Henry F. *The Life and Times of William Howard Taft*, Vol. 2. New York: Farrar and Rinehart, 1939.

Prothro, James W., and Charles M. Grigg. "What Do Americans Really Believe?" In Jay M. Shafritz and Lee S. Weinberg, eds., *Classics in American Government*. 1960. Reprint, Belmont, Calif.: Wadsworth, 1994.

Rakove, Jack N. *Original Meanings: Politics and Ideas in the Making of the Constitution*. New York: Alfred A. Knopf, 1996.

Rawls, John. *A Theory of Justice*. Cambridge, Mass.: Harvard University Press, 1971.

Rayback, Joseph G. *A History of American Labor*. New York: Macmillan, 1966.

Rees, Albert. *The Economics of Trade Unions*. 2nd ed. Chicago: University of Chicago Press, 1977.

Reich, Robert B. *The Work of Nations*. New York: Vintage, 1992.

Reisner, Mark. *Cadillac Desert: The American West and Its Disappearing Water*. New York: Penguin, 1993.

Remini, Robert V. *Andrew Jackson*. New York: Harper Collins, 1966.

———. *Daniel Webster: The Man and His Time*. New York: W. W. Norton, 1997.

———. *Henry Clay: Statesman for the Union*. New York: W. W. Norton, 1991.

Rhoads, Steven E. *The Economist's View of the World: Government, Markets, and Public Policy*. Cambridge: Cambridge University Press, 1994.

Ricardo, David. *The Principles of Political Economy and Taxation*. 1817. Reprint, New York: E. P. Dutton, 1973.

Ricci, David. *The Transformation of American Politics: The New Washington and the Rise of Think Tanks*. New Haven, Conn.: Yale University Press, 1993.

Riis, Jacob A. *How the Other Half Lives: Studies among the Tenements of New York*. 1890. Reprint, New York: Hill and Wang, 1957.

Ritter, Gretchen. *Goldbugs and Greenbacks: The Antimonopoly Tradition and the Politics of Finance in America, 1865–1896*. Cambridge: Cambridge University Press, 1997.

Roche, John P., ed. *American Political Thought: From Jefferson to Progressivism*. New York: Harper and Row, 1967.

———. *Origins of American Political Thought*. New York: Harper and Row, 1967.

Rodrik, Dani. *Has Globalization Gone Too Far?* Washington, D.C.: Institute for International Economics, 1997.
Roemer, John E. *Free to Lose: An Introduction to Marxist Economic Philosophy.* Cambridge, Mass.: Harvard University Press, 1988.
Rommen, Heinrich. *The Natural Law.* 1944. Reprint, Indianapolis: Liberty Fund, 1944.
Roosevelt, Franklin Delano. "Commonwealth Club Address." In Michael B. Levy, ed., *Political Thought in America: An Anthology.* Chicago: Dorsey, 1988.
Roosevelt, Theodore. *Autobiography.* New York: Charles Scribner's Sons, 1958.
———. *The Writings of Theodore Roosevelt.* Edited by William H. Harbaugh. New York: Bobbs-Merrill, 1967.
Rosecrance, Richard. *The Rise of the Virtual State: Wealth and Power in the Coming Century.* New York: Basic Books, 1999.
Rosen, Jeffrey. "The Unregulated Offensive." *New York Times Magazine,* April 1, 2005, 42–48.
Ross, Dorothy. *The Origins of American Social Science.* Cambridge: Cambridge University Press, 1991.
Rothschild, Emma. *Economic Sentiments: Adam Smith, Condorcet, and the Enlightenment.* Cambridge, Mass.: Harvard University Press, 2001.
Ryan, Michael, and Douglas Kellner. *Camera Politica: The Politics and Ideology of Contemporary Hollywood Film.* Bloomington: Indiana University Press, 1988.
Sabine, George H. *A History of Political Theory.* Rev. ed. New York: Henry Holt, 1937.
Salisbury, Robert H., ed. *Interest Group Politics in America.* New York: Harper and Row, 1970.
Salvatore, Nick. "Eugene V. Debs: From Trade Unionist to Socialist." In Melvyn Dubofsky and Warren Van Tyne, eds., *Labor Leaders in America.* Urbana: University of Illinois Press, 1987.
Samuelson, Paul. *Economics: An Introductory Analysis.* New York: McGraw-Hill, 1948.
———. *Economics from the Heart: A Samuelson Sampler.* New York: Harcourt Brace Jovanovich, 1983.
———. "Economics in a Golden Age: A Personal Memoir." In E. Cary Brown and Robert M. Solow, eds., *Paul Samuelson and Modern Economic Theory.* New York: McGraw-Hill, 1983.
———. *Foundations of Economic Analysis.* 1947. Enlarged ed. Cambridge, Mass.: Harvard University Press, 1983.
Samuelson, Robert J. "The Age of Inflation." *New Republic,* May 13, 2002, 32.
Sandel, Michael J. *Democracy's Discontent: America in Search of a Public Philosophy.* Cambridge, Mass.: Harvard University Press, 1996.
Sargent, Thomas J., and Neil Wallace. "'Rational' Expectations, the Optimal Monetary Instrument, and the Optimal Money Supply Rule." *Journal of Political Economy* 83, no. 2 (April 1975): 241–254.
Schaefer, Roberta, and David Schaefer. "The Political Philosophy of J. M. Keynes." *Public Interest* 71 (Spring 1983): 45–61.
Schattschneider, E. E. *The Semi-Sovereign People: A Realist's View of Democracy in America.* New York: Holt, Rinehart, and Winston, 1960.

Schickel, Richard. *D. W. Griffith: An American Life*. New York: Simon and Schuster, 1984.
Schlesinger, Arthur M., Jr. *The Age of Jackson*. New York: New American Library, 1945.
———. *The Age of Roosevelt: The Coming of the New Deal*. Boston: Houghton Mifflin, 1958.
———. *The Age of Roosevelt: The Crisis of the Old Order, 1919–1929*. Boston: Houghton Mifflin, 1957.
Schmookler, Andrew Bard. *The Illusion of Choice: How the Market Economy Shapes Our Destiny*. Albany: State University of New York Press, 1993.
Schneider, Herbert Wallace. *The Puritan Mind*. New York: Henry Holt, 1930.
Schullery, Paul. *Searching for Yellowstone: Ecology and Wonder in the Last Wilderness*. Boston: Houghton Mifflin, 1997.
Schultz, George P., and John R. Coleman, eds. *Labor Problems: Cases and Readings*. New York: McGraw-Hill, 1959.
Schumpeter, Joseph A. *Capitalism, Socialism, and Democracy*. 3rd ed. New York: Harper and Row, 1950.
Schwartz, Bernard. *Main Currents in American Legal Thought*. Durham, N.C.: Carolina Academic Press, 1993.
Schwarz, John E. *America's Hidden Success: A Reassessment of Public Policy from Kennedy to Reagan*. Rev. ed. New York: W. W. Norton, 1988.
Scott, William B. *In Pursuit of Happiness: American Conceptions of Property from the Seventeenth to the Twentieth Century*. Bloomington: University of Indiana Press, 1977.
Scull, William Ellis, ed. *The Great Leaders and National Issues of 1896*. Chicago: John C. Winston, 1896.
Semmel, Bernard. *The Rise of Free Trade Imperialism: Classical Political Economy and the Empire of Free Trade and Imperialism 1750–1850*. Cambridge: Cambridge University Press, 1970.
Sen, Amartya. "Democracy as a Universal Value." In Ricardo Blaug and John Schwarzmantel, eds., *Democracy: A Reader*. New York: Columbia University Press, 2000.
Shalhope, Robert E. *The Roots of Democracy: American Thought and Culture, 1760–1800*. Boston: G. K. Hall, 1990.
Sheldon, Garrett Ward. *The Political Philosophy of James Madison*. Baltimore: Johns Hopkins University Press, 2001.
Shenk, Joshua. "Limbaugh's Lies II." *New Republic*, August 8, 1994.
Shepherd, William G. "On The Nature of Monopoly." In Samuel Bowles, Richard C. Edwards, and William G. Shepherd, eds., *Unconventional Wisdom: Essays on Economics in Honor of John Kenneth Galbraith*. Boston: Houghton Mifflin, 1989.
Shove, G. F. "The Place of Marshall's Principles in the Development of Economic Theory." In James A. Gherity, ed., *Economic Thought: A Historical Anthology*. New York: Random House, 1965.
Silk, Leonard. *The Economists*. New York: Basic Books, 1976.
Simon, Herbert A. "Human Nature in Politics: The Dialogue of Psychology with Political Science." *American Political Science Review* 79, no. 2 (June 1985): 293–304.
———. "Methodological Foundations of Economics." In *Models of Bounded Rationality*. Vol. 3, *Empirically Grounded Economic Reason*. Cambridge, Mass.: MIT Press, 1997.

———. *Models of Bounded Rationality.* Vol. 2, *Behavioral Economics and Business Organizations.* Cambridge, Mass.: MIT Press, 1982.
———. *Models of Bounded Rationality.* Vol. 3, *Empirically Grounded Economic Reason.* Cambridge, Mass.: MIT Press, 1997.
———. "Satisficing." In *Models of Bounded Rationality.* Vol. 3, *Empirically Grounded Economic Reason.* Cambridge, Mass.: MIT Press, 1997.
Skinner, Andrew S. *A System of Social Science: Papers Relating to Adam Smith.* Oxford: Clarendon Press, 1979.
Skocpol, Theda. *Protecting Soldiers and Mothers: The Political Origins of Social Policy in the United States.* Cambridge, Mass.: Harvard University Press, 1992.
———. *Social Policy in the United States: Future Possibilities in Historical Perspective.* Princeton, N.J.: Princeton University Press, 1995.
Skowronek, Stephen. *Building a New American State: The Expansion of National Administrative Capacities 1877–1920.* Cambridge: Cambridge University Press, 1982.
Skousen, Mark. "Welcome Back, Professor." *Forbes,* September 22, 1997, 198.
Slemrod, Joel, and Jon Bakija. *Taxing Ourselves: A Citizen's Guide to the Great Debate over Tax Reform.* Cambridge, Mass.: MIT Press, 1998.
Smith, Adam. *An Inquiry into the Nature and Causes of the Wealth of Nations.* 1776. Reprint, New York: Modern Library, 1937.
———. *Lectures on Jurisprudence.* Indianapolis: Liberty Fund, 1982.
———. *The Theory of Moral Sentiments.* 1759. Reprint, Indianapolis: Liberty Fund, 1982.
Smith, James Morton, ed. *Politics and Society in American History.* Vol. 1, *1607–1865.* Englewood Cliffs, N.J.: Prentice-Hall, 1973.
Smith, Page. *John Adams.* 2 vols. Garden City, New York: Doubleday, 1962.
Smith, Rogers M. "Beyond Tocqueville, Myrdal, and Hartz: The Multiple Traditions in America." *American Political Science Review* 87, no. 3 (September 1993): 549–566.
———. *Civic Ideals: Conflicting Ideals of Citizenship in U.S. History.* New Haven, Conn.: Yale University Press, 1997.
———. "If Politics Matters: Implications for a 'New Institutionalism.'" *Studies in American Political Development* 6 (Spring 1992): 1–36.
———. *Liberalism and American Constitutional Law.* Cambridge, Mass.: Harvard University Press, 1985.
Spencer, Herbert. *First Principles.* 6th ed. New York: Appleton, 1912.
———. *The Man versus the State.* 1884. Reprint, Indianapolis: Liberty Fund, 1982.
———. *On Social Evolution: Selected Writings.* Edited by J. D. Y. Peel. Chicago: University of Chicago Press, 1972.
Spengler, Joseph J. "Economics: Its Direct and Indirect Impact in America, 1776–1976." *Social Science Quarterly* 57, no. 1 (June 1976): 49–76.
———. "The Political Economy of Jefferson, Madison, and Adams." In David Kelly Jackson, ed., *American Studies in Honor of William Kenneth Boyd.* Durham, N.C.: Duke University Press, 1940.
Stegner, Wallace. *Beyond the Hundredth Meridian: John Wesley Powell and the Second Opening of the West.* New York: Penguin, 1954.

———. "Wilderness Letter." In Page Stegner, ed., *Marking the Sparrow's Fall: Wallace Stegner's American West*. New York: Henry Holt, 1998.

St. George, Donna. "Americans Are Using Talk Radio to Carry Their Views to Congress." *Austin American-Statesman*, November 6, 1994.

Stigler, George J. *The Citizen and the State: Essays on Regulation*. Chicago: University of Chicago Press, 1975.

———. "The Intellectual and the Marketplace." In Adrian Klaasen, ed., *The Invisible Hand: Essays in Classical Economics*. Chicago: Henry Regnery, 1965.

Stokes, Donald E. "Spatial Models of Party Competition." In Angus Campbell, Philip E. Converse, Warren E. Miller, and Donald Stokes, *Elections and the Political Order*. New York: John Wiley and Sons, 1966.

Stouffer, Samuel A. *Communism, Conformity, and Civil Liberties*. 1955. Reprint, New York: John Wiley, 1967.

Stowe, Harriet Beecher. *Uncle Tom's Cabin or Life among the Lowly*. 1852. Reprint, New York: Paul S. Erikson, 1964.

Sumner, William Graham. *On Liberty, Society, and Politics: The Essential Essays of William Graham Sumner*. Edited by Robert C. Bannister. Indianapolis: Liberty Fund, 1992.

———. *What Social Classes Owe to Each Other*. 1883. Reprint, Caldwell, Idaho: Caxton, 1970.

Sundquist, James L. *Dynamics of the Party System: Alignment and Realignment of Political Parties in the United States*. Washington, D.C.: Brookings Institution, 1983.

Sunstein, Cass R. *After the Rights Revolution: Reconceiving the Regulatory State*. Cambridge, Mass.: Harvard University Press, 1990.

———. *The Partial Constitution*. Cambridge, Mass.: Harvard University Press, 1993.

Swedborg, Richard, ed. *Joseph A. Schumpeter: The Economics and Sociology of Capitalism*. Princeton, N.J.: Princeton University Press, 1991.

Sweezy, Paul M. "Power Elite or Ruling Class?" In G. William Domhoff and Hoyt Ballard, eds., *C. Wright Mills and the Power Elite*. Boston: Beacon Press, 1968.

Sweezy, Paul M., and Harry Magdoff. *The Dynamics of U.S. Capitalism: Corporate Structure, Inflation, Credit, Gold, and the Dollar*. New York: Monthly Review, 1972.

Taft, William Howard. "The Right of Private Property." *Michigan Law Journal* 3, no. 8 (August 1894): 215–233.

Taylor, John. *Arator: Being a Series of Agricultural Essays, Practical and Political, in Sixty-Four Numbers*. 1818. Reprint, Indianapolis: Liberty Fund, 1978.

Temin, Peter. *The Jacksonian Economy*. New York: W. W. Norton, 1969.

———. *Lessons from the Great Depression*. Cambridge, Mass.: MIT Press, 1989.

Thernstrom, Stephan. *The Other Bostonians: Poverty and Progress in the American Metropolis, 1880–1970*. Cambridge Mass.: Harvard University Press, 1973.

Thorsen, Niels Aage. *The Political Thought of Woodrow Wilson 1875–1910*. Princeton, N.J.: Princeton University Press, 1988.

Tindall, George B., ed. *A Populist Reader: Selections from the Works of American Populist Leaders*. New York: Harper and Row, 1966.

Tobin, James. "Macroeconomics and Fiscal Policy." In E. Cary Brown and Robert M. Solow, eds., *Paul Samuelson and Modern Economic Theory*. New York: McGraw-Hill, 1983.

Tomlins, Christopher. *Law, Labor, and Ideology in the Early American Republic.* Cambridge: Cambridge University Press, 1993.

Trevithick, J. A. *Inflation: A Guide to the Crisis in Economics.* New York: Penguin, 1977.

Trubowitz, Peter. *Defining the National Interest: Conflict and Change in American Foreign Relations.* Chicago: University of Chicago Press, 1998.

Truman, David B. *The Governmental Process.* New York: Alfred A. Knopf, 1950.

Tuck, Richard. *Natural Rights Theories: Their Origin and Development.* Cambridge: Cambridge University Press, 1979.

Tversky, Amos, and Daniel Kahneman. "Rational Choice and the Framing of Decisions." In Karen Schneer Cook and Margaret Levi, eds., *The Limits of Rationality.* Chicago: University of Chicago Press, 1990.

Twiss, Benjamin R. *Lawyers and the Constitution: How Laissez Faire Came to the Supreme Court.* Princeton, N.J.: Princeton University Press, 1942.

Van Deusen, Glyndon G. *The Jacksonian Era, 1828–1848.* New York: Harper and Row, 1959.

Veblen, Thorstein. *The Engineers and the Price System.* 1919. Reprint, New York: Augustus M. Kelley, 1965.

———. *The Instinct of Workmanship and the State of the Industrial Arts.* New York: Viking, 1914.

———. "The Limitations of Marginal Utility" (1909). In Philip C. Newman, Arthur D. Gayer, and Milton H. Spencer, eds., *Source Readings in Economic Thought.* New York: W. W. Norton, 1954.

———. *The Theory of Business Enterprise.* In Philip C. Newman, Arthur D. Gaye, and Milton D. Spencer, eds., *Source Readings in Economic Thought.* New York: W. W. Norton, 1954.

———. *The Theory of the Leisure Class.* 1899. Reprint, New York: New American Library, 1962.

———. "Why Is Economics Not an Evolutionary Science?" (1898). In James A. Gherity, ed., *Economic Thought: A Historical Anthology.* New York: Random House, 1965.

Von Der Muhle, George. "Robert A. Dahl and the Study of Contemporary Democracy: A Review Essay." *American Political Science Review* 71, no. 3 (September 1977): 1070–1096.

Von Mises, Ludwig. *Theory and History: An Interpretation of Social and Economic Evolution.* New Haven, Conn.: Yale University Press, 1957.

Vonnegut, Kurt. *Welcome to the Monkey House.* New York: Basic Books, 1974.

Walker, Jack L. "The Origin and Maintenance of Interest Groups in America." *American Political Science Review* 77, no. 2 (June 1983): 390–406.

Walters, Raymond, Jr. *Albert Gallatin: Jeffersonian Financier and Diplomat.* New York: Macmillan, 1957.

Walzer, Michael. "A Day in the Life of a Socialist Citizen." In Ricardo Blaug and John Schwarzmantel, eds., *Democracy: A Reader.* New York: Columbia University Press, 2000.

Wanniski, Jude. *The Way the World Works.* 1978. Reprint, New York: Simon and Schuster, 1983.

Warren, Charles. *Bankruptcy in United States History.* Cambridge, Mass.: Harvard University Press, 1935.

Wayne, Coston E., ed. *The Pullman Boycott of 1894: The Problem of Federal Intervention.* Lexington, Mass.: D. C. Heath, 1955.
Webster, Daniel. "Speech in Defense of the Tariff." In Michael B. Levy, ed., *Political Thought in America: An Anthology.* Chicago: Dorsey, 1988.
Wecter, Dixon, and Larzer Ziff, eds. *Benjamin Franklin's Autobiography and Selected Writings.* New York: Holt, Rinehart, and Winston, 1964.
Weinstein, James. *The Corporate Ideal in the Liberal State, 1900–1918.* Boston: Beacon, 1968.
Weir, Margaret. "Ideas and Politics: The Acceptance of Keynesianism in Britain and the United States." In Peter A. Hall, ed., *The Political Power of Economic Ideas: Keynesianism across Nations.* Princeton, N.J.: Princeton University Press, 1989.
Weisbrot, Mark. "Tricks of Free Trade." *Sierra* (September/October 2001): 64.
Weisskopf, Thomas E. "The Irrationality of Capitalist Economic Growth." In Richard C. Edwards, Michael Reich, and Thomas E. Weisskopf, eds., *The Capitalist System.* 2nd ed. Englewood Cliffs, N.J.: Prentice-Hall, 1978.
Welter, Rush. *The Mind of America, 1820–1860.* New York: Columbia University Press, 1975.
White, G. Edward. "The Path of American Jurisprudence." In *Patterns of American Legal Thought.* Indianapolis: Bobbs-Merrill, 1978.
———. *Patterns of American Legal Thought.* Indianapolis: Bobbs-Merrill, 1978.
White, Morton. *Philosophy, the Federalist, and the Constitution.* New York: Oxford University Press, 1987.
Whitman, Walt. "Editorials in *Brooklyn Daily Eagle*." In Michael B. Levy, ed., *Political Thought in America: An Anthology.* Chicago: Dorsey, 1988.
Wiecek, William M. *The Lost World of Classical Legal Thought: Law and Ideology in America, 1886–1937.* New York: Oxford University Press, 1998.
Wilentz, Sean. *Chants Democratic: New York City and the Rise of the American Working Class, 1788–1850.* New York: Oxford University Press, 1984.
Williams, T. Harry, ed. *Abraham Lincoln: Selected Speeches, Messages, and Letters.* New York: Holt, Rinehart, and Winston, 1966.
Williams, William Appleman. *The Great Evasion: An Essay on the Contemporary Relevance of Karl Marx and on the Wisdom of Admitting the Heretic into the Dialogue about America's Future.* Chicago: Quadrangle, 1964.
———. *The Tragedy of American Diplomacy.* 2nd ed. New York: Dell, 1962.
Williamson, Chilton. *American Suffrage: From Property to Democracy.* Princeton, N.J.: Princeton University Press, 1960.
Wills, Garry. *Explaining America: The Federalist.* New York: Penguin, 1981.
———. *Inventing America: Jefferson's Declaration of Independence.* New York: Random House, 1978.
Wilson, Francis Graham. *The American Political Mind: A Textbook on Political Theory.* New York: McGraw-Hill, 1949.
Wilson, Joan Hoff. *Herbert Hoover: Forgotten Progressive.* Boston: Little, Brown, 1975.
Wilson, Woodrow. *A Crossroads of Freedom: The 1912 Campaign Speeches of Woodrow Wilson.* New Haven, Conn.: Yale University Press, 1956.
———. "Freemen Need No Guardians." In Michael B. Levy, ed., *Political Thought in America: An Anthology.* Chicago: Dorsey, 1988.

Winch, Donald. *Adam Smith's Politics: An Essay in Historiographic Revision*. Cambridge: Cambridge University Press, 1978.

Wolfe, Alan. *The Limits of Legitimacy: Political Contradictions of Contemporary Capitalism*. New York: Free Press, 1977.

Wood, Gordon S. *The Creation of the American Republic, 1776–1787*. Chapel Hill: University of North Carolina Press, 1969.

Wood, Henry. *The Political Economy of Natural Law*. Boston: Lee and Shepard, 1894.

Wright, Gavin. *The Political Economy of the Cotton South: Households, Markets, and Wealth in the Nineteenth Century*. New York: W. W. Norton, 1978.

Wright, Robert. "Continental Drift." *New Republic*, January 17, 2000.

Yates, Michael D. "The 'New' Economy and the Labor Movement." *Monthly Review* (April 2001): 28–43.

Yergin, Daniel. *The Prize: The Epic Quest for Oil, Money and Power*. New York: Simon and Schuster, 1992.

Young, Iris Marion. "Justice and the Politics of Difference." In Ricardo Blaug and John Schwarzmantel, eds., *Democracy: A Reader*. New York: Columbia University Press, 2000.

Ziliak, Stephen T., and Deirdre N. McCloskey. "Size Matters: The Standard Error of Regressions in the *American Economic Review*." *Economic Journal Watch* 1, no. 2 (August 2004): 331–355.

Index

Abbey, Edward, 183
Abbott, Philip, 23
Abrams v. U.S., 155–56, 157
Action for Children's Television, 183
Adair v. U.S., 152
Adams, Abigail, 47
Adams, John, 5, 44–47, 295, 361
Adams, John Quincy, 65, 83
Adams, Samuel, 4
Adkins v. Children's Hospital, 153, 155, 193
African Americans: and the campaign of 1896, 136; and campaign of 1912, 172; and Civil Rights movement, 184; and critical legal studies, 264; and Dred Scot decision, 89; and the Left's redefinition of democracy, 256; opposition by Republicans to social equality for, 84–85; and the Populists, 129; position of, after 1898, 142; poverty of, during 1960s, 178; in South after Civil War, 99–100; and Voting Rights Act, 185
agriculture, 18, 33; and the common law, 92–93; depression of, after World War I, 175; and the hyperagrarians, 41; and Jefferson, 38, 52; monetary policies and, after Civil War, 126; prior to Civil War, 54; state of, after Civil War, 98, 99
Allais, Maurice, 270
Allen, William, 126
Allgeyer v. Louisiana, 120
Alperovitz, Gar, 234
American Bar Association, 116, 117, 122
American Economic Association, 106
American Enterprise Institute, 245
American Federation of Labor, 181; in the 1920s, 143; and the Populists, 129
Appleby, Joyce, 15, 37, 128

Appleton, John, 117
Aristotle, 110
Arnold, Thurman, 214
Arrow, Kenneth, 273, 278
Articles of Confederation, 23
Austin, Mary, 183
Austria, 222
Ayres, C. E., 214

Baer, George, 158
Bailyn, Bernard, 113
Bank of England, 33
Bank of the United States (B.U.S.), 47, 95; and Clay, 58; controversy over Second, 75–78; First, 33, 38–40; and Gallatin, 49; and Jefferson, 52
bankruptcy legislation, 90–91, 138
banks, 20; and "free banking" laws, 78; functions of, 75–76; Jackson's suspicion of, 77; and the Jeffersonians, 39; as special interests, to progressives, 162; suspicion of, prior to the Civil War, 62
Banning, Lance, 32
Baran, Paul, 232, 233
Barbary Pirates, 48
Bayard, James, 43
Beard, Charles, 131
Becker, Carl, 3, 213
Bellamy, Edward, 131–33, 163, 168, 198, 209
Bensel, Richard, 114
Bentley, Arthur, 201, 203
Biddle, Clement, 58
Biddle, Nicholas, 76–77
Blackstone, William, 5, 15
Blaine, James, 134
Blair, Frank, 80

Blatchford, Samuel, 120
Blaug, Mark, 270
Blyth, Mark, 199, 201, 251
Bolingbroke, Viscount, 13, 14
Brandeis, Louis, 156–58, 213; on interlocking directorates, 140; and Woodrow Wilson, 171
Braybrooke, David, xvii, 269
Brazil, 289
Bretton Woods Agreement, 179, 180
Brigham, Robert, xvii
Britain, 14, 18, 44, 98, 133; abandons gold standard in 1931, 176; and the American Civil War, 83; contrasts with U.S., 60; economic problems of, after WWI, 175; and Hamilton, 38; and the Phillips curve, 191; and Ricardo, 58; and trade policy, 51, 75; and War of 1812, 52, 53; wealth of, in 1860, 54
Brookings Institution, 139–40, 245
Brown, Michael, 201
Brown, Ron, 250
Brownson, Orestes, 63, 88
Bryan, William Jennings, 129, 135–38
Buchanan, Bruce, xvii
Buchanan, James, 89, 242
Buckley, William F., 228–30
Bull Moose Party, 169–71
bureaucracy: and Bellamy's utopia, 133; and state building after 1898, 143
Burgh, James, 15
Burke, Edmund, 87
Burnham, Walter Dean, xvii
Burr, Aaron, 32
Bush, George H. W., 248–49
Bush, George W., 248, 285

Calhoun, John C., 80; and slavery, 80, 88; and tariffs, 52, 58, 72, 133
California, University of, 242
Cambridge University, 149, 187
Canada, 283
Cannan, Edwin, 147
capitalism, 2, 5; "against democracy" and the modern Left, 255; and the alleged legitimation crisis, 245–46; attempt by the Right to redefine, 242–52; and the campaign of 1912, 172; and the common law, 93; defense of, by Sumner, 110–11; and the defense of slavery, 86; and democracy, 33, 36, 45, 48, 129, 151; at the end of the founding era, 53; and God, 158; and the Jeffersonians, 39, 43; new conservative strategy to defend, after New Deal, 121–213; and the Populists, 129; protection of, by judiciary, 115–25; rejected by Debs, 124; and social mobility, 88; Veblen's attack on, 164–68
Cardozo, Benjamin, 194
Cardozo, Jacob, 61
Carey, Henry, 61, 72–73, 75, 217
Carey, Matthew, 61
Carlton, Dennis, and Jeffrey Perloff, 283
Carnegie, Andrew, 108
Carr, David, 2
Carrington, Edward, 35
Carson, Rachel, 183
census, U.S.: of 1790, 18; of 1820, 54; of 1860, 54; of 1900, 100; of 1930, 139; of 1950 and 1970, 178
Center, the, 259–60, 264–67
Centinel, 28
Chamberlin, E. H., 187
Chamber of Commerce, U.S., 142
Charles, J. Daryle, 261
Charles River Bridge v. Warren Bridge, 94–95
Chicago, University of, 224, 242, 243, 275, 276
China, 240, 289
Choate, Joseph, 121–22
Civil War: cost of, 82; pensions for veterans of, 114
Clark, John Bates, 104, 148–49
Clark, William, 47
Clay, Henry: and bankruptcy legislation, 91; and the B.U.S., 58, 77; and the independent treasury policy, 80
Clayton Act, 140
Cleveland, Grover, 123, 135
Clinton, Bill, 250
Clower, Robert, xii
Cohen, Joshua, and Joel Rogers, 242, 252
Cohen, Lizbeth, 192
Coke, Edward, 4, 5
Collins, Robert, 184
Columbia University, 148
common law, the, 91–93; and Posner's jurisprudence, 276
Commons, John R., 214
Commonwealth v. Hunt, 93

INDEX 359

competition, 10, 26, 290; FDR's attitude toward, 198; and freedom of speech, 155–56; as issue in 1912 campaign, 171; "monopolistic" theory of, 187; in neoclassical economics, 147, 148; rejected by Populists, 128; and Schumpeter's theory of democracy, 206; and social Darwinism, 108
Congress of Industrial Organizations, 181
Conkin, Paul, 59
Connally Act, 200
Constitution, U.S., 14, 21, 22–24; and African Americans, 142; and the Dred Scott decision, 89; Epstein's interpretation of, 261–62; and globalization, 288; and the Jeffersonians, 38, 42; and the judiciary, 35; and Posner's jurisprudence, 276; and pre–Civil War jurisprudence, 93–94; and substantive due process doctrine, 118–20; and the tension between democracy and capitalism, 151
Consumers' Union, 183
contract, freedom of, 120–21, 192; and *Adkins* decision, 153, 155; and *Lochner* decision, 152; and neoclassical economics, 148; overturned as Constitutional doctrine, 193; and Posner's jurisprudence, 276
Cooke, Jay, 113
Cooke, John, 68
Cooley, Thomas, 118–19, 124, 152
Coolidge, Calvin, 142, 158
Cooper, Thomas, 61
Coppage v. Kansas, 152, 155
Cornell, Drucilla, 261
corporations: granted rights as persons by Supreme Court, 120; and pre–Civil War jurisprudence, 94; prejudice against, prior to Civil War, 76–77; as special interest, to progressives, 162
cotton, 55, 81
Crisp, Charles, 134

Dahl, Robert A., 203–6, 221, 260, 266
Daly, Herman, and John Cobb, 284–85, 286
Darrow, Clarence, 156
Dartmouth College v. Woodward, 94
Darwin, Charles, 107
Davis, John, 127
Debs, Eugene V., 123–24; and Bellamy, 131; and campaign of 1912, 168, 172–73

Declaration of Independence, 3, 23, 44; endorsed by Bryan, 135; Lincoln on, 84; parodied by the Declaration of Sentiments, 70; rejection by South of ideals of, 85; and slavery, 82–84, 87; as a specter haunting propertied classes prior to Civil War, 66
deflation, 126, 175
democracy, 2, 5, 15, 36, 37; alienation of modern conservative legal theorists from, 262; attempts to redefine, 240, 252–60; attempt to update theory of, after WWII, 202–8; attitude toward, by the Center, 259–60; Brandeis's views on, 156–57; and capitalism, 33, 45, 48, 151; change in discourse of, 69–70, 81; and disillusionment with mass public after WWII, 185; after 1896, 138; at the end of the founding period, 3; and globalization, 286; and government by experts, 162–63, 168; as imagined by Bellamy, 132; and the Jeffersonians, 39; Keynes's legitimation of economic, 189; and modern centrist jurisprudence, 264–65; natural law jurisprudence as a defender of, 194; polyarchal theory of, 203; and the Populists, 128; and Posner's jurisprudence, 276–77; potential of, to threaten property, 101, 117; processes of, and judicial scrutiny, 193; public ambivalence about inconsistency with capitalism of, 241; and public choice theory, 207; situation of, at beginning of 21st century, 267; Al Smith on the problems of, 162; substantive due process and, 119; and the suffrage prior to the Civil War, 66–70; triumph of, as standard of legitimacy, 240; universal endorsement of, after WWII, 184
Democratic Party, 44; after Civil War, 102; and corporations, 94; in 1811, 40; in 1816, 52; from 1830s to 1860, 62–63, 64, 65–66; and election of 1860, 89; and independent treasury policy, 80; and Keynesian economics, 192; and labor unions, beginning in 1930s, 181; and the legal profession, 92; Loco-Foco faction of, 79, 80; as mass party in 1827, 58; and modern economic ideologies, 242; and the Populists, 129, 134; and possible media bias, 258; post-FDR, 7; in 1790s, 21; and the tariff, 71
depressions: of 1893, 139; Great, 20, 186–87, 222

Derrida, Jacques, xi, 263
Dew, Thomas Roderick, 85
Dewey, John, 131, 196, 198
Dillon, John, 117
Dodd, Lawrence, and Calvin Jillson, 260–61
Doe, Charles, 115–16
Donnelly, Ignatius, 127, 163
Douglas, Frederick, 83–84
Douglas, Stephen, 58, 89
Downs, Anthony, 206–7, 278, 280
Dred Scott Decision, 89–90, 93
D'Souza, Dinesh, 251
Dworkin, Ronald, 265–66

Economic Recovery Tax Act, 248
economics, classical, 58, 61; defended by Henry Wood, 105–6; difficulties of, in 1870s, 144; and post–Civil War jurisprudence, 119, 122
economics, institutional, 164, 214–19, 271
economics, neoclassical, ix; antisocialism of, 147; beginnings of, 104, 145–46; and cardinal utility, 282–83; critique by, of Galbraith's theory, 218; defense by, of the concept of consumer sovereignty, 219; failure by, of empirical tests, 272–74; Galbraith's critique of, 215–17; and globalization, 282; and the Great Depression, 176, 186; and Keynesian theory, 188; as natural law, 146–47, 268–69; and Posner's jurisprudence, 275–77; and public choice theory, 278–81; and rationality assumption, 269–70; Veblen's hostility to, 163–64
economics, supply-side, 243–49, 291, 293; attack on, by Krugman, 248; and Republican Party, 248
Edelman, Marc, 282
efficiency, 146; and J. B. Clark on wages, 148; and modern economic theory, 268; as moral imperative, 147; and movements in asset prices, 273; and Posner's jurisprudence, 276; and Veblen, 164
Eisenhower, Dwight, 192
elections: of 1896, 134–38; of 1912, 168–74
Ellis, Richard, 1
El Salvador, 284
Elshtain, Jean Bethke, 259, 266
Emerson, Ralph Waldo, 70
eminent domain, 116

empiricism, xii
Engerman, Stanley, 56
entrepreneurs, 18, 32; and John Adams, 46; and the creation of wealth, 106; defense of, by Austrians, 223; denigration of, by Marxists, 253; FDR's attitude toward, 198; and the Jeffersonians, 29; and national aspirations after 1898, 141; and neoclassical economics, 243; Rawls's neglect of, 209; and supply-side economics, 243–49; undervaluation of, by the Left, 173; Veblen's view of, 166
environmentalism, 183
Epstein, Richard, 261–63, 290
equality, 45; Brandeis's views on, 157; in campaign of 1896, 135; change in discourse about, prior to Civil War, 70; before Civil War, 54; conservative explanations for lack of, 251; and the contemporary Right, 292; decline in, after Civil War, 99, 100; decline in, during 1990s, 238; after 1898, 139–40; and the leftist critique of capitalism, 254–55; and the Left's disenchantment after the New Deal, 213; of opportunity, 159; and ownership of land, 130; and post–New Deal liberalism, 196; and social Darwinism, 108, 112
equilibrium, economic, 147, 148; Keynes's critique of orthodox theory of, 14, 46, 188–89; and the neoclassical synthesis, 214; and pluralist political theory, 202–3, 205; Samuelson's contribution to theory of, 190

Federalist, The, 15, 22–28, 34–35, 44; and the hyperagrarians, 41
Federalist Party, 21, 42–44, 46, 47; and corporations, 94; and the legal profession, 92; policies of, stolen by Democrats, 52; and tariff of 1789, 51
Federal Reserve Board, 33, 174, 175; blamed by Friedman for causing Great Depression, 226; in Galbraith's theory, 217; policies in Great Depression, 176, 177; policies during 1960s, 180
Feldstein, Martin, 244
feminist movement, 239–40
Field, Stephen, 119–20, 124, 152, 154, 192
Fishkin, James, xvii, 295
Fitzhugh, George, 87–88
Fleischacker, Samuel, 25

Fogel, Robert, 56
Foner, Eric, 7, 88
Foster, William, and Waddill Catchings, 186–87
Foucault, Michel, xi, 263
Fourier, Charles, 132
France, 51, 137, 175, 270
Frank, Thomas, 254
Franklin, Benjamin, 4, 50
Free, Lloyd, and Hadley Cantril, 182
Free Soil Party, 65
Friedman, Milton, 219, 234; and the methodology of economics, 270–75; and public choice theory, 278–81; theories of, 224–26, 243
Friedman, Rose, 219
Friedman, Thomas, 287

Galbraith, James, xvii, 219
Galbraith, John Kenneth, 187, 214–19, 222, 234
Gallatin, Albert, 29, 47–50, 53, 96, 213
Gallatin River, 47
Garfield, James, 101
Garten, Jeffrey, 286
Genovese, Eugene, 257
George, Henry, 130–31, 163, 187
George Mason University, 242
Germany, 175, 180, 194, 218
Gide, Charles, and Charles Rist, 12
Gilder, George, 246–48, 251, 293
Glasgow, University of, 9
globalization, 237–38, 281–89; leftist skepticism of, 254
Goddard, William, 4
Goebel, Thomas, 15, 127
gold standard, 126; abandoned by Britain in 1931, 176; and campaign of 1896, 135, 137; formally embraced in 1898, 138; and Glass-Steagall Act, 177; Hoover's adherence to, 161; in international finance prior to Great Depression, 174; and neoclassical economics, 147, 176, 186
Gompers, Samuel, 129, 136
Goodwin, Craufurd, 282
Goodyear v. Day, 92
Gordon, Thomas, 15
Gouge, William, 62
Grant, Ullyses S., 114
Great Society, the, 247
Greeley, Horace, 73

Green, Daniel, and Ian Shapiro, 279
Gregg, Benjamin, xvii
Grotius, Hugo, 268–69
Grund, Francis J., 55
Guatemala, 284
Guild, Curtis, 136

Habermas, Jürgen, 245, 263
Hadley, Arthur Twining, 151
Hallett, Benjamin, 77
Hamilton, Alexander, 4, 14, 20, 29–36, 43, 53, 61, 78, 115, 229, 251, 288, 295; and *Federalist* #78, 35–36, 41; Gallatin's critique of, 48; and the impost, 50; and the Jeffersonians, 39, 41; and the post-1898 Supreme Court, 151; and the "Report on a National Bank," 33–34; and the "Report on Public Credit," 30–32
Hamilton, James, 75
Hammer v. Dagenhart, 153, 155
Hammond, James, 82, 88
Hansen, Alvin, 190
Harlan, John, 122
Harrington, James, 14, 62
Harrison, William Henry, 80–81
Hartz, Louis, x, 5–8, 12, 290
Harvard University, 73, 187, 190, 214, 247; Ethical Society of, 156; Law School, 156; Law School Association of, 122
Hausman, Daniel, 270
Hayek, Friedrich, 222–23
Held, David, 240
Heritage Foundation, 245
Hibbs, Douglas, 192
Hicks, John, 190
Hill, Thomas, 73
Hinich, Melvin, xvii, 280–81
Hoar, George, 136
Hobbes, Thomas, 87
Hofstadter, Richard, 22
Holmes, Oliver Wendell, 124–25, 153–56; fluctuation in reputation of, 194–95; and freedom of speech, 155–56; relationship of, to Brandeis, 157
Hoover, Herbert, 158–61, 176–77
Honduras, 284
Hoxie, Robert, 214
Hughes, Charles Evans, 169, 193
Hume, David, 15, 31, 32

immigration, 54, 100–101
imperialism, 134, 137, 141
independent treasury system, 79–80
India, 289
Indians, American, 49, 60, 85
inflation: caused by Keynesianism, charges Feldstein, 244; empirical studies of consequences of, 191; in Galbraith's theory, 216–17; and the gold standard, 147; and Keynesian theory, 191; in the 1980s, 236; and the oil boycott of 1973–74, 236; post-WWII, 179
Ingelhart, Ronald, 183
In Re Jacobs, 120–21
Insull, Samuel, 140
interlocking directorates, 140, 162
Interstate Commerce Commission, 114
Interstate Oil Compact Commission, 200
invisible hand, 10, 26, 27, 147, 291; and the contemporary Left, 292; and economic thought in the 1930s, 186; and Nozick's theory, 226; and public choice theory, 207; and Schumpeter's theory of democracy, 206; and slavery, 86
Iran, 236
Israel, 236, 289

Jackson, Andrew, 80, 213; and banks, 62; and the B.U.S., 77–78, 79; and trade policy, 58
Jackson, James, 39
Japan, 218
Jefferson, Thomas, 3, 15, 29, 31, 36–39, 44, 47, 161, 198, 229; and Gallatin, 49; ideas of, and the Virginia constitution of 1830, 66; Memorial, 36; and *Notes On Virginia*, 37; river named after, 47; and slavery, 36, 43; and suffrage, 19; and the tariff, 51, 74, 133
Jeffersonians, the, 14, 15, 35–40, 45; and entrepreneurs, 40; and Gallatin, 48; and hyperagrarians, 40–43; and Southern culture, 56; and trade policy, 51–52
Jevons, W. Stanley, 104
Johnson, Lyndon, 179, 192, 201
Judson, Frederick, 117
jurisprudence, ix; after Civil War, 115–25; prior to Civil War, 90–96; and critical legal studies, 263; fragmentation of modern, 260–67; modern, and Rawls, 209–10; natural law vs. positivistic traditions in, 153–54
jury, decline of, 92

Kansas Bar Association, 124
Kansas-Nebraska Act, 58, 89
Kennedy, John, 192
Kent, James, 66–67, 96, 118
Kershner, Jonathon, 274
Keynes, John Maynard, xiv, 20, 210, 242, 247, 274; and Henry Carey, 72, 73; criticism of, by Feldstein, 244; criticism of, by Friedman, 225–26; and "embedded liberalism," 199; modern Republican demonization of, 242; and neoclassical synthesis, 214; Samuelson's enlargement of theory of, 191; theory of, 187–89; theory of investment of, 243–44
Kloppenberg, James, 7, 16
Knott, Stephen, 36
Know Nothing Party, 65, 89
Kramnick, Isaac, 12
Kristol, Irving, 246, 260
Krugman, Paul, 217, 244, 248
Kuhn, Thomas, 186
Kuttner, Robert, 294

Labatt, C. B., 124
labor: changes in, after 1898, 141; "freedom of contract" of, 120–21; increasing prosperity of, after Civil War, 99; and the judicial injunction, 123, 135; long-term rise in productivity of, 139; in north prior to Civil War, 86–88; and questions about the creators of wealth, 106
labor unions: and African Americans, 142–48; attacked by J. B. Clark, 148; attack on, by Reagan administration, 251; after Civil War, 101–2; continuous decline of, through 1990s, 238–39; and the courts, 93; and Democratic coalition, 181; denounced by Arthur Latham Perry, 105; denounced by Henry Wood, 106; and economic thought during the 1930s, 186; first organizations of, 44; in Galbraith's theory, 215; and the new legal paradigm of the 1930s, 193; in 1920s, 143; opposition to, by Ricardo, 58; and the Populists, 128; and Posner's jurisprudence, 276–77; rise of, in 1930s, and decline of, beginning 1950s, 180–81; and social Darwinism, 109; state legislation supporting, 115
Lacan, Jacques, 263
La Follette, Robert, 153, 162, 213
Lasswell, Harold, 201

law, common, 19
"law and economics" movement, 195
Leach, De Witt, 84
Lee, Arthur, 18
Left, the: assumptions of, 131; and the belief that democracy is a sham, 233; change in ideas after New Deal, 213; evaluation of, 291–95; and the future of liberalism, 290; and globalization, 285–86, 288; during Progressive era, 173; redefines democracy, 253–60, 267, 290; and rule by an elite, 168; style of discourse of modern, 252
legal formalism, 121–22, 124, 143
legal realism, 194
Leggett, William, 63, 80
legitimacy, 1, 3, 14, 35, 45; alleged crisis of, in 1970s, 245–46; and attempts to redefine democracy, 240; and the B.U.S., 77, 78; and Civil Rights Movement, 184; and the contemporary Left, 292; and globalization, 287–89; and inequality, to the modern Left, 254–55; and C. Wright Mills, 221; and pre-WWII political science, 201; and social theory after the Civil War, 103
Lekachman, Robert, 192
Leopold, Aldo, 183
Levi-Strauss, Claude, 263
Lewelling, Lorenzo, 128
Lewis, Meriwether, 47
Lewis, Sinclair, 142
liberalism, x, 14–15, 17, 28; change in meaning of, during New Deal, 195–96; economic, 9–12; at the end of the founding period, 53; and equality, post–New Deal, 196–97; future of, 289–95; "growth" version of, after WWII, 184; and the Left's effort to redefine democracy, 256; modern, and influence of Holmes, 156; political, 2–8; and Populism, 127–28; and slavery, 86–87, 90
liberty, 21, 43; of contract, 109, 124; and equality, 112; in *Lochner* case, 154; and post–Civil War jurisprudence, 119
Limbaugh, Rush, 230, 249–51
Lincoln, Abraham, 213; and African Americans, 85; and Declaration of Independence, 84; and democratic capitalism, 96; and Dred Scott decision, 90; election of, 90; Hoover on, 159; and slavery, 85, 88

Lindblom, Charles, 259–60
Lippucci, Alessandra, xvii
List, Friedrich, xiv, 61, 74–75
Lloyd, Christopher, xii
Lloyd, Henry D., 163
Lochner v. New York, 152, 154
Locke, John, xiv, 2–12, 15, 18, 35–37, 42, 185; and Democratic Party prior to Civil War, 62; and Nozick, 226; and Rawls, 208; and slavery, 87
logrolling: and pluralist theory, 205; and the tariff, 51
Loomes, Graham, 270
Louisiana Purchase, 48
Lowell, Francis, 18
Lowi, Theodore, 205
Lowndes, William, 52
Lucas, Robert, 243, 274
Lutz, Donald, 3, 15
Lyon, Paul, xvii

Maclay, William, 38
Madison, James, 21, 44–47, 261, 295; and the *Federalist*, 22–29, 34; and the first B.U.S., 38–40; and Gallatin, 49; and the hyperagrarians, 40–41; and pluralist political theory, 203; river named after, 47; and "Vices of the Political System of the United States," 23–24; views of, on trade policy, 50, 51, 52, 74
manufacturing, 18, 33–34; growth in, after Civil War, 98; and the hyperagrarians, 31; and the War of 1812, 52–53
Marbury v. Madison, 35, 118
Marcuse, Herbert, 263
marginal utility, theory of, 145–46; and neoclassical economics, 148
market failure, 150, 222; vs. government failure, 225; and the leftist critique of capitalism, 254
market system: and J. B. Clark, 148; defense of, by Austrians, 223; defense of, by Friedman, 224–25; disrepute of, after WWII, 184; FDR's attitude toward, 198; and freedom of speech, 155–56; and Marshall's metaphor, 147; Marxism's denial of morality to, 253–54; rejected by Bellamy, 131–32; renaissance of support for, after WWII, 222–26; and Schumpeter's theory of democracy, 206
Marshall, Alfred, 104, 146–47, 243
Marshall, Charles, 117

Marshall, John, 35, 91, 94
Marx, Karl, xiii, 131, 220, 230, 259; and the "legitimation crisis" of capitalism, 245
Marxism, ix, 230–34, 271; historical undermining of the paradigm of, during 1980s and 90s, 253; and C. Wright Mills, 221; rejection of pluralist theory of democracy by, 204
Massachusetts Institute of Technology, 104, 190
maximization assumption, 146
McCain-Feingold Act, 293
McCarthy, Joseph, 229
McCloskey, Deirdre, 272
McCloskey, Herbert, 240–41
McCloskey, Robert, x
McCulloch, John, 59
McCullough, David, 45
McKinley, William, 137, 138
McKinnon, Harold, 194
McReynolds, James, 193
McVickar, John, 61
McWilliams, James, xv
media, 255, 258
Meister, Robert, 89
Mellon, Andrew, 176
Mellon, Richard, 140
Mengers, Carl, 104
mercantilism, 9
Mexican War, 64
Milkis, Sidney, 198, 201
Mill, John Stuart, xiv, 243; ideas of, prior to Civil War, 71; and jurisprudence, 116; and Arthur Latham Perry, 105; *Principles of Political Economy*, 59, 103–4
Miller, John C., 29
Mills, C. Wright, 220–22, 252, 259
Missouri Compromise, 42–43, 58, 85, 89
Missouri River, 47
Mitchell, Charles, 140
Mitchell, Wesley, 214
Moley, Raymond, 197
Mondale, Walter, 248
monetarism, 225, 243
monopoly, 222; attacked by J. B. Clark, 148; Brandeis on, 157; opposed by neoclassical economists, 186; theory of monopolistic competition, 187
Montesquieu, Baron, 3, 15
Moran, Theodore, 273

Morgan, J. P., 140
Morone, James, xv, 8, 163
Morris, Robert, 32
Mount Rushmore, 44
Mueller, John, 260
Munger, Michael, 280–81
Munn v. Illinois, 120

Nader, Ralph, 183
National Association of Manufacturers, 143, 220
National Civic Federation, 143
National Industrial Recovery Act, 197
"nationalist school" of political economists, 61
National Labor Relations Board, 180, 251
National Labor Relations Board v. Jones and Laughlin Steel Corporation, 193
natural law, x, 45, 115; and business, after 1898, 143; and economic theory, after Civil War, 103–13; and freedom of speech, 156; Hoover on, 159; and jurisprudence after Civil War, 125; and law, after 1898, 144–58; and the market, 60; and neoclassical economic theory, 268–69; and Posner's jurisprudence, 275–77; and quest for, in law during 1950s, 195; and redistribution of wealth, 59–60; and social Darwinism, 106–13
nature, state of, 9, 208
Nelson, John, 34
New Deal, the: and change in the meaning of "liberal," 195; Epstein's attack on jurisprudence of, 261–62; and the incorporation of organized groups, 183; intellectual incoherence of, 197; and legal realism, 194; and Nozick's theory, 247; and Reagan administration, 251; structure of polity that emerged from, 211
New Left, the, 184, 221, 234, 235
Newman, Samuel, 61
Newton, Isaac, 9–10, 110
New York State Bar Association, 122
New York University, 73
Nicaragua, 284
Nicholas, Philip, 67
Nietzsche, Friedrich, 87, 263
Nigeria, 289
Nixon, Richard, 178, 180, 192, 229
North, the: and the antislavery crusade, 84; and

banks, prior to Civil War, 78–79; as beneficiary of tariff, 75; business culture of, 55, 57; and the decline of juries, 92; free labor vs. slave labor in, 87; reaction of, to Kansas-Nebraska Act, 89; wealth of, in 1860, 54
North American Free Trade Agreement, 288
Nozick, Robert, 208, 210, 226–28; and Richard Epstein, 262

Ogden v. Saunders, 91
Ohio River, 21
Ohmae, Kenichi, 286
Olson, Mancur, 204, 207
Ordeshook, Peter, xvii
Ormerod, Paul, 273
Otis, James, 4

Palmer v. Mulligan, 93
Panic of 1837, 79
Parekh, Bhikhu, 240, 261
Peckham, Rufus, 120, 152
Pendleton, Edmund, 19
People's Party, 127, 128
Perry, Arthur Latham, 104–5
Phillips, Anne, 240
Phillips curve, 191–92, 226
Pickens, Francis, 86, 88
Pigou, Arthur, 149
Piven, Frances Fox, and Richard Cloward, 252–53
Plato, 132
Pocock, John, 13
Poe, Edgar Allan, 253
political science, ix; attempt of, to update theory of democracy after WWII, 202–8; and public choice theory, 208, 278–81
Poole, Keith, and Howard Rosenthal, 281
Populism, 125–29, 140; and Bellamy, 131; and election of 1896, 134; and pluralist political theory, 203; and racial conflict, 134
Posner, Richard, 261, 275–77, 281, 290
Post Office, 65
poverty: effectiveness of government in reducing, 1960s–90s, 237; Gilder's theory of causation of, 247; in 1929, 139; during 1960s, 178; "War on," 179
Prindle, Angie, xvii
progressivism, 161–68; attitude of, toward Holmes, 155; similarities and differences from socialists, 173
property, 2, 18–19, 20, 21, 46; defense of, and immigration, 101; defense of, and the legal profession, 92; embraced by Bryan, 135; and the post-1898 Supreme Court, 151–52; reconceptualization by courts of, after Civil War, 121–22
public choice theory, 207–8, 278–81
Public Citizen, 183
public interest, xiii; and Bellamy's utopia, 132; and campaign of 1912, 169, 171; and democratic discourse, 70; and interest-group theory, 202–3, 205; the Left as skeptical of achieving, after New Deal, 211; and neoclassical economics, 149; and rationality postulate, 146; and tariff of 1789, 51; and tariff of 1846, 73
public lands, 48
Pufendorf, Samuel, 4
Pulitzer Prize, 45
Puritans, the, 16

Quincy, Josiah, 52, 66

railroads: discriminatory rates of, after Civil War, 99–100; encouragement of, by Republicans, 114; as issue in 1896 campaign, 135; resentment of, by Populists, 126; as special interest, to progressives, 162
Rakove, Jack, 22
Randolph, John, 40–43, 47, 72
Randolph, Thomas Mann, 15
rational expectations theory, 243
Rawls, John, 208–10, 228, 264, 289, 293
Raymond, Daniel, 61, 62
Reagan, Ronald, 246, 248–49, 252, 253, 283–84
realism, philosophical, xi
Reconstruction Finance Corporation, 160
Reed, Thomas, 133
regulation, government: change in judicial doctrine of, in 1930s, 193; judicial doctrines regarding, 121, 192; Keynes's recommendation of, 189; and modern jurisprudence, 262, 266; and new meaning of liberalism in 1930s, 196; of petroleum industry, 199–200; and supply-side economics, 244–45

religion, 16, 26, 27; and campaign of 1896, 136; and party battle prior to Civil War, 65; and populist movement, 126; and slavery issue, 82–83, 84
Rennie, William Alex, xvii
republicanism, 12–16, 20–22, 28, 37, 127–28
Republican Party: and absorption of Whigs, 65; and African Americans in campaign of 1896, 138; anti-union nature of, 181; and antislavery ideology, 84; after Civil War, 102; and Civil War pensions, 114; and the Declaration of Independence, 84; and Dred Scott decision, 90; and economic theory, 61, 133; and Keynesian economics, 192; and modern economic ideologies, 242; as "normal" majority party after 1896, 136; performance of, in 1856 and 1860 elections, 89; and possible media bias, 258; and social mobility, 88; strain on, caused by imperialism after 1898, 141; and supply-side economics, 248
Ricardo, David, 58–59, 243, 282; and Bellamy, 132; impact of ideas of, prior to Civil War, 61, 71; and Mill, 104
Ricci, David, 245
Richie v. People, 121
Right, the: assumptions of, 131; evaluation of, 291–95; and future of liberalism, 290; redefinition of capitalism by, 267, 290; style of discourse of modern, 252
Riis, Jacob, 163
Robinson, Joan, 187
Rockefeller, Percy, 140
Roemer, John, 294
Roosevelt, Franklin, 178, 180, 209, 210; and change in the meaning of "liberal," 195–97; Commonwealth Club Address by, 198; and Keynesian economic prescriptions, 189
Roosevelt, Theodore, 130, 153; and campaign of 1912, 169–72; and special interests, 161
Rorty, Richard, xi
Rosecrance, Richard, 280
Ross, Doroth, 201
Rothschild, Emma, 11
Rousseau, Jean Jacques, 185
Rowan, John, 71
Ruffin, Edmund, 86
Russia, 155

Samuelson, Paul, 190, 191, 224, 226, 234; on free trade, 282; and the principle of redress, 294
Sandel, Michael, 15–16, 295
Saudi Arabia, 236
Say, Jean Baptiste, 19–20; and Henry Carey, 72; and economic thought in the early 1930s, 186; impact of ideas of, before Civil War, 58, 71; and Mill, 104; and neoclassical economics, 147; and Perry, 105; theory of, rejected by Keynes, 188; and Veblen, 164
Schattschneider, E. E., x, 204
Schmookler, Andrew, 254
Schumpeter, Joseph, 206, 243
Schwartz, Bernard, 261
Schwartz, Thomas, xvii
Sedgwick, Theodore, 36, 62, 65
service sector, 141
Shalhope, Robert, 12
Shaw, George Bernard, 130
Shaw, Lemuel, 93
Shays's Rebellion, 67
Sherman Antitrust Act, 114, 122
Short, William, 52
Sidney, Algernon, 15
Sierra Club, 183
Simon, Herbert, 270
Skidmore, Thomas, 62
Skowronek, Stephen, 143–44
Slaughter-House Cases, 119–20
slavery, 8, 21; Carey's theory of the abolition of, 72; and Dred Scott decision, 89–90; and the hyperagrarians, 42; number of slaves, 54, 55, 57, 82; political conflict over, 81–90; suppression as issue by Democratic Party, 58
Smith, Adam, xiv, 8–12, 19–20, 24–28, 30, 33, 50, 115, 157, 217, 242; and Darwinian theory, 107, 109; and Milton Friedman, 225; impact of ideas of, prior to Civil War, 58, 59, 61, 62, 65; and the Jeffersonians, 37; and jurisprudence, 116, 124; and Mill, 103–4; and neoclassical economics, 104; and Nozick, 247; and Perry, 105; and supply-side economics, 243; theories of, and U.S. tariff, 51, 71, 74; Veblen's critique of, 164; and Henry Wood, 106
Smith, Al, 162
Smith, Rogers, xiii, 7–8, 265
Smithson, James, 65

Smyth v. Ames, 151
Snow v. Parsons, 93
social Darwinism, 106–13, 119, 122
socialism, 6–7; and African Americans, 142; and Bellamy, 131–33; and Bryan, 135; criticisms of capitalism by, refuted by Henry Wood, 106; critique of, by Austrians, 223; differences between, and post–New Deal liberalism, 197; embraced by Debs, 124; explanation for lack of, in U.S., 65–66; FDR's attitude toward, 198; and the leftist attempt to redefine democracy, 256–57; in Marxist theory, 230; and the slavery issue, 86–87; as villain for legal profession, 117; as villain in public philosophy, 106; weakness of, after Civil War, 115, 130
Solow, Robert, 272
South, the: anti-union nature of, 181; and banks, prior to Civil War, 78–79; decline in economy of, after Civil War, 99–100; defense of slavery in, 85–87; economy of, 21; importance of slavery to, 81–82; political actions in states of, after Civil War, 115; and Populism, 125; and post–New Deal liberalism, 196; prior to Civil War, 55, 56, 57; representatives from, and tariff of 1789, 51; and the tariff, after Civil War, 133; as victim of tariffs, 75; wealth of, in 1860, 54, 57
special interests, 161, 170
Spencer, Herbert, 115, 159, 192, 212; and jurisprudence, 116, 124, 138, 152; and *Lochner* decision, 154; and neoclassical economics, 148; overturning of legal doctrine based on theories of, 193; theories of, 107–10
stagflation, 226
Stanford University, 242, 272–73
Steffens, Lincoln, 163
Stegner, Wallace, 183
Steward, A. T., 101
Stigler, George, 224, 226
stock market, 175, 237
Stone, Harlan, 193
Story, Joseph, 94, 95
Stowe, Harriett Beecher, 83, 85
strikes: denounced by Perry, 105; during 1890s, 102, 122, 123; and Haymarket bombing, 102, 116; and injunctions, 122; prior to Civil War, 55–56; Railway, of 1877, 102

structurism, xii
Sturges v. Crowninshield, 91
substantive due process: doctrine of, 118–20, 263; failure to revive of, 195; overturning of, during 1930s, 193; rejection of, by some legal thinkers, 124–25
suffrage, 19, 30, 46, 48; and democratic ideals prior to Civil War, 66–70; and party battle prior to Civil War, 65; and threats to property, 101, 116–17; and Voting Rights Act, 185; for women, 70
Sumner, William Graham, 110–13, 116, 131
Sunstein, Cass, 261, 266, 294
Sutherland, George, 153
Sweezy, Paul, 221, 232–33

Taft, William Howard, 122, 168–69
Taft-Hartley Act, 181
Taney, Roger, 89, 94–95
tariff, 34, 50–53, 115, 165; "of abominations," 58, 71; and campaign of 1896, 135, 137; and campaign of 1912, 170; and Civil War pensions, 114; denounced by Perry, 105; drop in, during twentieth century, 238; effect on South of, after Civil War, 99–100; of 1832, 58, 71; Hawley-Smoot, 176; opposed by classical economists, 59; and party battle after Civil War, 102; and party battle prior to Civil War, 65, 71–73; passage of Dingley, 138; and problems with international finance after WWI, 175; problems with support for, after 1898, 141; Raymond on, 61; and social Darwinism, 112–13; as subject of controversy, 60, 133–34
tax, income, 115, 119; increase of, in 1932, 177; and new liberalism of 1930s, 196; and supply-side economics, 244–45
Taylor, Jeremy, 269
Taylor, John, 40–43, 46–47, 62, 72, 86
technological change, 54–55, 139
Temin, Peter, 189–90
Texas, University of, ix, xvii
Thomas, Norman, 131
Thompson, Seymour, 124
Tiedeman, Christopher, 117
Tobin, James, 190
Tocqueville, Alexis de, xiv–xv, 118
Tolstoy, Leo, 130
Trenchard, John, 15

Truman, David, 202–3
Truman, Harry, 181
trusts, 106, 122; and campaign of 1912, 171; criticized by neoclassical economists, 148; as issue in 1896 campaign, 135
Tubingen, University of, 74
Tversky, Amos, and Daniel Kahneman, 270
Tyler, John, 80–81
Tyler v. Wilkinson, 93

unemployment: and globalization, 282; in Keynes's critique of orthodox economic theory, 189; during 1960s, 179; in 1980s, 236; and oil boycott of 1973–74, 236
UNESCO, 184
United Mine Workers, 200
United States v. Carolene Products, 193
United States v. E. C. Knight, 123, 193
urbanization, 55, 100, 139
utilitarianism, 144–45

Van Buren, Martin, 58, 78, 79
Veblen, Thorstein, 163–68, 209, 214, 217; and Bellamy, 131, 168; and Mills, 221
Vehake, Henry, 61
Virginia, University of, 15
von Mises, Ludwig, 222–23
Vonnegut, Kurt, 209
voter turnout: decline in, after 1960, 241; and disillusionment with democracy after WWII, 185; in 1824, 1828, and 1840, 69; in 1896, 137; and public choice theory, 207, 279

Walker, Francis Amasa, 104, 106
Walpole, Horace, 14
Walras, Leon, 104
Walzer, Michael, 257
Wanniski, Jude, 244
War of 1812, 40, 52, 64
Washington, George, 29, 51
water law, 93
Wayland, Francis, 61
Webster, Daniel, 118; and the B.U.S., 77, 78; and *Goodyear v. Day*, 92; and the independent treasury policy, 80; and trade policy, 58, 73–74
Weiskopf, Thomas, 233
welfare policies: attacked by Gilder, 247; in Britain, 59; denounced by Henry Wood, 106; effectiveness from, 1960s to 1990s, 237; and social Darwinism, 108–9
West, the: culture of, prior to Civil War, 56; monetary policies and, after Civil War, 126; overuse of water in, 183
West Coast Hotel v. Parrish, 193
Whigs, American, 61; attitude of, to banking issue, 79, 80; ideological conflict of, with Democrats, 64; and the legal profession, 92
Whigs, English, 3, 13, 15, 46
White, Morton, 22
White, William H., 192
Whitman, Walt, 63
Wiggen, Albert, 140
Wilbur, Jay, xvii
Wilbur, John, xvii
Wilderness Society, 183
Wilentz, Sean, 7
Williams, William Appleman, 232, 234
Wilson, Woodrow, 130, 155, 156; and Brandeis, 157; and campaign of 1912, 170–72; elected, 1912, 173; and special interests, 161
Winch, Donald, 11
Wirt, William, 83
Wolfe, Alan, 245–46
Wood, A. H., 80
Wood, Gordon, 13, 22
Wood, Henry, 105–6
World Trade Organization, 288, 289
Wright, Gavin, 56
Wright, Robert, 287

Yale University, 110, 151
Yellowstone National Park, 113–14
Young, Iris Marion, 256

Zaller, John, 240–41